Sin and the Unfolding of Salvation

David Gracey

Solid Ground Christian Books
Birmingham, Alabama USA

Solid Ground Christian Books
PO Box 660132
Vestavia Hills AL 35266
205-443-0311
mike.sgcb@gmail.com
www.solid-ground-books.com

Sin and the Unfolding of Salvation
*Being the Three Years' Course of Theological Lectures
Delivered at the Pastors' College, London*

David Gracey (1841-1893)

First Published in 1894 by Passmore and Alabaster in London

First Solid Ground Edition – June 2013

Cover design by Borgo Design
Contact them at borgogirl@gmail.com

> COVER PHOTO – The beautiful picture that graces the cover was taken by professional photo-journalist Karim Shamsi-Basha. Solid Ground is working on a powerful book by Karim entitled **PAUL and me:** *A Journey to and from the Damascus Road – From Islam to Christ.* This book is expected in the late summer of 2013.

ISBN- 978-159925-288-9

SIN AND THE UNFOLDING OF SALVATION,

BEING THE

THREE YEARS' COURSE OF THEOLOGICAL LECTURES

DELIVERED AT THE

PASTORS' COLLEGE, LONDON.

BY THE LATE

PROFESSOR DAVID GRACEY,

Principal of that Institution.

London:
PASSMORE AND ALABASTER,
PATERNOSTER BUILDINGS, E.C.

1894.
[ALL RIGHTS RESERVED.]

INTRODUCTION.

RIGHT glad am I to introduce these Lectures. What though I was not privileged to hear them delivered, I need have no hesitation in commending them, for I knew the lecturer, and to know him was to love him. I doubt not that his addresses form a fair portrait of himself. I am in the position of a chairman of a meeting who knows not what the speaker, whom he introduces to the audience, is going to say; but knowing the man himself, is quite at rest about the speech.

Would God we could still say, "Professor Gracey will now address the meeting"—and in some sense we can. "He being dead, yet speaketh." In introducing him—for he put *himself* into his discourses—I confidently expect sound and solid truth, expressed in terms that can be understood of all, and in language so chaste as to charm the ear of every reader.

Those who sat at his feet will have the great advantage of being able to supply, by aid of the good gift of memory, the graceful gesture, the rippling smile, the kindly eye of their translated teacher. To them these Lectures will be a memorial most precious of a man greatly beloved. But the book will be profitable to all, "for a blessing is in it."

There is no need of an elaborate "introduction" to a good meal. The host will do well to set the savoury viands on the board without ado, and bid the guests regale themselves. But let them first say grace.

I have heard of one who, being asked to open a public meeting with prayer, contented himself with saying, "For what we are about to receive the Lord make us truly thankful." It was not so inappropriate a petition as it at first sight appears to be. Let every reader "ask a blessing" on his perusal of this book, and it shall be granted unto him.

THOMAS SPURGEON.

PREFACE.

THE Author of these Lectures was no common man. As a Christian, a Scholar, and a Theologian all who knew him would assign him high rank. For over thirty years intimately connected with the Pastors' College, his influence upon the men there trained was unique, and with the history of that institution his name will ever be honourably and inseparably linked. It was partly the result of his utter devotion to his special work that he was not so well known among the leaders of religious thought as he deserved to be; although, any time that he addressed himself to other work, as, for instance, in the part he took in the discussion on the " Larger Hope," as conducted in the *Contemporary Review*, he clearly showed himself a " Master in Israel."

Mr. Gracey's special subjects were Classics and Theology, but he was also well acquainted with most other departments of learning. We have, sometimes, in thinking of the variety and abundance of his mental gifts, compared him to those mountains mentioned by Dr. Guthrie, whereon grows "every vegetable form peculiar to every line of latitude between the equator and the poles." Did space permit, we might say much more in praise of him, and those who knew him would not think it too much. Of the beloved Founder of the Pastors' College, Mr. Gracey said, in his last College Report,—" Eulogy itself fails to satisfy"; and so do many of us feel with regard to himself; certainly, in common with not a few, I shall ever esteem it one of the greatest privileges of life to have enjoyed the tuition and the friendship of such a man.

It may not be amiss to mention the following Biographical facts. David Gracey was a native of Ulster, having been born at Banbridge, co. Down, on September 24th, 1841. He was brought to the Lord during the great revival of 1859, and, not long afterwards, he renounced brilliant business prospects in order to enter Glasgow University, with a view to preparing himself for the work of the ministry. While studying at the university, and working as a city missionary, he had the privilege of hearing Mr. Spurgeon, on his visit to Glasgow, in 1861, and at once came under the spell of the great preacher, and rested not till he became associated with him in his noble work. Coming to the Pastors' College, as student and assistant tutor, he soon became fully engaged in tutorial work, and upon the retirement of the late venerable George Rogers, in 1879, he became Principal and Theological Tutor, in which capacity he continued to serve the College with credit to himself, and untold benefit to the students, until his lamented death on February 9th, 1893. At his death a general desire was felt among his old students for the publication of his Theological Lectures, and the present volume is the answer to that very natural desire. Those who had the privilege of hearing the Lectures delivered will welcome their production in enduring form; those who knew him as Tutor, but had not that privilege, will be specially pleased to read them for the first time. The wider circle of theological readers who did not know the Author personally, will find in the Lectures abundant proof of the ripe scholarship, the mature Christian thought, the theological lore, the historical research, the critical acumen, and the beautiful literary style which characterized our friend.

The Lectures, as first delivered, were necessarily prepared hurriedly, amid the press of other work, but even so, they bore no trace of haste or carelessness, but, like everything he did, carried the stamp of exactness and beauty; for of him, as of his great fellow-countryman, it might be said, "Everything he touched he adorned." I find, however, on comparing my notes of the earlier course with the Lectures in their present form, that some slight alterations have been made; thoughts have been more fully elaborated, sentences expanded, polishing touches added here and there, but there has been no change of importance. Even in their present form the Lectures do not fully represent the amount of teaching conveyed to the students in the class; for constantly questions would be asked on important points, and these would then, extemporaneously, be fully elucidated and elaborated. The Divisions of the Lectures are not, perhaps, quite what he would himself have left for publication; as read they were divided according to the exigences of the time of delivery; still, the leading divisions are his own, although the actual portion given in each Lecture cannot be exactly indicated.

We are persuaded that the volume will be a valuable contribution to the Christological literature of the day. Mr. Gracey ever gives prominence to the Person and work of the Saviour; though unfolding fully the dark and doleful character of sin, he does so under the light of the Gospel, and with the hope of the Gospel shining clear in view. Theology, in his treatment of it, is never a dry science, but a vital, palpitating reality, fresh and beautiful, attractive and inspiring. Having strong convictions, based upon the Word of God, which he hesitates not to express in clear and convincing language, he necessarily exposes and opposes with all his force the erroneous opinions which meet him in the way. He always, however, deals in a courteous and Christian spirit with those from whom he differs; always stating their case fairly, while with strong though gentle hand he demolishes their arguments. Sometimes, indeed, his swift, subtle strokes remind us of the scimitar of Saladin deftly dividing the silken kerchief, while anon, his heavy blows make us think of Cœur de Lion's battle-axe crashing through the bars of steel. While the Lectures will be specially interesting and helpful to students and ministers, they are also calculated to interest and instruct ordinary Christian readers, many of whom, we trust, will, from these pages, gain a clear idea of some of the most important points of Biblical Theology.

It will readily be understood that, had the Author lived to publish the Lectures himself, they would have been thoroughly revised; still, published as they are from the MSS. as he left them, we think they will be found quite worthy of his reputation.

It has been my pleasure to correct the proofs of those portions wherein Hebrew words occur; all the other proofs have been carefully examined by Mr. Gracey's sons, who have also, as far as possible, verified and noted the references to other works. It will be a cause of thankfulness to the numerous friends of the departed Principal to know that his sons are capable of doing such work so well.

It may be stated, in response to many enquiries, that it has been deemed advisable not to include the supplementary course of Lectures on Baptism in this volume, but, if practicable, they will appear in a separate form; since in them the subject of Baptism is treated in such a fresh way is to make their publication desirable. I may further say that among Mr. Gracey's MSS. there are many valuable Sermons, Addresses, and papers of which a selection might be published, should there be any desire expressed to that effect by his admirers. Meanwhile, this volume is sent forth as a cluster of the ripe fruit of a rare mind, with the earnest prayer that it may refresh and gladden many a heart. The book will be considered by many the best possible memorial of a man "greatly beloved"; and we trust it will also prove a tower of strength to the cause of Evangelical Theology.

ARCHIBALD McCAIG.

March, 1894.

CONTENTS.

	PAGE
INTRODUCTION	iv
PREFACE	v—viii

LECTURE I.
INTRODUCTION.

Introduction (1); Meaning and application of "Theology" (3); "Religion" and its relation to Theology (4); Summary of the intellectual movements which have acted and re-acted upon Christianity: public opinion (5—10) ... ...   1—10

LECTURE II.
SYSTEM, METHOD AND ORDER IN THEOLOGICAL STUDY.

System, Method and Order defined (11); Systematic study enjoined in Scripture (13); METHOD (14); *à priori* and inductive reasoning (15); Inductive method applied to Theology (16); Authority of Scripture (19). ORDER, its necessity and origin (21); The "Apology" (22). *Synthetical Systems*—Augustine, Aquinas, Melancthon, Calvin (23); Turretin (24); Limborch (25); Dr. Pye Smith and Dr. Dwight (26). *Analytical Systems* (27)—Jonathan Edwards (28); Dr. Chalmers (29)... ... ...   11—29

LECTURE III.
THE AIM AND SPIRIT OF THEOLOGICAL STUDY.

The Student's aim (30); personal and ministerial elements, and their proper relation (31); their influence on speculation and our hold on the Vital Truths (33); Spirit of Theological Study, and how obtained (37) ... ...   30—41

LECTURE IV.
SIN.

Reasons for first considering Sin (42); List of the chief Scriptural expressions for Sin (44); Old Testament expressions—their meanings illustrated and exemplified (45); New Testament expressions—$\dot{o}\phi\epsilon i\lambda\eta\mu\alpha$ (55); $\dot{a}\pi\epsilon\iota\theta\dot{\epsilon}\omega$ and $\dot{a}\pi\epsilon i\theta\epsilon\iota\alpha$ (56); contrasted with $\dot{a}\pi\iota\sigma\tau i\alpha$ (58) ... ...   42—59

LECTURE V.

NATURE OF SIN.

Principle of Sin (60); Sin not another form of good, Pantheism (61); True character of Sin lies in its relation to law (63); Protestant definitions of Sin (65); The immutability of the Law (66) ... ... 60—68

LECTURE VI.

SIN IN ITS RELATION TO LAW.

The requirements of law (69); Voluntary Acts; The Roman Catholic doctrine (71); all unrighteousness in Sin (74); Consequences of the doctrine (75); *Source of the Authority of Law* (77); Examination of the various theories (78); The two elements in Law; the Divine Understanding and Divine Will in perfect accord; the nature of Moral Law and Morality (85); Concluding observations (87) ... ... 69—88

LECTURE VII.

SIN IN MAN.

Total depravity (89); Classification of Scriptural teaching (91); Sin universal to the race (92), total in every individual (93), and inherent in our nature (94), from which it cannot be eradicated (95); Scriptural and other testimony (96) ... 89—98

LECTURE VIII.

THE CAUSE OF TOTAL DEPRAVITY.

Not to be be found in the line of man's moral growth and development (99), but to be traced to his fall from a moral integrity once perfect (100); The sin of Adam and its connection with the race (101) ... ... 99—105

LECTURE IX.

IMPUTATION OF SIN.

Preliminary considerations (106); must not be combined with the question of the salvation of infants (107); must rest on a basis of reality; Augustine's views (108); President Edwards' Theory (109): Analogy and contrast with the imputation of Christ's Righteousness (110); Scriptural doctrine (111); Analogy between Adam and Christ (112); The natural, federal and legal elements in Adam's headship (113); objections considered (116) 106–120

LECTURE X.

THE OUTLOOK OF SINNERS.

The risks and perils of sinners (121); The relation of God to sinners (123); the Christian Minister's duty (124) ... ... 121—124

LECTURE XI.

SALVATION.

The recuperative resources of nature (125); Salvation as a hope, speculation (126), doctrine (130), and mystery (131). The unfolding of Salvation in history (132), language and imagery (133) ... ... 125—134

LECTURE XII.

SCRIPTURAL EXPRESSIONS RELATING TO SALVATION.

Their meanings illustrated and exemplified ... ... 135—150

LECTURE XIII.

THE UNFOLDING OF SALVATION IN PROPHECY.

Old Testament prophecies concerning Christ (151); they increase in variety (154), grow in distinctness (155), and shed increasing light on the particulars of the Saviour's life and death (158). The application of these prophecies to Christ (160)... 151—163

LECTURE XIV.

THE SAVIOUR.

HIS PERSON (164); Christ is truly Man (166); He is truly God, having in Him a nature superior to the human (168); this superior nature being pre-existent to the human (169), is also Divine (170), and as such is the Deity of the Son of God, and being so, He is co-equal with the Father (171). Christ unites the human and Divine natures in one personality (175). This doctrine throws light on certain Scriptures (181), and on the acts and sufferings of Christ; it enables us to form some estimate of His rank (184), and indicates the homage due to Him (186) ... ... 164—188

LECTURE XV.

ANCIENT AND MODERN VIEWS AS TO THE PERSON OF THE SAVIOUR.

Earlier forms of error (189); Ebionites and Nazarenes, Docetæ and Valentinians (190); The Arian Controversy (191); Marcellus and Photinus, Apollinarius (192); Nestorianism (194); Eutychianism (195). The Council of Constantinople, A.D. 681 (197); Adoptionist Controversy (197); *The time of the Reformation* (198). Eucharistic Controversy (199). Servetus and Socinus (200). *Modern Speculations* (200); Swedenborg, Dr. Isaac Watts (201); Pantheism (203), Thomasius and Gess (204); Schleiermacher (205); Influence on present-day literature (206) ... ... 189—207

LECTURE XVI.

THE WORK OF THE REDEEMER.

It is a Manifestation and Representation (208), Christ is connected with the world as a world (211), man as a race (212), the Jews as a people (214), the Divine Law as a covenant of life (216), its precept (217), and penalty (218). His connection with the Redeemed (221); and relation to the Father (225) ... 208—227

LECTURE XVII.

THE RELATION BETWEEN CHRIST'S ENGAGEMENTS;
OR,
THE RELATION TO ONE ANOTHER OF THE VARIOUS TIES BY WHICH CHRIST IS BOUND.

The claims and responsibilities of those ties (228). Christ's relations are co-ordinate (229) and subordinate (230); Scriptural testimony (233). Christ in His mediatorial work is the Representative of the Redeemed (235); the demands entailed through this Headship—the Reconciliation of the race to God (238): its nature, method (239), and accomplishment (241); Why did Christ die? (243). The law of self-sacrifice (246). Christ's sufferings and death were penal (248), and also sacrificial (250). The nature of sacrifice (251). *Satisfaction* (257): its nature (258) and accomplishment (259). Scriptural testimony (260). *The Claims of righteousness* (261). Rectoral righteousness (262). *The Claims of law*: their nature (265) and extent (268) ... ... 228—270

LECTURE XVIII.

THE EFFECTS OF CHRIST'S RECONCILIATION UPON MEN.

They are fulfilled in the individual (271); Scriptural evidence (272). Sin is removed—sacrificially (273), by pardon (274), by Justification (275), and by Sanctification (277) ... ... 271—280

LECTURE XIX.

THE ASPECTS OF THE ATONEMENT.

Summary of the argument concerning the Atonement (281); it affords an adequate account of the sufferings and death of the Son of God (282); it reveals the true and perfect philanthropy of Christ's work (283); it brings out clearly the truth of the parallel existing between Christ and Adam (284); it reveals the true basis of the justification of sinners (285); it enables us to perceive the true scope and grandeur of Christ's work (287); it frees us from difficulty in presenting the Gospel to sinners (288), and enables every believer to perceive the direct personal love of Christ to him (291) ... 281—291

LECTURE I.

INTRODUCTION.

BRETHREN,—

I undertake the duties of this Chair with diffidence and yet with hope; with diffidence as to myself—my capabilities and my want of leisure, but with hope both in the Master whom we alike desire to serve, because we love Him, and in the fraternal regard which you have always largely accorded me. The desire which has brought you to this institution has been to know more of God, and to know better what you already hold, and my desire is, and prayerful effort shall be, to help you. I need not say to those who have been for some time at the College that it is not my manner to lord it over any man's belief or opinions. I may lament that others do not see eye to eye with me, I may pity their infirmity, I may pray that they may be converted, but I trust I shall never impugn their motives, or encroach upon the rights of private judgment. At the same time, I have certain fixed opinions and beliefs which I shall do my best to expound and enforce. There is a form of "sound words" which I consider it a duty to commit to faithful men. There are things most assuredly believed amongst us, and it were unfaithful to the office I hold, pernicious to your souls and to your ministry, baleful to the Churches and Evangelical religion, treasonable to the King and Head of the Church, if I did not deliver these tested and trusted truths with the accent of a firm conviction and the energy of belief. I trust I shall also know where to be silent, as well as where to speak, where to pause, as well as to proceed; and thus act in the spirit and prudence of the inspired words—"The secret things belong unto the Lord our God: but those things which are revealed belong unto us and to our children for ever, that we may do all the words of this law."[1]

---

[1] Deut. xxix. 29

But, my brethren, whether we pause in reverence, or advance in enquiry and discussion, my one prayer is, that I may through the grace of my Lord and Saviour be a helper of your faith. There is nothing that I would consider a greater reproach than to have weakened the faith of any brother in some truth of the Gospel. Faith is the staple commodity of the minister of the Gospel; and the measure of our faith is the measure of our capacity to serve our Saviour, and thus our fellow-men. If a preacher has not faith he has no good reason for entering the pulpit. Without faith on his own part, he cannot hope to promote faith in others. Faith is the one thing we wish to produce: for faith in Christ is salvation, faith among Church members is victory, faith between man and man is peace, progress, and prosperity. Without faith it is impossible to benefit man, as it is impossible to please God. Taking this view, I hold it a crime against the holiest and best interests of men for a man to become the mouthpiece of scepticism; and especially for a minister to become a mere advocate of doubts and negations. Such men reverse the Scriptural order, which is, "I believe and therefore have I spoken," and say, "I, *greater I*, doubt, discard, and therefore have I spoken." No worthier reason for its existence could many a volume give which has of late issued from the press. But we have not so learned Christ: we have one word to utter—*Believe*,—to the sinner, that he may have Eternal Life, to the believer, that he may go from faith to faith, and from strength to strength. I trust that the result of all our exercises here may be that we may be the better able to utter that word, with greater intelligence and with greater power.

Brethren, I count it a great honour to be permitted to trim those lamps that shall burn and shine in the sanctuary of God. It is, perhaps, a greater honour to burn and shine so that the wanderer, the lost, and the despairing may read the words of life and peace; but, my brethren, if Christian light is the stronger or clearer through aught I can do or say, I shall claim to enter into your joy over those precious ones recovered unto God.

"Every physician of generous principles," as Plutarch expresses it, "would have an uncommon ambition to cure an eye intended to watch over many persons, and to convey the sense of seeing unto numbers; and a musical instrument maker would, with uncommon pleasure, exert his skill in perfecting a harp, if he knew that it was to be employed by the hand of Amphion, and by the force of its music, to draw stones together for building the wall of Thebes."

Brethren, you are the eyes through which Christ is to gaze, and through which Christ is to weep over the miserable and the perishing. You are the harp to be touched by the hands of a greater than Amphion, and by the glad sound whereof, the walls of a fairer city than Thebes are to be built, even the heavenly Jerusalem, and the living stones of the heavenly temple charmed into harmony, and attracted so that they shall grow together into a habitation of God through the Spirit.

In so great a matter to do a little is a ground for rejoicing, but I am not so ill-acquainted with myself as to hope to succeed in that little unless God shall perfect His strength in my weakness. Pray for me, brethren. Pray continually that we may be helped together in this great undertaking. "*The Lord is our Refuge and Strength.*"

As we shall have frequent occasion to use the word Theology, and as it is a technical term for the subject in hand, it may be convenient to glance at its meaning and application. According to its strict etymology, it signifies *a discourse concerning God*, as he who composed or delivered that discourse was called θεολόγος, a theologian. It was thus the writers of treatises on the gods, or poets such as Orpheus and Hesiod came to be called θεολόγοι. Then turning from the pagan to the Christian, and rising from the false to the true, John the Apostle was called θεολόγος, because the Deity of the Saviour was his central theme. In later times Gregory Nazianzen enjoyed among his contemporaries the distinction of θεολόγος, because of his renowned orations on the same subject. From the nature of the case, *Theology* amongst the Christians developed a more varied and comprehensive meaning than the pagan mind had ever grasped. The Christian not only held discourse of God, but also received the Word of God. The Christian speaks of God because God has spoken to him. The one cannot be truly done without the other: without God, we cannot speak concerning God. From this view of the case, Turretinus held that *Theology* meant that doctrine which originally came from God, objectively treated of God, and finally led to God. Thomas Aquinas, some centuries earlier, had expressed the same thought, with equal clearness in his famous sentence:—"*Theologia a Deo docetur, Deum docet, Et ad Deum ducit*": God is the Teacher, God is the Theme, God is the end of Theology. Still widening, the term was applied, not only to God, but also to all the revealed divine relations to man, and especially to those relating to his Eternal Salvation.

It may seem strange that a word of such reputable origin and connections should in our day fall under reproach and rebuke, I had almost said execration. Leaving out of view the recent currents of opinion and styles of teaching, the dislike of the somewhat stable and stately word "*Theology*" seems altogether unaccountable. With these before us, all becomes plain. "Theology" is discarded, not because the new teachers have no theology to teach, but because they will not give their message the time-honoured name. Is it because their message is so raw, so ill-compacted, that it is not worthy of it? Is it because by doing so they would challenge a comparison between the old and the new? Is it because they hope that by simply presenting what they have to say in a nameless, unchristened fashion before the world, and incessantly puffing their contempt at Theology, they can unawares supplant the cherished truths of Evangelical Religion? Is it because they claim a higher epithet for their doctrines? Or is their collection of impalpable essences too fine for analysis, too delicate for use, too volatile and transitional to be stamped with a definite name? May there not be a combination of all these reasons, and many others that might be adduced, in the reiterated boastings and sneers against the word, which no man rejects who accepts the historical doctrines of vital Christianity, but which so many discard for the sake of some new-fangled notion? We hear of *exploded* theologies, of *obsolete, antiquated* theology, of theology that is effete and vanquished; but we have never yet heard of the time and place where the explosion occurred, nor of the valiant man who performed the deed. We have heard of the attempt ofttimes repeated, but always without success. The walls and bulwarks are there as of yore, only more venerable and venerated through this fresh resistance, for it is still true that "*no weapon that is formed against them shall prosper*" (Isa. liv. 17).

In former days objections were brought against the word because it was not found in Scripture; but the thing itself is there, and that is found in Scripture which is within its meaning, although not expressed by the current word for that meaning. A rival is now set up in the word *religion*, as if by exalting "religion" theology might be cast down. And since the words are put into competition, it may be as well to compare them.

We may view "religion," as James does (James i. 27), as expressing the mere external forms of piety. Religion thus dissociated from the devotion of the soul and the guidance of the reason, is always on the brink of falling into superstition. Those who oppose religion to theology will hardly be content with this narrow province of external offices for its action. They claim more; they claim the heart as well as the hand. They include in their notion the devotion of the Spirit and the practices of Christian life. Still we say the exposure to superstition is as inevitable now to the inner spirit, as it was before in the case of the outward practices. The spirit needs an informing truth to render its piety intelligent; and whence shall this truth be drawn but from that one Source, the God of truth, to whom all true and undefiled religion is ultimately directed? When we have enumerated all these elements, truth, devotion, practice, as essential to religion, all antagonism between religion and theology vanishes away. Religion, being primarily inspired truth from or concerning God, is consequently dependent upon theology, to whose special province the truth of or from God belongs. The true relation, therefore, of religion to theology is one of dependence; the rival, when set in her proper station, appears to be no more than the handmaid. Summed up in a brief sentence, Theology is the science of religion, religion the practice of Theology. While, therefore, none but an atheist will reject religion, we must expect to find sceptics opposed to any and every system of Theology.

Up to this point I have dealt with "religion," not so much as it has been defined and accepted among Evangelical Christians, but as it is being set in array against the truths of the Gospel, when these truths are thrown into a system and taught dogmatically. It is, however, but just to the position we take—the historic position of Evangelical Christendom—to quote a well-known definition in which this is clearly set forth. "The word Religion always denotes either a system of truths, of which God is the Great Subject, or a system of affections or conduct of which He is the Supreme Object."[1] Again, Dr. Fleming writes: "In all forms of *Religion* there is one part which may be called the doctrine or dogma, which is to be received by faith; and the *Cultus* or worship, which is the outward expression or mode of manifesting the religious sentiment." The use of "religion" in this comprehensive definition, either for the truths of revelation, or the practice of godliness, forbids the placing of it in antagonism to the truth, quite as emphatically as to the practice, while revealing its perfect accord with both. This inner, this essential harmony of Religion and Theology, of theoretical truth and practical godliness, having been once fully ascertained and recognized, it is not a difficult matter to discern their mutual relationships and their

---

[1] Dwight's *Theology*, Vol. I, page 1.

different spheres. They are both human embodiments of what is divine; Theology is the intellectual embodiment of truth in a system, religion the practical embodiment of truth in the life. The relation that Theology holds to religion is that of an architect's plan to the house that is being built; and the command from on high is that which was given to Moses, "*See*," said the angel, "*that thou make all things according to the pattern shewed thee in the Mount*" (Heb. viii. 5).

With this brief exposition and vindication of the term "Theology," I proceed to make some observations on the medium through which we have ofttimes to arrive at the knowledge of its Scriptural truths.

In looking at these truths we have not only to fix in mind the truths themselves, but to take into account the medium through which they are viewed. It matters much whether that medium is clear or whether it is coloured: whether it allows what is presented to appear as it really is, or serves only to distort and disguise, so that its true lineaments are not discerned. The stick that is straight in air appears bent when thrust into water, although it really remains as straight as before. The features of a landscape, under certain modifications of light and shade, may seem beautiful and fill the beholder with delight; but with an overcast sky that beauty may be turned to dulness and disgust. The Scriptures themselves warn us of this:—

"*Unto the pure all things are pure: but unto them that are defiled and unbelieving is nothing pure; but even their mind and conscience is defiled.*"[1]

"*Blessed are the pure in heart: for they shall see God.*"[2]

"*He that is spiritual judgeth all things.*"[3]

It shows us the result of using a faulty medium:—

"*The natural mind receiveth not the things of the Spirit of God: for they are foolishness unto him.*"[4]

"*The wrath of God is revealed from heaven against all ungodliness and unrighteousness of men who hold the truth in unrighteousness.*"[5]

Passing by the general treatment of this law, touching only on the one branch—so far as it applies to current opinion, we ask, How is this opinion formed? Like the deposit in the ocean bed, the result of the movements of the waters of many centuries, such is the public opinion of the world; and thus have many heresies arisen, as, making the story as short as possible, I will proceed to narrate.

---

[1] Tit. i. 15. [2] Matt. v. 8. [3] 1 Cor. ii. 15. [4] Job v. 14. [5] Rom. i. 18.

When the message of the Gospel was expounded to the nations, its centre was found to be in the Cross. This centre, indeed, was soon seen to be resting on many sublime, and to the pagan mind, altogether new truths—the unity of God, the unity of the race, the Divine origin, and the Divine government of the universe. With the message of Salvation, therefore, there went forth these vital attendant truths that smote to their overthrow the heterogeneous theories of the heathen world. Their philosophies, their religions, their moral notions and teachings all felt the shock and suffered in the ruin. The very process of refinement and development, which had set in six centuries before our Saviour's advent, had slowly prepared the way for the sudden climax and catastrophe of the ancient religions and philosophies. The excessive culture of their religions had led to weakness, and the development of their philosophies tended to their dissolution.

God of His free will had created all things: of His free mercy had offered man forgiveness: of His free love had come to save him from his sins: God was in Christ reconciled, and the Kingdom of heaven was come; and of this Kingdom the Christ, the Son of God, was King. In Him, all ranks, all races, all conditions of men were to find a Deliverer, a Friend and a Brother.

Based on a faulty foundation, the vaster the ancient superstructure grew, the weaker it became, till struck with the Divine force of the Gospel truth, the fabric was rent and fell to fragments. Then set in the reaction in the revival of paganism. Julian, the Emperor, attempted with all his resources and arbitrary power to reconquer for his idol gods their abdicated thrones and surrendered sceptres. But in the plains of Asia he fell, and with his expiring breath confessed, *Thou hast conquered, O Galilean.* The New Platonic School of Alexandria delivered their attack on the meagre doctrine of the "Barbarians," as they called the Christians. A wondrous mixture was that new philosophy with elements gathered from all systems of thought and religion, and well fitted to allure and intoxicate, but not to satisfy, the mind and heart! All the cleverness of able advocates, and the charm of eloquent expounders could not save it from utter failure in its attack upon Christianity.

What could not be done from without Christianity, was now attempted from within. The pagan and Jewish intellect, baffled in its external assaults, appeared in the very ranks of the faithful. It questioned the reality of Christ's person. It turned His divinity into a myth, or treated

His humanity as a phantom, and so sought to make Christianity itself a myth or phantom. These home-bred heresies, with their numerous descendants, were in time publicly silenced, if not radically removed from the soil of Christendom. Then Christianity entered upon the enchanted ground of the middle ages. In this era of her history the Church sought both to appear uniform in doctrine, and supreme in the temporal affairs of empires and kingdoms. Her success was greater in the former than in the latter. Thus in the "*Summa*," the great Theological work of Thomas Aquinas, the most eminent Doctor of the middle ages, we read that "The heathens, Aristotle and Plato, appear as witnesses to Christian truth ; so also in the great cathedrals, those most striking representations of the age, everything, even the most heterogeneous, the very world of demons and goblins contributed to the great yet simple edifice. And all this for the glorification of the Church, that supreme power on earth which held in one compacted unity the whole fabric of human society."

Yet in these halcyon days of Ecclesiastical power, the spirit of heathenism was rather latent than extinct, and it only required the balmy influence of the revival of letters to awaken it and send it forth over Southern Europe in refined immorality and cultured blasphemy. From the Papal Chair itself came the saying "How much the fable about Christ has profited us, is sufficiently known to all."

Had not Savonarola arisen in the city of the Medici, and afterwards Luther at Wittenberg, and Calvin at Geneva,—men of the highest culture, men who through the grace of God knew the true province of learning,—then the revival of letters had been but a muddy and pestilential inundation to everything lovely and good in morals and religion, instead of reviving, as it has done through the prudence and care of these Reformers, Christian truth, and refreshed Christian life.

The freedom of enquiry which the Reformers claimed and exercised, was taken advantage of by many restless and daring minds, who had nothing better than negations to oppose to the wholesome dogmatism of Evangelical doctrine. Faustus Socinus led this fresh revolt. He attacked the doctrine of the Trinity. His teaching in effect stripped the Incarnation of its true glory, and the death of Christ of its real efficacy, and left the world a teacher and exemplar, but bereft her of what she most required, a Redeemer and a Saviour.

The English Deists of the 17th and 18th Centuries next appear upon the scene, setting up a kind of natural religion, garnished with the moralities of that very Gospel which they wished to supplant. They denied all Divine revelation of a supernatural kind; and with such men for expounders of their negations as St. John Bolingbroke, Lord Herbert of Cherbury; and for their poet, such a man as Pope, it is little wonder that the movement spread alarm amongst the orthodox. The rise, however, of Whitefield and Wesley, with their great proclamation of the saving truths of the Gospel far and wide over the land, poured such a current of life through the weak and shrunken limbs of Religion, that it again arose and shook off the palsy of Deism.

The naturalism of the Deists was, however, echoed by the French. Through the peculiar characteristics of the French mind, what had been on this side of the Channel earnest and grave, became on French soil frivolous, flippant, sensual and atheistic. Voltaire turned Christianity into a jest, and his countrymen had not the courage to accept what he derided. He boasted that he would rid the world of it in a few decades; and the Revolution elevated a harlot as the Goddess of Reason. Clad in that deed of blasphemy and shame, we see the climax of the spirit of negation; we see a rehearsal for modern times, of God avenging the rejection of Himself, in the very way in which the Apostle Paul records, that God's vengeance fell upon the ancient heathen world, " *Their glory became their shame* " (ROM. i. 21—25).

By the publication of the famous *Wolfenbuttel Fragments* by Lessing, English Deism was translated to German soil; and by the connection of Voltaire with the Court of Frederick the Great, the minds of the higher classes in Germany received the subtle contagion of his scoffing infidelity. Passing through various phases, more or less transcendental, it arrived at length at the one-sided system of Kant, by which all the sublime verities of religion, virtue, and immortality, yea, the very existence of God Himself, were based upon man's subjective thought.

From these elements *Rationalism*, which reduces Christianity to the standard of human reason, sprang. It is but the exploded Deism of the past, gathered up and galvanized into activity again for the uses of the present day. Following in its rear comes *Pantheism*, devouring what Rationalism leaves untouched,—the doctrines of a personal God, moral freedom and the immortality of the soul. While affirming all to be God, Pantheism in effect, denies the existence of God, and thus do the extremes, Pantheism and Atheism meet. Hence, too, it happens that the Sceptical Systems, no matter how high their pretensions at the beginning, or how fascinating the charm of some passages of their course, are yet in their end contemptible. Their progress resembles the course of the river Rhine, which, rising amid the snows of the Rhætian Alps, flows through many a lovely landscape, and though washing with deep and rapid current many an ancient tower and stately city, yet with diminished wave sinks at last obscurely mid the mud-banks of Holland. So do these transcendental philosophies, when their course has run its full length, subside into the mud of Materialism.

I have endeavoured thus briefly to give you a summary of those intellectual movements that have acted and been reacted upon by the truths of Evangelical Religion. Their history is the record of the storms that have agitated the atmosphere of Christendom, and produced that unsettled, ever-changing element, which we call *public opinion*. It is the outcome and result of the conflict of many heresies with truth, and of a quality as yet *unstrained*. We all more or less inhale it, and it subtly thrusts itself between the vision of our soul and every truth which we contemplate. It has operated upon us from the dawn of reason; it may have mingled itself with our intellectual and spiritual life; it is certain to influence our investigation of the great and eternal themes to which we address ourselves. Its presence ought therefore to quicken our watchfulness over our own hearts, and our desire for the unction of the Holy One to give us the opened eye, that we may behold His wonders.

LECTURE II.

SYSTEM, METHOD AND ORDER IN THEOLOGICAL STUDY.

THUS far, I have endeavoured to ascertain the meaning and vindicate the province of Theology; to give a brief view of its great truths, and of the public opinion which these truths have daily to encounter, and through which we must approach their investigation. I come now to touch upon System, Method, and Order, as applied to the study of Theology. I apply the word *System* to the *connected study* of the truths of Revelation; *Method*, to the principles which should rule us in ascertaining those truths; and *Order*, to the position which individual truths should have in a systematic arrangement.

First, then, with regard to SYSTEM.

When we begin the separate study of a single truth, and pursue the investigation, so as to make it thorough and exhaustive, we are very speedily convinced that to comprehend it, we must extend our enquiry to other kindred and related truths. Our conception of the one may be very meagre and imperfect, not to say erroneous, till it is traced in its manifold relations and windings. Each of the great truths, or leading doctrines of Christianity, resembles a great river, of which a true conception can only be formed by tracing it through its various windings, and surveying it under different lights, till you see what branches it sends into adjacent lands, and what tributaries the neighbouring districts send into it, from what fount it springs, and whether that fountain is peculiar to itself, or common to other streams; into what sea it falls, and what lands it refreshes in its onward flow. In this process, we are advancing from the particular to the general, from the isolated study of separate parts to the unity, the breadth and completeness of a system. To this we are compelled by the laws that regulate our minds, and by the fact of our own researches and reasonings thereon. When we put together two texts referring to the same subject, we are laying the foundation of a System; it is a mere question of addition to make that System complete. And, reverting to the illustration just used, as it is necessary to have a view of the general system of the natural irrigation of a country before we can perceive the distinct relations and uses of one particular stream, so is it requisite to discern the general relations of a single truth before we can fully expound its individual and special functions.

The Chemist would be able to give only a very poor account of oxygen, if he were not able to describe its manifold combinations with other elements. The Physiologist could give but slender instructions on the various powers of the human hand, if he left out of view the diversified play of the related joints, muscles and nerves; nay, if he did not take into account the action of the distant brain, and the subtle and wondrous sympathy between that organ and the whole human frame. As element with element, joint with joint, and one set of nerves with another, so is truth joined with kindred truth, and every particular truth, in some degree, modified in its action by other truths.

If distinct truths be thus traced in their relations with due care, it will be found that while they lose nothing of their distinctness, that distinctness does not imply isolation; but that there are great principles transfusing and connecting the whole body of truths and all the individual parts. Justification is not severed from the Atonement, nor the Atonement from the operations of the Holy Spirit; but all are united under the rule of one great law, the law of Divine Love.

Even if a mistake should enter into the System, and the system be so far vitiated; yet a faulty systematic exposition of truth is preferable to an enunciation without system. The latter mode in effect dislocates Divine truth, and supplies no safeguard against exaggeration or caricature; whereas the practice of comparing, classifying, and drawing from the data of the Word of God their inherent principles is in itself right, for it supposes the unity of all the truths of revelation; and when errors creep in, as they certainly will, it has within itself the means of cure. The error is more easily detected and cast out; the mind gradually rises to a clearer insight, until the beauty and harmony of God's revealed truth are perceived, and the eye of man meets the eye of God, beaming out from the midst of all His words and works and ways.

By arranging truths together, so that their unity is made apparent, the advantage is not exclusively on the side of system. There is a reflex advantage on the side of the individual truths. These truths form the elements that build up the system; but by a grateful reaction, the System illumines all those elements. Truth gathers clearness, point and strength, when expounded with the definiteness that a system compels, and from the force one part lends to another. What a flood of light the federal leadership of Christ pours upon the whole doctrine of the justification of the ungodly by faith! How man's sin and Christ's Atonement reveal each other's stupendous magnitude!

Dr. Priestley goes even further than I have done in advocating System, and I the rather quote his words, as showing how his school, since his days, have swung round to the very opposite opinions to those he held. He says, "No branch of knowledge, religion not excepted, can be taught to advantage, but in the way of system."[1] In another passage he speaks in a similar strain,—"Without positive instruction, men would naturally have been mere savages with respect to religion; as without similar instruction they would be savages with respect to the arts of life and the sciences."[2] Despite the errors of Priestley's own system of doctrine, any candid mind must admit that, as to the value of system itself, his testimony is true.

Let no one suppose that, in advocating this connected study of truth, we are touching upon a plan unknown—much less alien—to the Word of God. Wherever we read in the discourses of our Lord of His reasonings, and of the reasonings of the Apostles, we have evidence, and even examples, of the systematic treatment of truth. That same Spirit that scattered truth in history and poetry, in type, metaphor, and syllogistic argument, has Himself laid down the rule "*that no prophecy of the Scripture is of any private interpretation,*"[3] and has Himself used the words, "*Comparing spiritual things with spiritual.*"[4] Not only does this method of study thus receive the very highest sanction; but the Sacred Volume affords us examples where it was practised with the happiest and best results. Was it not in this way that the risen Saviour drove away the darkness and despair from the bewildered and sorrowing disciples on their journey to Emmaus? "*Beginning at Moses and all the Prophets, He expounded unto them in all the Scriptures the things concerning Himself*";[5] and thus gave unto them a system of truth of which He Himself was the Centre.

---

[1] *Instit. of Religion*, Vol. I. Notes, p. 28.   [2] P. 25. Ibid.   [3] 2 Peter i. 20.
[4] 1 Cor. ii. 13.   [5] Luke xxiv. 27.

The sermon of Peter at Pentecost, Stephen's defence, the style of Paul's ministry in the Jewish Synagogues,—"*reasoning out of the Scriptures,*"[1]—the plan of study of the noble Bereans, the Epistles to the Romans, Corinthians, and Hebrews, all afford numerous and notable proofs of selecting, classifying, and eliciting from the scattered passages of Scripture their inner principles ; and, therefore, of treating truth in a systematic manner. Herein Christ and his inspired Apostles have left us an example that we should follow in their steps.

METHOD.

Taking it then as clearly established that truth should be studied systematically, it becomes us to ask, What method ought we to follow ? The diversity that meets us on every hand shows that we are here in the presence of no small difficulty. The disastrous effects that have in some quarters followed from the admission of a false method warn us to treat this matter with extreme caution. A false principle will vitiate all. I may remind you that we are not now speaking of forming a system of Ethics or Natural Religion, of doctrine as exhibited in history, or in any or all sections of Christendom, but simply and wholly of forming a system of Scriptural Theology. This being our aim, we cut off at a stroke, and abandon, that self-contradictory principle which acknowledges, side by side with the authority of the Bible, the authorities of tradition and experience in moulding doctrine. To us there is no such formula as *fons primarius et secundarius et æternus.* The Word of God is the primary and the only fountain from which we would draw. If we consult traditional or historic doctrine in their authoritative form, it is as that doctrine is formulated in the Bible, and as that tradition finds a record there. If we hearken to the inner voice of the heart of man, it is only as that voice finds expression, and is expressed, in the living oracles. If we admit development, it is the development of truth within the bounds of Revelation. There we find the root, the trunk, and the wide-spreading boughs of the tree of truth, and there also may pluck its rarest, most precious, and ripest fruits.

We hold, in its fullest sense, the axiom of Chillingworth, "The Bible and the Bible alone."

We keep to this strong and true position as against the Rationalist, whatever be the guise he may assume,—the Deistic type rejecting Scripture, the Dogmatic turning Scripture into a philosophy, or the

---

[1] Acts xvii. 2.

Transcendental putting his own speculations on a par with the Bible. We maintain this axiom as a bulwark against the Mystics, as well as against the Rationalists; against those who grope their way by feeling, as well as those who reach their tenets by laws of thought. The Rationalist evolves his system from his mind, the Mystic draws his from the emotions. The Rationalist will only accept what his reason can comprehend, the Mystic what his heart approves. Although thus diverse in operation, both Rationalism and Mysticism spring from the same wide error, in assuming that man, either in mind or heart, is at once the measure and the judge of Revelation. From this we indeed differ as widely as the poles; nor does our difference concern manner and forms only, for it is one of principle that affects the whole texture of faith. We cling to it as vital and fundamental; that Scripture is both a plenary source, and of supreme authority, in determining all moral and saving truth. We do not go to its pages to underline, erase, or correct their contents; but as disciples, to read with the heart and with the understanding, what the finger of God has written for our instruction and comfort. We go, not to infuse our ideas into its language, but to cast or recast our ideas in its heavenly mould, and to yield ourselves to be fashioned by its divine form of doctrine.

If, therefore, we put the question definitely, What principle shall we follow in deriving our system from the scattered and diversified facts of Scripture? there is only one answer to be given. The whole world of research is divided broadly into two methods, the *à priori* and the inductive. The former reasons from cause to effect, the latter from effect to cause. The former assumes the knowledge of the law that determines any given actions, the latter seeks from the actions to determine the nature of the law. We are all aware how universal and paramount, not only in metaphysics and theology, but also in natural philosophy, the *à priori* method was for centuries. We are also aware how thoroughly during its supremacy, it stayed progress, and spread darkness and confusion throughout every march of scientific knowledge. We all know how dire was the struggle in which the *à priori* was cast down, and the inductive principle went forth, as Hercules from his cradle, having strangled the serpent there, upon its mighty achievements in philosophy and science. Bacon cherished this new principle, and nurtured and trained it into vigorous activity, and to him the world is indebted for the light, the treasures and the might it has poured around the life, and placed at the feet of men.

When the inductive method is applied to the world of nature there are certain first principles upon which it proceeds:—

(I.) That the senses are trustworthy, and that their testimony may with certainty be relied on.

(II.) That the mental faculties are equally incapable of deception, but are true in all their operations of perceiving, comparing, remembering and inferring.[1]

(III.) That those self-evident truths which arise, not from experience, but from the constitution of our nature, are to be implicitly trusted: such as, that every effect must have a cause; and that the same cause, under like circumstances, will produce similar effects.

Such being the first principles of the student of nature, his first duty is to ascertain the facts that the wide domain of nature contains; to collect, compare and classify them. In this stage of his work he has nothing to do with hypotheses, he has only to see that his collection is complete, and his classification accurate. He now advances to the final stage, to deduce the general principles which underlie the facts, the laws by which they are determined.

When the inductive method is applied to Theology, certain first truths, not identical, but corresponding with the first principles of the naturalist, must be assumed. Such as, for example, that there is an essential difference between right and wrong; that nothing contrary to virtue can be enjoined by God; that sin deserves punishment; and other similar truths, that so manifestly bear the divine signature in the constitution of our nature, that no Revelation could be supposed to contradict them. Let it always, however, be borne in mind that into the ranks of these moral axioms nothing can be admitted simply on the grounds of individual persuasion, or arbitrary opinion. Only what is self-evident, what is universal, what is necessary, can be accorded the place of a first truth; and all things that cannot commend themselves to our mind by standing this threefold test, must be ruthlessly excluded, no matter how bright the names whereby they are endorsed. It is in this region that we must be chiefly on our guard against what it is the fashion to call "*intuitions.*" A vast amount of crude dogmatism that will not bear a moment's examination is thrust upon us under this name, mystic and imposing,—imposing only because it is mystic. If the old plain and unpretentious names, such as "opinions," "sentiments," or

---

[1] For examples of belief in adaptation see *Human Intellect*, Porter, page 611.

"convictions," were used, the world would more readily know how to deal with speakers and writers who seek to preclude criticism by the use of an indistinct and pompous phraseology, and strive to instil the idea that they have drawn from the clear fountain head, while all others have been condemned to sip at the muddy stream. The application of the threefold test will enable us to detect the true in the midst of the pretended moral axioms. Sad, indeed, would be the havoc on many a modern page—as chaff before the winnowing fan; or as Apollo treated prayer, according to the old translation :—

> "One half Apollo kept in mind,
> The other half he whistled down the wind."

With the recognition of these first truths must proceed the collection of the facts of Revelation. Whatever God has made known of Himself, or of man, must be ascertained. The record of all is in the Bible, and hence it is that the Bible is the Theologian's Universe, since all the facts of truth lie within its covers.

Narrowing as this does our labours, and simplifying our aims, it does not remove our difficulty with regard to the collection of the data for doctrine. The difficulties are peculiar, and require that the utmost diligence and care should be used. We are liable to mistake, or even not to see, the facts which lie before us. From this source alone innumerable errors have arisen.

Not only must we use diligence and care in collecting the facts themselves, but we must see that the collection is complete. We must take good heed, so that if possible nothing is omitted. The fact omitted may be that one which is absolutely essential. The suppression of a truth may be the suggestion of a falsehood. Of this, the history of every controversy affords glaring examples. Without going far afield, we have an example at hand sufficiently patent to all.

The Jews, in the time of the Advent, had formed their conclusions concerning the Messiah : He was to be openly David's Son, and issue from Bethlehem of Kingly dignity. He was to break the power of Israel's bondage, and raise the tribes to a pitch of earthly dignity they had never before reached, by making Jerusalem the centre of a universal kingdom. In the formation of their opinions, we now know how grievously they erred, and how tenaciously the error clung to even the disciples of our Lord. Now what was the reason of this error? An exhaustive collection of the prophetic testimonies concerning the Messiah had not been made. Evidence of His royal character only had been admitted, while the whole body of the facts of prophecy touching His sufferings had been excluded. It was only when the two were combined, when Christ was testified to be a King, and yet a Sufferer, the Anointed of the Father, and yet the Rejected of men, that the great mystery of godliness began to be unfolded, and the Spiritual redemption and Spiritual reign of the Messiah were expounded to mankind.

This example enforces the necessity for a complete induction of Scriptural testimony on any given doctrine. We must recognize all kinds and hues of testimony. We must give each its appropriate weight. We must not allow ourselves to fall into the habit of ignoring, perverting, or lessening the facts which seem to tell against our favourite opinion. Let the opinion be modified, let it be abandoned, sooner than a single undoubted jot or tittle of the Book of God should be impaired. When we read, "*No man can come unto Me, except the Father which hath sent Me draw him,*"[1] we hold that there is a necessity for this Divine drawing, in order that any man should come to the Saviour, notwithstanding what men may say of the natural good tendency of the human heart. When we read, "*Who His own self bare our sins in His own body on the tree,*"[2] we gather that no theory of the death of Christ that omits the bearing of our sins can be true. Sin-bearing must be taken into account if we would rightly understand the meaning of that tremendous event.

We advance another step in the application of the inductive method to Theology. True Science seeks her principles in the phenomena of Nature, she makes no attempt to evolve from the human consciousness, or to frame from the laws of thought, or glean from personal intuitions, the velocity of light, the laws of sound and electricity, or the properties of matter in any of its various forms. Science is powerless to impress any mere theory upon the actions of Nature, and speculations are worthless in her esteem without the corroboration of facts. In vain the alchemists of the middle ages tortured Nature to confess to a secret subtle fluid whose taste would charm away the ravages of decay and the approach of death. The theory was beautiful and seemed to do honour to her potency, but Nature refused the honour; and every element, in every combination, to this very day has resolutely declared, the elixir of life is not in me. The geographers of a former age conceived the theory of a North-West Passage to America. So sure were they that it must exist, and so great its probable advantages if it

---

[1] John vi. 44. [2] 1 Peter ii. 24.

did exist, that expedition after expedition was fitted out to make the desired discovery. Incredible sufferings were endured on the frozen seas, and around the ice-bound coasts of Northern Europe and America; but obdurate Nature could not be compelled to yield to speculation, the geographers were obliged to recast their theories and settle down in the belief that this Earth was actually formed without a practicable highway for commerce and intercourse between the old world and the new, in the direction of the North-West. Nature, in all her departments, refuses to take her laws from human lips. Man is not her master, but her scholar; and the more humbly he enquires, the more he learns. In the same way also when we approach the facts of God's written Book, our question should not be, What can we prove of Scripture? but, What do the Scriptures teach? When the statements on any given subject are gathered, like the various branches of the Golden Lamp in the Holy Place, What is the meaning that clearly shines therefrom? When the scattered parts are collected and intelligently arranged, What is the inner Divine plan that becomes apparent from the whole? What is the mind of God? That mind is the doctrine which we seek.

I say these things in reference to those who, like ourselves, accept the authority of the Bible as plenary and final. But if a man does not admit these two qualities in Scripture, let him define the authority he does allow—for certainly he must have some authority: and at the very least we claim for the Bible, apart altogether from its divinity, the very chief place in all literature concerning morals and religion. There is no book so original and piercing in its teachings. There is none so varied, copious, and profound in its knowledge of what is in man. There is none that has held so benign, so holy, and so sublime a view of God. As no other volume in the world, this has uplifted the curtain from the dark history of the past, and rent the veil of the future, unspeakably bright and unutterably terrible. As no other volume it has stirred the deep foundations of the human heart, and shaped the higher doctrines of mankind. And now as the light of knowledge is dawning on other portions of the globe, and is bringing into discredit the sacred writings of other religions, this volume appears like a true gem shining with brighter and yet brighter ray. All the world over, with the strongest minds it has the strongest influence, by the purest and tenderest hearts it is most prized, to the wisest and best of our race its wisdom is the most Divine. Without a rival and with undiminished power to bless, it is the angel's scroll unfolded across the heavens containing the Evangel of the nations. These things I claim for it apart from its Divine origin. If therefore a man puts his individual opinions into competition with Scripture, or counts them equal with, or superior to the sentiments of inspired authors, we know how to estimate his claims to our respect. But if a man clings to the shadow of Scriptural authority, is true to the word while false to the sense, takes the two-sided advantage of both, relying on Scripture when it supports his view, or rejecting it when against him,—then it is a more intricate task to make plain the position of such a theologian. It is difficult to strip him of the authority he assumes, and relegate his opinions to their real source. It is here that the wholesome rigours of controversy are beneficial, which, as the sharp east wind spurs the strength of the robust, and blasts the feebleness of the consumptive, cause truth to wax stronger and stronger, and vain speculations to pine away. The course formerly pursued by the Socinians, and the chastisement they received, afford notable examples of this. As Coleridge cannot be deemed other than an impartial judge of their conduct and its fate, I will cite his words : " Socinians," he says, " would lose all character for honesty, if they were to explain their neighbour's will with the same latitude of interpretation with which they do the Scriptures." " I told them,"—he adds, at a time when he was far ahead of them, as he himself informs us,—" I told them plainly and openly, that it was clear enough that John and Paul were not Unitarians."[1] Notwithstanding the scathing scorn these words imply, and the repeated exposures of the perniciousness of the Unitarian principle of dealing with Scripture, the practice has been revived and has spread much beyond the borders of their denomination. It is the old attempt, oft repeated, to mingle reason and Scripture in equal parts, so as to form a healing draught for the world's malady. It has failed. It is vain. It is impossible. It is as impossible for us to construct stable and harmonious systems by the admixture of self-devised doctrines and Scriptural proofs, as for the image of Daniel to be firm, resting as it did upon feet of mingled clay and iron. The one has no affinity with the other, and the time comes which ushers in a total overthrow.

Let any man bring his fixed beliefs, his self-formed axioms, and apply them to the teachings of the Word of God, it is not difficult to see the result, such is the overweening vanity man cherishes in the wisdom of his own conceit.

---

[1] Pearson : *Infidelity*, page 89.

If a man believes that a plurality of persons is inconsistent with a unity of essence, he must reject the doctrine of the Trinity.

If a man holds that creation is redemption, he must reject the Biblical account of man's fall, and the doctrine of recovery.

If a man denies the doctrine of federation, he must deny the imputation of Adam's guilt, and also the imputation of Christ's righteousness. Both original sin denied through our natural connection with Adam, and justification by faith in Christ, fall together.

Thus is devastation spread throughout the teachings of Scripture. These truths are ignored or explained away. But if Scripture speaks of plurality, as well as unity, in the Godhead, What authority is there for the one that does not support the other? If Scripture supplies us with a history of the fall of man, and commits itself in every conceivable way to that tremendous fact, and especially in the whole gracious plan of man's recovery, Of what validity ought our opposing theories to be thought worthy, to say nothing of our speculations and chance guesses? If sober judgment could speak in such a case, would it not meekly cast all self-derived fancies to the winds, and exclaim, "Let the living Oracles of God hold sway, both in thought and inquiry"? Would it not lead us reverently and humbly to bow with the child Samuel, and say, "*Speak, Lord; for thy servant heareth*"? (1 Samuel iii. 9.)

ORDER.

Having spoken of the method by which we arrive at a perception of truth, we now come to consider the order of arranging or studying the manifold truths of Revelation; and here we touch upon a branch of the subject of some importance. We all know the effect of grouping the figures in a picture, arranging the objects in a landscape, the arguments in a discourse—*callida junctura*—and even the words in a sentence. By one arrangement, the truly beautiful and excellent may be obscured, and by another, enhanced and illustrated. This holds good, also, of the arrangement or order of subjects in a System of Theology. Particular truths may be, by a false position, raised to an undue prominence, or depressed to a fatal insignificance. A tone is also imparted to the whole system, and all its teachings, which may be one of attraction or disgust. On the one hand, it cannot be denied that, by some arrangements, the dogmatic spirit comes into the ascendant, and gives to the whole an air of infallibility and finality that is the very antithesis of what our posture ought to be with regard to the great mysteries of the kingdom of heaven. We do not as yet command the whole prospect; we have not sent our line into the depth of the wisdom and knowledge of God, nor our intelligent scrutiny into the uttermost limits of the unfolding decrees of His lovingkindness and tender mercy; we have not found out the Almighty unto perfection. Hence, whatever system of theology we may form, these limitations ought to appear unmistakably in its very texture and arrangement. On the other hand, if the purely speculative, the polemical, and controversial are brought too much and too easily into the foreground, they cast a hazy and unhealthy atmosphere around, that must weaken and obscure all that follows. We are not afraid of giving the theoretical a place; but we object to that being either the first place, or the place where the foundation ought to be. After laying well the plain stones of the foundations of the Temple, as did that great architect, Solomon, we may then go on with him to the tracery of the Cherubim, and the finely-carved lily-work that adorned the Holy Place and the Most Holy.

It is even possible by the position we assign to obscurer themes—such as the origin of evil—to darken truths that are as clear as noonday. The discussion of the evidence of the existence of God—a fact which all Scripture never discusses, but assumes; the profound questions as to the inner life of God, a theme that has caused the strongest minds to pause with reverence rather than hasten with curiosity—has in some arrangements to be mastered at the very outset. One is launched upon the mysteries of the Trinity, at a time when he is seeking clearer light on the doctrine of justification; or is plunged into the stream of the evidences of Christianity, when it is more essential that he should be shown how to say, and to teach others to say, with heartier accent, "*I know whom I have believed, and am persuaded that He is able to keep that which I have committed unto Him against that great day*" (2 Tim i. 12).

It may now be as well to glance at the history of our subject; and although our glance be but hasty, it will put us in a better position for taking in the bearings of the whole question.

In the earliest centuries of Christianity we find nothing exactly corresponding to our modern "Bodies of Divinity", the nearest approach to this kind of composition being the ancient Apology. The Apology, however, if we may take as samples those of Justin the Martyr and Tertullian, was not framed for dogmatic, but defensive purposes. The order of arranging truths, and the relative weight attached to each individually, depended upon the varying order of the attack made at different times by the enemies of the Gospel. They were banners lifted up against the foe, pleadings addressed to the conscience of the world on behalf of the innocent who had been adjudged guilty, when as yet unheard. Their contents were therefore selected and fitted for instructing those without, better than those within the membership of the Churches.

The various treatises against the heretics of the period were of the same type. Tertullian directed his against Marcion, Irenæus in his great work attacked all heresies, while Clement of Alexandria, and even Augustine and Jerome, in their numerous productions kept up for the most part the same kind of fragmentary warfare against prevailing errors.

Augustine, however, who had so keen an insight into Divine things, began to perceive that the Christian teacher must do something more than demolish the untempered theories of heretical teachers. He must be constructive, as well as destructive. From the pen of the great Father we consequently have some of the first treatises which contain an orderly account of the truths of the Gospel, such as his *Encheiridion* and *De Civitate Dei*. These are far from complete, but the Church has not been slow to perceive the incalculable value of this type of composition. Ever afterwards the great eras of her history are marked by productions of this kind. After the interval of the "leaden ages," Augustine's example bears fruit in the sentences of Peter Lombard and in the *Summa* of Thomas Aquinas. Anselm also and Bradwardine prolong the line of descent until the days of the Reformation, when Melancthon, the well-matured theologian of the great German movement, appears to take up the task of didactic teaching. His great work, *Theologiæ Loci*, betrays in its conception and structure the masters from whom its author learnt, and the moulds in which his opinions were fashioned.

Immediately succeeding and seconding the efforts of the German Reformers came Calvin, who was gifted with a highly-constructive genius. His *Institutes*, dedicated to the French king, and published when he was only a little over twenty years of age, made a fresh departure in the study of Theology, and have left their impress more or less clearly upon every great treatise on the subject that has subsequently appeared. I will, therefore, be a little more minute in my account of the contents of this work. It is cast into four books, treating respectively—

(I.) Of the knowledge of God, the Creator.

(II.) Of the knowledge of God, as Redeemer, in Christ, who was first made known to the fathers under the Law, and to us in the Gospel.

(III.) Of the mode of receiving the grace of Christ; what fruit we thence derive, and what effects follow.

(IV.) Of the external means by which God calls us into the society of Christ, and there preserves us.

The great burden of Calvin's teaching is—God all in all.

Next to Calvin, the great works of Francis Turretin may be fairly ranked on the side of the Reformed Theology. To this place they are entitled both because of their intrinsic merits, and because of the influence they have exerted in shaping theological thought from the date of their publication, in 1679, down to the present day. Turretin was held in the highest esteem by the learned among his contemporaries, not only for his profound researches in Practical Theology *Theologicæ Arcana Scrutatum*—but for combining *Eruditionem Seculi* with *Scientiam Scripturari*, secular erudition with Scriptural knowledge. This praise is no more than just, if his treatise of Theology be taken in evidence. His *Institutio Theologiæ* is remarkable for its great elaboration, its polemical parts brought down to the times, and its rigid adherence to a logical and scientific form of treatment. The work is cast in three parts, each forming a quarto volume of about eight hundred pages. The colour of his opinions is reflected in the mode of distribution of his subjects. In the first part he treats of—

(1.) The province of Theology.
(2.) The Scriptures.
(3.) The Unity and Trinity of God.
(4.) Predestination.
(5.) Creation.
(6.) Providence.
(7.) Angels.
(8.) The state of man before the fall, and the covenant of nature.
(9.) Sin.
(10.) The free will of man in the state of sin.

SYSTEM, METHOD AND ORDER. 25

In the second part he treats of —

- (11.) The Law of God.
- (12.) The Covenant of Grace.
- (13.) The Person and State of Christ.
- (14.) The Office of Christ as Mediator.
- (15.) Calling and Faith.
- (16.) Justification.
- (17.) Sanctification.

In the third part he treats of—

- (18.) The Church.
- (19.) The Sacraments.
- (20.) The last Things.

By comparing this distribution of subjects with the arrangement adopted in the last great treatise of Systematic Theology that has issued from the Press, that of Dr. C. Hodge, it will be found that two hundred years have made little impression on Turretin's order.

A few years after the publication of Turretin's *Institutio*, there was issued at Amsterdam (1686) a work representing another school of doctrine. This was the *Theologia Christiana* of Philip Limborch. It contains an able and systematic exposition of that type of Theology held by the Dutch Remonstrants. Limborch divides his treatise into seven books, treating respectively of—

- (1.) The Sacred Scriptures.
- (2.) God, and Divine Works.
- (3.) Redemption.
- (4.) Predestination.
- (5.) The Precepts of the New Covenant.
- (6.) The Promises and Threatenings of the New Covenant.
- (7.) The Church of Jesus Christ.

Placing this order of themes in comparison with Turretin's, it cannot but be noticed how different is the position that the doctrine of Predestination obtains in the two systems. This difference is the key or index to the divergence in the views expounded by the two theologians. The prominent place Predestination holds in Turretin's order marks the strength of his Calvinism; the place subsequent to the Redemption, assigned to the same doctrine by Limborch, shows the modifying influence of Arminian teaching. With this difference, both the systems are formed on substantially the same principle.

The same manner of grouping the subjects pervades more or less the Theological Treatises and Bodies of Divinity that form connecting links between the times of Turretin and Limborch and our own. Each writer has some peculiarity of his own, while in the main adhering to these great exemplars. In Dr. Doddridge's Course, Pneumatology and Ethics are combined with Divinity proper, and in the latter, a large share of attention is paid to the Deistical controversies of the times. Dr. Pye Smith, in his *First Lines of Christian Theology*, approaches more closely to the favourite order of the Dogmatists of the present day. He has six books:—

(1.) On the Nature and Foundation of Christian Theology.
(2.) On the Deity.
(3.) On the Operations of Divine Will and Power.
(4.) On the Apostasy and Ruin of Man.
(5.) On the Redeeming love of God.
(6.) On the constitution, discipline, and ordinances of the Christian Church; its ultimate extent in the present world; and the consummation of the Divine Dispensations towards the race of mankind.

From this order the very perfect logical arrangement of Van Oosterzee varies but little. For the service that this accomplished theologian has rendered to the cause of Divine truth no praise can be deemed too high. First in his *Theology of the New Testament*, and then in his *Christian Dogmatics*, he has made contributions to Christian literature that have refreshed and quickened the believing and courageous thought of our own times, and will, doubtless, live to confer similar blessings on succeeding generations.

Glancing across the Atlantic, our kinsmen in America, with all their vivacity, show very little disposition to depart from established order. Dr. Timothy Dwight, President of Yale College, in his theological sermons, has introduced a very slight modification. He has arranged all his topics under three Systems:—

(I.) *A System of Doctrines*,—where he treats—
(*a*) Of the doctrines peculiar to natural religion.
(*b*) Of the doctrines peculiar to revealed religion.

(II.) *A System of Duties,*—divided into—
    (*a*) The duties of natural religion.
    (*b*) The duties of the Christian religion.
(III.) *A System of Dispensations,*—in which he treats of Death and its consequences.

This division is so extremely artificial on its very surface that it seems formed for the purpose of holding together compositions essentially disjointed and fragmentary, rather than for the orderly and proportionate exposition of one great central theme. The poverty of the scheme shows how little the grandson could appreciate the pregnant suggestions of the grandfather, President Edwards, in his *History of Redemption.* These suggestions, however, reached other minds gifted with an insight to perceive their value, and a vigour sufficient, at least, to attempt to derive some advantage from them.

Up to the time of Jonathan Edwards, Evangelical Protestantism had kept to the order I have exemplified with hardly an exception. All the Creeds and Confessions of Europe were formed after this fashion; and many more Systems of Divinity of the same mould might be added to those I have already mentioned. An order so widely diffused, so long established, and supported by such venerated and illustrious names, no man of judgment would lightly give up, or thoughtlessly disturb. The reasons for such a departure ought to be weighty and cogent. And certainly Jonathan Edwards, who may be credited with sounding the first note of such a change, was well entitled to the position of a sagacious leader, not to be moved by the vanity of mere novelty, but only by the attraction of solid advantages.

Why seek a change? If you look into the Systems to which I have referred, you will find they are formed on what is called the *Synthetical*, rather than the *Analytical* process. In the *Synthetical*, you begin, as in geometry, with the elementary principles, and from these compound the ultimate doctrines or conclusions of the science. In the *Analytical*, you begin with the objects of the phenomena which first solicit your regard, and then, by comparison and abstraction, are enabled to resolve them into their principles. It is evident that the Synthetical treatment demands a thorough and confident acquaintance with the subject-matter to which it is applied, and withal, a clear and correct notion of the primitive elements that enter into the investigation: or else lost in the stream of degenerate vaticination, some original flaw in the premises will be found to vitiate every deduction that may have issued from the infected fountain head. The Analytical, again, is more readily applicable to a subject, where instead of having the principles to set out with, it is necessary to seek them out, and thus, starting with the phenomena that are most palpable, or nearest at hand, end by a reverse process where the other begins. The latter method is surely more suitable for a science beset on every side with mysteries unfathomable—a science whose whole light breaks in upon us by partial and imperfect disclosures, and in which we vainly strive to find a ligament or connecting principle between one ascertained truth and another. With such a science we should feel inclined to proceed *modo indagandi*, rather than *modo demonstrandi*. Now, Theology we hold to be pre-eminently such a science— a science whose initial elements we cannot pluck from the dark recesses of the eternity that is past, and whose ultimate conclusions we cannot follow to the like dark and distant vistas of the eternity before us. We can, therefore, only explore it to the confines of the light that has been made to shine around us. There it is our duty to stop, intruding not into the things which we have not seen, but waiting in humble expectancy for the day of a larger and brighter manifestation.

The work in which Edwards applied this humble principle of analysis to Systematic Divinity is, as I have mentioned, his *History of Redemption*. "In it," as Rogers says, "we have little more than a rough sketch of a magnificent design." Edwards' own son tells us how his father's heart was set on the prosecution of this design.

The three main propositions into which he divides his work are as follows :—

(1.) "That from the fall of man to the Incarnation of Christ, God was doing these things which were preparatory to His coming, as forerunners and earnests of it."

(2.) "That the time from Christ's Incarnation to His Resurrection was spent in procuring and purchasing redemption."

(3.) "That the space of time from the Resurrection of Christ to the end of the world is all taken up in bringing about or accomplishing the great effect or success of that purpose."[1]

While not expressing his reasons, his work supplies them. It brings into immediate prominence the truths of the Gospel, the glad tidings of salvation in Jesus Christ. His Theology consists in the

---

[1] Vol. 1., page 536.

unfolding of Redemption, like the brightening of the bow of promise and hope upon the cloud of human sin and misery gathering and darkening through advancing generations.

Andrew Fuller came next with his suggestion and promise, never fully completed, of working out a systematic exposition of Theology of which Christ should be the centre. Every doctrine was to be viewed in relation to Christ. His own letters, however, show how difficult is the consideration of Christ in immediate connection with every theme necessary to the comprehensive study of systematic Divinity. His fifth and sixth letters prove that it was to him at least an impracticable task. The plan which Mr. Fuller left incomplete, Mr. Steward has carried out in his *Mediatorial Sovereignty*.

Dr. Chalmers commenced his professorial lectures on the customary plan, but felt his position unhappy as he advanced. The transitions from subject to subject were too violent, and the order conveyed a suggestion of mastery over mysteries that accorded little with his frame of mind. He wished to have an order that would in some greater degree go hand in hand with practical Godliness, and be to a considerable extent a reflection of the experience and relation of a believer with regard to the Gospel. He therefore arranged his course of lectures in such a manner that, after an introductory inquiry on the metaphysics involved in his subject, he touched upon—

(1.) *Natural Theology.*
(2.) *Evidences of Christianity.*
(3.) *Subject matter of Christianity.*
      (*a*) The disease for which the Gospel remedy is provided.
      (*b*) The Remedy.
(4.) *The Trinity.*

Believing this order of subjects to be on the whole the most clear and helpful, I propose for the most part to adhere to it in my succeeding lectures.

LECTURE III.

THE AIM AND SPIRIT OF THEOLOGICAL STUDY.

I DO not now intend to touch upon the aim and spirit of the Gospel Ministry. My purpose is simpler and nearer to each of us in our present circumstances. It is to view and review the aim and spirit with which we can most profitably carry on our present inquiries after a fuller knowledge of Divine truth. I put *aim and spirit* together, because it appears to me they act and react upon one another. Our aim controls our spirit, and our temper of mind modifies our aim. I propose to first consider the aim, and afterwards deal with the spirit.

If any one of us were asked the question, What is your aim in studying Theology? The answer that would most naturally rise to the lips would be, In order to become a better preacher of the Gospel. That answer I hold to be in general correct. It describes our employment as it would appear to an onlooker. It describes it, however, for that very reason, from the outside, and gives expression only to the superficial part of our purpose. The heart of that purpose is not reached, much less laid bare. It is the heart of that purpose which indeed more immediately and intimately moves us in our efforts.

This will be seen if we put another question, Why do we labour to become better preachers of the Gospel? No full or satisfactory answer can be given to this second question which does not give the chief prominence to our individual love and devotion to our Lord and Saviour. Our aim is therefore more immediately personal, and only remotely professional—the professional is grafted upon the personal, and our service to Christ grows out of our salvation by Christ. It is not an unnecessary refinement to draw this distinction, nor is it a distinction without valuable practical effects on the whole tone of our work. It is quite possible that, to some minds, such a statement of the case would wear the hue of refined selfishness rather than of consecrated benevolence. Such a misapprehension will vanish in a moment when we remember that the growth of true Godliness means the decay of the selfish principle. Men impressed with a morbid distortion of the Christian life may withdraw to some hermitage or monastic cell, and make the cure of their own souls the isolated aim of their efforts. Such is not Christianity, if Christianity means Christ-likeness. Christ was a man of "the people," and dwelt among the people, although infinitely above them. No man was so infinitely unselfish, or so divinely individual. To grow up into Him in all things is therefore the ideal of a true personal Godliness.

These remarks will, I trust, clear away the misapprehension that to make personal godliness the nearer aim is not the same thing as introducing a doctrine of selfishness.

To put the matter in other words, we do not become students of Divinity merely because we have chosen the ministry as a profession; but we enter the ministry of the Gospel, because by becoming Christ's we have made the seeking and unfolding of His truth our main object in life. Woe is unto us if we preach not the Gospel. We feel we cannot keep a conscience void of offence before God unless we engage in this work. We cannot say with its full meaning that the love of Christ constraineth us, unless our lives take this direction. The Call is in our souls, and we feel the work of grace within us is retarded while that call is disobeyed. If we would further the growth of our own piety, we must follow the call. And so conversely, if we would further the calling, we must strengthen the work of grace. Deepened piety makes the call the louder.

As thus acting and reacting upon each other we see the personal and ministerial elements in those burning passages of Paul's addresses. "*Take heed therefore unto yourselves, and to all the flock, over which the Holy Ghost hath made you overseers*" (Acts xx. 28), is the order in his appeal to the Ephesian Elders. To Timothy, he says, "*Meditate upon these things; give thyself wholly to them; that thy profiting may appear to all. Take heed unto thyself and unto the doctrine; continue in them: for in doing this thou shalt both save thyself, and them that hear thee*" (1 Tim. iv. 15, 16). How interwoven, how inseparable his own personal godliness was in all his ministry of truth we gather from such words as these, "*That I may win Christ,*" . . . . . "*that I may know Him, and the power of His resurrection, and the fellowship of His sufferings, being made conformable unto His death; If by any means I might attain unto the resurrection of the dead*" (Philip. iii. 8, 10, 11). "*Every man that striveth for the mastery is temperate in all things. Now they do it to obtain a corruptible crown; but we an incorruptible. I therefore so run, not as uncertainly; so fight I, not as one that beateth the air: But I keep under my body, and bring it into subjection: lest that by any means, when I have preached to others, I myself should be a castaway*" (1 Cor. ix. 25-27).

Our Lord has Himself observed this relation of the personal to the ministerial: when the seventy returned exulting in their conquests over the enemy, and our Lord entered into their joy, He immediately added the warning note: "*Notwithstanding in this rejoice not, that the spirits are subject unto you; but rather rejoice, because your names are written in heaven*" (Luke x. 20). Of this relation our Lord was Himself the most illustrious example, for it is said of Him, "*Though He were a Son, yet learned He obedience by the things which He suffered*" (Heb. v. 8). "*For it became Him, from whom are all things, and by whom are all things, in bringing many sons unto glory, to make the Captain of their salvation perfect through sufferings*" (Heb. ii. 10).

Even when we turn to what might be called purely ministerial exhortations, individual godliness appears as the root of ministerial usefulness: "*Study to shew thyself approved unto God, a workman that needeth not to be ashamed*" (2 Tim. ii. 15).

In these passages while the individual and official are distinct, they are yet related, and that in a very important manner: the one being preparatory to the other. Our inquiry into the truths of God is first for the information, upbuilding and sanctification of our own hearts and understanding,—for the strength of our own life, its holiness and conformity to Christ, for the support of our own faith in trials, the consolation of our own spirit in troubles and sorrows, for the removal of our own fears, and getting the mastery over our own doubts and sins. Then, because the truth of God means these things to us, we can handle it for the salvation, edification, enlightenment, and comfort of others.

This order serves to combine the practical and the theoretical, the speculative with the vital, and a man's own interest in the truth with his official exposition thereof.

It also puts these in their right order: he is a penitent before he is a preacher; a believer before a teacher: he is a disciple before he becomes a critic; he has seen, tasted, and handled, before he discourses, declares or expounds. It shows the necessity for first becoming acquainted, and then keeping up the acquaintance with the King that reigns in Salem's towers, the God who shines in Zion's Temple, before, like the Psalmist, we venture to "*walk about Zion, and go round about her; to tell the towers thereof, and mark well her bulwarks;*"[1] and to say, "*This God is our God for ever and ever: He will be our Guide even unto death.*"[2]

This order will make our speculations reverent, our discussions wholesome and conducive to godliness. Our enquiries and criticisms will not be like the withering blast of an east wind, that blights or parches everything fair and tender; but like the refreshing breezes from the south, that open the delicate blooms and diffuse the fragrance of the renovated plants and flowers.

It is an order that need not deter us from *proving all things;* but it will enable us *to hold fast that which is good.* It will protect us from the cultured trifling of those who are ever learning, and never coming to the truth: for it will enable us, having first come to the truth, even to Christ who is the Truth, to ever learn to profit there.

No more fruitful source of error, heresy, rationalism, infidelity and religious and moral decay, has been found within the boundaries of Christendom than that caused by the severance of the speculative from the practical, or the treatment of theological study rather as a matter of science than of life. The words of Dr. Arnold on this point are weighty and far-reaching. "There is in the rationalists," he says, "a coldness and irreverence of tone, and so apparent an absence of all feeling of their own personal relations to God as men and as sinners, while they are discussing, like indifferent spectators, His dealings with mankind in the abstract, that their intellectual fault is greatly aggravated by their moral defects. If we look for the cause of these defects, we shall find it in their exclusively literary habits, and in their want of Christian intercourse with their fellowmen, and especially with the poor; so that the Bible has presented itself to their minds more frequently in connection with their studies than with their practice."[3]

The truth of God is not to be apprehended fully in all its branches as one would learn a mathematical proposition, for "*If any man will do His will, he shall know of the doctrine, whether it be of God, or whether I speak of Myself.*"[4]

---

[1] Psalm xlviii. 12.   [2] Psalm v. 14.   [3] *Sermons*, Vol. I, p. 57.   [4] John vii. 17.

34 SIN, AND THE UNFOLDING OF SALVATION.

This insight into His truth is to be obtained only by communion with Christ. Apart from communion with the personal, living Christ, it is impossible to know His Word. Without Him we can do nothing. He still breathes the power, and still opens the understanding to the Scriptures. And as he that maintains fellowship with Christ must be holy, so is heart holiness a necessary condition for apprehending the truth. The carnal mind cannot perceive the native loveliness of the truth of God. The truth is holy, and this holiness of truth is revealed to the pure in heart alone.

Affinity, or a kindred feeling for the truth of God, opens out into an attractive power and receptive faculty for that truth. Even in the lower sphere of the natural world, that fine observer, Humboldt, demands such a pre-requisite. "For it is the inward mirror of the sensitive mind," says he, "which reflects the true and living image of the natural world. All that determines the character of a landscape—the outlines of the mountains, which, in the far-reaching distance bound the horizon; the dark shade of the pine forests; the sylvan torrent, rushing between overchanging cliffs to its fall—all are in antecedent, mysterious communion with the inner feelings and life of man."[1] And so, for a much greater reason, when in the Word of God, the grand and varied scenes of Divine truth are unfolded to our view, the thoughts which are suggested, the ideas we form, the emotions awakened, are all determined by the "mysterious communion" of our own inner life with the doctrines of revelation.

When we consider the tenor and the nature of the great truths of which Theology treats, it is not difficult to see that he, and he alone, who lives in fellowship with Christ can maintain full sympathy with these truths. Without such a sympathy, without a heart moved and swayed by the doctrines of the Gospel, there will be here and there an intellectual recoil and revolt from some which are the most vital. The themes of Theology are the most exalted and most profound that can engage the mind of man. "*The angels desire to look into these things.*"[2] All other themes are but the creatures of time, and earth, and sense; these are heavenly, of the soul, and eternal. All others are but as the fitful wind, the transient shower, and passing cloud, that may leave a temporary trace on the surface of the ocean; but these are the ocean itself; the ocean's depth, the ocean's vastness is in them; and all the melody of its deep-toned music rises and swells upon the believing soul.

---

[1] *Aspects*, Vol. I, p. 208.   [2] I Pet. i. 12.

Here is unfolded to us what may, in our present state, be comprehended of God, His inner life and outward manifestations: His relations to the world and to man, the innocent and the fallen creatures of His hands. Here is brought to light the sad and terrible reality of man's sin. But not upon our darkness only does "the lamp from off the eternal throne" cast its gracious bow. The heavenly ray makes visible the approach of a Deliverer. The sacred history first brings before us the ruins of Jerusalem, the decay of its beauty, and the overthrow of its bulwarks, and of the Temple, its joy and glory; and then shews us Nehemiah amidst them all as their restorer. So, too, theological truth reveals a greater than Nehemiah, One who bowed the heavens and came down, not contemplating the ruins of a city, but of a world; not the ruins of a generation, but of a race. It reveals the Son of God travelling in the greatness of his strength, mighty to save, mighty to restore the moral wastes, and rebuild among mankind the ruined temple of true and spiritual worship of the Father Everlasting. It reveals the mystery of the Incarnation of the Second Person of the Trinity—the Bridal of the earth and skies; His righteous life, His vicarious and atoning death; His resurrection, and entrance as the Great High Priest into the Heavenly Sanctuary, there for ever to make intercession for all who come unto God through Him. It reveals the descent of the Holy Spirit as the gift of the ascended Christ, by whose vital powers of light and love the soul is renewed in the image of God. It shews the laws of support and progress. It makes known the duties of the individual believer to the Saviour, and his relation to others of the pilgrim band, the host of God and the Church of the living God. It reveals the laws of organisation and action, their history and their triumph. It carries us forward to the confines of time, the very limit of the long struggle between eternal goodness and man's ingratitude, eternal love and man's rebellion, and leaves us not till we hear the note of the trumpet of God's eternal power and justice sounding upon the scene. Then comes to pass the saying that is written "*He that is holy, let him be holy still: and he that is filthy, let him be filthy still.*"[1] The bliss and the glory of the New Jerusalem shall encompass the people of God for ever, and the unbelieving be cast forth "*into outer darkness; there is weeping and gnashing of teeth.*"[2]

These are the vital and far-reaching themes which Theology handles. It presents them not as the fully-penetrated and thought-out deductions

---

[1] Rev. xxii. 11.   [2] Matt. xxii. 13.

of human reason, not as the result of human experience, not as the intuitions of the human mind, nor upon the ground of human authority. It presents them on the authority of the Scriptures, because they are contained in that Revelation of God to men. In dealing, therefore, with these themes, what is needed above all things is a heart that shall vibrate in union with Christ, who is the centre and crown of them all. We need to strive after His holiness, and especially to cultivate a teachable and humble mind. By humble mind, I do not mean a mind, weak, lax, negligent, or doubtful concerning what is held or received, but the consciousness that, although we know something, after all, we know but in *part*. Although we may be taken up the mountain of vision, yet all we can see of the infinite God is but part of His ways—the eye, as yet, cannot pierce to the breadth, and length, and depth, and height of the love of Christ. We must own that, notwithstanding all the unfoldings of divine wisdom and grace, that "*Eye hath not seen, nor ear heard, neither have entered into the heart of man, the things which God hath prepared for them that love Him.*"[1] God is infinite, we are finite; He is Almighty, we are weak; He is enthroned in holiness, we are stained and darkened with sin. He inhabiteth Eternity, we dwell in the shadows, infirmities and obscurity of time, earth and sense. How wonderfully is the declaration of the prophet applicable—"*My thoughts are not your thoughts, neither are your ways my ways, saith the Lord*"!"[2]

In proportion as we realize the truth of these remarks, we shall be more and more inclined to infuse our personal spiritual life into the investigation of truth. By doing so, this great advantage will accrue; we shall be able to invert the order, and infuse the truth more abundantly into our spiritual life. The truth will thereby become assimilated to our being. It will be made incarnate in us. It will be in us the living truth of God. And just as every particle of matter in our frame obeys the private law of our life, so, in a somewhat similar way, the movement and action of the truth will be controlled in us, according to the special characteristics of our own individuality. The truth becomes incarnate, and exerts its influence and achieves its victories through the peculiar powers of our own humanity. And as plainly as we can see the distinguishing features of the minds of Matthew, Mark, Luke, and John impressed indelibly in their records of Christ's life and doctrine, so, in the exhibition of Christ and Christian teaching by all

---

[1] 1 Corinthians ii. 9.   [2] Isaiah lv. 8.

really great and successful preachers in all ages, the marks and signatures of the men are visible in their portraiture of their God. This is so plain that it can hardly be said with greater truth or emphasis, the Gospel *according to John*, the Gospel *according to Luke*, than the Gospel *according to John Calvin*, the Gospel *according to John Wesley*, the Gospel *according to Jonathan Edwards*, or the Gospel *according to Charles Spurgeon*. It is a common salvation; but each has his own Evangel. The verity of the characters of these, and of all real witnesses for Christ, and the fact that they have Christ for their common Centre, are seen, not by their testimonies being parallel, but by their very divergence from one another. Each witness traces his own line, but all are seen to be drawn from the same Centre, Christ. The divine is the Centre, the human at the circumference. The display of the Gospel may be made as wondrous, as glorious, and as overwhelming to the imagination as Ezekiel's representation of the Cherubim by the River Chebar; but even these were not complete without the "likeness of the face of a man," and the "hand of man."

To reach this mastery, or, rather, total submission of mind and heart to truth, is no easy task. By some indeed it is never reached; no doctrine ever takes root in their minds, but only rolls about upon the surface. Or, if they do take firm hold of a doctrine, having themselves so imperfectly understood it, they expound it to others with so little skill, and enforce it on such insufficient grounds, that adherents are disgusted, and opponents provoked. This is betrayal, not by enemies, but by friends. A tremendous anxiety lest the very appearance of a reproach should be cast upon the least truth taught by Christ leads every true friend of His to surrender himself to calm and patient investigation, that he may assuredly discover, and be able to display and to defend, the essential properties, tendencies, and relationships of Gospel doctrine.

To do this, a man must shake himself free from indolence of spirit and of mind. He must cultivate that nimbleness and alacrity ot soul that starts to obey at the first faint call. Truth treads with lightning footsteps—a moment's delay and the bright vision vanishes for ever. Who has not found that at times when, in deep meditation, he has been pursuing some high and holy theme, he has arrived at a point where it seemed to branch off into meanings and affinities, so glorious as to astonish, so real as to convince, and yet so indistinct as to baffle his understanding altogether? What is it, then, we want in such moments?

What Herschel wanted when he gazed upon that bright tract that stretched across the midnight sky—the power of vision. And just as he with ever-extending reach of sight resolved luminous vapour after vapour into groups of distinct worlds, till through the shining strata of the Milky Way, he pierced to the blue and cloudless ether beyond; so, as the vision of the mind grows purer and more powerful, those tracts of thought that were at first full of nothing but flitting shadows will become peopled with the veritable and living forms of truth. This explains what we often observe, that only one man dares to utter what many may have conceived. He speaks because to him it is a verity: others are silent because to them it is but a phantom.

But whence is this far-reaching vision to be obtained? First, *from the light that shines from the countenance of Christ;* next, from what we advocate—*constant and diligent exercise in all the branches of discipline that sharpen the soul, till, by reason of use, it is able to discern clearly the mysteries of the Kingdom.*

Once more: Is not this advance to higher mental attainments connected most intimately with the development of a higher spiritual life? I am aware that many sever the spiritual from the rational, and even go so far as to give a broad hint that growth in grace would be much more rapid and sure were the intellect allowed to sink into neglect and decay. But why dig an impassable gulf between reason and piety? From those who hold this idea in its full-blown dimensions, I should like to enquire, Whence would spring the development of their piety, if their reason left them? Of this one thing I feel fully convinced, that those studies which refresh, nourish, and stimulate the roots of the mind, and cause it to shoot upwards and spread with greater luxuriance, do not, by necessary consequence or invariable law, inflict sterility and death upon the soul. On the contrary, in the majority of individuals, especially in those in whom the law of progress is strongly operative, the spirit begins to pine into inactivity and inanition, unless led by the intellect as its unwearied forerunner, ever on the wing to new regions of research, where it may gaze upon other aspects and other evidences of Divine wisdom, power, and love. To the truly devout man, in proportion as you increase the strength, and enlarge the range of his mind, so do you multiply and magnify the reasons and opportunities for his devotion. For if this be not so, How is it that, when encompassed with doubtful disputations, when beset with difficulties concerning the evidences of revelation or doctrine, the man instantly sinks spiritually distressed and disabled? On the other hand, How comes it that often a single ray of certain knowledge sends power and joy into the very centre of his soul? Does not he who is struggling towards a clearer apprehension of dwelling, living and acting in unbroken harmony with God in Christ, often feel himself like one seeking to pierce through the mazes of a tangled wood, and reach the shores of the lake that spreads its broad expanse of deep blue waters many a league in front. He can now and then see through openings between the trees the crested waves sparkling in the golden beams of day, or hear their melodious murmurings resounding from the beach, but the thicket holds him back, the thorn tears, and the tall trees cast around him their dense gloom of shade. That longed for tranquility and freedom of soul is not to be gained without a struggle with puzzling questions, without summoning up all the energies of the mind to cut through the intercepting intricacies, and disperse the lingering shades of error.

Lastly, Does not advancement in study give stability of character and steadfastness in the work? It not unfrequently happens that when a young and ardent spirit is led to devote himself to the ministry of the Gospel, he is carried away by a strong torrent of enthusiasm, so sudden and so overpowering as to leave little room for reflection, for sounding the depths of his own heart, for thoroughly estimating his powers, or sifting his suitability. The original impulse at length spends its force, and reaction begins to set in : his calling may still appear the best and highest course of life, the most holy and most Godlike, and the very sphere where a thousand others might play their part with applause and success. For him, however, in particular, the strain becomes too great, and he sinks under repeated efforts to raise his faculties to meet the imperative demands of his task. Where he does not fail utterly, the apprehension of doing so operates almost as powerfully as the reality. It arrests his progress, or flings him backward many a weary league, disappointed and dispirited, to his first starting-place. His first feeling is to give up—in despair, if true at heart, in disgust, if insincere. Yet this despondency may be only the isolation of a newborn independence. He has begun to estimate, to compare and decide and act, less by the example of others, and more by the persuasion within his own breast. He may have gradually drifted beyond the reach of the great influence which at first aroused, and afterwards perhaps overshadowed his enthusiasm, and now be warmed only by the feeble flame of his own devotedness. He is free, but he is alone. His very first sensation of liberty is of its solitariness rather than of its strength. It is the first hour of conscious weakness, but also the first of personal power. It is the first moment of perceptible wavering, but the last of parasitical dependence. The cause of this dejection becomes its cure. The effort of groping out one's own groove in belief and action, though at the beginning it may be wearing and wasting to the spirit, yet afterwards raises the whole mental and moral nature of the man to the unmistakable tone of vigour and robustness. The foundations of a true and distinct character are laid: his vagueness of views begins to vanish. While for a season around his character may float in confusion many impressionable, fitful, variable and contradictory feelings and opinions, yet the centre is sound and solid, and assimilates to itself all that is of a kindred nature in the surrounding mass; like the sand mingled with the salt sea and tossed to and fro, down and up, in the waves before it finally settles down and forms with its once shifting, now immovable grains, the rock that is to endure from age to age.

Only when a man has fought his way to an enlightened and positive apprehension of the reality and vitality of the Gospel; only when its essence has become incorporated with his being; only when he has made his ministry his own, and begins to work from a basis of his own, does he begin to feel the irresistible sway of full conviction, and have a sense of the unutterable responsibility and grandeur of the Gospel ministry. Service to Christ is no longer an intermeddler with his nature; it is the law of his existence. To him to live is Christ, and should that service lead to sacrifice, it is not unexpected. It is even so that he has learned Christ. To die is gain. He stands unmoved: suffering is the complement of service; he is prepared for either. Francisco Pizarro, the conqueror of Peru, in the memorable crisis of his career, when the Spanish envoy found him with his followers, enduring the most bitter distresses on the dreary island, almost naked, and well nigh famished, and offered them food, raiment, and immediate convoy home, would not even in those extremities forsake his purpose. The hero when all were silent, stepped forth, and drawing his sword, traced a line with it on the sand from east to west. Then turning towards the south: "Friends and comrades," he said, "on that side are toil, hunger, nakedness, the drenching storm, desertion and death; on this side, ease and pleasure. Their lies Peru with its riches; here Panama with its poverty. Choose, each man, what best becomes a brave Castilian. For my part, I go to the south;" so saying he stepped across the line. The constancy of the dauntless Castilian is the constancy of every brave servant of Christ, but touched for a nobler purpose and aspiring to a Divine reward. He reduced millions of his kind to misery and slavery, we would raise the soul to heaven. He sought the perishable wealth of this world, we seek the amaranthine crown of righteousness.

LECTURE IV.

SIN.

It requires but a little direct meditation on the appearances of human life to make a man conscious of the presence of some foreign element therein. Whether we regard that life as spread abroad in the vastness of a nation, shaping itself in the diversity of types or families, or throbbing within the narrow limits of the individual existence, this strange force betrays its presence. From the most ancient times history exhibits its existence following the race as a spectre, and every human heart to-day more or less distinctly mirrors its fatal features. Its touch in some way breaks the harmony, taints the purity, disturbs the peace, mars the beauty, embitters the sweetness, depraves the perfectness, and dims the glory of the life of man in this world, and surrounds the thoughtful soul with unspeakable apprehension with regard to the world to come. Various are the forms under which Scripture describes this thing, but there is one name that is universal and generic,—SIN. Sin is the all-spread disease that enfeebles our race. For the following reasons, therefore, I propose to direct our inquiry first upon Sin.

(I.) *Because the Gospel is a remedial system; and to comprehend the remedy it is needful to understand the disease.* I do not mean by this that any investigation of sin as the great plague of mankind, however profound or prolonged, would ever have suggested to man the true and only remedy which a righteous and loving God has found. Man, the diseased one, never could have found the sure method of cure for his disease. That is God's prerogative, and only possible to the All-wise, the All-good and the Almighty. Nor do I mean to deny that the knowledge of the Divine remedy opens up to the mind a deeper and wider view of our great malady. On the contrary, I hold that it is only possible to form a true estimate of what sin is under the light cast upon it by the humiliation, sufferings and death of the Son of God. The fierce light that shines from the Cross can alone penetrate and reveal the vast extent and heinousness of man's transgression; and the death of the Son of God alone affords an appreciable base line for its measurement. Sin never appears so exceedingly sinful as when it places the thorn-wreath on the brow of the Holy One and the Just, and drives the spear into His breaking heart. The delirium of its fever reached its height in the cry, "*Let Him be crucified.*" There is discoverable in the Crucifixion, if we could read its meaning, the attainment of Sin's maturity.

At the same time, if there is no sense or knowledge of the evil by itself, there will be no resort to the Physician; if the physician does not make an accurate diagnosis of the complaint, there will be no intelligent application of the healing balm. To apply a better than Gilead's balm is to be our great and delightful business in life.

(2.) Our next reason for here treating of Sin is, *because this subject is near to every one of us.* We have not to make a pilgrimage to investigate this subject. As each life has its own sin, and as sin forms a part of Divine Revelation, it is that part which not only touches, but actually rests upon our constitution and condition. It is here where the Divine is first made known to us. By reasoning and imagination, we may rise into the more elevated regions of the Divine decrees, the control of the infinite over the finite spirit, the essence and the constitution of Deity, and find matter in all for adoration, instruction and humility. All these themes belong to the heavens—the cloudy, airy, or starry heavens—of theology; we are men upon the earth. I do not say that these sublime truths move us not, or move us little. What I wish to convey is, that the centre of their influence is far removed and infinitely high, whilst the form in which that influence reaches us, and is first discernible in us, is in relation to our sad condition as fallen sinful creatures. It is in our sin, alas! we first come consciously into contact and conflict with God, into conflict with His law of holiness, and, blessed be His name! into contact with His law of love. In our disease we consciously touch the hand, the mind and heart of the Great Physician. Not in the disquisitions of the Pharisee, but rather in the publican's cry, "*God be merciful to me a sinner*"![1] do we show a vital apprehension of God our Redeemer.

(3.) I may urge in the third place, that as it is his *sin* that first

---

[1] Luke xviii. 13.

engages the mind of the inquirer for salvation, so we may with profit survey more thoroughly the nature, phenomena, and extent of sin, before we address ourselves to seek a fuller knowledge of the salvation that is in Christ. Our theory thus follows the order of our experience.

(4.) Finally, I claim this to be the *Divine order.* The sin was committed before the promised Seed was announced. Sin was allowed to reveal itself in the variety and virulence of its nature before He came, whose task it is to make an end of sin, and bring in an Everlasting Righteousness. The *Divine* Book, our supreme authority, tells us of that which is natural, and afterwards of that which is spiritual : of the first man who was made a living soul, then of that other, who was a quickening Spirit; of the first who was of the earth, earthy, and lastly of the Lord from Heaven.

Our course being thus clearly in accordance with Scripture, we proceed to investigate the meaning of the words which Scripture employs to describe the moral condition of man. And here a mournful wealth of language and imagery meets the view. A mere list of the chief words runs to considerable length. Passing by for the present the ideas these words may convey of the effects of sin, the sorrow and pain, shame and desolation, wrought in its course, we look simply at the way in which they represent what sin is in itself.

It is described as :—חָטָא—*Chata*—missing the mark.

ἁμαρτία, missing the mark.

עָוָה—'*Avah*—the distortion of right.

עָוֶל—'*Avel*—the turning away from the right course.

עָבַר—'*Avar*—the crossing over or transgressing.

רַע—*Ra'*—the breaking up of what is good with ruinous crash.

פֶּשַׁע—*Pesha'*—the revolt from rightful authority.

מַעַל—*Ma'al*—the betrayal of a trust.

אָוֶן—*Aven*—emptiness, nothingness.

אָשָׁם—*Asham*—negligence mingled with ignorance.

παρακόη, disobedience of a voice.

ἀνομία, non-obedience of a law.

παρανομία, transgression of a law.

παράπτωμα, a falling away.

סוּר—*Sur*—departure from God.
ἀδικία, want of justice.
ἀπείθεια, want of obedience.
ἀσέβεια, want of reverence.
κακία, evil in its principle.
πονηρία, evil in its practice.
ὀφείλημα, indebtedness and guilt before God.

Taking this list as representative rather than complete, we begin with the words that may be regarded as generic, חָטָא and its corresponding ἁμαρτία: these words are both translated sin, and very few others either in Old or New Testament are so rendered. The literal meaning of the verbal forms of these words is to miss the mark. In this sense Homer uses ἁμαρτάνω of Diomede in the pursuit of Dolon, the Trojan spy.

ʾΗ ῥα, καὶ ἔγχος ἀφῆκεν, ἑκὼν δ'ἡμάρτανε φωτός, (Il. X. 372.)

"He spake, and hurled the spear, but purposely *he missed* the man." In this same sense the sacred historian uses חָטָא of those skilful slingers of the tribe of Benjamin: "*Among all this people there were seven hundred chosen men lefthanded; every one could sling stones at an hair breadth, and not miss*" (Judges xx. 16). In a secondary sense *way* takes the place of *mark*, and both words are used of *missing the way*.

From this sharply defined meaning, obtaining in relation to what is physical, the transition was easy and natural to the region of morals. Here חָטָא and ἁμαρτάνω describe the sinner as " missing the divine aim of life." How complete this failure was in closest proximity to the very cradle of our race! We have only to make one remove from Adam, and find it in the history of Cain, his firstborn son. After the sacrifices had been offered, and the token of God's favour given to Abel, after envy had risen into hatred, and hatred had stained its hands red in a brother's blood, what was the feeling that brought irresistible torture upon his conscious soul? Was it not the sense of vast and irretrievable *failure to hit the mark* at which he aimed? Failure in the sacrifice, failure in the envy, failure in the deed of blood; and according to God's forewarning voice, this huge failure of Cain's, crimsoned over with moral guiltiness, made its lair like a beast of prey before his very door (Gen iv. 7). He missed God, and then went out from His presence, a wanderer in the wilds.

In order to perceive how deep is the sense of moral guiltiness this word conveys, one need read no more than the first four verses of the fifty-first Psalm. At the words of Nathan, the scales had fallen from the king's eyes, and the mean, selfish success of his sin stood convicted as a gross failure with regard to God. It is true that other sides of his evil course are there deplored : its disloyalty to God, the true King of Israel, in קשע : its utter wrong in עון ; the ruin and desolation it brought to the family concerned in רע. But it is in חטא he laments how sadly he had missed the divine purity. From his *sin* he therefore prays to be purified ; it was his *sin* that was ever before him. "*Against thee, thee only, have I sinned.*" Bitter as is the grief of David, it needs but the prophet's word to plunge all hearts into the same penitence, for all have committed the same dark error: "*All have sinned, and come short of the glory of God*" (Rom. iii. 23).

The word עוה has several renderings in the LXX, the chief being ἀνομία, ἁμαρτία, ἀδικία ; but not one of these exactly marks the form of its meaning. It means to *bend, make crooked;* and as a noun is admirably represented by our *wrong, i.e.*, that which is wrung out of course. Its native force is seen in Isaiah xxi. 3: "*I was bowed down at the hearing of it*"; where the surroundings show that the bending is of one writhing in pain. Its moral use appears in Esther i. 16. As a distortion of the right, it was brought by one of the king's wise men as the point of the charge against Vashti the queen : "*Vashti the queen hath not done wrong to the king only, but also to all the princes,*" etc. So lofty an example of wrong would infect all the wives throughout the Empire with perverseness of conduct towards their husbands. The conduct of Jonathan, in transferring his sympathies from his father's to David's cause, is stigmatized by that angry and disappointed parent with the indignant words, "*Thou son of a perverse rebellious woman*" (1 Sam. xx. 30). From Saul's standpoint such conduct appeared a distortion of nature. When Shimei, the son of Gera, met the returning king at the fords of Jordan, after having cursed him in his flight from Absalom, he plays the clever politician in entreating the king not to remember nor take to heart "*that which thy servant did perversely the day that my lord the king went out of Jerusalem*" (2 Sam. xix. 19). Such may be the form that the evil deeds of His people may assume to God Himself, Solomon apprehends in his dedicatory prayer (1 Kings viii. 47); and Daniel, in his confession, acknowledges the apprehension to be too sadly realized : "*We have sinned, and have committed iniquity,*" i.e., *acted perversely* (Dan ix. 5).

We come now to עול. With this and the foregoing word there is this in common: they both contain the idea of *bending* or *distorting*. It would seem, however, that diverse notions have gathered round the different stems. As we have seen עָוָה is the wresting of the right into a wrong, the turning of the Grace of God into lasciviousness; whereas עָוֵל is the bending aside from the right, the turning away to lasciviousness in the very presence of that Grace, and notwithstanding all its persuasiveness: "*Let favour be showed to the wicked, yet will he not learn righteousness: in the land of uprightness will he deal unjustly, and will not behold the majesty of the Lord*" (Isaiah xxvi. 10). The excellence of the surroundings in this case enhances the obliquity of the deeds of evil men, as a perfectly straight line shows up the bendings of one that is crooked, or rather as the pitiful care of the husbandman in sparing, digging about, pruning the barren tree makes its ultimate barrenness all the plainer. In a negative phrase, Malachi ii. 6 observes this same relation of עָוֵל to the law of God: "*The law of truth was in his mouth, and iniquity was not found in his lips.*"

The famous passage in Ezek. iii. 20 exhibits in a marked manner the same peculiarity of usage: "*When a righteous man doth turn from his righteousness, and commit iniquity, and I lay a stumblingblock before him, he shall die.*"

In the word רָע, Sin is announced by its noise and uproar. The central signification is *breaking up, crashing ruin*. In contrast with the fruit of the spirit which is peace, and with righteousness which is quietness and assurance for ever, this brings the "*crash as of the thunder,*" (Job xxxvi. 33), and "*a noise of war in the camp*" (Exod. xxxii. 17). It renders visible the sin in its consequences. It exhibits the rough exterior of wrongdoing, and expresses the ruin of what is good and desirable in man and society. It depicts the action of evil as the dashing in pieces of a potter's vessel (Ps. ii. 9); as the rattling roar of a consuming flame (Jer. xi. 16); as the rumbling noise that accompanies the earthquake (Is. xxiv. 19); as the discordant wailing of unbelieving discontent that swelled upwards from the tents of the murmuring Israelites (Numbers xi. 10). Readily, therefore, on the lips of the newly rescued and still trembling Lot does it echo the "Crack of Doom" which had just burst so awfully over the cities of the plain: "*Behold now, thy servant hath found grace in thy sight*" ...... and he pleads, "*I cannot escape to the mountains lest some* evil *take me, and I die*" (Gen. xix. 19).

The vociferous cry of "Stop Thief!" with all the suggested

consequences of lawless times, well illustrates the combined harshness and violence of the word. In this way it occurs in the bitter parable of Job. The sorely tried patriarch, as he turns upon his revilers, depicts their contemptibleness in the words, "*whose fathers I would have disdained to set with the dogs of my flock. . . . . . They were driven forth among men—(they cried after them as after a thief)*" (Job xxx. 1—5). From the shout and clamour at the detested presence of a thief in a camp, רֵעַ easily passes into the rough alarm of war. It was the tumultuous sound of the host of Israel, calling to conflict with the Philistines, that smote upon David's ears, as he came to the camp (1 Sam. xvii. 20). It was the loud cry of the tribes as on the seventh day they encompassed Jericho, and the city's walls fell before it (Josh. vi. 20). It takes nothing from the violence of its meaning to find it in these two instances used as the battle cry of the people of God, and as such used in a righteous cause. Inasmuch as war is essentially, according to James, born of evil,[1] and calamitous to mankind at large, the war cry in any mouth is the symbol of that calamity, wherever the silent, hidden principle of evil travels throughout this world, the רֵעַ, the din of strife and crash of ruin break out sooner or later around its steps. To accommodate well-known words: "Whenever it moves in anger, desolation tracks its progress; whenever it pauses in amity, affliction mourns its friendship." Still more literally accurate and pictorially terrible do the words of God, through the lips of Isaiah, blend all the features in the Divine indictment of sinners: "*Their feet run to evil, and they make haste to shed innocent blood: their thoughts are thoughts of iniquity; wasting and destruction are in their paths. The way of peace they know not; and there is no judgment in their goings: they have made them crooked paths: whosoever goeth therein shall not know peace*," Isa. lix. 7, 8 (cf. Prov. i. 16; Rom. iii. 15).

It is impossible to dismiss רֵעַ and its cognate words without giving some consideration to רָשָׁע, a word bearing some resemblance in sound, and a much greater in meaning. Their similarity lies in this, that they both contain the notion of *din, noise;* but the noise of רָשָׁע is the noise of tumult. Its central idea seems to be *quick motion*, or *agitation*, and it describes sin in its activity, its ceaseless energy. Hence *wicked* (quick) is our wonted rendering. And the perturbation that sin in this form produces, is as vast as "the trouble of the sea." "*The wicked*

---

[1] Cf. James iv. 1.

are like the troubled sea, when it cannot rest, whose waters cast up mire and dirt. There is no peace, saith my God, to the wicked" (Isa. lvii. 20, 21). Job consoles himself with the prospect of the grave, for "There the wicked cease from troubling; and there the weary be at rest" (Job iii. 17).

Changing the point of view, עָבַר enables us to contemplate sin in relation to law. Its primitive sense is *to pass over*, and is thus applied very often to the crossing of a stream, a bank or boundary. It has its equivalent in the Greek παραβαίνω. Raised into the moral sphere, it supposes the existence of law. The command is the boundary line of God. Where there is no law, there is no transgression, עָבַר, or παράβασις. It matters not in what sense law may be regarded, whether as spoken by God in Eden to Adam, or uttered by our Saviour on the Mount of the Beatitudes; as written by the finger of God on the Tables of Stone at Sinai, or written by the same finger in the constitution of our nature all the world over, law in some way is supposed to exist as the embodiment of the will of supreme and sovereign authority, by which our lives should be regulated. עָבַר is the violation of that authority; it is man's reply to the royal word, "Thus far shalt thou go, and no farther;" and means, "So far shall I go, and as much farther as I like." If I were merely illustrating the form of idea contained in the word, I might quote the words of the Archbishop of York, when, in his rebellion against Henry IV., he was accused of—

"Ill translating himself
Out of the speech of peace, which bears such grace,
Into the harsh and boisterous tongue of war."

His reply was:—

"We see which way the stream of time doth run,
And are enforced from our most quiet sphere
By the rough torrent of occasion."

Though no "torrent of occasion," however violent, can excuse man's going beyond his proper sphere, yet עָבַר marks the fact; it is his passage of the limit set by God. Therefore, although this word reveals some of the dread consequences of sin, which we may see in other words of this sad category, there is centred in it a bold contempt of the Divine will, which fills the devout mind with horror. With a deep sense of the heinousness of "man's first disobedience," the apostle expresses Adam's act of sin by that word παράβασις (Rom. v. 14); and with a corresponding feeling of abhorrence, Hosea charges the people of his day with sin of as deep a dye : "*They like Adam have transgressed the covenant*" (Hosea vi. 7).

In connection with these ideas of law and authority, but with a still darkening shade of guiltiness פֶּשַׁע gives expression to sin. It views man as a sinner in the immediate presence of God. With עָוֹן, the law, the command or covenant intervened, and it is with this that man comes into collision; but with פֶּשַׁע, even the law is removed, and man confronts God face to face. This is plain from the original and habitual sense of the word, which is *to fall away from, to break away, to revolt.* This is well conveyed in 2 Kings viii. 20 : "*In his days Edom revolted from under the hand of Judah, and made a king over themselves.*" It is man's revolt from his King, the King in a state eternal and invisible. So David, himself a king, bewailed the arbitrary act of his kingly power as a revolt (פֶּשַׁע) against God, the King of all. And Isaiah adding the parental to the kingly character of God, gives edge to that pathetic complaint: "*Hear, O heavens, and give ear, O earth: for the Lord hath spoken, I have nourished and brought up children, and they have rebelled against me*" (Isa. i. 2). Our King-Father may but too truly impeach the world as having "*added rebellion unto their sin*" (Job xxxiv. 37).

Tracing still the footsteps of sin along these darkling ways, we strike into a denser gloom. To his sin man has added transgression, to his transgression revolt, and to his revolt he has joined treachery; this we find expressed in the word מָעַל. Its native meaning is *to cover*, and thence *to act covertly, to deal treacherously.* It contains all the essential evil of עָוֹן and פֶּשַׁע, and has this in aggravation, that it wraps around all the mantle of concealment and deceit. It was this mantle of deceit that was the especial object of Paul's loathing repudiation, as it was an essential part of the equipment of Achan's sin. "*For neither at any time used we flattering words, as ye know, nor a cloke of covetousness; God is witness*" (1 Thess. ii. 5). But Achan moved among his brethren wearing a fair seeming of honesty around his faithlessness, girding the cloak around his covetousness, and clinging to it until it was rent in shreds from off his sin. The tenacity with which Achan held to the guise of innocence gives a vivid view of the essential falsehood of sin in this form. The open repulse before the gates of Ai indicated the presence of a secret sin in the camp of Israel, but Achan still concealed his treachery to God. The Divine voice left no doubt as to the evil having been committed: it announced to

Joshua, "*They have even taken of the accursed thing, and have also stolen, and dissembled also, and they have put it even among their own stuff*" (Josh. vii. 11). Still the dissembler wore his fair guise. Not until they were taken "man by man," and the lot fell upon Achan the son of Carmi, did he confess his faithless deed: "*Indeed I have sinned against the Lord God of Israel*" (verse 20). The mixture of evil qualities found in this sin, as seen in the terrible case of Achan, prepares the mind for the implacable severity of Ezekiel's denunciation. When the grievous trespass has been committed by the land against Jehovah, the people are warned that He shall smite them in such hot displeasure that the presence of Noah, Daniel or Job could not turn away the penal stroke (Ezek. xiv. 13).

Speaking of מָעַל, which supposes concealment, I may bring under notice אָשָׁם, which also contains an element of secrecy. This secrecy is not of the same kind; the difference seems to lie in this, that the former describes the wilfully concealed transgression, while the latter is rather the unwitting act of sin, the sin of ignorance. Let us not suppose, however, that the measure of ignorance that may be in the sin excludes any of the guilt thereof; the ignorance itself is a guilty thing. This אָשָׁם not obscurely shows.

Its original application is to negligence in *going*, carelessness in *gait*, as of a faltering, jaded, slow-paced camel, who saunters along without regard to his steps. The LXX have used very frequently πλημμέλεια as its representative in their version; thus adding to the false step of the Hebrew word, the idea of a false note, the jarring sound, the harsh dissonance of sin among the harmonies of righteousness. The fault in music however may arise from want of care, as well as the error in going, and thus we are led to this want of care as the very kernel of the meaning of the word. Negligence has nothing in common with righteousness. To watch as well as to pray is the mark of the holy; to be "circumspect," to take heed to their ways; but with the inconsiderate of heart there is a certain easy irreverence or profanity, that seems ineradicable from their nature. This is the seed of the sin of ignorance, being itself sin. Hence it was that the sin of ignorance needed to be expiated by death, and for it as for others of a different hue, "*without the shedding of blood there was no remission.*" In Leviticus v. 5 (*vide* verse 17); iv. 13, 22, 27, the mode of expiating this sin is commanded, whether the whole congregation have fallen into it, the ruler or the common people. Nor is the equity of the Divine procedure herein unappreciated or unreflected in the laws of nations. "Ignorantia juris, quod quisque tenetur scire, neminem excusat" is as much the maxim of our own law, as it was of the Roman. What a lurid glare does the action of this same principle of justice cast upon the strangely chequered life of Œdipus, King of Thebes, in the Greek tragedy. When probing the cause of the wide curse that withered all the happiness of the land he detected himself to be "the murderer of the man whose murderer he sought"; it takes nothing from his dread doom that he perpetrated all his nameless crimes of parricide and incest unwittingly: Justice follows him with "a foot swift as the storm" and "springs upon him all armed with fire and lightnings." The bringing of the evil deed to light brings all its guiltiness before the eye of justice. It is true some sense of the wrong may awaken misgiving in the breast of those who do the wrong, before or while they do it, but the dim light of their heedless hearts is not then enough to force conviction home.

This phase of אשם is aptly exemplified in the case of Joseph's brethren. When they sold him only Reuben pleaded, "Do not sin against the child." But when Joseph, as ruler of Egypt, having imprisoned them for three days, demanded that they should bring down their younger brother, then they said one to another, "*We are verily guilty concerning our brother, in that we saw the anguish of his soul, when he besought us, and we would not hear; therefore is this distress come upon us*" (Gen. xlii. 21). The "winters of memory," that in that moment of conviction seemed to roll over these brethren in guilt, recalled their sin out from the darkness and silence of years, and invested it with new and unthought-of terrors. With similar feelings of horror does the apostle recall the blasphemy, the persecution, the injury he did in ignorance and unbelief. But it was a horror that through Divine mercy was dissolved into tearful penitence and grateful love. Instead of expressing itself in the bewilderment of the agitated patriarchs, it bursts into a doxology for the grace, the longsuffering, and mercy shown to him, the chief of sinners, "*Now unto the King eternal, immortal, invisible, the only wise God, be honour and glory for ever and ever*" (1 Tim. i. 17). He that sinned by blasphemy in ignorance regarded himself as the *chief of sinners*. He did not therefore mitigate his sin because of ignorance; much less did he represent his ignorance as guiltless, but joining it with unbelief showed that it needed mercy. "*I obtained mercy, because I did it ignorantly in unbelief*" (verse 13). He stands out as a representative of that class, for whom the Lord prayed, "*Father, forgive them; for they know not what they do*" (Luke xxiii. 34); of whom Peter speaks, "*I wot that through ignorance ye did it, as did also your rulers*" (Acts iii. 17). This ignorance was relative; it was not so dense as to exclude all the light of truth shining from the character, and words and works of Jesus; there was a light they rejected, and for that they were responsible, and on that account were without excuse. But the light of testimony was not of that kind which a man rejects who commits the sin against the Holy Spirit, and therefore left room for the intervention of mercy. They knew enough of Jesus to lead them to receive and adore Him, had it been a mere question of knowledge; but they knew not that Jesus was the "Lord of Glory" (1 Cor. ii. 8). Upon this limitation of their knowledge, though not sinless, even in spite of its sinfulness, our Lord bases His plea to his Father, and Peter his argument addressed to the multitude. Such pleas and arguments are not inconsistent with the charge made by the same apostle, "*By wicked hands ye have crucified and slain*" (Acts ii. 23); and afforded by Stephen, "*Ye do always resist the Holy Ghost*" (Acts vii. 51).

The last of the list of Hebrew words to which I now refer is אָוֶן. It is rendered very variously in our version: as *unjust* (Prov. xi. 7); *unrighteous* (Isa. x. 1); *sorrow* (Ps. xc. 10); *mourning* (Deut. xxvi. 14); *affliction* (Job. v. 6; Hab. iii. 7; Jer. iv. 15); *evil* (Prov. xii. 21); *false* (Prov. xvii. 4); *mischief* (Ps. xxxvi. 4; lv. 10; Ezek. xi. 2); *wicked*, or *wickedness* (Job. xi. 11; xxii. 15; xxxiv. 36; Ps. lix. 5; Prov. vi. 12, 18; etc.). But the most frequent rendering is *iniquity*, as in Micah ii. 1, "*woe to them that devise iniquity.*" "*The calling of assemblies I cannot away with; it is iniquity, even the solemn meeting*" (Isa. i. 13). If we inquire, Whence has this word אָוֶן such a versatile power? the answer is in a high degree remarkable. The most probable and natural root of אָוֶן is in אַיִן, which means *nothing;* and hence אָוֶן comes to signify *nothingness, emptiness, vanity*. We should remember, however, that it is not Solomon's favourite, and famous word for *vanity*, which is הֶבֶל, and means a *breath, thin air* or *mist*, and as such giving name to the shortlived but saintly *Abel*, the first in whom our earthly life expired, and rose as an exhalation to the sky. The "thin air," the dewy mist, or the viewless wind, according to Solomon, is the appropriate description of the residuum of all "the fever and the fret" of earthly toils and worldly ambitions. But when these toils and ambitions are tainted with evil, some word less substantial still, some more ghostly sound (*exigua vox*) is needed to delineate their expression and outcome, and such is אִין, *emptiness, mere vacuity of good, the utter negation of real being.* Sin robs life of its substance and weight in the esteem of God, and degrades all our laborious existence to a nonentity in the Divine account. "*They conceive mischief, and bring forth vanity!*" (Job. xv. 35.) "*Behold they are all vanity; their works are nothing*" (Isa. xli. 29). "*What fruit had ye then,*" inquires Paul of the Romans, "*in those things whereof ye are now ashamed?*" (Rom. vi. 21.) And sins are called the "*unfruitful works of darkness*" (Eph. v. 11). There is no ingathering to the great garner of the future, no fruit for God or for eternity. "*He that soweth iniquity shall reap* VANITY" (Prov. xxii. 8), *i.e.*, utter nothingness in the scale of all excellence. The idolatry of Israel turned Bethel, *i.e.*, the House of the Mighty God, into Bethaven, *i e.*, the house of nothingness: for an idol is nothing in the world, and they that follow it are like unto it in the esteem of God. No matter how beauteous may be life's forms, how bright the halo around our earthly lot, if left to the touch of sin, all the glittering pageantry is dissolved, and nothing is left in the eye of God, but the blank negation of His goodness and holiness. From this negation sin has sprung; the first dark day is nothingness, and when its span of action is spent, *its last is danger and distress.* The danger and distress arise from that "fearful looking for judgment," when every sin shall be weighed in the balance of the Sanctuary, and the Eternal Judge shall say of every sinner as of old of Belshazzar: "*Thou art weighed in the balances, and art found wanting*" (Dan. v. 27).

The Greek words I will handle more briefly. The meaning of several of them I have glanced at in dealing with the corresponding Hebrew expressions. For the rest, with two exceptions, I refer you to Trench's *Synonyms of the Greek Testament*.[1] These two are ὀφείλημα, and ἀπείθεια; and of these Trench gives no description. They are, however, words of considerable note and deserve some attention.

ὀφείλημα.—In a general way ὀφείλημα represents the commercial side of life; the intercourse of man in bartering and borrowing, in sale and traffic. The derivation of ὀφείλημα is from ὀφείλω, which originally has the simple meaning, "I owe, I am indebted." By its form it is equivalent to τὸ ὀφειλόμενον, *i.e.*, that which is owed, and the latter is actually used in this exact sense in Matthew xviii. 30—34. From material

---

[1] pp. 36, 231, 233, 303: for ἀσέβεια see *Old Testament Synonyms*, Girdlestone, pp. 133 135.

indebtedness arises the notion of *moral obligation*. The debt is what is due; what is due turns an obligation into a *duty*. "*The borrower is servant to the lender*" (Prov. xxii. 7), is Solomon's view of the case. In the same vein the apostle (Gal. v. 3) writes of him who is circumcised, that he thereby becomes a "*debtor to do the whole law.*" In the admission that that one rite is a matter of binding obligation, he admits that he is bound by the whole law. He cannot admit circumcision to be a Christian duty, and then exclude any other Mosaic rite from the list of those things which he ought to do. The law is one, and in this sense indivisible. That this is of its very essence, James shows in the case of the transgressor, if he "*offend in one point, he is guilty of all*" (James ii. 10). So here with Paul, he that receives the benefit of circumcision, he that fulfils the law in that particular, renders himself accountable for all. The privileges, the promises, the blessings of the law are, so to speak, so many loans to be paid back to God in the coin of its duties. All the blessings of life, if we enlarge our view beyond the reach of the Mosaic law, will be seen to have this counterpart of duty. (Cf. Rom. xv. 27.)

It would be, however, too slight a view of ὀφείλημα to take it as denoting simply *obligation*, it goes much further. It specially notes the *failure to discharge obligation*—that which is due, but not paid. At this turn of its meaning we derive no aid from classical writers, nor even from the Greek version of the Old Testament. With regard to the latter, it is not a little remarkable that, with all its wealth of imagery, the Septuagint does not once use ὀφείλημα of sin. We are obliged to fall back principally upon the New Testament usage. Its very first occurrence there is with the intensity of meaning I have just named—*failure to discharge duty*—in our Lord's Prayer (Matt. vi. 12). If we were to insert the classical sense of "obligation," "what is due," in this passage, it would acquire a meaning at utter variance with our Lord's intention. How foreign it would be may be shown by quoting the prayer of Apollonius of Tyana, ὦ θεοὶ δοίητέ μοι τὰ ὀφειλόμενα.[1] Between the claim of merit here put forward, and the voice of confession in the model Christian prayer, a whole world of moral meaning seems to intervene; yet the verbal expression is almost identical—ὀφείλημα =ὀφειλόμενα.

But what is our warrant for giving so dark a hue to the word on the lips of Christ? Christ Himself: (Matt. vi. 14 and Luke xi. 4).

---

[1] O Gods, give me those things that are due to me.—*Tholuck on Matthew, loc. cit.*

By comparing these expository remarks of our Lord, we find He regards ὀφείλημα as equivalent to ἁμαρτία and παράπτωμα.

Even this meaning of failure, or dereliction of duty, does not satisfy all the uses of this word. It indicates that duty has not been rendered, and also that duty is still *to be discharged*, that is, by satisfaction. He to whom this debt is reckoned is not absolved from his liability to pay in the future, because of his failure in the past, or because he has now nothing to pay withal. Our Lord has shown that the debtor is still in the just grasp of the great Creditor. In the parable, Matt. xviii. 25, he is commanded to be sold, and all that is his, in order to make satisfaction for that great debt. When the unforgiving servant has his own forgiveness cancelled, he is delivered *to the tormentors*, "*till he should pay all that was due to him*" (verse 34).[1] These passages prepare the way for that dread denunciation wherein all the penal consequences of guiltiness hover over those who are impenitent debtors to God (Luke xiii. 4, 5).

Thus, then, our indebtedness has its basis on what is natural and physical; thence it rises to the intellectual and the moral, where it merges into that guiltiness which is exposed to the penal terrors of an All-holy God. How divinely becoming, as it is infinitely needed, is, therefore, the petition, "*Forgive us our* DEBTS."

We now come to Ἀπειθέω and Ἀπείθεια.

All the other words which we have been considering depict sin before it comes in contact with the Divine remedy. The word we now handle represents sin as touched, but not healed, by the hand of Mercy. On the contrary, "the body of sin," when so touched, as by Ithuriel's spear was Satan, although squat as a toad, rises into surprising proportions and new malignity. It may seem to some that sin, in this form, had better be examined after dealing with the offer of the remedy; but, on second thoughts, you will find that, in the midst of people who habitually hear the Gospel, this is the very pith and poison of all their sinfulness. Were they to receive Christ as offered in the Gospel, the expulsion and annihilation of sin in its myriad forms would, after all, be only a matter of detail. Christ firmly seated in the citadel puts such a curb upon sins, that, like abashed culprits, they can only hide in the dens and caves, and mutter and peep in the dark places.

Ἀπείθεια is the abstract noun derived from ἀπειθέω, or ἀπείθομαι, which is compounded of a privative and πείθω, *I persuade*. The noun

---
[1] Cf. Matt. v. 25.

is not of frequent occurrence in the New Testament, and is not once found in the Septuagint; but the verbal forms occur often in both. In all material points the meaning of the noun corresponds with that of the verb, but in several passages where the latter is used, there is greater vividness, owing to the antithesis of the context.

It is impossible for us rightly to estimate ἀπείθεια without briefly contrasting it with its opposite, πίστις. The root of πίστις is also in πείθω; and it describes the positive, as ἀπείθεια does the negative result of persuasion. Both words have this in common, that they suppose the Gospel to be a grand persuasive, and in this they are true to its essential character. It is God's master argument addressed to man, every advance made, every victory won, is through its persuasiveness. It is not, however, of that kind of argument born of the syllogism, but the logic of compassion and redeeming love, which says in its attack, "*Come now, and let us reason together*,"[1] and in its triumph, "*I drew them with the cords of a man, and with the bands of love.*"[2] Faith (πίστις) is our acquiescence in the Divine persuasiveness; it is our persuasion resting on God's great persuasives. God reasons, we yield; God persuades, we believe. In its exercise we show that both heart and understanding are by irresistible reasonings brought into captivity to Christ.

The opposite of all this "obedience of faith" is comprised in ἀπείθεια. It is not simply unbelief, but the disobedience of unbelief. It is not simply want of faith, unbelief, non-persuasion, but it is the persuadableness of the "carnal mind" rising into direct rejection of Mercy's pleas and pleadings.[3] When Paul entered into the Synagogue of Thessalonica "as his manner was" and on three Sabbath days reasoned with the Jews out of the Scriptures, we read (Acts xvii. 4) that "*some of them were persuaded* (ἐπείσθησαν) *and cast in their lot with Paul and Silas.*" But (verse 5) the unpersuaded ones (ἀπειθοῦντες) did not remain neutral; immediately their unpersuadableness turned into strenuous and violent opposition.

In Romans x. 21 we see ἀπείθεια ripening into "gainsaying," putting word against word, man's against God's—"*All day long have I stretched forth my hands unto a disobedient and gainsaying people.*" The description of the early results of Paul's preaching at Ephesus brings out the character of ἀπείθεια still more forcibly. We read (Acts xix. 8) that "*He went into the synagogue and spake boldly for the space of three*

---

[1] Is. i. 18.   [2] Hos. xi. 4.
[3] Cf. Jno. iii. 36; Acts xiv. 1, 2; 1 Peter ii. 7, antithesis of πιστεύω.

months, reasoning (disputing) and *persuading the things concerning the Kingdom of God.*" With what effect did his persuasions fall? "*Divers were hardened and disobeyed* (ἠπείθουν, verse 9), *and spake evil of that way before the multitude.*" The unpersuadableness that we have seen elsewhere putting word against word, here opposes bad to good. "Gainsaying" has turned into slander of "God's unspeakable gift." Is it to such stubborn rejectors of the Gospel that the same Apostle alludes, when writing to these Ephesians (ch. ii. 2) as "*children of disobedience,*" moved by the energy of the mighty spirit which is the Prince of the power of the air? Again he warns them (ch. v. 6) lest by "*vain words*" they be seduced into the company of the "*children of disobedience,*" and so be exposed to the coming wrath of God. The phrase occurs, if we accept the old reading, singularly enough in the epistle, written at the same time, and borne by the same messenger to the Church at Colossæ,—a community resembling the Ephesians in this, as in so many other respects (ch. iii. 6), that they, too, had their "*children of disobedience*" hanging on their borders. Always indeed hovering around the light, wherever it is raised, these disobedient ones will be found, dashing like the moth with feeble wing through the heavenly beam to perish amidst its brightness.

In the passages to which we have alluded, it may be observed that the English Version sometimes gives "unbelief" or "unbelieve," instead of disobedience and disobey, by which I have rendered the words in all cases. The same irregularity runs throughout the English Version of the New Testament in its treatment of these words. It is not a little perplexing, too, as it gives the same translation—unbelief and unbelieve—of ἀπιστία and ἀπιστεῖν, where they refer to man's relation to the Gospel. While such a reading is correct enough, we must here be on our guard, and not sink the stronger ἀπείθεια in the weaker ἀπιστία. That there is this difference in strength will readily appear by examining the texts and contexts containing the words.

Wherever ἀπείθεια is used it includes ἀπιστία; but in all cases where ἀπιστία is employed, there is not the matured ἀπείθεια. It is true, in some cases, as in Hebrews iii. 19, that the context gives intensity to ἀπιστία, but generally we may take ἀπιστία to be the native unbelief of man before hearing the Gospel, which is overcome when the Gospel is received; but ripens, when rejected, into ἀπείθεια. That this is the relation of ἀπιστία to ἀπείθεια, as the Apostle used the words, will appear by comparing Hebrews iii. 8, 10, 12, 18 and 19; and iv. 2. Here the

Israelites perish on account of "a heart of unbelief" which, unsanctified by the reception of the glad tidings, grows callous, and leads to apostasy and sins of disobedience. In these descending steps, *disobedience* is the last. The sinner, in that stage, appears in another part of this same Epistle (chapter vi. 7, 8): "*As the earth which drinketh in the rain that cometh oft upon it . . . but that which beareth thorns and briars is rejected, and is nigh unto cursing; whose end is to be burned.*"

It results, too, from ἀπιστία being the root sin, that we find the lingering remnants of that native unbelief now and then reappearing in the occasional acts of those who, in character and disposition, are believers. The distressed father cries, "*Lord, I believe; help thou my unbelief*" (ἀπιστία—Mark ix. 24). This was the "unbelief" of the disciples after the Resurrection, which drew down upon them the upbraidings of their risen Lord (Mark xvi. 14). This unbelief on their part one Evangelist traces to their very joy and wonder at His appearance (Luke xxiv. 41).

But ἀπείθεια is never toned down by such surroundings; it is always without excuse. That which provokes it into being takes away the excuse of its existence. Were it the sin against law, we might imagine the law too severe; or, against rule, we might find an excuse in its sternness; or, against power, we might possibly find an apology in its despotic severity. There remains, however, no such palliation of ἀπείθεια; for, unlike all other forms of sin which we have considered, this springs into being, and confronts God, when He stoops, in His "gentleness," to raise the poor out of the dust, and the needy from the dunghill, to set him among princes, even the princes of His people.[1] It is the beggar's refusal of that heavenly dignity. It is the stubbornness of man that will not yield to God's way of blessing, when He, the Ancient of Days, seems to lay aside the splendour of His throne, and come to sinners in His Son, *beseeching* them to be reconciled unto God. It is the scorn of Eternal Love, Love's sacrifice, and all Love's sweet reasonableness. It is the thrice-ribbed ice of sin that will not melt beneath the warm beam of heavenly pity. It is the triple steel that will not be pierced by the golden-headed arrows of Mercy; the adamant that will neither rend nor dissolve at the expiring cry of the Son of God.

---

[1] Psalm cxiii. 7, 8.

LECTURE V.

THE NATURE OF SIN.

IN illustrating the words used by Divine Revelation for Sin, I have taken occasion to set in array the representative facts of Sin. In doing so, I have endeavoured to dispense as much as possible with mere speculation, and to employ the forms and colours of the Word of God. My object has been to fill the mind with Biblical ideas before we come to form any theory of Sin. Such a course will also secure to us the advantage of a better test by which to try any theory that may be propounded. We can more clearly see whether the facts are fairly and fully interpreted by the theory; whether any foreign element is introduced, or any essential element excluded. It is, indeed, denied by some, of the very highest standing, that the states and acts of sin can be referred to any one single principle. "It is the opposite of holiness," says Dr. Hodge,[1] "and does not admit of being reduced to any one principle, either the love of the creature or the love of self." But it is overlooked in this statement that in the unity of holiness there lies an available argument from analogy, for the unity of the principle of sin. Sin is stated to be the opposite of holiness. If holiness can be reduced to one simple principle, Why should not also its opposite, Sin? It is principle against principle. For the soundness of this conclusion, we have not to discuss the question of the reduction of holiness to one simple principle. That has been put beyond all argument. Our Lord himself has reduced all moral and all legal righteousness,—that is, all that stands before the eye of the Eternal Judge as the great opposite of Sin,—to one simple principle, and that principle is love : "*Love is the fulfilling of the law*" (Rom. xiii. 10).

---

[1] *Theology*, Vol. I, p. 149.

The incalculable gain our Lord's great induction has brought to morals and to truth, affords a *prima facie* incentive to those who seek for a single root-principle underlying all the manifold manifestations of evil. It at the same time suggests, if it does not guarantee, success in the attempt. This remark, however, I make only by the way; it may, nevertheless, be useful to keep the subject in mind as we advance. I shall return to it again, when we have followed out our present main purpose, which is to trace and to delineate the Nature of Sin.

In all the examples that have been brought forward, and in all that might be adduced, sin supposes the existence of what is good and right, of which it is in some way the direct opposite. It is never, however, the opposite on equal terms. There is not a moment's countenance given to the Manichean doctrine that Good and Evil exist in the Universe as eternal contraries, each having an equal legitimacy in its independent eternal existence. In Scripture, the evil-doer is dependent even in his evil deed. Sin is subject to the good even while it resists it. Good and right are always endowed with command. The right does not always struggle, sometimes baffled and defeated. It is lifted up to the dignity of a standard, which no sin can ever lower. It is expressed in the enactments of law, which no transgression can abrogate. It derives its vitality and its strength from Him, who is the Being of Beings, the Judge of all: who causes the wrath of man to praise Him, and the remainder of wrath He restrains.

Sin thus being subordinate, while it is opposed to the right and good, and opposed, while it is subordinate, it follows that sin cannot be another form of good. Refine sin as you may, and remove from it all that grossness that awakens loathing, you cannot elevate it into even the lowliest brotherhood with the good. The more refined it becomes, the subtler and more concentrated is its aversion, just as the phylacteried Pharisee offered a bitterer rejection to Christ, the Holy One of God, than did the abandoned publicans and sinners of Jerusalem. The right owns no kindred with the wrong. No bond acknowledged in Revelation or in the conscience can bind them. Their only relation is that of mutual repulsion.

I call your attention the more earnestly to this irreconcilable enmity sown between these opposing principles, because it is at this point of this, the moral system of Scripture, that Pantheists, nd those tinctured with their opinions, make their fiercest onslaught. Pantheists acknowledge no innate difference. In their view, evil is "the shadow of good;"[1] "with God evil itself is good."[2] "Evil and good are God's right hand and left."[3] "If the whole phenomena of the universe," says Pearson, "be one chain of necessary development, if man and his actions are strictly inevitable pulsations of the one great source of being, then what is properly called moral evil has no existence. The Emerson school tells us that it lives only in dogmatic theology. 'Evil, according to old philosophers,' says the author of the *Representative Men*, 'is good in the making. That pure malignity can exist, is the extreme proposition of unbelief. It is not to be entertained by a rational agent; it is Atheism; it is the last profanation ..... the Divine effort is never relaxed; the carrion in the sun will convert itself to grass and flowers; and man, though in brothels, in gaols, or on gibbets, is on his way to all that is good and true.'[4] This may accord with the generous spirit of the Indian Vishnu, but Christianity and it are wide as the poles asunder. The *Festus* of Mr. Bailey, a poem of great power and of a religious spirit, is pervaded by this bad pantheistic theology. The following is but a specimen :—

> " 'The soul is but an organ, and it hath
> No power of good and evil in itself,
> More than the eye hath power of light or dark.
> God fitted it for good ; and evil is
> Good in another way we are not
> Skilled in.'[5]

Hence the notion that all religions are good, but that Christianity is the best. And the conclusion 'All souls shall be in God, and shall be God, and nothing but God, be.'[6] Dr. Strauss moves in the same plane, though far ahead, when he says, 'Human kind is impeccable, for the progress of its development is irreproachable. Pollution cleaves only to the individual. It does not reach the race and its history. The human race is the Christ, the God-made man, the sinless one, that dies, rises again, and mounts into the heavens.'[7] The consciousness of guilt becomes on this system a delusion. The sense of responsibility, which is a fact in the natural history of man, is belied. And that voice, which comes from the recesses of our moral nature, pointing us from a judge within the breast, to a Judge without and above, is silenced. That God is ever educing good from evil is true, and that the ministry

---

[1] *Festus*, p. 173.   [2] Ibid.   [3] Ibid, Proem, vii.
[4] P. 68, *Swedenborg; or, the Mystic*.   [5] *Festus*, p. 48.   [6] Ib. p. 109.
[7] *Leben Jesu*, last chapter.

of evil, mysterious though it be, is made under this benign supremacy to subserve most important purposes, agrees at once with experience and Scripture. But that evil has no positive existence, that it is only good in another way, is as repugnant to our natural sentiments as it is opposed to Christianity. We will persist in calling this course of conduct bad, and that opposite course good; and can never act on the belief that both were alike things of fate and necessity, or that each agent is a structure formed by inevitable laws, and part or particle of God. When this creed prevails, the foundations of the earth will be out of course. Only let this doctrine leaven the mass of the community and the result will be a deluge of sensuality and crime." [1]

Seeing, then, that sin is subordinate, while it is opposed to the law of God, and distinct and diverse, while it subserves the purposes of good, it becomes us now to look more narrowly into the requirements of that law, the rejection of which is sin.

When Scripture speaks of the good with which sin clashes, it is not good, as a "factor" or principle in our nature, contending for its own development, or for the mastery over all that opposes it. It is good, erected into a standard by the Author of Nature, to which we must be conformed, and expressed in a law to which we must render obedience. That law is objective. Its commands bear inwardly upon us from without and from above. It has this objective character; for only under a law of this kind could true moral obedience be given. That course of conduct which is the result of yielding to our own inner impulses, and has no eye to the Divine requirements, is destitute of the essence of morality in its true Scriptural conception. The obedience of mere impulse is the obedience of necessity; but moral obedience is the obedience of a free agent, who reverently recognizes the Divine command, and is moved by the spring of its impulse to its accomplishment. Accordingly, in the very earliest phase of Adam's life in Eden, we behold him determining his actions under a Divine command. Though he was undefiled, and the impulses of his heart were pure, yet the imposition of an external command was needed to give to the action of those innocent impulses the quality of moral obedience.

It does not take away from the validity of this conclusion to say that the sense of duty is within. Duty is not law; but duty supposes law. Law is Divine, duty human; law the expression of Divine will, duty our translation of that expression for the guidance of our will. The

---

[1] Pearson, *Infidelity*, pp. 41, 42.

apostrophe of the poet is as true in its definition, as it is sublime in its expression, when he says :—

> "Stern Daughter of the Voice of God !
> O Duty ! if that name thou love
> Who art a light to guide, a rod
> To check the erring, and reprove ;
> Thou who art victory and law,
> When empty terrors overawe ;
> From vain temptations dost set free,
> And calm'st the weary strife of frail humanity."

In the opening line he shows Duty's descent, its dependence upon "the Voice." The subjective sense of duty vindicates the objective law.

Referring again to the happy life of Eden, and the harmony that innocence exhibits between duty and desire, and desire and law, we may draw a further inference from the then existence of law. We may warrantably conclude that if the external objective law existed, conditioning the life of our innocent and unfallen parents, the existence of law now enforcing its commands objectively upon us, cannot be an evidence of our fallen condition. But while the existence of law yields not this evidence, it comes with copious abundance from the *contradiction* we offer to that law.

The fact of this *contradiction*,—the jar of inclination with duty,—the conflict between the sense of what we ought to do and the feeling of what we like, reveals how miserably mankind are out of joint with the law, of their well-being. Even however in this "gate of tears" a ray of consolation is discernible. That contradiction to the law of God, so deep-seated, so intertwisted with the fibres of our being, as to become a second nature, while it is the mark of our sin is also the proof that sin is not native to us. It is something foreign to our true selves, and hence its disturbing power. And as it has been imported, it may be expelled. The Divine method to prepare for this expulsion has been not to arrest, not to allay the disturbing power of sin, but to ferment its trouble and to intensify its disorder. Thus the Divine kindness and forbearance were concerned in this plan, as well as the Divine wisdom.

Man turned adrift by his own wilfulness from the "open vision" of his duty, required, if restrained at all, additional exposition of his duty. His deepening darkness of mind and error of life demanded increasing plainness and clearness and copiousness of law. As the perils to which he hastened increased, the beacons were multiplied to warn him of his danger. As from age to age he sought out "many inventions" in sinning, the Divine goodness pursued him in unfolding the manifold ways of rectitude and safety. In a word, "*the Law was added because of transgressions*" (Gal. iii. 19). And that full and comprehensive expression of the Divine law was given through Moses in order to shed its light upon the transgressions of men and leave no doubt as to their crimes. Just as sin spreading from its parent stem grew manifold and various, and sent out its wide branches, shedding its poisonous fruit into the darkness of isolation from God; so God kept continually unfolding His Law of Righteousness iike an ever-increasing light, so as to reveal sin as sin, and let all mankind know the true nature of the deadly fruit that grew upon its baleful branches.

Need we put the question—Was sin checked by this outstretching of the lines of the law? A still more stubborn resistance was evoked. Sin revives at the approach of law, and starts into new vigour of antipathy at the sound of its trump. "*When the law came, sin revived, and I died.*"

I have endeavoured to enumerate some of the particulars of the relation of sin to law. We have seen that sin as a single principle is opposed to good,—to good as a standard and supreme law. Consequently evil has no legitimate rights, nor is it another form of good. The relation of sin to duty was seen by considering the objective character of the law, which creates the sense of duty by requiring conformity to its precepts. Finally, it was seen that sin did not give rise to law; but as law had existed during the innocency of man, so the same Divine goodness that instituted it then, led to its further revelation, as man more deeply needed its light in the wandering mazes of his sin.

Up to this point I have refrained from giving you any precise definition of sin. But in order to illustrate our position, and connect it with historical evangelical doctrine, I will put you in mind of some of the definitions of Protestant divines:—

Melancthon: "*Defectus vel inclinatio vel actio pugnans cum lege Dei.*"
Gerhard:[1] "*Discrepantia, aberratio, deflexio a lege.*"
Calov: "*Illegalitas, seu difformitas a lege.*"
Baier:[2] "*Carentia conformitatis cum lege.*"
Buddeus: "*Violatio seu transgressio legis divinæ.*"

---

[1] *Loci Theologici* xx. i. 3.   [2] *Compendium Theologiæ* (1739), p. 346.

Baumgarten: "*Transgressio legis, seu absentia conformitatis cum lege.*"

Vitringa:[1] "*Forma peccati est disconvenientia actus, habitus, aut status hominis cum divina lege.*"

Pye Smith:[2] "*Any neglect, contempt, or violation of the wise, just, and benevolent law of God.*"

Stein:[3] "*Want of the agreement of voluntary actions with supreme moral excellence.*"

Arndt:[4] "*Whatsoever is contrary to the Holy Will of God.*"

The Larger Catechism:[5] "*Any want of conformity unto, or transgression of any law of God, given as a rule to the reasonable creature.*"

These are samples, which might be easily multiplied, of the briefer definitions by Protestants. In looking closely into them, it cannot fail to strike us that in every one of them there is either expressed or implied the existence of a law, as a rule and standard of the obedience which is due. These definitions further suppose that the true character of sin is discovered in relation primarily to law. They also, by giving a fixed character to sin, attribute by parity of reason a fixed character to the law. This agrees with the old Protestant doctrine of the law determining the actions of moral agents, which is, that it is "*immutable, equal to all, and universal.*" Nothing less can be assigned as the essentials of law, if we would hold a truly rational conception of law, and one which is consistent both with itself and with Scripture.

Having so far given my unqualified adherence to this fixed character of law, it is needful to ask the exact meaning of the quality of immutability. Is this quality to be accorded to the principles of the law, or to the expression of those principles? If it is meant that the law has the same fulness and variety of expression at one time as at another (for example, under Noah as under Moses; in Patriarchal times, as from the lips of our Saviour), then I hold it will be very hard, it will indeed be impossible, to make out in this sense the immutability of the law. But if it is meant that the principles of righteousness embodied in the law, as revealed during any given period, are the same as for any

---

[1] *Doctrina Christianæ Religionis*, x. 7. [2] *Theology*, p. 370.
[3] *De Satisfactione Christi*, p. 13. [4] *Von wahren Christenthum*, p 470
[5] Answer to Quest. xxiv.

other period,—that the quality of righteousness does not vary with time, nor the requirements of righteous law with changing dispensations,—then I hold that nothing less than such an immutability as this will comport with the nature and majesty of moral law. That this immutability of principle is in complete harmony with multiplicity and variety of expression and application may be shown by many and cogent proofs. It appears first in the Mosaic legislation. The Ten Commandments, or ten 'Words,' as they are called, stand to the rest of the Mosaic code as immutable pillars, bearing the whole weight of the varied ceremonial structure, the social, the civil and national enactments of the Jewish kingdom. What may be found in the remotest deductions or minutest applications of this great code may also be traced in principle to these ten "Words." In them lies the indestructible germ, whence all the manifold ordinances grew.

It appears, secondly, in our Saviour's identifying His doctrine of righteousness—the righteousness of the Kingdom of Heaven—with the requirements of the moral precepts of Moses. He came not to destroy, but to fulfil the law. And none has affirmed the immutability of law with such emphasis as He. Yet He regarded it as perfectly consistent with this immutability to reduce all its precepts to two, or rather to one principle, that of love. Herein our Lord has given a further demonstration of the truth of what I am advancing.

Admitting then this immutable character of the law, combined with the different degrees of its revelation, it is clear that transgression of its commands, under one form of expression, would be transgression of its precepts under any other form, because the Eternal principle would be thereby violated. Hence what was sin under the Mosaic law, would have been sin before the days of Noah; and what was sin in the times of the Patriarchs would be sin in Christian days; what was sin in the Jew would also be sin in the Gentile. For no man of any tribe or class, in any period or in any dispensation, has existed or does exist exempt from the requirements of law. The apostle therefore had no hesitation in arguing from the disobedience of the Gentile to the law written on his heart, as well as from the disobedience of the Jew to the law given at Sinai, to the shutting up of both Jew and Gentile under sin. In so doing, he identified the principle of the Natural Law, as it is called, with the principles of the Mosaic, and regarded all sin as the "*transgression of the Divine law.*" The law being thus immutable, it is also vindicated as being the same for all, and universal.

Of course there are those who maintain what has been called an accommodation, a stooping on the part of the law to human infirmity. And they allege particular instances in proof. But if one will take the pains dispassionately and without prejudice to examine these instances, it will be found that instead of the law bending or stooping from its lofty purity, it shows an effort to uplift the people concerned from lower practices and customs to nobler forms of life. The people are levelled up; the law is not let down.

LECTURE VI.

SIN IN ITS RELATION TO LAW.

WE have seen that the true character of sin is to be found in its relation to the law of God. That law being unvarying in its requirements, it becomes us now to ask more particularly how far these requirements extend. Do they reach to the character as well as to the act? To the disposition as well as to the will? Is the law satisfied by anything short of a perfect conformity, both in condition and deed? Or, to put the questions from the opposite standpoint, Is sin to be restricted to the volition only, and not to be predicated of those states of the soul that lie behind the acts of the will? Is it sin to transgress, and is it also sin not to comply with the demands of law?

It will be seen at a glance, that these questions go far beyond the theoretical. They enter into the experimental and practical, and vitally affect religion at its very source.

Comparing the claims of the law with the actual life of men, we might conclude, as some have done, that the law represents no more than an ideal purity. Its perfection has never been realized, except only in the one Man, who could say of every act, "*Thus it becometh us to fulfil all righteousness.*"[1] Inasmuch, however, as that one real Man fulfilled *all righteousness*, the ideal holiness ripens into the actual for evermore. He fulfilled that law, too, as satisfying its normal demands upon man. This is the view of the Old and New Testaments. Obedience is possible, for "*The man that doeth these things shall live by them.*"[2]

It follows, therefore, that the law not merely lights us onward towards the pure and good and perfect, but also *obliges* us to purity, goodness and perfection. Its demand is, "*Thou shalt love the Lord thy God with all thy heart, and with all thy soul, and with all thy strength, and with all thy mind; and thy neighbour as thyself*" (Luke x. 27).

This act of love being the supreme exercise of the faculties of a moral agent, has also for its object the holiest of Beings, God, and in its measure or degree embraces the whole of our being, both disposition and volition. Here, therefore, if anywhere, in this trinity of perfections, the perfect service of love to the perfect God by our complete powers, we have the ideal of the perfection of the law. And yet it is this ideal that is enforced as the standard of our actual obedience.

It is impossible to escape the reach of this command by pleading inability. All inability to love God resolves itself into unwillingness, and for that unwillingness every moral agent is responsible. It is his gravest condemnation.

It is equally illusory to urge the differing capacities of moral agents. We admit the capacity of the child is below the capacity of the man, and that of the man below the capacity of an angel. But these differing grades do not turn aside the edge of the command. The child is to render perfect obedience as a child: the man, as a man: and the angel must serve with an angel's love. In all cases it must be *with all thy heart.*

As the measure, therefore, is *with all thy heart*, etc., anything short of that measure is a failure in the eye of the law; and the conscience in the presence of that law will charge home that failure as an offence. To offer unto God a love that is not our supreme affection, is to offer unto Him an affront. Hence it is that the waning of the first love of the Church at Ephesus is called a "*fall*,"[1] and the lukewarm Laodiceans are on the point of being "*spued out of His mouth.*"[2] The older Theologians on these grounds maintained the axiom, *Omne minus bonum habet rationem mali.* If a man should observe the "weightier matters of the law," he is not thereby set free to treat with indifference the "least of the commandments." Even the tithing of the mint, the anise, and the cummin is *not to be left undone.*[3] Should he have paid all his dues unto God save "one farthing," that payment is good so far as it goes, but it does not go far enough; the good is *too little*, and has in it the form of evil. For that "one farthing" we have the "verily" of Christ that the defaulter shall not escape.[4]

We are now in a position to more directly answer the question, Is

---

[1] Rev. ii. 5.   [2] Rev. iii. 16.   [3] Matt. xxiii. 23.   [4] Matt. v. 26.

sin attributable to the disposition, or is it restricted to the acts of the will? If the arguments just advanced are founded on truth, there can be only one answer. Love is not only an act of the will, but is also an *affection* of the soul. Clearly the law lays claim to it in both these respects. But if the demands of the law press beyond the volition, and enter the region of the *affections*, there is no reason why the *passions* and *appetites* should be excluded from its control. All the principles of action are in this way determined by the law of God, as well as the voluntary acts themselves.

This will be still more evident if the senses in which the word voluntary has been used in reference to this matter are borne in mind. "The first and strictest sense makes nothing an act of the will, but an act of deliberate self-determination, *i.e.*, something which is performed *sciente et volente*. Secondly, all spontaneous, impulsive exercises of the feelings and affections are in a sense voluntary. And thirdly, whatever inheres in the will as a habit or disposition, is called voluntary, as belonging to the will."[1] Passing by the metaphysics of these definitions I look at them only as they belong to theology.

The inconvenience of having a narrower and a broader sense for voluntary acts is very considerable, and is likely to lead to confusion. But we must take these things as we find them. The chief point of interest lies in the manner in which the claims of the Divine law are adjusted to these definitions. If we accept the wider meaning of the second and third definitions, and admit that all voluntary acts are in either of these senses determined by the law, then we add provinces to the rule of law altogether unacknowledged by the narrow range of the first definition.

The Roman Catholics for the most part prefer the more restricted sense, and limit the demand of law to the scanty act of determination. By so doing they put the whole body of concupiscence in the soul beyond the Divine jurisdiction: and where there is no law there is no transgression. Concupiscence, the staple and material of all sin, is with them not of the nature of sin. This they do partly in order to preserve the vicious harmony of their doctrine of baptism with the facts of human nature. The baptismal wave removes sin, but it does not wash away concupiscence. Thus as it is untouched by their sacraments, it is tolerated by their theory of law. By this method we arrive at this astonishing contradiction. Paul says he had not known sin unless the

---

[1] Hodges' *Theology*, Vol. 2, p. 186.

law had said, "*Thou shalt not covet.*"[1] He felt and owned, therefore, that the law reached to his desires. But the Roman Catholics altogether reject the bridle of the law upon desire. The law of God demands love—love "*with all the heart,*" etc., and certainly love is among the emotions of the soul. But by surrendering only the deliberate act of the will to the law, they deny to God the spontaneous spring of the affections, and that silent flow of sacred emotion which having become habitual bears the soul in unconscious, as well as conscious moments, onwards to the Divine presence. All this is certainly included in " with *all* thy heart," etc.

Whilst observing these contradictions in the authoritative expositions of Roman Catholic Theology, it ought to be remembered that it was not left to Protestants alone to point them out. Long before Protestantism arose, and ever since it has made its voice heard, the various sects of Mystics and Pietists existing within the Roman Catholic Church have, by making the affections of the heart the main factor and requirement in religion, uttered a practical protest against the doctrine which gained currency from the Papal chair.

From Bernard to Madame Guyon and Faber there is an unbroken strain of unofficial Roman Catholic teaching which declares in impassioned prose and poetry, that God requires the love of the heart; and this is in perfect agreement with the whole of Evangelical Christendom.

There are others who maintain the same limitations of law as the Roman Catholics, but they do so for different reasons. These are the Pelagians, and those who, in this respect, follow them. Discarding the notion of Sacramental purity, they insist on an original purity as pertaining to each individual on coming into the world. This theory leads them to the same practical contradiction that besets the Roman Catholics, and compels a similar limitation of the demands of law to the voluntary act. They thus stand equally opposed to the facts of experience, and the teaching of Scripture.

It would be easy to trace still further the pernicious tendency of this theory, and show how it extends to the very foundations of morality. Fixing the limits of the law's claims upon the bare act of the willing faculty, to the exclusion of the disposition, this theory implies a particular character in all morality, and especially in its supreme law. That character is its arbitrariness. If the morality be of the act, and not of the disposition, the law that enforces it must be of the same

---

[1] Rom. vii. 7.

description—arbitrary, and with no foundation in nature. An act of the Supreme Will might, therefore, reverse all morality, turning virtue into vice, and vice into virtue.

The danger thus planted in the way of practical religion, because it is so near, is the more alarming. The first rise of evil in the soul is allowed to take place without being condemned as evil. If the first is allowed, where is the authority or guarantee for censuring the second, third, or fiftieth inroad of envy, pride, malice or cupidity, when every wave belongs to the same tide of sin? The theory mystifies conscience, and leaves it completely at fault, unless it keeps a wonderfully good memory. But with the Apostolic injunction, "*abstain from all appearance of evil*,"[1] the course of duty is plain, and the soul is brought round into a proper antagonism towards evil, both root and branch, both the first blade, and the very shadow it casts in advance.

From these various considerations, the conclusion to which we come is, that as the law extends its rule over the whole empire of the soul, volition and passion, transitory emotion and habitual disposition, so it condemns as sin anything in any of these provinces that does not submit to its authority. It condemns the sudden rush of passion that hardly seems to pause for the behest of the will, as well as the act that the will slowly sanctions under the full blaze of knowledge. It condemns the minute incursive acts which, like drops of water, unite to make up the continual course of conduct, although they seem not to require a distinct volition for their several performance, as well as those rare and prominent acts that require a great and sustained effort of the will. The nether currents of feeling and thought are required to flow in the channel of Divine precepts quite as truly as the upper currents of conviction and purpose. The character that does not square with the requirements of law in this respect is under condemnation as certainly as the overt act of transgression.

It is only possible on these grounds fairly to understand the reasonings of Scripture which proceed from the character to the act: "*If the righteous scarcely be saved, where shall the ungodly and the sinner appear?*" (1 Peter iv. 18.) The flood was brought upon "*the world of the ungodly*" (2 Peter ii. 5). In Jude (v. 15), the ungodliness of the character spreads to deeds and speeches, and to the very manner that these ungodly sinners observed. The character appears in Rev. xxii. 11, where, in the fixed state, "*the unjust are to be unjust still.*" On this

---

[1] 1 Thess. v. 22.

same view alone do our Lord's appeals come with meaning and force: "*Do men gather grapes of thorns, or figs of thistles?*" (Matthew vii. 16.) "*Either make the tree good, and his fruit good; or else make the tree corrupt, and his fruit corrupt*" (Matthew xii. 33). "*A good man out of the good treasure of the heart bringeth forth good things: and an evil man out of the evil treasure bringeth forth evil things*" (Matthew xii. 35). It is because of the inseparable connection between the open deeds and words, and the inner character, that even the lightly-spoken "idle word" renders a man accountable in the day of judgment. It is the straw on the stream that shews the way it is flowing, the thistle-down that reveals the thistle's presence.

We may now conveniently put the second question: Is that only to be called sin which is transgression of the law, or are we to put the brand also upon those states where there is a want of conformity with law? A little reflection will show that in this question the same principles are at issue as in the previous one. The only difference is that the discussion is removed to the broader domain of practical life. There reappears the false notion that the claim of God does not extend to the whole of our being, but that there is a certain portion marked off as a kind of neutral territory. From this, it is supposed, God does not gather any tribute, and there is no expectation that any should be paid. But the word neutrality is unknown to morals. Where righteousness is in question, to be indifferent or neutral is to commit sin. For man to obtain the benefit of this want of conformity to the will of God, he must abdicate the grand prerogative of his nature. He must subside into the passiveness of a stock, or stone, or other senseless thing, and present a mute and brute negation to the law of intelligent holiness. This is impossible. His prerogative of bearing the image and superscription of God, be it to his glory or to his shame, cannot be abandoned. It is not enough to say he does not oppose God; if he has not rendered himself unto God, it is defect of duty and treason. Nor is the crime lessened by trying to deface that image, or any lineament thereof, or endeavouring to erase a single letter of that Divine signature. That would be to disinherit God of His own portion in our nature. Everything in that nature is God's by indefeasible right, and He ought to be served by His own. "*He that is not with Me is against Me*"[1] is the Saviour's alternative, and the world for these two thousand years has not succeeded in finding a practical middle course.

---

[1] Matt. xii. 30.

Nor can there be such a middle course. In morals, a defect implies opposition. A want of conformity to the law of God is only another phrase for refusal of compliance with the law of God. The negation of love is hatred; of obedience, transgression. Not to be in fellowship is to be "*alienated from the life of God*"[1]; to be "*without God in the world,*"[2] is to be at "*enmity against God.*"[3]

There are two definitions of John, which, if taken together, like two infallible witnesses, corroborate these positions. It would seem that there were some in the Churches of Asia Minor who held that there might be a want of righteousness of a sinless character. To these John declares "*All unrighteousness is sin*" (1 John v. 17). There were others who were inclined either to limit or tone down the claims of Divine law, and to make some allowances for sinful practices, because they were not expressly forbidden by the letter of the Ten Commandments. To such John says, "*Whosoever committeth sin transgresseth also the law; for sin is the transgression of the law*" (1 John iii. 4). The matter then stands thus: to this question, What is unrighteousness or want of righteousness? John replies, It is sin. To the further question, What is sin? John answers, It is transgression of law—it is $\dot{a}\nu o\mu\acute{\iota}a$, lawlessness, outlawry. The sinner is an outlaw, with regard to the dominion of God. The connection of this definition enhances its force. The sin here in the mind of the Apostle is anything short of that spotless purity which has its perfection in Christ—"*As He is pure*" (1 John iii. 3). He that is not in accord with this purity is the sinner, who in his sin is also a transgressor of law. The principles of these passages are so interwoven into the very texture of the teachings of Scripture, that it is in vain to search for shelter or tolerance, upon the score of pure legality, for anything that does not fully satisfy the law in character and condition, as well as in act. The axe is laid to the tree, root and branch. The decree is gone forth from the Throne against "*All ungodliness and unrighteousness of men*" (Romans i. 18). Under the piercing light of that decree, "*All the world is become guilty before God*" (Romans iii. 19).

Important as this doctrine is in itself, it is equally important in its bearing. It affects several matters vitally connected with practical religion.

First, *It regulates our judgments as to the possibility of attaining sinless perfection in this life.* Perfectionism rests on the supposition either that the law does not require absolute conformity, and entire freedom from

---

[1] Eph. iv. 18.   [2] Eph. ii. 12.   [3] Eph. ii. 16, and Rom. viii. 7.

the taint of sin, or else that sin can be affirmed only by the acts of the will. But when it is seen that there is nothing in the character or deeds of a man but must submit to God; when it is found that all our life and being must be raised to the supreme standard of the law; when any failure to render loving service *with all the heart, etc.* . . . is sentenced as sin, then the whole ground is removed from under the feet of perfectionism. The glorious image falls, as did that image Daniel saw. The motives of sin, which are in the members of every son of Adam, only expire with this vile body's dying pang. So long as those motives survive, perfection is impossible.

Secondly, *It enables us to see that man never can plead the merit of his life as ground for acceptance with God.* If perfection be beyond his power, for a greater reason Salvation never can be his as a reward of his own works. The law gives no reward to those who in a single particular fail. The man who doeth the things of the law, and he only, shall live by them. For "*Cursed is everyone that continueth not in all things which are written in the book of the law to do them*" (Galatians iii. 10). But as no fallen man has continued in all these things, if any man is to be saved, it must be as a gift, and not as his due. Salvation must spring from the free mercy of God, and in no wise depend upon the desert of human virtue. The infinite grace of the Saviour alone opens the door of hope to a fallen world.

Thirdly, *There is no scope left for works of supererogation.* If man cannot fulfil, much less can he go beyond the law. According to the Roman Catholics, the specific enactments of the law touch us only at certain points distant from each other: these enactments are for all. But between these distant points, what they term *precepts* intervene. These precepts may or may not be adopted by us. We may or may not abstain from marriage: we may or may not choose poverty, and follow a monastic life, or pursue similar eclectic virtues, which are all of the nature of " virtues seeking adventures." But if any should obey such precepts, all such obedience, being beyond the common limit, and so not required by themselves, goes into a fund of merit available for others. Of this fund, the Church, owing to the communism of saints, and by virtue of the power of the Keys, is the Sovereign Custodian and Dispenser. Now if the commands of the law, either in spirit or letter, encompass the whole of our capacities and life, even as the waters of the ocean encircle and wash on every part the shores of the dry land, Where is there an opening, a dry passage through the waves, for the practice of these adventurous virtues, the superfluities of the saints? Besides, as they admit that their holiest saints were tainted with "venial sins" to the end of their days, it seems a peculiar kind of Spiritual Economy which allows men to be over-righteous, while they are yet not righteous enough, to accumulate saintly savings, while they are not able to pay their own sinful debts. God acknowledges no merit, till all demerit is removed. Even in the case of His own Son, not till He had said, "*Thus it becometh me to fulfil* all *righteousness*," was His approval expressed in the sublime words, "*This is My beloved Son in whom I am well-pleased*" (Matthew iii. 15, 17). With regard to all others, that Son, from His self-knowledge, has shown the measure that shall be meted out to them. They shall not emerge into the liberty of merit, before they are entirely discharged from their guilt. They shall not come out thence till they have paid the *uttermost farthing* (Matthew v. 2ℓ).

Thus, then, the figment of perfection while in this imperfect body in this sinful world, the pharisaic dream of salvation through the works of the law, and the fond speculation of the funded savings of saintly virtue, so full of gain to the Romish Church, all shew their unscriptural and irrational character when the touch of the Divine Law is closely applied. They cannot abide the test.

The Source of the Authority of Law.

We have ascertained pretty clearly and fully this great truth, *that sin is the negation and violation of the Moral Law*. It becomes us now to put the further question, *Whence does the Moral Law derive its authority? Why should it be the Sovereign Arbiter of right and wrong?* It will be seen at once that this involves a matter that both theoretically and practically goes to the very foundation of morals and religion. In vain we trace the breadth of the Commands, if we in the slightest degree weaken the force of the imperative, the *ought*, and the *must*, that breathes in the least of them. Even if we prove them each to be the voice of God, it is no slight matter to ascertain in what way they are that voice.

As might be expected, there are many explanations of such a theme. We may collect the chief under four heads.

(1) Some trace all law to the *merum Arbitrium Dei*.

(2) Some go further, and hold that as the will is determined by the ideas of the understanding, it is in the understanding we find the original fount of law.

(3) A third, and more recent school goes outside both the Divine Will and Understanding, and grounds all morality upon a metaphysical necessity, an ideal eternal law of righteousness, existing independently of the Will of God.

(4) A fourth view may be distinguished as combining the first two above-mentioned, and asserting the "indistinguishable identity" of the Divine Understanding and Divine Will on the authority of law.

(1) With regard to the first view, that the moral law is based solely upon the Will of God to the exclusion of the Understanding, I may say that it is both ancient and recent. Duns Scotus stoutly maintained it, and had many followers. The chief reason given in its support is that in this way alone can that absolute freedom be truly attributed to God, which was necessary in His creative work. Ernesti, among modern Divines, has given it his adhesion largely on the grounds that there are in Scripture some moral arrangements of universal authority, which have their basis entirely in the Divine Arbitrariness.

This view has its origin in a false notion of freedom. It is supposed that an agent can act with freedom just in proportion as notion or intelligence is severed from the will: if the severance is complete, the freedom is absolute. The contrary is, however, the case. "A human action, whether it be good or evil, is so much *the more free*, the more clearly the agent knows what he wills, and wherefore he wills it; and so much the less free, when he merely wills in order to will."

In addition to this misconception of the nature of liberty, we may charge this theory with practically cutting off God from the nature and constitution of His Own Universe. If the law of moral agents results from a *will*, the reason for whose action is within itself, or what is the same thing, owns no reason, then the law of moral agents has no necessary connection with the intelligence of God. That law is no longer the mirror of the nature of Deity. With equal consistency, if this theory be true, God might have laid down the reverse of every precept, and turned all virtue into vice, and all vice into virtue, by saying, "Thou shalt steal, murder, covet"; and also, "Thou shalt have other Gods before me." Yet all this might be done, without the Divine Character being concerned. The idea is monstrous. God would become an empty abstraction; the origin of His law a tyranny.

Such exhortations as, "*Be ye holy, for I am holy*" (1 Peter i. 16), would be rendered meaningless; and even the wrong of sin as a

---

[1] *Christian Doctrine of Sin:* Müller, Vol. 1, p. 99.

transgression of law extenuated, because it would not thereby necessarily be an act of violence done to the intelligence and nature of God and the moral constitution of His Universe.

(2) On the contrary it is urged by the advocates of the second theory, that sin is not evil because it is forbidden by the law; but it is forbidden by the law because it is evil. They accordingly derive the moral law from the Divine Understanding to the exclusion of the Divine Will, just as the previous theorists affirmed the Will of God to be free from the influence of the understanding.

Let us keep distinctly before us, in comparing the contents of a law with the ideas of the mind originating that law, that while there may be a perfect correspondence and identity, yet this correspondence does not destroy the generic difference between a law and a mental idea. All the world recognizes this distinction. The mental conception, as such, is within, and affects only the being in whose mind it exists. But when the conceptions of the Divine Mind became law, they had an imperative bearing upon external Creation. What was it that transformed them into that imperative and determining force? The *fiat* of the Divine Will. It was the creative *Deus vult* that transformed the conceptions of the Divine Will into symbols of Divine Majesty, binding upon all the Universe. This *fiat* of the Divine Will is an essential constituent of law. We acknowledge the same principle in the formation of human laws. The mind of Parliament is not the law of the country simply as the mind of Parliament. The will of the Sovereign expressed in the imperial words, *Regina vult*, is essential to make it legally binding upon the citizens.

That this commanding power resides in the will is fully recognized in some of the latest definitions of law. The Duke of Argyll says: "The idea which lies at the root of law in all its applications is evident enough. In its primary signification, a 'law' is the authoritative expression of human Will enforced by Power."[1] Take away the element of the Sovereign Will, whosesoever that may be, from a law; and in that act you degrade it from being a law to the mere level of a record or statement. The legal status is gone. Remove the Divine Will from the Law of Righteousness, and refer that law to the sphere of the Divine Mind, and we then behold the Divine conception of righteousness; but that conception is not a law. It is the source whence the contents of the law spring, and the seat of all primal principles of right; but the

---

[1] *Reign of Law*, p. 64.

Supreme Volition is essential to give these sovereign sway over Creation and all outside the Divine Mind. Scripture avows this again and again. When representing the Divine purposes as supreme in the control over all affairs, it is the Divine Will that is the symbol of that supremacy. "*Who hath resisted His Will?*" (Rom. ix. 19.) He "*worketh all things after the counsel of His own Will*" (Eph. i. 2). "*According to the good pleasure of His Will*" (verse 5). But lest any should say that these, and the great number of kindred passages, do not touch the point, as they refer to the purposes of God, and not to His righteousness; I reply by saying that Scripture holds the same language when the law alone is concerned. "*Behold thou art called a Jew, and restest in the law, and makest thy boast of God, and knowest His will*" (Rom. ii. 17, 18). "*Not every one that saith unto Me, Lord! Lord! shall enter into the Kingdom of heaven; but he that doeth the will of my Father which is in heaven*" (Matt. vii. 21). "*This is the will of God, even your sanctification*" (1 Thess. iv. 3). Passing by the abundant other passages deriving their binding force from the Supreme Will, I close with what may be regarded as the most important instance that even Scripture affords. It is that respecting the death of our Lord, which occurs in Hebrews x. 7. No satisfaction could ever be rendered to God in the carnal sacrifice of bulls, etc.; and no effectual redemption wrought by them, as God had no pleasure in them. Hence the Son came, and having His will in accord with the Divine Will, and the law of His God hid in His heart, He offered up to that Will "*one sacrifice for sins for ever.*" (verse 12). This gave infinite satisfaction. It fulfilled all righteousness, by fulfilling that Will. It obtained eternal redemption for us. Thus the Will of God represents His moral character in the supreme moral transaction of the Universe. It is vain to seek to turn aside the force of this evidence, by making the Will of God equal to the purpose that Christ should die; even then it must include satisfaction to law. So that doing *the Will* would necessarily be satisfying the law of His righteousness.

When we reflect upon the exceeding riches of the Divine grace, the manifold wisdom, and the manner of love that lay behind that *Will*, and remember that the Apostle regarded *Will* as the true symbol of all this moral wealth, we need not fear to refer the law to the Divine Will as well as to the Divine Mind,—to the Volition as essentially as to the Understanding of God. The true position is that righteousness, as an idea, belongs to the Understanding; while as a law, it pertains to the Will.

(3) The third theory is that which traces the standard of Moral Excellence beyond the Will and Mind of God, to a metaphysical necessity external to God. This absolute righteousness becomes personal in God: He is at once its most perfect Exponent, and its most illustrious Subject. The expounders of this theory go to the extreme of saying that this ideal righteousness would reveal itself to, and bind the conscience of man, *although there were no God.*

Dr. Dale avowedly repudiates this theory, and yet uses language perilously near to its error. Amongst other sentences of the same complexion, this one occurs in his 9th lecture:[1] "Righteousness gains an infinite support when it is known that God requires us to be righteous; but even in the absence of that knowledge, conscience confesses that the Law of Righteousness has an external and necessary authority." The infection even enters some of his nicest discriminations. Speaking of God's relation to law, he says: "His relation to the law is not a relation of subjection, but of identity." . . . . . "In God the law is *alive;* it reigns on His throne, sways His sceptre, is crowned with His glory."[2] The rift becomes wider when he adds: "It is possible to conceive of the authority of the eternal Law of Righteousness apart from God. An Atheist knows the meaning of the word *ought*, and may confess that the obligations of duty are absolute. But apart from the authority of the eternal Law of Righteousness as expressed in the Divine Will, it is not possible to conceive of God."[3]

Now I accept Dr. Dale's disavowal heartily. But he seems to repudiate this "godless basis" of ethics as one would abjure sea-bathing, while he was yet dripping with the brine. Like Milton's lion, "pawing to get free his hinder parts" from the "grassy clods,"[4] he seems unable to get clear away from this ideal law, independent of God. His jealous regard for the authority of conscience would seem to tie him down to a cast of expression which is quite appropriate in others, but unfortunate in him, since he rejects their principles.

It is possible to vindicate the rights of conscience, precious as they are, at too great a cost. Necessary as the authority of conscience is to the authority of righteousness, yet there is a truth infinitely more essential, and that is the existence of God, the Framer of the conscience of man. What can be the tendency of arguing for the power to conceive of the Eternal Law of Righteousness apart

---

[1] *On the Atonement*, p. 368.   [2] Ibid, p. 372.
[3] Ibid pp. 372-3.   [4] *Paradise Lost*, Book vii.

from God, and then producing in evidence the Atheist who knows the meaning of the word *ought?* Whose is this *ought* that the Atheist knows? Is it his own or the borrowed language of the godly? Did this *ought* that he claims arise out of his Atheism? If so, what is its meaning? Do Dr. Dale's "moral sceptics" obtain their morality from their scepticism? Do his "virtuous Atheists" gather their virtue from their Atheism? Let the question be put where unadulterated Atheism has flourished without restriction, if any such spot can be found. Let the question be put in a favourable case, where the idea of God was not quite obliterated, but only depraved—and what is the reply? Inspiration gives it in Romans i. in the hideous revolt of man against whatsoever things are pure, whatsoever things are lovely and of good report among men. If you want to know the unequivocal meaning of an Atheist's "*ought,*" if you want to trace his conception of the eternal Law of Righteousness apart from God; if you want to perceive his sense of its binding force upon the conscience, that dark page opens up a woful wealth of information. There the ancient Atheist evolves his "ought" from his Atheism, unlike his modern successor, who steals the Christian's "ought" and ideas of absolute law. In simple verity, Atheism of itself knows no law of righteousness, no "ought" beyond utility; it requires the idea of a God to lift utility out of the mud of materialism into the pure dignity of unbending law. When, therefore, Dr. Dale brings in his "Atheist's ought" to shew us how conscience may learn its duty from an ideal law of righteousness, apart from God, he is vitiating his whole reasoning process by equivocal terms. His clever antithesis, that we can conceive of law apart from God, but not of God apart from law, becomes when analysed by these tests, in part a pretty ringing of the changes upon words, and for the rest suggests that God is infinitely less essential than the law to the virtue of His universe!

It will not help Dr. Dale to fall back upon the position that a man may give up the mental acknowledgment of the existence of God, but cannot thereby silence the voice of conscience. This I admit. But conscience is not law; it is the organ of the eternal Law of Righteousness within our breasts. Nor can he fairly appeal to the authority of Bishop Butler as sustaining his extreme view. Bishop Butler's object, in his sermons on Human Nature, was not to shew the relation of Conscience to the eternal Law of Righteousness, but the rightful supremacy of conscience over the other faculties and emotions of the soul. To quote his own words, "This part of the office of conscience is beyond my present design explicitly to consider."[1] Whatever reference to the subject in hand the Bishop makes, is therefore incidental; but it is none the less valuable on that account as evidence of his sentiments. "Conscience," he says, "does not only offer itself to shew us the way we should walk in, but it likewise carries its own authority with it, that it is our Natural Guide, the guide assigned us by the Author of our Nature."[2] Here there is no severance of the function of conscience from the existence of God. It acts, because it is of God; and its magisterial rule gathers force because it has an ultimate reference to God. This is brought out in a striking manner, in the famous passage in the second Sermon (p. 21). "There is a superior principle of reflection in every man, which distinguishes between the internal principles of his heart as well as his external actions; which passes judgment upon himself and them; pronounces determinately some actions to be in themselves just, right, good; others to be in themselves, evil, wrong, unjust; which, without being consulted, without being advised with, magisterially exerts itself, and approves or condemns him, the doer of them accordingly; and which if not forcibly stopped, naturally and always of course goes on to anticipate a higher and more effectual sentence, which shall hereafter second and affirm its own."

When Dr. Dale quotes this passage, he bestows upon the first part of it great and deserved approbation; but with regard to the latter part of it, he, in effect, takes its evidence out of court. But this part we insist ought to be heard in evidence. And for this reason: Conscience grows in influence over our actions in proportion as it more vividly anticipates that "higher and more effectual sentence." In other words, its rule is more absolute, the clearer is its vision of God. "The idea of the moral cannot be truly apprehended and understood, without the idea of God,"—this is the just sentiment of both Rothe and Müller.[3] These distinguished men also go so far as to say, "that morality necessarily involves relation to God, and that it, *ceteris paribus*, is so much the more perfect, the more completely this relation is co-conditioned with it."[3]

But enough has been said to show that the normal and true testimony of conscience points, not to a law of righteousness apart from God, binding to duty, but ultimately to the Eternal Author both of conscience and of law.

---

[1] *Sermons*, Vol. 2, p. 21. [2] Ibid, p. 29.
[3] Müller, *Christian Doctrine of Sin*, Vol. 1, p. 102, note.

I turn briefly to the passage (page 372) where Dr. Dale repudiates the notion of God being subject to law : " His relation to the law is not a relation of subjection, but of identity." I will not here put the question, If there is this relation of identity between God and the law, how comes it about that the moral Atheist who admits the existence of law does not also necessarily recognize God ? To his mind the identity would appear, for some reason, not to be very manifest. But is it quite clear to any mind what is meant by this phrase ? What is this "relation of identity " ? We cannot say that the person who was the fervent Evangelist of Methodism had the relation of identity, or—what is I suppose the simple equivalent—was identical with the person who laid down the laws of its organization. We can say that the autograph of Queen Elizabeth in the Library of the British Museum has the relation of identity with the autograph of her Majesty exhibited at the Guildhall. But we cannot say that Charles was identical with John Wesley. Nor can we say that the autograph of Queen Elizabeth has the relation of identity to herself. The first would be a case of mistaken identity ; the second, a confusion of thought or language, or both. The signature is one, the Queen another, but they are not one and the same. And so with regard to the law and God. The law is one, God is another ; but the law is not God, nor is God the law.

In the subsequent phrase (page 372), in which Dr. Dale seeks to invest the law with the splendours of Deity, he virtually degrades it. "It reigns on His throne, sways His sceptre, is crowned with His glory." Has Deity abdicated? Has God left a law to sway His sceptre ? I had thought God reigned on His own throne, swayed His own sceptre, was crowned with His own glory, and "*would not give it to another.*"[1] If this be only Dr. Dale's way of phrasing the sublime Scriptural truth, "*Justice and judgment are the habitation of Thy throne*" (Ps. lxxxix. 14), I humbly think that he has not improved upon the original. I prefer the language of Scripture, and I can follow its clear, intelligent expressions of this grand theme without the fear of being impaled upon some dark supposition. " *The Lord is King for ever and ever* " (Ps. x. 16). " *He doeth according to His will in the army of heaven, and among the inhabitants of the earth: and none can stay His hand, or say unto Him, What doest Thou?* (Dan iv. 35.)

In this way I come to the conviction that it is not safe to morals, neither is it Scriptural nor rational, to attribute to an ideal law, existing

---

[1] Isa. xlii. 8.

apart from God, the supreme authority over conscience. God is the Lord of conscience, and He rules it by His law. It is not the law through God, or in God; but God in and through His law, Who is the moral Governor of all.

We have discussed three out of the four answers given to the question, *Whence does the Moral Law derive its authority?* We have seen good reasons for rejecting the theory that traces the law up to the arbitrary act of Divine Will. We have not been able to admit that the Divine Understanding, separated from the Divine Will, is the fount of law as law. Nor can we allow a metaphysical necessity, external to Deity, as the origin of that which subordinates all, Deity itself not excepted. Only one theory remains, and that I regard as giving a true account of the eternal source of the authority of the Law of Righteousness. It is that theory which acknowledges two elements in law, intelligence and binding force; it refers the *intelligence* to the Divine Understanding, and the *binding force* to the Divine Will. To the adoption of this theory the course of reasoning we have pursued has led us; and the arguments raised against the three other theories are, directly or indirectly, available for the support of this view. I will not, therefore, repeat what has been said, but simply add the following thoughts.

(1) *This theory is in harmony with just views of the perfection of Deity.* It represents the Divine Understanding and the Divine Will in perfect accord; but it shows each working in its own sphere: the Infinite Intelligence framing the idea of righteousness, and the Absolute Will transmuting that idea into a binding rule of right upon all creation. On the other hand, by referring Law either to the Will or to the Understanding exclusively, the supposition of a schism between the Divine Intelligence and the Divine Volition is raised. If you lean to the Will only, you suppose the Will might be *fettered* by the Understanding. If you choose the Understanding only, you suggest that there might be in the Divine Will that quality of *arbitrariness* which is the defect and the vice of fallen man. Both of these suppositions are utterly unworthy of the infinite harmony of the attributes of Deity; and, in being so, condemn themselves. They arise not from the simple contemplation of the All-perfect One; but seem in this particular tainted with the thought, unconscious perhaps, that God is such an one as ourselves.

(2) *This theory agrees with the nature of Moral Law.* There are at least two distinct elements in law, instruction and authority. The

ancient name **Torah** has the primary meaning of instruction : " *The commandment is a lamp, and the law is light*" (Prov. vi. 23). Besides shedding its light upon the path of duty, it also enforces its precepts by an authority, unquestionable and infinite. To the Intelligence of God we appropriately trace the light of the law; to the Will, its authority.

(3) *This view is further strengthened by the nature of morality.* No act or course of action can be termed moral from which the exercise of reason or will is excluded. A man must see why he acts, and he must will the act, before he can be accountable for it. Blot out his intelligence, or arrest his voluntary action, and he is no longer a moral agent. This is admitted on all hands, and it seems to me that this admission carries with it a far-reaching consequence. It points to the very foundations of all morality. For that which is the standard and rule of morality cannot be deficient in any element essential to the act of obedience. If we examine closely, we shall see there is Element answering to Element : the Divine corresponding to the human : and that as truly as the seal corresponds to the impression. Above our poor reason rises the infinite mind of God ; before our conscience is arrayed the holiness of God ; and in view of our will is set forth His majesty—the majesty of the King Eternal, immortal and invisible. Hence it follows : "*The law of the Lord is perfect, converting the soul : the testimony of the Lord is sure, making wise the simple. The statutes of the Lord are right, rejoicing the heart : the commandment of the Lord is pure, enlightening the eyes. The fear of the Lord is clean, enduring for ever : the judgments of the Lord are true and righteous altogether*" (Ps. xix. 7—9).

I therefore point to God as the Author of the Law of Righteousness, in such a way that it is not the mere arbitrary dictum of His Will—not singly the conception of His Understanding ; but the conception of His Understanding, the expression of His holy nature, armed with all the authority of His Will. It is the mirror of Deity ; and over it is inscribed for everyone that looks therein, the command "*Be ye holy for I am holy*" (1 Peter i. 16).

If, therefore, a man asks why he should obey the Law of Righteousness, I will not trouble him with notions of utility, or the good of greater numbers, questions all doubtful and obscure, I refer him to God : to God as the wisest, the purest, the kindest, the most powerful Being in the Universe : the Creator, the Ruler, the Redeemer, the Judge of all. Whether a man hears the whispers of that Law of Righteousness, in his own conscience, its broken utterances in the experience of daily life, or trembles beneath the sound of the trumpet, and the voice of the words from Sinai, the whisper is at one with the trumpet, and both summon our spirits into the presence of the Eternal throne.

I add the remarks—(1.) That if the view I have taken of the origin of law is correct, it follows that wherever the dominion of God extends, this Law of Righteousness is the rule of His government. As that dominion extends throughout the Universe, this **Law** must be supreme in all worlds and over all moral agents, however high or low in the scale of being. The law of gravitation is not more certain in its reach over all matter; the laws of light, as operating here, are not more truly exemplified in the faintest rays that reach our Earth from the most distant stars; than is the existence of one standard of righteousness throughout the domain of creation. It is the same Power that fashioned distant Jupiter as fashioned this Earth: the same wisdom and goodness that fixed the bands of Orion, and loosed the sweet influences of the Pleiades, that also bind and loose the Winter's cold and balmy air of Springtime over our glades: and shall that attribute of Righteousness, and the law expressing it, be regarded as variable, and changing with the changing source? Impossible. Wherever the throne may be erected, there "*Justice and judgment shall be the habitation of His throne*" (Psalm lxxxix. 14).

(2.) We may remark that we have great reason to hold that a clearer revelation of this law is made in other worlds than in our own. In this world the right is often obscured—good is put for evil, and evil for good. The general darkness of mind, hardness of heart and sinfulness of life prevent us from beholding the awful majesty of the Divine Law, and feeling the terrors of the Lord. But along with the departure from earth there will be a departure from all the shades that now hide the piercing light of Eternal Justice. There will be "*a revelation of the righteous judgment of God,*" says the Apostle.[1] According to the words of the Psalm,[2] "*A fire shall devour before Him, and it shall be very tempestuous round about Him. He shall call to the heavens from above, and to the earth, that he may judge his people.*" And yet again, John says, "*Behold, He cometh with clouds; and every eye shall see Him: and all kindreds of the earth shall wail because of Him*" (Rev. i. 7). "*It is appointed unto men once to die, but after this the Judgment*" (Heb. ix. 27; see also Rev. xx. 11-15).

---

[1] Romans ii. 5.   [2] Psalm l. 3, 4.

(3.) In conclusion, I would point out the woful state of impenitent transgressors of this Law of Righteousness. In this world, if a man offends against the law of one country, he may escape to another; but he that offends against the law of God can enter no country where that law does not exist. The sinner can pass into no society where it is suspended, no world where it is abrogated. Its principles are diffused through all creation. And just as the law is diffused, so also is the accumulation of moral force against the transgressor. By being opposed to the law of God, he is a rebel in arms against the Universe. Sooner might he succeed in pulling down the heavens, than in securing happiness by violation of that law. "*Heaven and Earth shall pass away, but My words shall not pass away,*"[1] says Christ. At the centre of all the moral system of the Universe, the loving God is enthroned, sustaining, energizing and vindicating all. In the words of the Psalmist, we may say, "*Whither shall I go from Thy spirit? or whither shall I flee from Thy presence? If I ascend up into heaven, Thou art there: if I make my bed in hell, behold, Thou art there. If I take the wings of the morning, and dwell in the uttermost parts of the sea; Even there shall Thy hand lead me, and Thy right hand shall hold me. If I say, Surely the darkness shall cover me; even the night shall be light about me. Yea, the darkness hideth not from Thee; but the night shineth as the day: the darkness and the light are both alike to Thee*" (Psalm cxxxix. 7-12).

---

[1] Matt. xxiv. 35.

LECTURE VII.

SIN IN MAN.

THIS branch of our subject follows in due order after describing the Nature of Sin. It compels us to deal with the problems *How* and *How far* Sin affects mankind. Under the former head comes up the great question of the origin of the corruption of our race; under the latter, the extent of our depravity. With this latter, I first propose to deal.

I do not hesitate to use the word adopted by Evangelical Divines for centuries, and affirm that, owing to the presence of sin in man, his depravity is *total*. This, I take to be the only word that adequately expresses the measure of our corruption. To this conclusion every unprejudiced mind must come, if one would accurately observe the actions of man, correctly trace the history of the race, honestly listen to experience, and truly interpret the language of the Word of God.

At the same time, the phrase, "total depravity" requires, like all such general terms, to be used with discrimination. Depravity supposes a state of integrity, as sin supposes a former condition of uprightness. When our nature, therefore, is spoken of as being totally depraved through sin, it ought never to be taken in such sense as to mean sin has become truly natural to us. Sin in our nature is a foreign element; but so closely interwoven as to become a second nature, supplanting our original nature—still it is foreign. The more anyone becomes a sinner, the less he is a true man. The progress of depravity is, therefore, the progress of what is unnatural, of what is contrary to the Divine Ideal. Our very form of speech bears this out. An unnatural mother, an unnatural father, an unnatural child, are terms that in the judgment of mankind, mark depravity of the uttermost degree. But still it is depravity, and "never the divinely created manhood." It is sin, subjugating and enslaving our manhood, but not annihilating its properties and faculties. This is what I take the "total depravity" occasioned by sin to be. It is the turning of all aside from the original purpose—putting the "world out of joint", as our great poet expresses it.

It is not meant, however, that because every man is totally depraved, he has therefore gone as far in sin as he possibly can. Sin in our nature is a reigning power, but it does not therefore at once exhaust all our activities. The lost have not added to their iniquity their last iniquity; and even Satan has not sinned his last sin. Sin impresses a character in us, and that is complete; but sin also instigates action, and that goes on to eternal ages.

Finally, the proper use of the term "total depravity" does not forbid us to acknowledge whatever actions of a praiseworthy kind we observe in the unbelieving and heathen world. This doctrine in no sense requires us to obscure the rays of "original brightness", that may linger around human deeds. As I have stated it, it compels us to expect and to acknowledge some traces of faded virtues. We need not blot out a single good feature of the worthy deeds of heathendom, we can accept and praise all; but we must accept and praise all at their right value. Honesty obliges us to recognize the many virtues of Socrates, the best of heathen; but the same honesty requires us to note his vices and idolatry. Common honesty forbids us to degrade the honest conduct seen every day in worldly men at home, in the office, in the circle of friends, and in every walk of life, into a hollow hypocrisy, thinly varnished over with the appearance of truthfulness. But common honesty also compels us to take these honesties and amenities of life for just what they are meant to be and naught else,—deeds between man and man, without any primary reference to God.

Now it is the absence of this reference and relation of the life to God that furnishes the clue to the real condition of a man. If he sees not God in his life and deeds, he is an alien to God; he is without God; he is at enmity against God. Hence it is, that notwithstanding his being an amiable father and friend, and just man of business, he may be what the apostle found himself to be, though as "*touching the righteousness which is in the law blameless,*"[1] "*sold under sin;*"[2] in other words, totally depraved. The man virtuous in his own, and in the world's esteem, may be utterly sinful in God's sight.

This paradox arises from the twofold relation of man; first to God, and secondly to his fellowmen. While his conscious loving relation to

---

[1] Philip. iii. 6. [2] Romans vii. 14.

God is severed by sin, his necessary relation to man and this world survives. This point is worthy of further remark.

As sin does not destroy our existence, so it neither stops the duties, nor severs the present relations of our existence. The sinner is still a member of human society. He loves life, and will therefore seek to sustain it. He loves happiness, and will therefore cultivate it. He loves society, and will therefore tighten its bonds, adorn its intercourse, and strengthen its safeguards. From causes such as these may spring and be cultivated the good qualities of the man, the citizen, the father, the friend, the merchant, or the patriot. From these, too, may arise the arts, the poetries, and philosophies that refine, adorn, and elevate life: such worldly virtues have no value in the scale of Divine esteem, if God is excluded.

But admitting all these excellences, they do not represent the full fruitage of all his nature. He is destined for a life beyond the boundary of time and earth, and for a society other than that of this world; and if his earthly temporal virtues hold not those futurities in view, they are radically defective. A failure here is as fatal as it is complete. It brings all life down to the dust. So-called virtues become but splendid vices. Thus, when the young Ruler refused to go the whole length in true virtues, our Saviour pointed out that his past keeping of the Commandments lost by that refusal all its seeming righteousness. What is more, by not going far enough these very virtues are likely to be in actual antagonism to the true Divine idea of existence. Perhaps it was so with this young Ruler, as we know for certain it was the case with the majority of the Pharisees. With their very virtues they opposed God. They went about to establish their own righteousness, "*not submitting themselves to the righteousness of God*" (Rom. x. 3). The existence of worldly virtues, therefore, does not make any argument against man's total depravity; it but helps to complete the proof of the doctrine.

The view thus presented of the corrupting influence of sin in our nature is so truly sad and terrible, that we ought not to receive it unless supported by the most cogent proofs. Our great proof is derived from Scripture, as we proceed to show, classifying the various passages under three heads.

(1) All those passages which expressly teach it:—"*And God saw that the wickedness of man was great in the earth, and that every imagination of the thoughts of his heart was only evil continually*"

(Gen. vi. 5). "*There is none that seeketh after God. They are all gone out of the way*" (Rom. iii. 11, 12). "*Every one of them is gone back: they are altogether become filthy; there is none that doeth good, no, not one*" (Ps. liii. 3). "*The carnal mind is enmity against God: for it is not subject to the law of God, neither indeed can be*" (Rom. viii. 7). "*The whole world lieth in wickedness*" (1 John. v. 19).

(2) Those Scriptures which declare that it is impossible for carnal men to do anything pleasing to God:—"*Without faith it is impossible to please God*" (Heb. xi. 6). "*To be carnally minded is death*" (Rom. viii. 6).

"If they that are in the flesh did any part of their duty towards God, or if what they did were good and virtuous in His sight, so far as it goes their minds would be subject to the law of God, and being such they might and would please Him. God is not a capricious or hard Master, but is pleased with righteousness wherever He sees it."

(3) Those Scriptures which speak of the whole of goodness or virtue as comprehended in *love*—the love of God and our neighbour. (Matt. xxii. 37, 39; Rom. xiii. 9, 10; Gal. v. 14; Jas. ii. 8; 1 John. iv. 7; etc.).

I have endeavoured to show that we must not take a lighter view of the corrupting effect of sin, because sin is not natural to man, neither because it is not at its climax, nor because there still survive in mankind certain excellent traits of conduct, which are called Virtues. The depravity of our nature is not diminished by any of these considerations. I can understand the feelings of those who would wish to paint out some of the darker lines of our moral ruin; but no false tenderness should allow us to disguise for a moment the sad and terrible fact of our total moral corruption—provided that fact can be well established—seeing the acknowledgment of it is so closely connected with our recovery.

That our nature is wholly depraved through sin is made sadly plain by the following evidence :—

(1) As regards the human race, there is no tribe or people to be found not subject to death. Now the presence of death proves, according to the Apostle, the presence of sin. It proves the presence of sin, not merely as a factor in human history, but as a supreme dominating power—*sin reigning unto death*. All that is meant by this, the poets and sages of the Ancient World have essayed to narrate in their confessions and lamentations.

Horace, the Epicurean poet of luxurious Rome, asserts: "*Nam vitiis nemo sine nascitur*" (*Sat:* Book I., iii. 68). Propertius says that no man is born without sin, and that every man is naturally vicious. Laertius, in his *Vita Aristippi*, asserts that there is an evil disposition that is implanted and grows up in men. Plutarch declares that there is a fatal portion of evil in all when born, from whence come the depravity of the soul, diseases, etc. Cicero laments "that men should be brought into life by nature as a step-mother, with a naked, frail and inferior body, and with a mind or soul prone to lusts."

It may, however, be said, that these are unfavourable examples, and do not show human nature to the best advantage, because the true knowledge of God had been obscured in these nations. I therefore turn to an example liable to no such objection. I turn to a people, in whose midst, as a great writer (Renan) has said, the doctrine of conscience was developed, as amongst the Greeks was cultivated the idea of the beautiful, and among the Romans the science of law. Of this people the Apostle Paul has said that they had an advantage over all other nations in every way that could conduce to righteousness. They were chosen from others, blessed above the rest of mankind, redeemed of the Lord by special displays of mercy and power, kept by unchanging faithfulness, and taught by miracles, laws, admonitions, and persuasions,—surely these privileges justify the exultant words of their departing legislator: "*Happy art thou, O Israel: who is like unto thee, O people saved by the Lord!*" (Deut. xxxiii. 29.)

And what was the result notwithstanding these privileges? The prophet chronicles the first stages of the disappointment: "*Your goodness is as the morning cloud, and as the early dew it goeth away*" (Hosea vi. 4). I say this was only the first stage; if we would trace their sin up to its fatal climax, we must witness the scene at Pilate's Judgment Hall; we must mark their gift of a thorn-crown to the Son of God, and listen to the cry, "Crucify Him," "Crucify Him." That cry was the cry of the most religiously enlightened, the most religiously scrupulous of all nations under heaven. This religious people consummated, under the guise of their religion, the world's greatest sin— the Crucifixion of the Son of God. If there was such a complete alienation of heart from God on the part of such a nation, what can we expect in the case of the rest of the inhabitants of the earth? From one we may know all.

(2) Not only is this depravity universal as to the race, but in every individual it is total. The same Scripture that declares "*All the world*

is guilty before God,"[1] also affirms that "*There is none righteous, no, not one*."[2] The scope of this charge becomes apparent, if we bear in mind what alone can fitly be assigned as the seat of sin in man. It cannot be our material or sensuous nature, for that would remove from sin its essential moral element: it cannot be the heart severed from the understanding, nor the understanding severed from the affections and conscience; the one would take away the rational, as the other would remove the moral and voluntary ingredient of sin. But the soul, as an indivisible unit, the seat of habitual and emotional powers, of conscience and will, is the seat of sin in man, and as such is the centre of control, and the source of contagion. Intellect and heart, will and physical frame, all become the instruments of unrighteousness. Every member of the body feels the corrupting taint, and enters into the degrading drudgery: tongue, throat, lips, eyes, mouth, feet, and hands. Every emotion and every faculty are turned aside into aversion from God. "Man loves to *think*, and cannot live without thinking; but he does not love to think of God; '*God is not in all his thoughts*.' Man delights in *activity*, is perpetually in motion, but has no heart to act for God. Men take pleasure in *conversation*, and are never more cheerful than when engaged in it; but if God and religion be introduced, they are usually struck dumb, and discover an inclination to drop the subject. Men greatly delight in hearing and telling *news;* but if the glorious news of the Gospel be sounded in their ears, it frequently proves as unwelcome as Paul's preaching at Athens. In fine, man feels the necessity of *a god*, but has no relish for the true God. There is a remarkable instance of this in the conduct of those nations planted by the King of Assyria in the cities of Samaria. They were consumed by wild beasts, and considered it as an expression of displeasure from the *god of the land*. They wished to become acquainted with him that they might please him. An Israelitish priest is sent to teach them the manner of the god of the land. But when he taught them the fear of Jehovah, His character and worship do not seem to have suited their taste; for each nation preferred the worship of its own gods (2 Kings xvii.)."[3]

(3) This depravity unfolds itself at such a time, and in such a way, as to show that it is not from imitation, but is inherent in our nature. The blight is in the opening bud, as well as in the full-blown flower of our life. The careful observer is never for a moment deluded by the poetic fiction of the snowy sinlessness of childhood. "Certainly there

---

[1] Rom. iii. 19.   [2] Ibid, v. 10.   [3] *Works:* A. Fuller, p. 301.

is a sort of innocence in a child—its very naughtinesses are often almost lovable; but in the midst of all its innocence and loveliness, an ominous background is often seen"—so says Luthardt.[1] The language of Scripture gives body to these fears. The earliest date for its bursting forth is Youth. "*The imagination of man's heart is evil from his youth*" (Gen. viii. 21). If we take "youth" here to indicate what is called the dawn of reason, another passage will carry us up higher, even to man's birth: "*The wicked are estranged from the womb: they go astray as soon as they be born, speaking lies*" (Ps. lviii. 3). Lest we should imagine this referred to a separate class, the children of wicked men, we have the children of the righteous described as "*Transgressors from the womb*" (Isa. xlviii. 8). Of "man" universally it is affirmed in Job, "*Man is born like a wild ass's colt*" (Job xi. 12); and David particularly, the child of godly parents, though cared for of God from his mother's knee, yet mourns the inborn taint, "*Behold I was shapen in iniquity*" (Ps. li. 5). This, his lamentation, is not in extenuation, but in aggravation of his sin. The depravity is the greater in his eyes, the deeper its roots are in his nature entwined about the fountain of his being and nurtured there. With him, as with many a thousand others, his manhood bore the poisonous fruits of those evils that in childhood and youth lay dormant as germs in the soil of his heart. And probably, if only our eyes were opened to penetrate the depths of our nature, "we should at length feel that there is no sin of which the germ and possibility is not within us."[1]

(4) Another evidence of the total depravity of our nature is seen in our inability to eradicate it. Sin germinates early, and it lives late in every individual, as in the world at large. Its presence may be detected and an effort made to remove it—for so far the action of our moral sense avails us. But the light of conscience, however vividly it may reveal, never removes our sin. It may condemn and inwardly torture the sinner; but no man is morally purer or stronger for all these inward "penal fires." An outward strictness of conduct may be produced, but the core of evil remains untouched. Where conscience fails, the power of will has no better success. Even this imperial faculty cannot stem the torrent of the inclination. We have examples of this in widely different men—the Roman poet and the Christian Apostle. Horace, with a complacent sigh, confesses his feebleness, "I know and approve the things that are better, but I follow those that

---

[1] Luthardt: *Fundamental Truths*, p. 188.

are worse." In the earnest moral struggle of the Christian Apostle, this cultured acquiescence gives way before a vehement indignation of expression, but the indignation nevertheless of defeat—"*O wretched man that I am!*" (Rom. vii. 24.)

It is well to pause over this acknowledged failure: it is typical. Paul had the culture of which some affirm that if it were universal it would altogether purify mankind. He had the better moral knowledge for which Socrates longed as a sure antidote for moral evil. By the one he was moulded as a member of society on the most refined models; by the other he became a Pharisee. He had learned to discipline his habits and control himself; but neither culture nor moral knowledge and discipline, nor all combined, could save him from the moral collapse he so passionately deplored. They left him lamenting "*in me (that is, in my flesh) dwelleth no good thing;*"[1] and no wisdom of later times has attained a better result.

Those who, like Schiller, fondly dreamed that it is through the beautiful, that door of dawn, that we are to enter the lands of moral freedom, have found the fair hope sink into the bitter mortification of Guizot, "*nous avons méconnu le mal inhérent à notre nature.*" After all these centuries Job's challenge remains unanswered, "*Who can bring a clean thing out of an unclean?*" (Job xiv. 4.)

(5) Having touched upon the experiences of Paul, I may also refer to the universal experiences of the best of men as testifying to the complete defection of our nature from God. The nature of this testimony is peculiarly strong. Not only do the best teachers of Ethics among the Ancients admit that such is the case; but the most holy of the saints of both the Old and New Testaments are as copious as they are sorrowful in its acknowledgment. So much at one are they in this sad confession, that there is not a single voice raised to the contrary. Nor is this concurrence of opinion brought about by slight or superficial views of what is in men, by imitation, or by artificial exaggeration. It comes through the individual shame, the grief and deep remorse of every one of the witnesses. The "*groaning*" of the Prophet, the "*woe*" of Isaiah, the "*abhorrence*" of Job, who, according to the estimate of God Himself, was perfect and had not his like in all the earth; these all attest it. Every true penitent takes the same view of himself as these holy men did. Indeed I might go almost as far as saying that the degree of attainment in holiness by believers may be measured by their

---

[1] Rom. vii. 18.

readiness to admit their own utter sinfulness. "It is a strong presumption," as A. Fuller says, "against the contrary doctrine, that the light-minded and dissipated part of mankind are generally its advocates; while the humble, the serious, and the godly as generally acknowledge with the Apostle, 'that fulfilling the desires of the flesh, and of the mind, they were by nature children of wrath, even as others' (Eph. ii. 3)."[1]

(6) I adduce finally the testimony of Scripture. So voluminous and varied is this, that I can attempt little more than orderly arrangement. It is found in nearly every conceivable form. It appears as history—the history of the race in its wanderings from the gates of Eden to the gates of the New Jerusalem. We have the history of the race as a whole, and of particular nations; of distinct families, and of separate individuals, some of whom shine out with the most stainless characters among mankind. And yet, as the Record runs, before the flood came to destroy, "*all flesh had corrupted his way upon the earth;*"[2] so now, though Christ has come to save, the Apostle declares, "*the whole world lieth in wickedness (the wicked one)*" (1. John. v. 19).

This evidence occurs in the form of vivid descriptions, and terrible impeachments, as in Isaiah (chapter i.). It is heard in plaintive elegy and lament, as in Psalm li., and Isaiah liii. It appears in close and vigorous reasoning, as in Romans i. and iii., and Ephesians ii. You hear it in the passionate eloquence of the Baptist in the desert as he addressed the multitudes; and in the calm teaching of the Saviour to the ruler of the Jews, "*That which is born of the flesh is flesh*" (John. iii. 6).

Even when the fairer qualities of our nature are portrayed and insisted upon, there is not the slightest hint of denial of the inner core of evil. When the Apostle on Mars' Hill used the words of one of the Grecian poets to describe the Divine descent of man, "he did justice," as Van Oosterzee says, "to the æsthetical worth of heathenism, as well as to its religious aspirations; but beneath this transparent robe he sees a corruption whose depth, with firm hand, he probes and lays bare."[3]

When our Lord speaks of "*the whole who need not a physician*" (Matt. ix. 12), these are not the sinless and the perfect. When He describes the "ninety and nine," these are not the subjects of that Kingdom which is righteousness, and peace, and joy in the Holy Ghost. When, in contrast with the wandering prodigal, He introduces

---

[1] *Works*, p. 301. [2] Gen. vi. 12.
[3] Van Oosterzee, *Theology of New Testament*, p. 267.

the elder brother who had ever been at home, he is not a perfectly obedient one, "but an unloving brother, whose self-righteousness is yet more repulsive than the unrighteousness of the other."[1]

Nor is the indirect evidence less convincing than the direct. Every passage that speaks of Redemption by Christ supposes that man needs such a redemption, and is utterly unable of himself to give unto God a ransom: else why should there be this unspeakable expenditure of suffering on the part of the Son of God? Every sentence that tells of the work of regeneration by the Holy Spirit implies the utter degradation of man. Every passage that urges the need of Divine enlightenment supposes a dense moral darkness, through which unaided we cannot burst. There is not a single text that insists on the necessity of the quickening energy of the Spirit of God; but suggests a spiritual death from which no man can effect for himself a resurrection. We gather this evidence, too, from those Scriptures which "declare the utter impossibility of carnal men doing anything to please God; such as, '*Without faith it is impossible to please God*' (Heb. xi. 6); '*To be carnally minded is death*' (Rom. viii. 6); '*Because the carnal mind is enmity against God: for it is not subject to the law of God, neither indeed can be. So then they that are in the flesh cannot please God*' (Rom. viii. 7). If they that are in the flesh," continues A. Fuller, "did any part of their duty towards God, or if what they did were good and virtuous in His sight, so far as it goes, their mind would so far be subject to the law of God, and being such, they might and would please Him; for God is not a capricious or hard Master, but is pleased with righteousness wherever he sees it."[2]

Wherever, in the Word of God, love is declared to be the "fulfilling of the law," there is a verdict universally recorded against men. For as the ungodly cannot have the love of God within them, whatever love they may have is robbed of its essential relation, and so they are destitute of true virtue. To all this may be added the broad bearing of the mission of our Lord, which was to seek and to save that which is lost. The command to repent and to believe compels the conclusion, that men have sins of which they must repent, and reasons which incite them to believe. And as the command is universal, "*God commandeth all men every where to repent,*"[3] so we may infer that all are smitten with that disease from which faith, in the name of Jesus, opens up the only remedy.

---

[1] Van Oosterzee, *Theology of New Testament*, p. 93.   [2] *Works*, p. 302.   [3] Acts xvii. 30.

LECTURE VIII.

THE CAUSE OF TOTAL DEPRAVITY.

WE have seen that the sinfulness of mankind is such that no one, at any time of his life, escapes the taint, and that all are thereby completely estranged from God. It becomes us now, with this terrible fact before us, to seek after its cause. How comes such depravity to be there? Judging from the magnitude of the effect, no slight cause can satisfy us as being adequate. An effect so universal must have a cause equally universal: an effect so constant must be produced by a cause equally persistent. It is well to keep these essential requirements of the true cause in mind, as we open up the enquiry. Many theories are before us; but they may all be broadly grouped into two classes. First, *those that seek the cause of man's depravity along the line of his moral growth and development.* Secondly, *those that place the cause of it in his fall and degeneracy from a moral integrity once perfect.*

In the first group, the general view comes prominently forward that man began the race of life far distant from the attainable goal. He began in more or less imperfection, but would rise to be perfect. Faults were unavoidable in this his upward struggle, and hence his sin.

It requires little reflection to perceive that theories of this class are not only inconsistent with the Bible account of man's sin, but are directly opposed to it. Scripture does not for a moment acknowledge that there is any kind of necessity for sin, whether you place that necessity in the limitations of our nature, or in its weakness. Depravity is more than a limitation, and sin more than a weakness, both before the bar of conscience and the Word of God. If you place the necessity in the prior development of man's sensitive nature, you are not on better ground; for sin survives the period which ought, according to the theory, to bring about the proper equilibrium of man's powers. In its more insidious, but not less heinous forms, it belongs not to the flesh but to the mind. Pride and envy have their root in the soul. If you try to account for man's being a sinner by affirming that moral good always casts a shadow, you do one of two things. You give as a reason for the existence of his sinfulness that which is not sin; or else you remove the culpability from the very nature of sin.

To conclude this enumeration; if you assign imitation as a reason for the universal spread of sin, the cause is inadequate. The statement of Scripture is backed up by the most abundant proofs: "*All we like sheep have gone astray; we have turned every one to his own way*" (Isaiah liii. 6). Man is no mere copyist in his sin. "No one can remember his first evil deed, still less his first sinful thought."[1] No one has proved his original purity by retaining it. But the purest of men will confess to the upspringing of impurity in the heart and imagination even in their holiest moments.

Besides these particular objections to these, and kindred theories of this group, there is this general condemnation of them all: they are at variance with the facts of man's existence as given by inspiration, and also with the principles of redemption. The Bible knows of no ascent without a descent; no return to God without a departure from Him. The course of Christ, the Redeemer, is parallel with the course of man, the sinner, and defines it: He bowed the heavens and came down. "*That He ascended, what is it but that He also descended first into the lower parts of the earth?*" (Ephesians iv. 9.) And man, to whom and for whom Christ stooped so low, had also descended, had fallen; else we know not if Christ would ever have stooped, or redemption been possible.

It is therefore along the downward, and not on the upward course of man, that we may expect to find the cause of the depravity of the race. We turn accordingly to the second group of theories, that is, to those which place the cause of the sin and sinfulness of mankind in the fall of Adam. It will readily be seen that here both Scripture and good sense are on their side.

There is no mistaking the testimony of Scripture on the subject. Its most distant, as well as its most direct references point to one great event as the fountain of all the sins and miseries of mankind. In one of the earliest references in the inspired Volume, Adam appears as

---

[1] *Christian Dogmatics*, **Van** Oosterzee, p. 401.

the arch transgressor of his race : "*If I*," says Job, "*covered my transgressions as Adam, by hiding mine iniquity in my bosom ?*" (Job xxxi. 33.) Hosea makes it the burden of his charge against the sinners of his time, that they had sinned after the similitude of Adam's transgression: "*But they like Adam have transgressed the covenant*" (Hosea vi. 7). In his more incidental, as well as in his graver allusions, the apostle Paul clearly indicates that all human sin was connected with the sin of our first parents. It appears incidentally in his reasons for the silence and submissiveness of women in the Churches: "*For Adam was first formed, then Eve. And Adam was not deceived, but the woman being deceived was in the transgression*" (1 Timothy ii. 13, 14). It comes out in his monitions addressed to the Corinthian converts : "*But I fear, lest by any means, as the serpent beguiled Eve through his subtlety, so your minds should be corrupted from the simplicity that is in Christ*" (2 Cor. xi. 3). It is beyond controversy one arm of his great arguments in 1 Cor. xv. and Romans v., which are two of the most momentous pieces of logical deduction with which the world has ever been favoured. In the one, he reasons as from an undoubted premise . "*As in Adam all die.*" In the other, he argues with equal certainty from "the one man's offence," "the one man's disobedience," "the one man by whom sin entered into the world."

Upon the discussion of the nature of the connection between the depravity of the race and the sin of Adam, I do not now enter. I bring forward these passages to establish the *fact* of the connection, as one of the axiomatic truths of Scripture. These inspired allusions will serve another and more immediate purpose that I have in view. They form a luminous commentary on the original narrative, and throw a light thereon by which we may read it aright. Under that light, we shall be enabled to read the account given in the third chapter of Genesis in all the simplicity of a real history. The stamp of reality and literalness comes out unmistakably under the light of the various references to the detailed and moving incidents of that great tragedy. I do not mean that a reader of this history must suspend his judgment as to its reality, until he hears what the rest of Scripture has to say on the subject. I hold that, without the help of any comment, a plain, unprejudiced reader will be struck with the air of reality pervading every part of this narrative. The connection in which it stands, the coherence of the different parts of the account, the improbability that a fable, or myth, or parable should be so introduced, all go to produce the conviction that this is veritable history, of the same literal nature as that in whose company it is found.

Now, the special value of the Scripture references is not so much to convey this view to our mind, as to corroborate it, and to prevent us from taking another. We have thus in them a gauge of interpretation; and everything below that gauge must be discarded. That standard is the full acknowledgment of both the real and the literal element in the narrative. By its application, we must reject all those explanations which tell us, first, that we have here a historical *mythus* or fable, *i.e.*, a fictitious narrative founded on some historical fact; or, secondly, that it is a history " infallibly true " without being real—whatever that may be—originally existing in the form of a Saga, then encased in a hieroglyphic, and at length disentombed by Moses; or, finally, an allegory, founded on fact or not, whose object may be to convey certain views of the experience of man in the process of transition or development.

Were these interpretations capable of defence on their own merits— and they have all been long ago exploded, although they are continually being revived in some form or another,—yet they cannot be upheld against the Scripture I have quoted. This is especially very clear from the incidental references from the two Epistles of Paul. The advocates of this theory would lead us to believe that the Apostle founds his teaching, in both cases, not on what they would call the kernel, but on the shell of the real history; as if the Apostle were not able to discern by reason of use, between things so different as kernel and shell! As if Paul had no inkling of the "Higher Criticism" reserved for more advanced times: as if the writings of Philo, the literary father of these fanciful expositions, were not extant in Paul's time, and he were quite in ignorance of their contents. The fact is, that what is now called the "Higher Criticism" was rife in the times of the Apostle; he despised it, and in its stead gave a plain and literal interpretation. By this way he shows, in both the cases cited, that the very minute details of the narrative contain or reflect great truths that are wrought into the very fabric of our nature.

As the scene of the temptation opens before us, we can hardly help comparing it for a moment with another scene not now laid in an Eden of delight, but in a wilderness and savage haunt of wild beasts. And there is this to note in the comparison, that it is not from the baptismal wave, it is not from the severe and prolonged fast of forty days, it is not from the austerities of self-denial in any form, as that other and more godly Man comes to be tempted of the Devil; but amid the bliss of Eden, and from the sweets of wedded happiness, that Adam and Eve enter into the conflict and trial. As, however, the favour of the Father shone over the austerities of Him who "fulfilled all righteousness," so also the beams of the Divine delight fell upon the happiness of our first parents, enhancing every previous gift. These favours and endowments were such as one might well suppose would render Adam proof against the tempter. He was made in the image of God—with a nature invisible and spiritual like the Divine, and capable of holding communion with the Father of Spirits. He was placed in a position suited to his native powers, exalted to the sovereignty of all creatures, and the world at large. His central seat of government was fitted up by the hand of God. There was employment assigned that would train and develop, without exhaustion or fatigue, his bodily strength and faculties of mind. He was made acquainted, through the kindness of the Creator, with the various orders of animals subject to his control. His unexpressed desire had been anticipated in the formation of Eve,—

> "Fairest of creation, last and best
> Of all God's works."[1]

"Thus superior to all creation, he is yet allied to all creation"; and in his alliance, he is the bond connecting God more intimately with His works, and Earth more intimately with Heaven. Thus honoured and furnished, man enters upon the encounter. The temptation turns upon the one Divine restriction, itself an honour, as it notes the responsibilities of his headship of the world. And yet with every incentive to be true to his God, to be faithful to his trust, with every consideration from reverence, obedience, gratitude and love, man swerves from his duty, and disobeys his God. Eve, "by the spirited, sly snake," is gradually enticed out of her native sphere of thought and desire, and absorbed in the tree, and the soaring ambitions that have been evoked by its fair fruit: thus does she stain her soul, and sin in spirit, ere yet she takes and eats of the forbidden tree. "As soon as the woman had succumbed to the serpent, she became," says Delitzsch, "the serpent to her husband. The tempted one, in her turn, became a tempter; and Adam abides not in himself and in God, but in the sight of the enticing fruit in the hand of the beloved one. Every thought of God's love, of the death

---

[1] Milton, *Paradise Lost*, Book IX.

which He had threatened, vanishes from his mind; and thus he incurs an equal sin."

> .... "He scrupled not to eat
> Against his better knowledge; not deceived,
> But fondly overcome with female charm.
> Earth trembled from her entrails, as again
> In pangs; and Nature gave a second groan;
> Sky loured; and, muttering thunder, some sad drops
> Wept at completing of the mortal sin
> Original."[1]

If it be remarked by way of diminishing the offence—thereby arraigning, at the same time, the equity of God—that it was, after all, only the eating of an apple, then obedience was the more easy; and the equity of God is vindicated in imposing so slight a prohibition as the test of virtue. Had it been some very arduous task, there might have been some reason for complaint; now there is none. But it is altogether misleading to attempt to estimate this act mechanically. The inherent virtue of the act is not to be judged by any of the laws of physics. This we must seek in its character. In this act, slender as it is, we cannot but be struck with a deficiency of that love which makes God its chief joy, and with the uplifting of self in opposition to God. We need go no deeper in the analysis than this to enable us to comprehend how such an act could be the rupture of the bond binding man to his kind Creator, seeing it was the deliberate violation of law, and therefore the severance of that tie which held man to life, and all the joy and glories thereof. How complete, as well as sudden, this severance was, appears even in the glades of Eden. It appears before the accusing voice of God is heard. It is felt before the sinful pair are confronted with the holy presence of their Judge. The fair robe of innocence is rent. They feel their shame: they dread their God. This kindling shame, and this cowering fear, proclaim the destruction of the harmony between body and spirit; between their present and their past; between reason, too, and awaking conscience; between themselves and God. It is but a step into the trial scene, and the destruction of the harmony between man and woman becomes visible. At the note of alarm, they shift the blame, and the one accuses the other. To these natural consequences are swiftly added others of a penal kind. These latter involve in appropriate suffering every participator in the sin. Upon the tempter, the man, the woman, and all their posterity, and even upon inanimate nature, as associated with human kind, the curse falls.

---

[1] Milton, *Paradise Lost*, Book IX.

Now, it is in the parallel lines of these dire consequences we see the connection between the sin and misery of the world, and the one transgression of Adam. It is quite true, as Dr. Chalmers grants, that it is not in this account said, "that Adam's first sin entailed a sinfulness, not only on himself, but on all his posterity."[1] But it is equally true, as Von Baeder remarks, "The fall of man was a cosmic event, as when a kingdom falls with its king." The consequences to creation ensue from man's position of headship and sovereignty over it. Linked inseparably with his destinies, as it is crowned in his person, external nature would have shone in man's virtue, as now it sinks in his fall. What was a gracious ordinance of God, by which Man and Creation were mutually honoured and blest, becomes, when permeated by sin, a source of misery and calamity. The kingdom suffers in the ruin of the king. "*The whole creation groaneth and travaileth in pain together until now*" (Romans viii. 22).

These consequences, therefore, come upon their posterity through Adam being the first man, and Eve the mother of all living. Here, as in the wider domain of nature, the family share the fortunes of their parents; but here, also, there is a closer bond than that which exists between mankind and creation, by virtue of which all those qualities which go to fill up the character of the fallen parents are transmitted to their descendants. This character of Adam is called "his own likeness," "his image" (Genesis v. 3): "*And Adam lived an hundred and thirty years, and begat a son in his own likeness, after his image.*" This was "his own," in contrast with "the likeness of God" in which he was created. It was "his own," self-developed, with the Divine lineaments all faded therein, and the new features of his sinfulness grown into prominence. And this was the character he transmitted to the race. Let it be borne in mind, also, that this transmission takes place through the action of a law of our nature whose influence in innocence would have been fraught with good, and nothing but good. Yet this law of natural descent (Genesis i. 28), in itself so excellent and salutary, has become, through the perversion of sin, the channel by which the virus of evil is conveyed to the whole race. "*By one man's disobedience many were made sinners*" (Romans v. 19). And thus, by man's headship of creation, "Creation is made subject to vanity"; by his headship of the human family, their life is poisoned in its springs, and their character of righteousness for ever forfeited.

---

[1] *Institutes of Theology*, Vol. I, p. 412.

LECTURE IX.

IMPUTATION OF SIN.

I HAVE endeavoured to set forth in some adequate manner the terrible fact of the utter and universal sinfulness of man. I have tried to state, as clearly as possible, the evidence of Scripture connecting this depravity with the sin of Adam. It now remains to consider *how* the transgression of our first parents involved all their posterity in guilt; or, in other words, on *what principle* the whole human family are dealt with as sinful on account of the sin of their disobedient progenitor. The Scriptural way of explaining this great mystery is by *imputation*. But "imputation of sin" itself needs to be explained, both because of the inherent difficulties of the subject, and of the no little obscurity that has been thrown thereon by many Theologians. It must, however, be distinctly and constantly kept in view, that whatever difficulties may be found in any theory of imputation of sin, yet the great difficulty does not lie there, but in the *fact*, the undeniable, stubborn fact, of the universal dominion of sin and death over the entire race, both infants, as well as full-grown sinners. The disproving of any form of imputation does not disprove this fact; nor does the weakening of any method of explanation diminish, in any degree, its terror. It looms beyond all theories, and remains permanent in its fatal hold on mankind, whatever theories may rise into favour or fall into decay.

If, therefore, one explanation of imputation be rejected, some other must be adopted that will better account for the facts. And it is reassuring to know that in this, as in other great moral problems, the light is on the Christian side. "No system of philosophy," says Dr. Philip Schaff, " has ever given a more satisfactory explanation than the great Divines of the Church. Outside of the Christian redemption, the fall, with its moral desolation and ruin, remains an impenetrable mystery."[1]

It will be remembered that the word, taken from the New Testament as the Scriptural basis of the doctrine of the imputation of sin is λογίζομαι; but there is a peculiarity in its use which seems to have escaped notice. While it is constantly used of the imputation of righteousness, in a positive sense, it is never once used in the New Testament other than negatively of the imputation of sin. The constant use in connection with the imputation of sin is, as you have it in Romans iv. 8, "*Blessed is the man to whom the Lord will* not *impute sin.*" Where sin is *positively* described as imputed, the verb καθίστημι is used, as in Romans v. 19 : "*For as by one man's disobedience many were made sinners, so by the obedience of one shall many be made righteous.*" As λογίζομαι means to count or reckon, to reckon anything to a person—not necessarily implying that the thing reckoned really belongs to him—the view καθίστημι gives of the matter is most important. According to its current usage, it means, to place one in an office or condition : we read of making one a ruler or judge ; and also of making one's life miserable. "The choice of expression in Romans v. 19," says Cremer, "rather arose, partly from its not being simply the moral quality that is referred to, but, above all, the thence resulting situation of those who are sinners."[2]

With these considerations before us, I would now add one or two hints as to our forming a theory of imputation. We must beware—

(I.) Of combining this question with the salvation of infants.

(II.) Of adopting any explanation which, resting on what is a purely artificial arrangement, has no basis in reality.

(III.) We must not expect imputation of sin to agree in all particulars with the imputation of Christ's righteousness, although the principle is the same in both cases.

(I.) It matters not into what you resolve this, or how you may propose to account for it : there it is behind and above all the streams of life. So vital is the union with Adam, that it requires no conscious consent on the part of any of his descendants to involve them in guilt ; also, so vital is it, that it always issues in their acts in conscious transgression. Even if we were to agree with the New School Calvinists of

---

[1] *Lange on Romans*, p. 195.
[2] *Biblico-Theological Lexicon of New Testament Greek*, p. 311.

New England, and so reject imputation altogether, the admissions they make would necessarily bring us back to it. They admit that the first moral choice of all is universally sinful. The alienation of heart from God, herein supposed, cannot possibly be the normal condition of a moral agent; neither can it be a condition to which the Holy Creator is indifferent; much less can it be one which He regards with favour. We are driven, therefore, to the conclusion that it is one that He, as Moral Ruler, views with displeasure; and also that it is one which, in itself, bears the mark of His deep displeasure. Even in this modified view of man's condition, as presented by the New England Calvinists, we have all the deep significance of imputation conceded. The moral agent is at the beginning of his career, as the Apostle describes him, "*A child of wrath*."[1] His being without God is penal.

As this state is universal among men, we have the whole race, whether living or dying, in a penal condition at infancy, without their having done anything individually to deserve the penalty. Whence comes the penalty? Some offender must have acted in full consciousness to have deserved it. Some crime must have been committed to call it down. The crime must have been antecedent to the penalty; and the offender must have been the first of mankind. And, again, I say, considering who He is that metes out this penalty, it must be infinitely just.

(II.) In the second place, we must not accept any explanation of imputation which makes it out to be merely an artificial arrangement, without a corresponding basis in nature and in fact. The guilt of the race is too tremendously real a matter to be accounted for by a legal or any other kind of fiction.

The great point of difficulty has been, and is, where to place or find the proper basis of reality. Augustine placed it in the organic unity of the race. In this unity he recognized a two-fold relation of the human family to Adam's sin :—

(1.) *A Germinal relation*: all men were germinally in Adam when he fell: "*Omnes fuimus in illo uno, quando fuimus ille unus.*"[2] All were in the loins of Adam when he was condemned; as all the Israelites were in the loins of Abraham, when he paid tithes to Melchisedek.

(2.) Sin bears the relation of *propagation*; Adam vitiated the race in himself as in the root. As Anselm, expressing this view, has said, "In Adam, a person made nature sinful; in his posterity, nature

---

[1] Ephesians ii. 3. [2] *De Civitate Dei*, viii. 14.

IMPUTATION OF SIN.

made persons sinful—*Persona corrumpit naturam, natura corrumpit personam.*[1]

Thus the full Augustinian theory is, that we sinned in Adam, and also that Adam sins in us.

With more or less modification, the Divines of the Reformation, both Lutheran and Calvinistic, accepted this theory. The modifications consisted in some laying greater stress on mediate, others on immediate imputation. The Dutch Theologians of the Seventeenth Century broke away from the realistic and natural basis of Augustine, and in its stead laid down a judicial arrangement called the Covenant of Works. Adam was the representative; all mankind the constituents; and the act of Adam was in consequence binding upon all his descendants. When, too, in addition, it is explained that imputation proceeds without regard to the natural condition, but simply through the legal relation, no one can wonder that the doctrine, so stated, has been stigmatized as a "*judicial artifice.*"

Justly dissatisfied with this exaggeration of the *immediate* and *legal* elements of the doctrine, Jonathan Edwards recalled attention to the broader, deeper and more Scriptural view, in which the immediate and mediate, the legal and the natural, are blended together. "Indeed," says he, "the derivation of the evil disposition to Adam's posterity, or rather, the *co-existence* of the evil disposition, implied in Adam's first rebellion, in the *root and branches,* is a consequence of the *union* that the Wise Author of the world has established between Adam and his posterity; but not properly a *consequence* of the *imputation* of his sin; nay, is rather *antecedent* to it, as it was in Adam himself. The first depravity of heart, and the imputation of that sin, are both the consequences of that established union; but yet in such order, that the evil disposition is *first*, and the charge of guilt *consequent*, as it was in the case of *Adam* himself."[2]

This broad and sober statement of the case, contrasts favourably with the extreme view which Dr. Hodge sometimes allows himself to suggest, and at others to express. Calling Edwards' theory of the unity of the race, "pantheistic nonsense," he argues on the latter part of this quotation thus: "If the loss of original righteousness and inherent depravity are penal, they suppose antecedent guilt, that is, a guilt antecedent, and not *consequent* to the existence and view of the depravity."[3] Though this extremity of reasoning

---

[1] *Encheiridion*: C. 26.   [2] *Works*, Vol. 1, p. 221.   [3] *Theology*, Vol. 2, pp. 207-8.

appears to occupy rather the same position in Dr. Hodge's theory, as he says *mediate* imputation does in President Edwards' works,—that of an excrescence, yet as such it ought to be dealt with.

Observe then, that Dr. Hodge states that "guilt is antecedent, and not *consequent*, to the existence and view of the depravity." Now, it must, I think, be granted that they to whom anything is imputed, must, when the imputation takes place, be viewed as being in existence. You cannot impute either sin or righteousness to one who does not exist. A person must be regarded as existing in fact, or in design: if in design, the existence considered must be one identical with what it would be in fact. In what condition could mankind be regarded as existing in design? Not certainly as righteous, for they never were so in fact, but as unrighteous. The words have a real significance, "*Adam begat a son in his own likeness and after his image.*"[1] The clean does not come from the unclean: that which is born of the flesh, is flesh. Now, apart altogether from the question of imputation, every individual since the fall of Adam is, by nature, and, in fact, according to the teaching of these Scriptures, in a condition identical with the condition of fallen Adam. If individually in the same moral condition, is it not more rational to expect that all the responsibilities or penalties should be the same, and should come in the same order? But the facts of our existence correspond with the design thereof. It therefore follows that the imputation in design with regard to the future descendants of Adam must proceed on the same principles as the imputation of guilt to Adam himself. This brings us to the position of Jonathan Edwards; *first* the evil disposition, and the charge of guilt *consequent*. Beyond all doubt, the evil disposition exists in his children as it did in Adam; and it would be as absurd to suppose it to be ignored in the Divine reckonings in the one case as in the other. If this be taken into the account, it will necessarily occupy the same position in the one as in the other. The depraved nature will be viewed as preceding the charge of guilt. Imputation of sin is therefore no legal figment, but has a terribly real basis in the universal corruption of our race, which is the result of our union with Adam.

(III.) Our other point was, that we must not expect to find the imputation of sin agree in all particulars with the imputation of Christ's righteousness. In a general manner, the one illustrates the other, because the principle is the same in both. But it is not always safe to

---

[1] Gen. v. 3.

argue from the particulars of the one to the particulars of the other. There are points of correspondence; but there are also lines of divergence. The Apostle Paul, the inspired expounder of the doctrine, while he was clear in revealing the similarities, was also very careful in pointing out some of the dissimilarities. In Romans v. 15—17, he draws three broad and important distinctions: the first (verse 15) is a distinction as to *degree—intensity:* the second (verse 16) is a distinction in *kind:* the third (verse 17) is also a distinction in *kind.* Where the Apostle thought it necessary to limit and explain, let us not be less careful. Holding fast the grand analogy between Adam and Christ, the natural and spiritual Heads of mankind, let us also pay good heed to the particulars where the analogy ceases and a contrast sets in.

These remarks have been intended to clear away some misconceptions, and to prepare the way for a brief examination of the doctrine as it is presented in Scripture. Although it is in germ in the opening chapters of Genesis, and is illustrated in many of God's dealings with man; yet it is in Romans v. that the doctrine occurs in set form for the first time in Scripture. It is not till Christ is fully revealed, that Adam is fully made known. It is not till the believer's relation to the Second Man is graciously brought to light, that the sinner's relation to the first man is rendered visible. God, in mercy, withholds the eye from the despair of the ruin, till there is proclaimed to the lost the good news of the Saviour. It is at length the light that surrounds the footsteps of the Redeemer, and shines from His person as He descends into the lower parts of our degradation, that makes our misery appear in all its length and breadth of horror.

And as with Revelation at large, so is it with the Apostle's argument. It is not till he has told us of justification, of reconciliation, of peace, of joy in God—in a word, of the restoration of the soul to live to God through the death of the Lord Jesus—that he turns our gaze upon Adam. Then, too, it is for the purpose of strengthening our confidence in the effectual energy of this new life of godliness, and enhancing by contrast the grace and glory of Redemption. He uncovers the hidden vital bond that binds the believer to Christ, and to awaken the very highest anticipations as to the effects thereof, he points to the mortal link with Adam. It is probably for this reason that some expositors have regarded this passage (Romans v.) as an episode. It is a transition, rather, and recalls another transition. Herein is brought up into parallel and contrast the passage of believers in Christ from the death of sin to the life of godliness, and the passage of our race in Adam from the delights of Eden to the condemnation and sorrows of death.

While in the earlier chapters the Apostle was pressing home on Jew and Gentile the charge of guilt, he dropped not a hint about the headship of Adam. But now that he is showing the sure efficaciousness of the Redemption of Christ in all who are united to Him by faith, he brings forward the effectual working of sin as an analogical proof. Let it be also borne in mind that it is the same faith which has been so vividly illustrated in chapter iv. that is here assumed as the vital bond with Christ, just as natural descent is the mortal link with Adam.

The analogy between Adam and Christ is that due to the doctrine of imputation, and it is distinctly affirmed in chapter v. Adam, in verse 14, is called a figure, a type "*of Him that was to come.*" The natural foreshadowed the Spiritual head. For the most part the order in which the influence is described as flowing between the head and the members is the same throughout. It is the head that communicates bane or blessing, condemnation or righteousness. Sin in Adam diffuses death to all his posterity: righteousness in Christ brings life to all believers. But the remarkable phrase (verse 12)—"*inasmuch as all sinned*"—may be taken as a proof that here also the Apostle keeps in view the fact that the race, by virtue of its unity, may be said to act in the head, as well as the head in the members. The phrase seems an echo of the doctrine distinctly stated in 1 Cor. xv. 22: "*In Adam all die.*" In 2 Cor. v. 14 the same ascending line of virtual action is reasoned from: "*For the love of Christ constraineth us; because we thus judge, that if One died for all, then all died.*" So also in Gal. ii. 20: "*I am crucified with Christ.*" "Dying in Adam"; "Dying in Christ"; "Being crucified with Christ"; and all similar expressions indicate an ascending line of relation to the Head, just as clearly as the descending line of relation is shown when it is said that "*by one man sin entered into the world, and death by sin; and so death passed upon all men*" (Rom. v. 12). My object, however, is to point out that the Apostle does not altogether exclude the ascending line, though dwelling principally on the descending. By recognizing both we obtain a clear view of the relation of the members to both the natural and the Spiritual Heads of mankind.

I pass on to trace the separate course of Adam's sin, as drawn by the Apostle. In verse 12 there is a comprehensive statement, the particulars included in which are explained in the following verses of the chapter. The statement is—by means of one man sin comes into the world; by means of sin comes death; and then, as from the root, death spreads to every branch of the human family. The explanation is given in the double bearing of Adam's sin, the natural and the legal. The Apostle first shows the natural, or moral working of sin. In verse 12 he expresses this by the phrase, "*by means of one man*"; but, in verse 15, he uses the narrower and more definite term, "*the transgression of one man.*" Thence death spreads to all. In verse 16, the legal bearing of sin is brought to view, that is, the action which God as Judge takes with regard to it. Judgment is pronounced on the occasion of the one man, which in result is condemnation. Further definition limits the reason of condemnation to *the one transgression*. On the one hand, the natural effects proceed from the *one man*, and from his *one offence*: on the other, the legal consequences ensue in an exactly similar manner from the *one man*, and from the *one transgression*. The legal follows the natural, and is dependent upon it. There is not first the legal, and then the natural; but there is first the natural, and afterwards the legal. The two are kept distinct; but they both in parallel lines help forward the Apostle's argument to its sum and conclusion in verse 19: "*By one man's disobedience many were made sinners.*" In this one expression "were made," or constituted sinners, we have both trains of consequences united, the natural and the legal. If we ask how they are united, the vital phrase in verse 12 supplies the answer, "*inasmuch as all sinned.*"

If I have given in the foregoing a true account of the Apostle's meaning, it will follow that Scripture teaches that there are two elements in the headship of Adam,—the *natural* and the *legal*.

(I.) With regard to the natural, it needs no words of defence or advocacy with those who accept the Bible account of the origin of man. Nor can those who hold the theory of evolution rationally deny the transmission of natural qualities by those who first attained the rank of humanity. In that first pair the species attained at length to such a degree of fixity as has since pertained to it. With regard to the explanation of this natural element in Adam's headship, sufficient has already been given in the previous lecture.[1]

(II.) In considering the second or legal element, it will be convenient to do so under two aspects, the representative and the purely

---

[1] P. 102, *et seq.*

legal. From one point of view these are the same, but from another they present sufficient points of dissimilarity as to merit separate notice.

By "federal," or representative, I do not mean anything of a mechanical association, or external character, or which would imply a separate and independent starting-point for every individual of the race. I mean the representation which is inseparable from the position of one who is the first of a race, all the members of which are derived from him, and therefore linked together by living ties. The unity of the race makes the first of the race representative, and his acts influential upon all the others. Were there any break in the line of descent, or deflection of any of the streams from the original source, or some more potent power counteracting the first impulse, so far the influence of the actions and character of the first man might be thwarted or averted. This actually takes place in Christ, the New Man. The work of Christ refers not to our being, as such, but to the ruin and guilt of our nature. Our nature, viewed in itself, is still transmitted from the first Adam; and it is transmitted bearing his stamp, so that we bear the image of what he became, and the results of what he did. In his course of life he drew the outline, filled out the character, and developed the mould, for all succeeding members of his family. The first oak that ever grew developed in its sturdy trunk and spreading branches the fashion and the form of the oaks of a thousand forests of the world, and infallibly transmitted them in the living germs enclosed in its acorns. Varieties there may be, superinduced by various causes, but all the essentials of the oak character exist in every member of the oak family. The youngest sapling lives over again the life of the ancient patriarch of the forest. So with Adam, he shewed what was in man; the characters of our humanity were expressed in his life, and that so that not one of all the race would have done better than he with his exact surroundings. Surroundings which, as Edwards says, were the best imaginable.[1] In this sense Adam was truly representative, and his headship most vitally federal; and thus is brought out a most profound reason why it is, that *by the disobedience of this one man as many as are of the race were made sinners* (Rom. v. 19).

(III.) The *legal* element in this headship will appear, if we view Adam's representative relation to law. So far as he dealt with law,

---

[1] Cf. *Works*, Vol. I, p. 222.

so far was he legally and morally our head. This element in his position, when properly weighed, is as inseparable as his representative, or natural headship. He could not be natural without being federal; nor could he be federal without being our head in the eye of law. Had he obeyed, his obedience would have benefited us through the vital link of his natural and federal relation. He would then have been in a position of transmitting a nature unfallen, perfected and approved. But sin intervening turns his legal relation into the medium of condemnation, and all the race receives a heritage of guilt. Let it, however, be observed, that this guilt is charged home upon no one, for the single reason that Adam sinned. The race became thus immediately guilty; but in every individual there is a personal reason, in the alienation of his heart from God, and in the open violation of law. "*For that* all *have sinned*" (verse 12), is the Apostle's method of presenting this doctrine is evident for two reasons: (1) the position of the doctrine in his argument, and (2) his statement of the doctrine.

By tracing imputation to the root-doctrine of federation, which sustains it, we can the better see its reasonableness. Briefly put, sin is imputed to us because of our union with Adam. But a due consideration of the threefold nature of that bond of union,—the natural, the federal and the legal, helps us to justify more clearly the ways of God in dealing with man in this matter. The truth it conveys runs thus: I could not be a man without this union with Adam; I could not be in union with Adam without sharing his fallen nature; I could not share his fallen nature without incurring the legal relations and responsibilities with which it is encumbered.

It will be seen that this view of the case places every son of Adam in the same position as Adam was by his fall. It supposes he has had his probation when Adam was tried; he has sinned when Adam sinned; he has lost what Adam lost; and has suffered in Adam's condemnation. Whether any *injury* is done to any man hereby, we shall see presently; but now it is the time to enquire, How stood the matter with Adam in that act which was the ruin of our race? This will show us what is ours in consequence of that act. Was he charged with a double guilt, first of the sinful disposition, and then of the external act? Or was not rather the disposition, included in the external act, giving to it its proper character of morality? "The external act he committed was no otherwise his than as his heart was in it." The act was therefore one, and the guilt chargeable was in consequence one and simple; and such is the guilt inherited by all his family. We are not first treated as guilty on account of our depravity, and then because of our union with Adam; a double charge would thus rest upon us— as Adam was in his condemnation, so are we.

Thus it is seen that the imputation of sin follows every recipient of human nature. It would be as impossible to suppose a man to whom iniquity was not imputed, as to find a man who did not derive his nature from Adam. That nature is received by none in its integrity, and therefore none can be justly treated as innocent. Sin is laid to the account of all, because sin is in all.

To this way of stating the doctrine there are certain objections. It is urged that the transference of a corrupt nature to all is owing to an antecedent legal imputation of sin. As the circumstances are, the transference of an evil nature can only mean the giving of existence. But the giving of existence to the descendants of Adam cannot be a judicial condemnation of the race. The continuance of the race is nowhere described as a judicial, much less as a condemnatory act of God. Nor can the justice of God, taken by itself, sufficiently account for the perpetuation of mankind under all the conditions disclosed in history. We might as well seek to trace up the analogous case of regeneration, by referring it to the judicial act of God in justification. Regeneration is to be traced to the renewing of the Holy Ghost; justification to the act of God, as Judge. So also the continuance of our race is to be attributed to the Sovereign Will of God. When properly considered there is also compassion in the act. It is an act of mercy that subserves the very highest Divine purposes concerning mankind. The children of Adam are not multiplied because of the displeasure, but because of the good pleasure of God.

Secondly, it may be urged that this way of presenting imputation of sin is not in keeping with the analogy of the imputation of Christ's righteousness. It may be said that the freedom of the Divine grace in justification is compromised, because it may be inferred, that if the imputation of sin supposes subjective corruption, so the imputation of righteousness may also suppose subjective righteousness. Here it behoves us indeed to move with care, as we are beset with difficulties. That God justifies the ungodly is the cardinal doctrine of the Evangelical system; and it becomes us to guard and maintain it with a holy jealousy. But, at the same time, let us beware of false alarms; and let us avoid an overstrained statement of this vital truth. The chief thing to be kept in view is the *ground of the imputation*—either of sin or righteousness. When we clearly recognize, that on the one hand guilt is imputed to his posterity on the ground of Adam's sin; and on the other, that righteousness is imputed to sinners on the ground of Christ's work, we have the key to the whole situation. We can then survey the inseparable conditions of these two analogous acts; and chief among them are union and participation with the respective federal heads. As are the heads, so are the members. There is a perfect community of condemnation with Adam, and of righteousness with Christ. This community must be maintained most strenuously in both cases, to preserve imputation from being a mere "legal figment." It is of especial importance to do this on the side of justification, in order to prevent Antinomianism obtaining a foothold. The Gospel promises justification to the ungodly; but it knows nothing of putting a man legally in the position of righteousness while he is without Christ, and an unbeliever or disbeliever in Him. No unbeliever is justified. While in unbelief he is a "*child of wrath*" judicially. It is only when he believes, that his legal standing is changed. Justification is unto, and upon all them that believe. It is a justification in Christ; and faith is the vital link between the believer and Christ. Now what faith, or spiritual union in Christ, is in those to whom righteousness is reckoned, the tie of nature is in those to whom sin is imputed. But, as in the one case there is no union with Adam without corruption of nature, so in the other, there is no union with Christ without faith, and there is no faith in Christ without regeneration: "*If any man be in Christ, he is a new creature*" (2 Cor. v. 17). Thus, when the due limitations or conditions are observed, the analogy between the imputation of sin and the imputation of righteousness is complete and perfect. The Divine order of procedure in the one, explains and enforces the Divine order in the other.

Passing from these objections brought against this method of stating the doctrine, I proceed to notice those that are advanced against the doctrine itself, in whatever form it is stated.

(1) It is alleged, that this doctrine leaves the whole race foredoomed in its inherited depravity. I admit it. But to what does the

admission amount? It simply amounts to the acknowledgment of the unity of the race. Upon this unity the federation of Theologians and the scientific law of heredity both rest. To declaim against these, is to declaim against the very framework and texture of our existence. We could no more suppose our race without these laws, than we could suppose the world of matter existing without the law of gravitation. But imputation arises as necessarily out of federation, as federation does out of the unity of mankind. In the innumerable benefits imputation brings, we freely consent that it is good; it is only when suffering comes in its track that we complain. The suffering, however, arises not from the law considered in itself, but from the perversion of it through sin. Sin turns the channel that had been prepared for the Stream of Life into a course for the waters of bitterness, of pollution and death.

(2) An objection may be raised on account of the individual, as well as on the part of the race. Even admitting the beneficence of the law of federation, it may still be urged that men individually have some reason to be discontented in possessing a sinful nature, without having had a chance of being different. This objection may be taken in one of three forms.

(a) It may be taken as another form of finding fault with the conditions of Adam's probation. From this point of view it may be answered with Jonathan Edwards [1]: First, "that it is reasonable to suppose, that Adam was as *likely*, on account of his capacity and natural talent, to persevere in his obedience, as his posterity (taking one with another) if they had all been put on the trial simply for themselves." And, secondly, "there was a *greater tendency* to a happy issue, in such an appointment, than if every one had been appointed to stand for himself; especially on two accounts. (1) That Adam had stronger motives to *watchfulness* than his posterity would have had; in that, not only his own eternal welfare lay at stake, but also that of all his posterity. (2) *Adam* was in a state of complete manhood, when his trial began. It was a constitution very agreeable to the goodness of God, considering the state of mankind, which was to be propagated in the way of generation, that their *first father* should be appointed to stand for all. For by reason of the manner of their coming into existence in a state of *infancy*, and then coming so gradually to *mature* state, and so remaining for a great while in a state of childhood and

---

[1] *Works*, p. 222.

comparative imperfection; after they were become moral agents, they would be less fit to stand for themselves than their first father to stand for them."

"If any man notwithstanding these things shall say, that for his own part, if the affair had been proposed to him, he should have chosen to have had his eternal interest trusted in *his* own hands: it is sufficient to answer that no man's vain opinion of himself, as *more fit* to be trusted than others, alters the true nature and tendency of things, as they demonstrably are in themselves." [1]

(*b*) This objection, from the standpoint of the individual, may be resolved into a complaint against our very existence. We could not exist, except as descendants of Adam; but we could not be descendants of Adam, and at the same time have an isolated, independent existence, as if we were not so descended. We could not have the possibilities of angels, and retain the advantages of being men. Thus the objection is a cry after the impossible. It is something more. It betrays an utter insensibility to the glorious possibilities of individual life, and that not the best or holiest under the actual constitution of mankind.

"In the human race especially," says Lacordiare, "each man contains a posterity in himself whose term is not assignable, and which makes of its generations one united assemblage in which no single member can lose his place without drawing after him the multitude of his descendants. To suppress a single man is to suppress a race; to suppress a wicked man is to suppress a people of just men who may spring from him. For good and evil are entwined together in the changeable course of mankind; a virtuous son succeeds to a bad father; and the ancestor but too often contemplates, in his distant progeny, crimes which to him were unknown. Now, the glance of God, perceiving at once all the successions of life, all the regenerations of good in evil and of evil in good, no destiny appeared solitary to Him; so that, in cutting it off from the anticipated Book of Life, He would but cut off a course unworthy to be continued. In His sight, Adam, a prevaricator, included the whole posterity of the Saints. To refuse being to him because of his crime, even had that crime never obtained pardon, would have been to destroy in him all the merits of the human race. How could the goodness of God have required such a sacrifice? How could it have required that the wicked should have been preferred to the just, that life should be withdrawn from those who would make good use of

---

[1] *Works*, p. 222.

it, because of those who would have turned it into a curse instead of a blessing?

"I know God, I love Him, I hope in Him, I bless Him in life and death; why should the fault of one of my ancestors, eternally foreseen by Divine goodness, have intercepted my birth, and not have permitted me for a single day to respire in the mystery of liberty from whence my beatitude might result? Why should I have been condemned to nothingness because one of my forefathers would have abused his existence? Where in this would have been justice, wisdom, or goodness?"[1]

(c) We have to deal with the complaint of a hardship that should now be removed. There is no man discontented with his state of sinfulness who may not find a remedy and release. When the bondage of iniquity came, there came with it the hope of a Redeemer. If he would be free, he has but to cry, and the Deliverer will run to his relief. If he would have not merely the chance, but the certainty of holiness, he has but to stretch forth his hand to Him who is mighty to save. He is not far from any one of us who can " Be of sin the double cure, Cleanse us from its guilt and power."

These have been the circumstances of the continuance of the race from the beginning. The clear beams of the Saviour's grace and power are indeed around us in these latter days; but from the very first the light shone. The hope of a "better man" was the lamp that shed its rays over the path our first parents took from the gates of Eden. In advancing ages, this hope was the refuge to which patriarch and prophet pointed. All through the dark and troubled flow of human history, the clouds have gathered in the heavens; but every cloud has had its silver lining, and upon the cloud the gracious bow of promise has been shed, casting its radiance upon the gloom. There its light has been discernible, ever widening, and showing more distinctly the throne of the Heavenly Grace; while from the throne comes the voice of Eternal Love, " *O Israel! thou hast destroyed thyself; but in Me is thine help*" (Hosea xiii. 9).

---

[1] *God*: pp. 87—9.

LECTURE X.

THE OUTLOOK OF SINNERS.

BEFORE passing on to consider the Divine Remedy, it may be of some value to give a brief summary of the chief miseries and dangers of men under the disease. What are the risks and perils sinners run, of which we are bound to warn them? What is the charge we have to urge against them? How are we to make the accusation good to reason and conscience?

The Apostle could say, " Knowing *therefore the terror of the Lord, we persuade men*" (2 Cor. v. 11); for he had received visions of the grandeur of God withheld from us. Awed himself, and deeply impressed with what he had seen of the terror of God's glorious majesty, and of the resources of His power and righteousness, he might infuse the same awe into others. But it is not needful so to be wrapt in vision, before we can be filled with a reverent sense of the unspeakable glory of God's perfections. The manifestations and proofs of these are around us, within us and above us, in teeming abundance, and can be readily comprehended by all those who have eyes to see, ears to hear, and hearts to understand.

Thus, in pressing upon men those persuasions that ought to move them to a sense of the terror of their condition, it is not needful to explore what is remote, or enquire into that which is veiled and concealed. It is not needful to fetch arguments from the undiscovered heights, or unrevealed depths. There are sufficient, and more than sufficient, nigh to all mankind, if taken to heart, to force from every one the cry, " *God be merciful to me a sinner.*"

It is not always necessary to darken the impeachment, in the case of those who have exaggerated the ordinary conditions of sin by violent crimes, by long continuance of evil practices, by neglect of the light, by rejection, by opposition or blasphemy of Divine Mercy. So clear is the condemnation of such, that no reasoning is needed, no doubt is left concerning their position. Nor—in order to make evident the sinner's helpless state—is it necessary to lay special stress upon the trouble of sinners in affliction: their want of a stay and support in the great shocks and calamities of life; their perplexity in reverses; their terror and despair at the approach of death. The ordinary case of the reputable and prosperous man who is yet without God, will, if examined in the light of the plain truths of revelation, supply enough and to spare of materials for alarm and conviction.

This is the character with which we have most frequently to deal; and in dealing with him, let his due be given him. Let him have credit for every excellence he may fairly claim. Let no virtue that is his be taken away. Yet what is he though clothed in the scarlet and fine linen of his prosperity, if he stands in this world " without God " ? If without God ($\mathrm{\ddot{a}\theta\epsilon os}$), in the darker sense, what is life to him? Where is the nobility of existence? What separates him from the brutes that perish? What is the hope of his destiny? At most, and as the case is, at best, the fires of life—no matter how high they may burn—must die out in everlasting darkness. But, since no assurance of such a conclusion can be so sure as to silence and remove doubt, what then? What if there be a Hereafter? What if there be a God? If the doubt as to His existence be not well founded, what then? The Materialist is in the world of Spirits; the Atheist is in the hands of the living God.

If we regard this same reputable individual as " without God," in the milder, commoner, less odious sense, what have we? A creature who owns to a Creator, and yet rejects his control; a man who receives God's daily bounties, and yet excludes that very God from the love and gratitude of his heart. "*A son honoureth his father, and a servant his master: if then I be a Father, where is Mine honour? And if I be a Master, where is My fear? saith the Lord of hosts*" (Mal. i. 6). There is some consistency in living " without God," when God's existence is denied; but the verbal admission only enhances the guilt of the denial in deed and life. Of the two, this milder atheism is exposed to the charge of greater inconsistency, though it shuns the wicked boldness and folly of him who says, " *There is no God.*"

If we take the case of the man who has been roused to think and to enquire; the more he enquires, the worse his state will appear. The more closely he questions his own conscience, the more fearful looking for of judgment will there be; the more the sight of conscience is cleared, the more terrible its apprehension; the more its voice is opened, the louder are its threatenings and thunders.

If from the book of conscience the enquiring sinner turns to the page of Revelation, the prospect darkens immeasurably over his sin. The relation of God to sin comes into view. We may look on this as sevenfold :—

(1.) HE OBSERVES IT: "*For the ways of man are before the eyes of the Lord, and He pondereth all his goings*" (Prov. v. 21).

(2.) HE MARKS IT: "*If I sin, then Thou markest me, and Thou wilt not acquit me from mine iniquity*" (Job x. 14).

(3.) HE REMEMBERS IT: "*For her sins have reached unto heaven, and God hath remembered her iniquities*" (Rev. xviii. 5).

(4.) IT PROVOKES HIM TO JEALOUSY: "*And Judah did evil in the sight of the Lord, and they provoked Him to jealousy with their sins which they had committed, above all that their fathers had done*" (1 Kings xiv. 22).

(5.) IT PROVOKES HIM TO ANGER: "*Thou hast walked in the way of Jeroboam, and hast made My people Israel to sin, to provoke Me to anger with their sins*" (1 Kings xvi. 2).

(6.) HE RECOMPENSES IT: "*And first I will recompense their iniquity and their sin double*" (Jer. xvi. 18).[1]

(7.) HE PUNISHES IT: "*And I will punish the world for their evil, and the wicked for their iniquity*" (Isa. xiii. 11).[2]

If therefore with these truths in view, the sinner tries to sever the connection, he finds it impossible. His *abhorrence* will not break the link; his *resolves* will not remove the tyranny; his *scrupulous care* cannot guard against surprise; his *struggles* will not overcome it; his *mortification* will not stay it; his *confessions* will not banish it; his *tears* will not wipe it out; his *penances* and *sacrifices* cannot atone for its wrong. Affliction hardens, and prosperity inflames it. It flourishes under the brightness of earthly joy, and thrives beneath the shade of human sorrow. It keeps on its course, through disquiet, through fear, through sore travail of spirit, in apprehension of the greater disquiet in the dread unknown.

To the man thus conscious of his state, recollections of the past add new alarms. Memory traverses bygone years, and at its touch,

---

[1] Cf. Rev. xviii. 6.   [2] Cf. Amos iii. 2.

former transgressions come into life and being again. It needs no trump of angel, no voice of God; memory is that trump and voice. By its power, the years that are gone give up the sins that are in them; and there in long array people all the dark retrospect. If he looks upwards, he finds that this surrounds the throne of the Father Everlasting with terrors of lightning and thunder; arms the Cherubim at the gates of Bliss; rends the realms of woe from the abodes of joy, and fixes the impassable gulf between. It is memory that digs the hell of the transgressor deep in unutterable gloom, and fills it with pangs that shall never die. In the midst of all, there springs up fresh within the breast that living instinct which stretches after continuity of being which is corroborated by the intimations of the Word of God—it brooks no terms, and shudders at nothingness. This instinct of immortality forbids and rebukes the desire for nothingness, even as it rises; it links us to being, even as our inability to renovate or atone, links us to all the moral guilt, pollution, and suffering of our sinfulness.

These are the dolorous truths we have to proclaim :—

Faithfully: for we have to bear in mind our commission from God, and the danger and peril of our fellow men.

Tenderly: for sinners, with whom we have to reason, are sufferers as well; they are patients as well as transgressors. Their sin is their disease.

Clearly and fully: for the sin of man is the dark base line of measurement—so far as we can conceive—of the Redemption of Christ.

Preparatorily: for the declaration of man's sin is but to introduce and make ready for the declaration of God's free mercy in Christ Jesus, and to lift men to the hope of the Gospel. In this, the great example set us is the method of the Holy Spirit Himself, whose special work it is to convince of sin—all in relation to Christ. Every line leads up to Him: every arrow shot at the heart is dipped in the blood of Calvary, and is meant to bring the sinner to the feet of the Lamb of God who alone takes away the sin of the world.

LECTURE XI.

SALVATION.

We have long been poring over the dark and blotted page of the sinfulness of our race, we now turn the leaf to trace the bright lines of redeeming love. Every phase of man's misery is a proof of the need for some system of restoration. Nor is the hope of some kind of rectification quite absent from mankind, though it may be traced to different sources. Dim and uncertain at best, or else most earthly when most definite, this hope is in some form the heritage of the race. It is fed by our natural desires after happiness and certain good. It is cherished by the lingering rays of traditional promises. It is strengthened by an intelligent view of life in its myriad forms, around and below, if not above us.

There is not a living organism around and beneath, however low its place may be in the ranks of existence, but what is endowed with some *vis medicatrix,* some native healing power. When the branch is snapped in the wind, this inherent restorative energy presses together the wound and wraps up the part with layer upon layer. When a bone is broken, or the flesh is bruised or torn, the secret-healing virtue—the basis of all medical science—forthwith exerts itself to effect a cure. Even in the oyster—a member of so low an order—to what perfection is the healing art carried! To salve the lacerated wound, and protect itself in future from the injury caused by the grain of sand it has incautiously imbibed, you know how it spreads over the obnoxious grain coating after coating of pearly substance, until it becomes at length the gem that a monarch might prize.

If, turning from the open page of Nature as it is, we were to lift up the stony records of this world as it has been, we should see evidences of restoration on a scale as vast as the globe. Change after change has taken place in the outward conformation of the earth's crust; dynasty after dynasty of fish, reptile, bird, and beast has passed away; but the earth has ever risen from her ruins, each time clothed with a brighter beauty, and after every desolation has been reinstated with the more exuberant joy of a higher life.

Still there is this to be said, that in all these realms of research where we may view the recuperative resources of nature, there is a point beyond which they cannot avail. This healing virtue copes with injury, if the injury is not too great; but it is utterly powerless in the presence of death. It cannot revive the dead, nor restore an extinct race. Prizing with due care all the hopefulness it yields, it must be confessed that it is but the hopefulness that springs from analogy, not from identity. Those Orders in nature that afford the analogy do not share with man that moral nature, by the fortunes of which his destinies are supremely swayed. In none of our researches have we evidence of a race of moral agents being restored when once fallen. It is at this point, the point of most distressing perplexity the oracle is silent: and when we ask for life we encounter death. So doubtful, too, is the evidence that man's own history affords on this subject, that Bishop Butler knows not whether to call what he gleaned therein, "the darkness or the light of nature."[1] But it is in this dubious darkness that the Dayspring from on high visits us.

If the hope of restoration to God is thus uncertain—our right is out of the question—for a much greater reason the views we may form (*à priori*) of the nature of the restoration must also be vague and inadequate without revelation. The task some have set themselves, in some respects a noble one,—to deduce from the nature of God and from the nature of man, the essential elements of a remedial plan—is far beyond the compass of our powers. We cannot sound the depths of the Divine nature, of the Divine Government, of the Divine resources; they are infinite and eternal. We cannot even sufficiently explore the mysteries of our own existence, or explain our own history. There may have been floating ideas of a remedy; but no human intellect could ever have conjectured the precise nature of the remedy provided by Christ's Atonement. I argue that man could not do it, because man did not do it. That there was a faint idea in the common practice of sacrifice, I admit,—I admit with the claim that this practice is of Divine origin. That there was also the notion, engendered by

---

[1] *Analogy*, page 144.

ancient Divine promises, that a great Deliverer should come, is also true. But then there appears to have been a radical defect in the conceptions of this Coming One, and this defect was most glaring where the two ideas of sacrifice and deliverance were separately most clear and strong, *i.e.*, among the Jews. The defect to which I allude is, that none combined these two notions and made them meet in the person of a Redeemer. No one saw that the Divine remedy was deliverance through sacrifice; that Christ Crucified is the wisdom of God and the power of God. This was the mystery kept hidden from the ages. This, as far as a defined devotion went, was absolutely new to the world. Its germ, its dim shadow lay on the prophetic page. But till He came, till the Cross was an accomplished fact, till the Holy Spirit was given, not even the Apostles and future preachers of the great truth grasped its substance and saw its bearings.

This historical fact may be used to regulate our approaches to this subject. It may save us the pains, and perhaps the presumption, of setting up *à priori* conceptions as to what the character of Deity required, or what His government demanded before sinful man could be uplifted. On the whole question of restoration all was hazy. The spirit, therefore, that becomes us is one of humility. "When we think of the eternity before, and on the still more baffling mystery of the eternity behind us—when we think of the wondrous God who unites both, and comprehends both—when we think of the universe on which He sits enthroned, stretching far beyond the ken of human eye, onward and outward to the viewless depths of immensity—Is it, we ask, for the creatures of our little sphere and our little day, to sit in judgment on the principles or policy of that high administration which reaches to all ages and embraces all worlds? Our becoming attitude is surely that of learners; and our proper business, when studying the volume of nature or the volume of revelation, is not to excogitate truth, but to receive it."[1]

On this point I add another argument for the spirit of humility. Supposing man, by searching, had found out what was the true and only remedy, the incarnation and death of the Son of God, how could he have demanded or even desired such a gift? To utter the desire would have turned supplication into blasphemy. If it had been uttered, who could trace the bent of the Divine mind thereon, or hope that God would give a gift so unspeakably great and precious, to a race so sinful?

---

[1] Chalmers' *Institutes of Theology*, Vol. 2, pp. 4, 5.

The infinite compassion of our Redeemer has not left us thus to lift helpless hands in the darkness, and cry in the night; but rather to adore and wonder that what was beyond the competence of all creatures to ask, was yet not beyond His love to bestow.

Turning from the Divine side to the human, from the high requirements of the moral rule of God to the demands of the sinner's need, we must bear in mind that even here *à priori* speculation cannot walk with steady step. We cannot certainly infer the existence of a supply from the existence of a want. Our subjective feelings do not of themselves imply the existence in external nature of that object which can give them satisfaction. "The mere feeling of hunger," reasons Dr. Chalmers, "would not of itself suggest even the notion of food, and far less afford any demonstration of its reality. The mere feeling of thirst, apart from the sight or the appearance of water, would be no argument for the existence of this element in the world. The mere painful affection of a want arising from the organic structure of the lungs, when the needful aliment of breathing was not supplied to it, would convey no intimation to us, either of the certainty or probability of an atmosphere. We could not thus find our way by an inferential process from the experience of certain felt wants, to the reality of certain counterpart objects. . . . . We must have both the feelings and the objects brought within our reach. We must have the sensation of the one, and, distinct from this, we must have the knowledge of the other. Or, to express it differently, we must have observation for both; and observation or experience too, ere we can know the adaptation between them. And then, to be sure, there do come into our possession the materials of a most glorious argument; and from the adaptation between the fruits of the earth and the sustenance of its living generations, as well as their intense and universal cry of hunger—of water, that cheap and common bounty, to the sensation universal too of thirst—of air, compounded as it is, to the apparatus of respiration in all animals, none of whom could breathe or exist in any other—of light to the eye—of sound to the organs of hearing—in short, of the many thousand objects in the world to the wants, and the susceptibilities, and the powers of the innumerable living creatures upon its surface."[1]

The application of this argument is in keeping with the argument itself. I give it in Dr. Chalmers' words: "Now, we have felt wants in

---

[1] Chalmers' *Institutes*, Vol. 2, pp. 9, 10.

our mental as well as in our corporeal economy. More especially, there are the unutterable longings of a spirit, conscious-stricken because of iniquity, and in sore distress under the agonies of a present remorse and the dreary forebodings of an unprovided eternity. I do not see why, in the physical department, we should isolate ourselves from the world, and then put our ingenuity to the task of guessing from the knowledge of our wants, and our wants alone, what the objects might be in the outer panorama which are suited to them. And neither can I see why, in the moral department, we should isolate ourselves from the Bible, and thus making a voluntary abridgment of the data within our reach, put ourselves on the rack of speculation—and that for the purpose of trying how well we can guess, from the wants too as before, and the wants alone, whether there be a revelation at all, and then what be the likeliest doctrine there to meet the appetencies and the needs of our moral nature. I would make short work of it. I would neither address myself to the first enquiry with the world shut out, nor would I address myself to the second enquiry with the Bible shut out. I would go forth at once on the volume of nature, and thence learn from the adaptations there to man's bodily wants, that there was a Divinity in the world. And I would go forth at once on the volume of Scripture, and might also learn there from the adaptations to man's moral and spiritual wants, that there is a Divinity in the Word. More particularly would I lay immediate hold on that which professes to be the bread of life come down from heaven, or the precious doctrines of Jesus Christ, and Him Crucified. I would at once make trial of it."[1]

Thus we take it as fairly proved, that a certain knowledge of the nature of the remedy can only be had from an experience of that remedy itself. The sweetness of honey can only be known by tasting it.

The drift of these observations is to impress on the mind the infirmity and utter insufficiency of human speculations on this matter of such vast and vital importance to humanity. If doubt hangs over the very hopes of restoration, as far as reason can see; if we cannot argue from the nature of God or man to the nature of the remedy; if the doctrine of the Cross is an absolutely new doctrine in the world; if we cannot reason from the felt want to the existence of the objective satisfaction; if, discovering its existence, we dare not (for it would be in us impious) demand its application; I think it is very clear that the powers of speculative reason in the domain of redemption must be very limited.

---

[1] Chalmers' *Institutes*, Vol. 2, pp. 10, 11.

It is very clear that in this province, where we have reason alone to light our way, we should advance with cautious footsteps; and only there indulge in the feeling of certainty, where we have a "*thus saith the Lord.*" To the question, What is God, and what is man? individual reflection, even without the light of revelation, can get much nearer to an answer than if the question be proposed, What has God done for the deliverance of a sinful world? Here, neither speculative thought nor empirical investigation can of itself help us much farther. God alone can procure Salvation; but He alone, too, can make known to the sinner whether He gives it, and if so, how He will do it. Salvation the Saviour describes as a "heavenly thing," and its knowledge we can obtain from heaven alone.

SALVATION AS A DOCTRINE.

We have been considering Salvation as a hope and as a speculation; we now proceed to view it as a doctrine. Regarding Divine Revelation as a whole, Salvation is its central doctrine. In the New Testament, which fills up with its substance the shadow and outline of the Old, this is the one distinguishing and absorbing feature. It is not one among many truths brought down to us; it is the one around which all others cluster, and from which they gain their life and support.

In the Pagan systems of religion subsisting throughout Europe, the underlying idea was a kind of deification of nature. In Mohammedanism, it is difficult to decide whether the essential tenet is, that God is one, or that Mohammed is His prophet. But Salvation is the burden of Christianity. Clear and precious light it sheds on collateral problems, on the nature of God, the course of Providence, virtue and immortality. But it comes not into being for the purpose of adding to our knowledge of these great themes. It came to reveal the heart-rejoicing and world-renewing fact, that a real salvation had been provided, not by the intervention of man, but by the mercy of God. The very reason of the existence of the Gospel is that it reveals the power of God unto salvation. This constitutes it "good news" and "glad tidings to all people," and "worthy of all acceptation." The doctrine of Salvation is the very heart-blood of our religion. It is the very central sun, of which all other truths are emanating beams. It is the eye of the Gospel, to use Dr. Miller's beautiful figure, which like that of a portrait, is uniformly fixed on us, turn where we will. Recognizing thus fully the prominence of Salvation, we shall find it difficult to exaggerate its importance, or give undue weight to it in delivering the message of Christ. We shall feel that, whatever doctrine we may preach, if we do not preach Salvation, we do not preach the Gospel. And, as in preaching, so in studying, Salvation is the one engrossing theme. All true advancement in the theoretic and systematic knowledge of the great remedial scheme of God will have its spring in the advancement of our own personal experience and knowledge of the saving power of Christ. Ever going forward, with the consciousness of what is involved in being ourselves sinners saved by Divine compassion, we will instinctively feel the reverence with which we ought ever to handle the deep mysteries of God.

Salvation as a Mystery.

Here I may observe we ought to be prepared for mysteries in Salvation. The fact of Salvation may be evident enough; the way of Salvation may be most divinely simple, so far as we are practically concerned. These simplicities are the glory of the Gospel, and it will be the glory of our ministry to keep them unclouded before the people. Yet, without contradiction, great is the mystery. The fact is one thing, the doctrine is another. Life, as a fact, is the most commonly simple of all simple things; but Life, as a doctrine, as a science, is one of the deepest mysteries in which the mind can be engaged. And if science is speechless before many of the problems the life of a common nettle may suggest, can we expect to see to the end of the inner working of salvation upon the hidden life of the spirit of man? In nature, in the course of Providence, in the constitution of the soul of man, and in the existence of sin in mankind, there are admitted mysteries. Salvation has to do with these mysteries, is interwoven with them all, and can we expect that it should in all respects be plain and transparent? Not only is Salvation a graft upon mysteries; but it is itself the chief of the Divine works, and, as such, the chief of all mysteries. Here Deity concentrates the essence of His wisdom; and His eternal love adds the crown to all the other works of His hands. Marvels and wonders therefore may be expected on every hand. "If Redemption is really a Divine work it must as such have its mystery; if it is the greatest of all God's works, we know that the highest mountains cast the longest shadows." We may rejoice at the plainness and brightness of the lines that come near to us, but we must not be disconsolate with Daniel, if the vision shades off into deepening gloom. The Apostles were obliged to cry, "*O the depth of the riches both of the wisdom and knowledge of*

God!"[1] "*Now we see through a glass darkly;*"[2] "*Into these things the angels desire to look.*"[3] We may well be content with the part vision of the Apostle, and the unfulfilled desire of the Angels. These elevated and holy ones waited, where they could not enter; believed, where they could not see; and adored, where they could not understand to perfection.

Salvation in its Unfolding.

(I.) *In History.*

If we enlarge our vision to the utmost bounds of human history drawn for us in the Word of God, we shall see the one increasing purpose of redemption running through the ages, and widening "with the process of the suns."

We perceive the great family tree of the human race throw out its branches in all directions over the earth. But there is one branch that receives the special care of the great Husbandman; it is the race of Abraham. There is one bough on that branch enriched with a special promise; it is the tribe of Judah. From that one bough, there is unfolded to the day, that precious Blossom, whose fragrance perfumes all the universe; there is brought to maturity, that precious Fruit, which is the life of mankind,—Jesus Christ the Lord.

If we follow the course of Israel as a nation, we shall find Salvation shadowed forth on a scale as large as their history. In those miraculous deeds by which their deliverance from Egypt was accomplished; the slaughter of the first-born, the sprinkled blood of the paschal lamb, the passage of the Red Sea, the wonders and mercies of their desert wanderings, and the entrance into their promised inheritance, the vast type is begun, which throughout their national course is continued, until the temporal shadow vanishes before the Eternal Substance.

Turning our eyes from the events of their history, if we scrutinize the constitution of Israel, we shall meet this great truth on every hand. When the tribes are formed into a people, and a religious and civil code is given, the whole atmosphere is filled with symbols, images and types, teeming with ideas exhibiting redemption in partial and manifold glimpses. In the divinely-appointed ritual of the Temple, every implement and every vessel, every act and every word, were charged with the lessons of Salvation. The light, however, is not narrowed down to the prescribed forms of worship. The intimations of the

---

[1] Rom. xi. 33. [2] 1 Cor. xiii. 12. [3] 1 Pet. i. 12.

coming redemption cover a wider area than the curtains of the Tabernacle, or the gates of the Temple. They pass beyond all the limits of ritual, and overflowing into the common affairs of the people, give a tone to the every-day usages of society. This truth of Salvation is embodied in the time their sacred year began. It is found in the three chief festivals of the year. The year of Jubilee shews it to be in their system of land-tenure, and in their regulations of the liberty of the subject. The cities of refuge reveal it in their administration of justice. Their very garments were to tell it forth, and the post of their doors proclaim it. The tracery of redemption, like the fair lilywork on the pillars of Solomon's Temple, is to be discerned over all the history of God's peculiar people. That tracery was there, not only for its lines of beauty, but also for its lines of light. It was a kind of Divine hieroglyphic, yielding up as the Rosetta stone its wealth of meaning to those who found the key. That Key, then, as now, was never absent from the believer. The Key is Christ.

(II.) *In language and imagery.*

Although this seems to retrace in some respects the ground we have gone over, it is in reality another and a wider field. I mean to present here some gleanings from the wide range of ideas used of Salvation apart from any race or people. In these gleanings we shall find the intimations of Salvation prepared for man, as suffering from the misery and the peril of sin. Many sided as his ruin is, equally so is Divine restoration. The Saviour comes where the sinner is.

The variety of imagery employed has yet another reason, which is thus rendered by a writer of the present day. "Transcending, as the benefits (of Salvation) do, all human thought, and failing to find anywhere a perfectly adequate expression in human language, they must still be set forth by the help of language, and through the means of human relations. Here, as in other similar cases, what the Scripture does is to approach the central truth from different quarters; to exhibit it not on one side but on many, that so they may severally supply the deficiencies of one another, and that moment of the truth which one does not express, another may." [1]

These images are gathered from a wide range. They are taken from the *material* world. The lost piece of money is found; [2] the believer as a living stone is built upon the true Foundation, and so the

---

[1] Trench: *New Testament Synonyms*, p. 278.   [2] Luke xv. 9.

holy temple grows.[1] They come from the *vegetable* kingdom. The vine-branch is nourished with the sap of the True Vine;[2] the wild olive is, by grafting on the true, reclaimed contrary to nature from its wildness.[3] From the domain of *animals*, we see the lost sheep as traced and brought back with joy.[4] From *national life:* ye who were not a people are now the people of the living God.[5] From *physical evil:* Christ is the great Physician,[6] the Lord, the Healer;[7] and the Quickener of those who were dead.[8] From *social relations:* the slaves sold under sin are redeemed not with corruptible things;[9] the prodigal is welcomed home from his distant wanderings.[10] From *legal affairs:* we are redeemed from the curse of the law.[11] From the *intellectual world:* the eyes of the understanding are enlightened.[12] From our *Moral and Spiritual nature:* ye must be born again.[13]

In a word, the Salvation is represented as taking effect in all man's powers and faculties. It rectifies his relation to law, to his fellow men, to God, to the world, to all the high purposes and responsibilities of life. It contemplates the complete recovery of every believer from all taint of sin, the eradication of evil from the world, the expulsion of Satan, the restoration of the glory of God in the new heavens and the new earth. Therefore it is, that all things are made to contribute, in their manner and measure, to the full expression of that Mercy that comprehends all.

---

[1] 1 Peter ii. 5, Eph. ii. 20-21. [2] John xv. 1-15. [3] Rom. xi. 24. [4] Luke xv. 5.
[5] 1 Peter ii. 10. [6] Mark ii. 17. [7] Exod. xv. 26. [8] Eph. ii. 1.
[9] 1 Peter i. 18. [10] Luke xv. 20. [11] Gal. iii. 13. [12] Eph. i. 18.
[13] John iii. 7.

LECTURE XII.

SCRIPTURAL EXPRESSIONS RELATING TO SALVATION.

IN the last Lecture we observed how Scripture fills the whole atmosphere of life with ideas of redemption; we come now to the study of some of those words which may be considered almost technical in the science of Salvation.

In treating these words, I do not confine myself to one line of enquiry. It will be pertinent to note, whatever the etymology, the primitive signification, the broader usages or ultimate applications of the word, may contribute to a full insight into the Scriptural notion of the recovery from sin. I am well aware how misleading bare etymologies may be, and therefore I shall not keep to their narrow groove; yet under a temperate and judicious treatment, even these may yield some light. Here we cannot despise any light, however dim or flickering. To give to each contribution, so far as we can, its due place; to combine all, and bring them to bear on one another, is wisdom in us, even as it is the mark of Infinite wisdom "to give line upon line and precept upon precept." In the literature of a single word, we often find the unfolding of a great idea, the development of a great principle. Of this, the first word in our list is an eminent example:—

גאל (GOEL). When we read in Romans xi. 26, "There shall come out of Zion *the Deliverer*, and shall turn away ungodliness from Jacob," this word *Deliverer* is the representative of גאל, and as such, it carries us back into the midst of those primitive practices and institutions, which fostered and shaped in patriarchal and Mosaic times, the expectation of redemption. As the Apostle uses the word, or rather its equivalent (ὁ ῥυόμενος = גאל), it is true that it is endued with the wealth of its richest meanings, but that does not prevent it from being traced backwards to lowly connections and humble affairs. "The fundamental signification of the stem," says Fuerst, " is to separate from something, to divide off, whence to untie"; and he translates, "to loose, to set free what was bound or fettered." Rare as is this meaning (and be it remembered the primitive meaning of many words is often rare in literature), there are three passages that may fairly be claimed in its favour, viz, the Septuagint rendering in Job iii. 5; and Ezra ii. 62, and Nehemiah vii. 64. In these two latter, the Vulgate gives as the equivalent, "*ejecti sunt.*"

In Leviticus we are in the full stream of the common meaning, given in our version, *to redeem.* The more primitive signification *to set free,* receives however, several illustrations in chapters xxv. and xxvii. In the former (verse 25, etc.), there are set forth the regulations by which the encumbered inheritance, or the enslaved Israelite (verses 48-9), is to be set free. In chapter xxvii., we see in succession the way of setting free the animal (verse 13), the house (verse 15), and the field (verse 19), that had been bound by the vow of consecration.

But as we survey these instances of redemption, we observe a new and important element come into operation. The person concerned is not always able to discharge his obligations; and bondage or alienation of property may therefore ensue. To avoid this calamity the tie of brotherhood and kindred is invoked. The persons next of kin—the Septuagint has ἀγχιστεύς, ἀγχιστεύω, words very beautiful in their breadth of meaning—is charged with the duty. The rich kinsman is to help the poor, the strong to assist the weak. In Lev. xxv. 35-42, we have the precept, but the Book of Ruth in its pictorial history, shews how beneficial the principle may be, and how nobly the *Goel* may put it into practice. The appeal to the tie of kinship is answered by the generous Boaz, by the preservation of the family rights, by paying off outstanding claims, and finally by marriage.

The sacred union of the family may however be threatened by other forces of dissolution than poverty. It may be threatened by violence or death. And when any member fell under the blow of an assassin, such was the method of patriarchal justice, that the next of kin was charged with the stern duty of executing the murderer. Until the *Goel* had inflicted vengeance upon the criminal, he was, as Jahn expresses it, considered *infamous.* Jahn even goes the length of supposing that on this very account, the name *Goel* or *polluted* (taking the alternative root) was applied to the next of kin. The true explanation is much simpler, and is found in the original meaning assigned to the root by

Fuerst. The murderer fastens an injury upon the family of his victim, and the avenger, the *Goel*, sets his family free. Or to seek a closer analogy: as in the case of debt, the *Goel* frees the family property by paying off the encumbrances, so, in the case of culpable homicide, he clears the right and justice of the family by paying off the murderer with the death penalty.

Moses did not found this system of revenge; this "wild justice" as Bacon has termed it. It already existed in all its native wildness, and his effort was to restrain and regulate it, by infusing into it something of judicial calm. He provided especially that the unwitting manslayer might be within reach of safety from the avenger of blood, by the humane institution of the Cities of Refuge.

How eminently expressive the typical meaning of these Cities of Refuge is, we well know; but we must not allow the grace that provided them to raise any prejudice in our minds against the equal grace that invests the character and duty of the *Goel* or Redeemer. Were we to do so, type would seem to clash with type, and the Redeemer be at variance with His own redemption. To avoid such confusion we have only to bear in mind that the Cities are appointed against the infirmities, not against the rights of the Redeemer, or blood avenger. Where his rights are clear, as in the case of actual murder, no city's gates, no temple's shrine, no divine altar can bar his entrance or arrest his hand. Joab, the son of Zeruiah, is cut down from the very horns of the Altar of God.

But when the Lord stoops to perform the work of *Goel*, all the human infirmities melt in a moment from the office. His abundant kindness too, or as the Apostle calls it—"*the philanthropy of God*," comes into view as He sustains this character. He, the strong, interposes on behalf of the weak; the rich, to free the poor; the just, to vindicate the wronged and oppressed. He, as our near neighbour, taking the idea of the Septuagint, turns aside to act the neighbour's part.

It is with this feeling of neighbourly nearness that the exhortation is given: "*Remove not the old landmark: and enter not into the fields of the fatherless: For their Redeemer is mighty; He shall plead their cause with thee*" (Proverbs xxiii. 10, 11). In Psalm xix. 14, David calls the Lord, "*his strength and his Redeemer.*" In Psalm lxix. 18, he prays, "*Draw nigh unto my soul, and redeem it.*" It is not without significance that the very first time it occurs in Scripture, it is applied to Jehovah. This prime instance is in the blessing pronounced by the venerable Israel upon Joseph's sons, "*The Angel which redeemed me from all evil, bless the lads*" (Genesis xlviii. 16, and cf. Isaiah xli. 14).

In the Old Testament, however, the most famous display of God's kindness to His people, as their *Goel*, was in delivering them from the bondage of Egypt : "*I will redeem you with a stretched out arm, and with great judgments*" (Exodus vi. 6). This great national redemption furnished the type of a still greater. And when prophets struck their harps to the glories of the Coming One, no sweeter sound than Redeemer fell from their strings: "*Thus saith the Lord, the King of Israel, and his Redeemer*" (Isaiah xliv. 6). It is promised at chapter xlix. 26, "*All flesh shall know that I the Lord, am thy Saviour and thy Redeemer, the Mighty One of Jacob.*"[1] It was the deep blessedness contained in this word that roused the heart of the suffering Job : "*I know that my Redeemer liveth*" (Job xix. 25). "Whatever view may be taken of this passage, whether we regard it as a prediction of the Messiah's coming, or an intimation of the doctrine of the resurrection, or as referring to a temporal deliverance from disease and trouble, one point is clear, that Job expresses his deep conviction that there was a living God who could and who would take his part, and extricate him from all difficulties."[2]

It was the grandeur of the Lord, advancing towards him in vision, as Redeemer, that caused the prophet to put the question, "*Who is this that cometh from Edom, with dyed garments from Bozrah? this that is glorious in His apparel, travelling in the greatness of His strength?*" (Isaiah lxiii. i.) That the wondrous glory of this appearance belongs to Him as Redeemer, is put beyond doubt by verse 4, which asserts, "*the year of my redeemed is come.*" If you trace the prophet's unfolding of the work of Redemption, you will find, in verses 8 and 9, the old ties of kinship brought distinctly into view : "*Surely they are my people ; children that will not lie ; so He was their Saviour.*" The natural bond of blood-relationship which the rich kinsman was to own by releasing his poorer brethren, and the strong in freeing from peril or magisterially wiping off the family dishonour, gives shape to the hope, and form to the idea of the spiritual and eternal Redemption of mankind. By sowing such thoughts in the minds of His people for generations, God was tacitly owning or teaching that the *right* of redemption

---

[1] Cf. also Isaiah xliv. 6, 22, 23, 24 ; xlvii. 4 ; xlviii. 17 ; xlix. 7, 26; lii. 3.
[2] Girdlestone : *Old Testament Synonyms*, pp. 193, 194.

lay in the tie of kindred, and thus preparing the mind for that event which should make the lowliest believer the brother of the Son of God. The Incarnation was the glorious fruition granted to these awakened desires. "*Forasmuch then as the children are partakers of flesh and blood, He also Himself likewise took part of the same; that through death He might destroy him that had the power of death, that is, the devil, and deliver them who through fear of death were all their lifetime subject to bondage*" (Hebrews ii. 14, 15). "*In all things it behoved Him to be made like unto His brethren*" (verse 17). And let us remember that it is unspeakably true with respect to our "high-born Kinsman," our "Elder Brother," in the skies:—

> "No distance breaks the tie of blood;
> Brothers are brothers evermore;
> Nor wrong, nor wrath of deadliest mood,
> That magic may o'erpower.
>
> "Oft, ere the common source be known,
> The kindred drops will claim their own,
> And throbbing pulses silently
> Move heart towards heart by sympathy.
>
> *   *   *   *
>
> "So is it with true Christian hearts;
> Their mutual share in Jesu's blood
> An everlasting bond imparts
> Of holiest brotherhood." [1]

פָּדָה (PADAH). The next word translated to redeem is פָּדָה. The primary meaning is *to loose*; and it is cognate with פָּרַד to cut, as if the idea were to loose by cutting. As גָּאַל is employed in circumstances very like those in which פָּדָה is used, it is rather difficult to fix the exact shade of meaning which makes the one differ from the other. We have seen how vividly the person of the Redeemer is set before the mind in גָּאַל; whereas in פָּדָה the attention is fixed rather upon the act of deliverance, and especially as that act has a relation to the threatening dangers from which one is delivered. Our word *rescue* has similar surroundings; it is the vigorous and prompt act by which one is saved from the brink of danger or ruin. When Jonathan had been detected transgressing the king's command, and in consequence put under the stern sentence, "*Thou shalt surely die, Jonathan*," then the people took up the cause of the hero of the day, and "*So the people rescued Jonathan, that he died not*" (1 Sam. xiv. 44, 45). With the

---

[1] Keble: *Second Sunday after Trinity*.

same sense of impending destruction, Job prays, "*Redeem me from the hand of the mighty*" (Job vi. 23). When David felt himself free from the constant pressure of danger, through the overthrow of Saul's army, his feelings found expression in his description of God—"*As the Lord . . . . . who hath redeemed my soul out of all adversity*" (2 Sam. iv. 9).

The law of the sanctification of the first-born of Israel brings פָּדָה, *redemption*, into contact with *sacrifice*, and the instrument of redemption generally. Yet here the presence of overhanging is not overlooked. On the contrary, the law is designed to put the nation in perpetual remembrance of their first-born being rescued from the stroke of the destroying Angel, while the first-born of all the Egyptians perished. The law was enjoined at their first halting-place on their way from Egypt, while the exceeding great and bitter cry of the Egyptians was still ringing in their ears: " *All the first-born of man among thy children shalt thou redeem* " (Ex. xiii. 13, 15). They were to do this by means of sacrifice; but the slaughter of a victim as the price of their redemption was an acknowledgment that they themselves were guilty of death. Escaping from that death by the shedding of blood, they were sanctified unto God; and to him they were themselves to be as "living sacrifices." In Isaiah xxix. 22, it is applied to Abraham in a remarkable manner, but here, as elsewhere, alarms of danger are present in the surrounding verses.

From these physical and ceremonial usages, the transition of פָּדָה to what is spiritual is easy, and here its force of suggestion as to impending danger comes fully out. " *The Lord redeemeth the soul of his servants* " (Ps. xxxiv. 22). " *None of them can by any means redeem his brother, nor give to God a ransom* (כֹּפֶר = atonement) *for him; (for the redemption of their soul is precious)* . . . . *But God will redeem my soul from the power of the grave* " (Ps. xlix. 7, 8, 15). " *With the Lord is plenteous redemption, and He shall redeem Israel from all his iniquities* " (Ps. cxxx. 7, 8). In all these and similar passages, sin or its consequences form the alarm, and constitute the falling destruction.

יָשַׁע (YASHA'). The native meaning of יָשַׁע is, to be spacious, ample, broad. In the Hebrew mind the idea of ample space was connected with freedom and safety, just as the opposite notion of narrowness and strictness was equivalent to danger and distress. What David says in Ps. xviii. 19, and Ps. xxxi. 7, 8, might be set down as an exact definition of the word, though the word itself does not occur in either passage: "*He brought me forth also into a large place.*" "*Thou hast known my soul in adversities : And hast not shut me up into the hand of the enemy : Thou hast set my feet in a large room.*" The signal deliverance wrought for Israel when hemmed in by the mountain and the tower on either side, the deep sea in front, and the pursuing army of Pharaoh behind, is set forth by this word : "*Fear ye not, stand still, and see the salvation of the Lord, which He will shew you to-day*" (Exod. xiv. 13). The release from the galling Midian yoke to the ample rights and liberties of a free people is promised in the same word : "*Go in this thy might,*" said the Lord to Gideon, "*And thou shalt* SAVE *Israel from the hand of the Midianites*" (Jud. vi. 14). And when, too, the trump of a greater Deliverer than Gideon is heard, the hopes fostered by that glad sound are clothed still in the same imagery. In Isa. lxii. 8-11, the end to be achieved by the coming of the Saviour recalls in its description the dark days of Midian when no man was free to reap his own harvest, or gather the fruits of his own vines : "*The Lord hath sworn by His right hand and by the arm of His strength, surely I will no more give thy corn to be meat for thine enemies ; and the sons of the stranger shall not drink thy wine, for the which thou hast laboured*" . . . And why? The Lord hath proclaimed "*Say ye to the daughter of Zion, Behold thy Salvation cometh.*" Zechariah in describing the coming of Zion's King, associates with the salvation He brings the same large liberties. No sooner do the joyful hosannahs that welcome His approach die away, than we hear of the royal grace in the enlargement of the oppressed : "*By the blood of thy covenant I have sent forth thy prisoners out of the pit wherein is no water*" (Zech. ix. 11). So again in verse 9, is seen how He is *just* and has *salvation.*

How emphatic is the use of this word in Isa. xxxv. 4 ! The prophet using the return of the exiles from Babylon as the substratum of his thoughts, pictures in glowing language the return to God of the whole ransomed Church. Their presence pours gladness over the wilderness ; their footsteps leave the desert blossoming as the rose ; springs issue from the arid sands ; cooling waters take the place of the deceptive mirage ; and the lion and ravenous beast hurry away from the path of the pilgrim bands. But when in the midst of all this scene of rejoicing, it is observed by Omniscient Pity that there are some timorous spirits and trembling hearts that cannot taste the universal joy, a special message is sent to them from the Throne, and the essence of that consoling message is contained in the word *Salvation :* "*God will come*

142   SIN, AND THE UNFOLDING OF SALVATION.

. . . . *and* SAVE *you*" (verse 4). This includes all—the return, the glory of Zion, the song and the everlasting joy.

In these examples it may be noticed how constantly the word inclines to give prominence to the positive nature of the blessings bestowed by the Saviour. It is not merely a release from pressing danger or suffering. Of course, there is necessarily brought within view the evil from which the Saved have escaped. It is neither the act of escape, nor the evil escaped, but the condition of safety they have reached, which is the prime thought embedded in ישע, and its kindred forms. These other ideas are incidental and subordinate; this is essential to the word. If at any time emphasis is laid on the danger, it is for the purpose of throwing the greatness of the Salvation into bolder relief.

As the attainment of this positive Salvation, in contrast with the various misfortunes of this present life, is beyond unaided human power, it is not very surprising to find ישועה (salvation) attributed to God alone. Jonah expressed the creed of every pious Israelite, concerning both temporal and eternal things, when he said, " *Salvation is of the Lord*" (Jonah ii. 9). Isa. xliii. 11, expresses the same thought with all the force of a Divine declaration: "*I, even I, am the Lord; and beside me there is no* SAVIOUR."

From the positive character of Salvation naturally grew the idea of the permanent and the eternal (cf. Isa. xlv. 17, and Heb. ix. 12). With such attractive and inspiring qualities was that Salvation invested, which was associated with the coming of the Messiah. "It is," says Cremer, "opposed to God's wrath, and implies deliverance from guilt and punishment, and at the same time all positive blessings coming in the place of distress and sorrow."[1]

It is peculiarly called "THE *Salvation of God*" (Isa. lvi. 1, and li. 6 and 8). The phrase is "*My Salvation,*" God being the speaker. As far back as patriarchal times it had this high distinction, and is shewn in the pause of Jacob's blessing, when he exclaims, "*I have waited for Thy* SALVATION, *O Lord*" (Gen. xlix. 18). That we do not strain the words by taking them in a Messianic sense, is shewn by the paraphrase of the later Targums (*Jerusalem* and *Jonathan*)—" My soul waiteth, not for the deliverance of Gideon, the son of Joash, for that is but temporal; not for the redemption of Samson, for that is transitory; but for the Redemption of the Messiah, the Son of David, the Redemp-

---

[1] Cremer, *Biblico-Theological Lexicon of New Testament*, Greek, p. 533.

SCRIPTURAL EXPRESSIONS RELATING TO SALVATION. 143

tion which Thou, through Thy word, hast promised to bring to Thy people, the children of Israel : for this Thy redemption my soul waiteth, for Thy salvation, O Lord, is an everlasting Salvation." [1]

This ישׁע of the Old Testament is represented for the most part by σώζω in the New; and the latter, though differing from the former in the radical idea, bears to it in common usage a very close resemblance. Σώζω comes from the root of σῶs, sound, whole; and means to make sound, to heal. Thence it branches out into the meanings of *to save*, to preserve, in any and every case of man's exposure to danger. Throughout its various connections the positive element of safety, as in ישׁע, is paramount. There are instances where it verges on the meaning of ῥύομαι, I rescue, I deliver, as in Peter's sinking cry, "*Lord, save me*" (Matt. xiv. 30); and the jailor's, "*What must I do to be saved?*" (Acts xvi. 30.) Yet even in these examples its native meaning is easily distinguishable: a safe condition in both cases is the object of desire. The relation of σώζω to ῥύομαι Homer has defined very clearly. Ulysses says to the herald Medon,—

Θάρσει, ἐπεὶ δή σ' οὗτος ἐρύσσατο καὶ ἐσάωσεν [2] (*Odyssey*, xxii. 372)

So when Hector springs to life again, after having fallen under Telamonian Ajax, it is said,—

'Αλλά τις αὖτε θεῶν ἐρρύσατο καὶ ἐσάωσεν [2] (*Iliad*, xv. 290).

In these passages ῥύομαι refers to the deliverance from the danger, σώζω to the subsequent safety.

That this distinction is strongly marked in the New Testament also, will be seen in 2 Tim. iv. 17, 18: "*And I was delivered* (ἐρύσθην) *out of the mouth of the lion And the Lord shall deliver* (ῥύσεται) *me from every evil work, and will preserve* (σώσει) *me unto his heavenly kingdom.*" Where, however, σώζω is made to cover the whole ground, the rescue as well as the safety, as in James v. 20, σώσει ψυχὴν ἐκ θανάτου, it is the ultimate fact of safety that it chiefly presents. When the devils are cast out of the man of Gadara he is *rescued;* but when we see that rescued one clothed and in his right mind sitting at the feet of Jesus, he is *saved*. When we observe the prodigal coming to himself, and leaving the swine trough and the far country, there we see his *rescue* from his misery; but when we trace him till he is within the Father's gaze and the Father's arms, till he shares all the blessings of the Father's home—

---

[1] Keil and Delitzsch, *On Pentateuch*, Vol. I, p. 404.

[2] "Be confident since he has *freed* thee and *saved* thee."

[3] "But some one of the Gods has again *liberated* and *preserved* Hector."

the best robe, the ring, the joyous banquet—then we see his *salvation*. The very memory of misery and sufferings is steeped in the bliss of present and abiding safety. An ancient Greek hymn very happily expresses this view :—

> " Safe home, safe home in port !
> Rent cordage, shattered deck,
> Torn sails, provisions short,
> And only not a wreck :
> But oh, the joy upon the shore
> To tell our voyage-perils o'er !
>
> " The prize, the prize secure !
> The athlete nearly fell ;
> Bare all he *could* endure,
> And bare not always well :
> But he may smile at troubles gone
> Who sets the victor-garland on.
>
> " No more the foe can harm :
> No more of leaguer'd camp,
> And cry of night alarm,
> And need of ready lamp :
> And yet how nearly he had failed,
> How nearly had that foe prevailed !
>
> " The lamb is in the fold
> In perfect safety penned :
> The lion once had hold,
> And thought to make an end :
> But One came by with wounded side,
> And for the sheep the Shepherd died.
>
> " The exile is at home !
> O nights and days of tears,
> O longings not to roam,
> O sins, and doubts and fears !—
> What matter now (when so men say)
> The King has wiped those tears away?
>
> " O happy, happy Bride !
> Thy widowed hours are past,
> The Bridegroom at thy side,
> Thou all His own at last !
> The sorrows of thy former cup,
> In full fruition swallowed up." [1]

Salvation is therefore not a bare exemption from evils, but a possession of the positive blessing of Christ's Redemption. They to whom the blessings are given are called οἱ σωζόμενοι, those that are being saved. And the Apostle says of himself " *the Lord will save me*

---

[1] *Hymns of Eastern Church*, translated by J. M. Neale, D.D.

SCRIPTURAL EXPRESSIONS RELATING TO SALVATION. 145

unto His heavenly Kingdom"[1]—σώσει εἰς τὴν βασιλείαν—*i.e.*, He will bring me safe through into His heavenly Kingdom. How near this view of Salvation before the Apostle's mind assimilates to the ancient Hebrew idea, it is not difficult to see. The heavenly Kingdom is the "broad place" into which the Saviour brings His people—the place of ample and assured liberty for Christ's freemen.

Finally, I notice the use of יָשַׁע in the proper name *Joshua*, which through the Greek became *Jesus*. The successor of Moses bore the name Joshua in contrast with Moses, in that while Moses led the people out of Egypt, the house of bondage, Joshua led them into Canaan. Moses was the deliverer, Joshua the salvation of God. To the Antitype, the Incarnate Son of God, the name Jesus is given "*For He shall save His people from their sins.*"[2] But as salvation from sin requires both the work of a Moses and a Joshua combined, Christ is in His single Person the Antitype of Moses and Joshua. He is the Deliverer and the Saviour in one. He is in the fullest sense the Captain of our Salvation. He shall not fail or be discouraged till He has led all the weary who come to Him to the rest that remaineth for the people of God.

כָּפַר (CAPHAR). In the foregoing word nothing was defined or implied as to the way or means of Salvation. But in כָּפַר we touch upon a group of words, whose main object in Scripture is to declare with great plainness the way and means of salvation from sin. Among all such words כָּפַר is first in importance. In our Version its renderings are by no means uniform. The chief is *to make atonement*, and the passages where this occurs most frequently, are Exodus xxx. and Leviticus xvi. In Exodus xxix. and Leviticus iv., v., xii., xiv., and xv., we also find many examples of this usage of the word. The other renderings given are, *reconcile, make reconciliation, purge, cleanse, put off, pacify, appease, expiate* (in margin), *pardon, forgive, disannul, be merciful*, and in one passage, *to pitch*. Of the derived nouns, כֹּפֶר has its chief renderings in ransom (eight times), and in satisfaction (twice); כִּפֻּרִים in *atonements* and atonement, as in Leviticus xxiii. 27, 28; xxv. 9; כַּפֹּרֶת is always the *Mercy Seat*.

In order to find our way through this network of meanings, let us begin with the radical notion of the word, which is *to cover over*. The ark, we read, was covered over with pitch (Gen. vi. 14, where both verb and derivate noun כֹּפֶר occur). In Isaiah xxviii. 18, we read,

---
[1] 2 Tim. iv. 18.   [2] Matt. i. 21.

"*And your covenant with death shall be disannulled*"; if we substitute "covered" for "disannulled," we have a literal description of the way in which a written covenant was obliterated, as the writing was covered over and deleted by drawing the style over it. A village is called כָּפָר or כֹּפֶר, because it was a covering or shelter to the inhabitants. The hoar frost is called כְּפוֹר (Simonis' opinion), because it covers the ground (Ex. xvi. 14).

As it begins to emerge from its strict literal sense into ceremonial and moral applications, it appears in two forms, first as a human, and secondly, as a divine act. As a human act the covering may be extended to the offended, the offender, or the offence. (1) The face of the offended is described as being covered. Jacob with his princely gifts *covered* (Gen. xxxii. 20, *Heb.*) the angry face of his brother Esau so effectually that the injuries of the past were hidden from view. (2) The offender is said to be covered by sacrifice (as in Lev. iv. 20, etc., *passim*), and hence the meaning of *reconciliation* or *atonement* (Lev. xvi. 6, etc). (3) The offence itself is covered, as in that famous prophecy in Daniel, concerning the death of our Lord, "*to make reconciliation for iniquity*" (Dan. ix. 24).

Perhaps the most frequent usage is that which brings both the offender and the offence under the one sacrificial covering, as in Leviticus v. 16 and Numbers vi. 11. In all such passages our translators have the uniform rendering, "*to make atonement,*" except where once or twice they have "*to reconcile*", or "*to make reconciliation*."

On turning to the word as it expresses a *divine act*, we find our version gives quite another set of renderings. It is in this connection *to purge, to pardon*, or *to be merciful*. "*As for our transgressions, Thou shalt* PURGE *them away*" (Ps. lxv. 3). "*Lo this hath touched thy lips . . . and thy sin* (*is*) PURGED" (Isa. vi. 7). The perfect appropriateness of this rendering of כָּפַר, when used of God, lies in the one only medium through which Divine pardon or cleansing from sin comes to us. In this same sole medium also the human act of "atoning" and the Divine act of "pardoning" find their meeting place. Sacrifice is the one only "covering" for sinners, from the Divine and consequently from the human point of view; and "*without the shedding of blood is no remission*."[1] These ideas are brought together in this very order in Leviticus xvi. 30, where the work of the great day of Atonement is summed up: "*For on that day shall the priest make an atonement*

---

[1] Hebrews ix. 22.

for you, to cleanse you, that ye may be clean from all your sins before the Lord."

As the institution of sacrifice is of God, the covering for sin therein provided may be truly attributed to God. Over and above all human thought and act God in this way covers sin; yet it is at the same time in and through the human act. It is man, not God, that offers the victim on the altar. It is by man's hand the blood of the sacrifice is shed, and the blood is sprinkled. Keeping it then distinctly before our minds that sacrifice as an act is human, but as an institution is Divine, it will appear perfectly consistent to attribute the "covering" of sin thereby both to man and to God.

But there are other reasons to be taken into account. Though the institution of sacrifice derives its origin from God, yet no single observance of it can be supposed to be independent of God's approval and acceptance. Every act must be well-pleasing in His sight, or else have no value to the suppliant. Of this, Cain and Abel afford a remarkable example. When, however, the sacrifice has met with the Divine approval, that approval is shown in granting what the worshipper had in view, *i.e.*, pardon, cleansing, purging from his sin. And thus God in pardoning may be said to own the covering of the blood, which the suppliant has offered, to refrain to break through that covering, and so to seal it as a covering indeed. No sacrifice could be truly said to be an effectual covering until it had borne the scrutiny of God, and had been ratified by Him. The Divine scrutiny and ratification, or acknowledgment, were signified in the acceptance of the sacrifice offered as a covering. The acceptance showed the covering to be effectual. Then came the blessedness of the man whose sins were covered.

Before leaving כָּפַר, and the great family of words which have sprung from it, there is one which demands separate treatment. It is the noun כַּפֹּרֶת (Capporeth), the name given to the covering of pure gold that was over the Ark of the Testimony (Exodus xxv. 17). It is translated into Greek by ἱλαστήριον, and into English by Mercy-seat. So important a part of that typical worship was this golden covering, that we find the Holy of Holies is called after it, the "House of the Covering" (1 Chron. xxviii. 11; cf. 1 Kings vi. 5). Upon this the Cherubs had their stand, and upon this they bent their continual gaze. Over it, and between the cherubic wings, dwelt the bright cloud, the Shekinah of the presence of Deity. But its pre-eminence arose not from its awful surroundings alone. It was not the pure gold, the underlying Tables of the Law, the outspreading wings; it was not even the overhanging cloud, nor all these typical and symbolic forms combined, that conferred upon it this singular pre-eminence in the Tabernacle and Temple of Jehovah. It was because that here the whole sacrificial acts of all the year and all their worship culminated. It was because that upon this golden covering the sacrificial covering for sin fell in crimson drops. It was because that here the blood of the bullock slain for the priests, and the blood of the goat slain for all the people, were "once in the circuit of the year," on the great Day of Atonement, sprinkled seven times amid clouds of sweet incense by the High Priest. This was the climax of that ceremonial worship: higher it could not rise. This act brought the pure gold, covering the Holy Law, sprinkled with the innocent blood shed for the people's sin, perfumed with the fragrance of grateful odours, beneath the immediate presence and gaze of Deity. And down from this summit of ceremonial sacrifice, and outwards from this inmost centre of typical atonement, came the beams of Jehovah's favour, shining over the people. Above every other covering, therefore, was this most eminently the covering for sin. Well did the most Holy Place itself bear the title of the "House of the Covering."

From what has been said about כַּפֹּרֶת we can understand why the LXX should render it by ἱλαστήριον, and our own Translators by "Mercy Seat." Between these renderings there is this difference: the Greek word according to its strict etymological forms denotes the *place of propitiation*, and in its wider use, *a propitiatory sacrifice;* but in both senses the view given is from the human side. The English word "Mercy Seat" gives, on the other hand, a Divine point of view. The ark-covering is the dwelling place of Mercy.

But what is of more importance, we can perceive how truly the great central type exhibits the Antitype, and how exactly the real has filled up the outlines of the shadowy. Christ, the Apostle tells us, is "*set forth to be a propitiation ('Mercy Seat') through faith in His blood*" (Rom. iii. 25). The Ark with its golden covering, containing the Law of God, becomes under this light a most expressive figure of the True, of Him who, being "holy, harmless and undefiled," could say to the Father, "*Thy law is within my heart.*" The blood sprinkled thereon tells us of Him who made His soul an offering for sin, and by that one offering once for all obtained Eternal redemption for us. His life and death both meet here. His life of purity in the refined gold: His death in the sprinkled blood. He is thus the true Covering, the true

Propitiation, the true Atonement, the Mercy Seat, the Throne of Grace, to which we may "*come boldly that we may obtain mercy and find grace to help in time of need*" (Heb. iv. 16). Uplifting our eyes from the earthly sanctuary to the heavenly we see what was in type local to Zion, made in substance universal to the world. The "glory" that once pertained exclusively to the Jews is now made to shine from the true Ark-covering, in beams of pardoning mercy, freely unto all tribes and peoples and tongues.

In justification for thus giving, in Rom. iii. 25, the sense of "Mercy Seat," rather than the meanings of "expiatory sacrifice," or "means of propitiation," to ἱλαστήριον, I note that in the only other place where it occurs in the New Testament (Heb. ix. 5) it has this meaning. In the LXX ἱλαστήριον is the uniform representation for the Ark-covering. The words, "in his blood"="his own blood," are in strict keeping with this view. For only the blood, and not the sacrifice itself, came into contact with the Mercy Seat. It is in this connection that the words "set forth" have their full significance. The meaning is to manifest, to expose to the gaze of all, (προέθετο = *ad spectandum proponere*). The veil is rent, the way to the Most Holy Place is made clear. Christ, as the "Mercy Seat," is made manifest by God to the believing eye of all mankind. Lastly, there can be no doubt about the Shekinah resting on Him. "*We beheld His glory*,"[1] says John; and another says, "*He is the brightness of the Father's glory.*"[2]

The general bearing of the typical coverings of sin and sinners is not fully recognized unless we grasp the fact that it is always implied there is One Presence from which sin and sinners are covered. The sinner is not covered from his neighbour, his king, the nation, or the priest, but from Him who is of purer eyes than to behold iniquity. The transgressor is sheltered by the death of an innocent victim, as by an invincible shield, from the sword of Eternal Justice. Not to recognize this thrice Holy Presence, in which the sinner can appear only through atoning blood, would lead to a fatal misconception or denial of the great truth that underlies all sacrifice.

Excluding the element of Divine Justice, whence could we derive an adequate reason for the sufferings and death involved in sacrifice? If goodness or compassion alone be in the practice, sacrifice would seem to cause a gratuitous waste of happiness and life. Mercy can find no 'sweet savour of rest" in the tears, the agonies, and the expiring cries

---

[1] John i. 14. [2] Heb. i. 3.

of the innocent. On the other hand, not to recognize the Divine Compassion in the institution of sacrifice, would expose us to the danger of attributing to the God of Salvation a harsh and stern indifference that could only be melted down and won to love mankind by costly offerings and dying victims. Such was the character of Pagan deities. But the provision of sacrifice makes it abundantly evident that God is already working towards the sinner's pardon and relief. All through the course of anticipation and preparation, what Abraham said to Isaac on the way to Moriah holds true, "*My son, God will provide Himself a lamb for a burnt offering.*"[1] And in the one true Sacrifice, it is not more distinctly clear that He takes away sin, than that He is the *Lamb of GOD*. It is because the philanthropy of God has so large a share in the provision of redemption, and is the first fountain whence it springs, that Scripture avoids stating in direct terms that God is appeased or propitiated. Yet it is equally evident from Scripture that there is wrath to be averted from sin, and that that wrath is of God. It is in things pertaining to God that Christ made expiation for our sins (Hebrews ii.). And it was *unto God* that He offered Himself through the Eternal Spirit.

At this turn of the subject which brings into view the Justice of God, we are able to see the point of contrast between כָּפַר and λυτρόω, and the kindred words by which it is rendered by the LXX, and represented in the New Testament. The full idea of redemption is not a mere release, but a release obtained through the payment of a ransom. And as in the case of sin, sacrifice was the only covering or atonement, so also was sacrifice the only ransom. It was the same Divine Justice that regarded the sacrificial covering, that also received the sacrificial ransom. The element of Justice thus confers upon λυτρόω, I redeem, an appropriateness as a representation of כָּפַר, I cover or atone. We are "*not redeemed with corruptible things, as silver and gold. . . . . But with the precious blood of Christ, as of a lamb without blemish and without spot: Who verily was foreordained before the foundation of the world*" (1 Peter i. 18—20).

To sum up, the love of God provides a covering for sin, but His Justice demands that the covering should be by sacrifice.

---

[1] Genesis xxii. 8.

LECTURE XIII.

THE UNFOLDING OF SALVATION IN PROPHECY.

THIS subject is so vast that in a single Lecture I can hope to touch upon only a few of its main branches and those too, but lightly. I prefer however to do this, rather than pass it by altogether; for even a hint or two may be a help to wider and deeper researches.

That all the prophets gave witness to Christ is to the Apostles of the nature of an axiom (Acts x. 43). They never hesitate to appeal to the prophecies in support of the Gospel they preach. They claim to say "*none other things than those which the prophets and Moses did say should come*" (Acts xxvi. 27). They simply ask, as Paul asked the King in his defence, "*King Agrippa, believest thou the prophets?*" (Acts xxvi. 27.) To any one who admitted the Divine authority of the prophets they had no difficulty in preaching, as Philip did to the Eunuch, Christ from the prophetic page. For this task the Apostles were specially fitted by our Saviour's instruction, and fully enlightened by the help of the Holy Ghost. In that last solemn interview with our Lord before His ascension, it is said in reference to this very point, "*Then opened He their understanding, that they might understand the Scriptures*" (Luke xxiv. 45). And, as if to leave no doubt on our mind as to what was here intended by "the Scriptures," our Lord Himself gives the most minute of all the enumerations of the divisions of the Old Testament, that is anywhere to be found in the New. He gives the three recognized divisions which have come down to our own day: "*These are the words which I spake unto you while I was yet with you, that all things must be fulfilled, which were written in the Law of Moses, and in the prophets, and in the Psalms, concerning Me*" (Luke xxiv. 44). By thus specifying these three sections of the Old Testament Canon our Lord by implication claims each book of the Canon as part, after its kind and in its degree, of the great prophetic revelation of Himself. Viewed in this way, "the entire Old Testament," as De Wette has observed, "is one great prediction, one great type of Him who should come and is come."

That to the apprehension of the Apostles the Old Testament was teeming with allusions to Christ and His Salvation, their writings very fully shew. Take as an example the use made, in the Epistle to the Galatians, of the history of Isaac and Ishmael, and the references in that same passage to Sinai and Zion. I adduce an example of this sort rather than one of the many well-known quotations of verbal prophecies, and for this reason, the verbal prophecies are more obvious, and few could miss their bearing on Christ, but to the minds of those specially illuminated men Christ appeared in Scripture where there was no verbal mention whatever made of Him.

The less elaborate and more incidental references in these Epistles prove the same thing. In the Old Testament history of Moses' flight from Egypt we read nothing of "*the reproach of Christ*"; but in Heb. xi. 26 we read that he esteemed "*the reproach of Christ greater riches than the treasures in Egypt.*" In reading the account of the many occasions on which Israel provoked God in the desert, there is no mention made of a single one of these being directed against the Messiah, yet the Apostle exhorts the Corinthians, "*Neither let us tempt Christ, as some of them also tempted*" (1 Cor. x. 9). I would not pay so much heed to this passage, if it stood alone. But it comes in close connection with that remarkable description of the thirsty Israelites drinking from the smitten rock: "*They did all drink the same spiritual drink: for they drank of that Spiritual Rock that followed them; and that Rock was Christ*" (1. Cor. x. 4). To men who could thus so freely use places, personal history, and national events, in a Messianic sense, the Scriptures must have appeared as one vast and varied panorama of Divine Salvation.

I make these observations fully conscious of the wild extravagance in which some have indulged, in spiritualizing Scripture. But as I am speaking as unto wise men, judge ye what I say. No man of well-balanced mind will venture to rival the Apostles in this matter until he has first obtained their training and power of vision. Destitute of that illumination, as many of us confessedly are, it may be often safe to use

THE UNFOLDING OF SALVATION IN PROPHECY. 153

many things out of the Old Testament by way of illustration, which we dare not hazard as interpretations. Perhaps too, in this humbler course, we shall not be very far away from the true genius of the more ancient Scriptures.

To resume : Within or alongside the general appeal made to the Old Testament as a whole, there is a special appeal made to the testimony of that prophetic line which began with Samuel, and ended with Malachi. Peter has this in view, when he says, " *Yea, and all the prophets from Samuel, and those that follow after, as many as have spoken, have likewise foretold of these days*" (Acts iii. 24). Samuel instituted the schools of the prophets, which besides exerting such a vast influence upon contemporaneous history, formed the link between the giving of the Law and the preaching of the Gospel. This prophetic race of men, nurtured within the bosom of the Mosaic dispensation, pointed in their ministry to a dispensation of greater glory, and to a Deliverer greater than Moses. They developed the seeds of truth already sown in venerable promises, and showed what precious fruit they would one day bear. Their rise makes an epoch in the preparation for the Saviour. From that period we can trace a growing dissatisfaction with mere ceremonial religion. They see depths and wonders in the Divine law not to be expressed by ritual, not to be realized by burning victims or fragrant incense. They grow more and more convinced " *that Lebanon is not sufficient to burn, nor the beast thereof sufficient for a burnt offering*" (Isa. xl. 16) to Him before whom "*all nations . . . . . are as nothing; and they are counted to Him less than nothing and vanity*" (verse 17). They learn to sing "*Sacrifice and offering* Thou didst not desire," and then to echo the glad cry, "*Lo, I come, in the volume of the book it is written of me*" (Ps. xl. 6, 7). Thus Christ, the Beloved, the Church then might sing "*standeth behind our wall; He looketh forth at the windows, showing Himself through the lattice*" (Cant. ii. 9). The husk was visibly breaking, and the grain appearing. The spiritual grows up amid the carnal ; the very law is a Schoolmaster to bring us to Christ.

Having thus called attention to the wider and more definite prophecies in which Salvation is unfolded, I wish now to point out three things :—

(I.) The growth of variety in the course of Prophecy.

(II.) The growth of the distinct personality of the Saviour.

(III.) The growth of particulars of His life and death.

(I.) *The growth of variety in the predictions of Salvation.*

This variety ought to be taken as a matter of course where many men in different ages handled the theme. But it is not always so taken, and I therefore call attention to it. The prophecy of Salvation growing up throughout different ages, and in connection with different kinds of events, bears the impress both of these as well as of the men by whom it was delivered. The same in substance in all, it is yet by all fashioned into a manifold diversity. As the vine, though essentially the same in every land, yet changes in some aspects, by changing soils and suns and seasons. So the prophecies of Christ bear some tincture and flavour of the times and circumstances in which they spring up. This we can admit without in the least compromising their entire Divine inspiration.

Moses in his last charges to Israel described Christ as a Prophet resembling, yet greater than himself: "*The Lord, thy God, will raise up unto thee a Prophet from the midst of thee, of thy brethren, like unto me*" (Deut. xviii. 15, etc.). With singular appropriateness Balaam beholds Christ coming as the "*Star out of Jacob, and as a Sceptre out of Israel*" (Numb. xxiv. 17). In the midst of the convulsions that shook the kingdom in the days of Ahaz, occasion is taken to give that remarkable prophetic description: "*Therefore the Lord himself shall give you a sign; Behold a Virgin shall conceive and bear a Son, and shall call His name Immanuel*" (Isa. vii. 14, cf. ix.). At the building of the second temple, and in reply to the feeling of disappointment that weighed down the people, the message comes, "*The glory of this latter house shall be greater than the former, saith the Lord of hosts.*" And why? "*The Desire of all nations shall come, and I will fill this house with glory, saith the Lord of hosts*" (Hagg. ii. 9 and 7). From musing on the reign of Solomon, his peaceful son, David, sings, in Psalm lxxii., of the Prince of peace. Every stanza of that sublime poem confesses a Greater than Solomon is here. And if Psalm xlv. be a marriage ode, yet the voice has a higher tone than the human, Divinity shines out clearly in "*Him who is fairer than the children of men*" (verse 2). Contrasting the "good matter" of this Psalm with other equally inspired songs, we gather that the prophecies grew upon the great sorrows as well as upon the great joys of the Psalmist. He knew both joy of the brightest and sorrow of the darkest kind. Thus was he furnished forth to sing, "*My God! My God! why hast Thou forsaken me?*"[1] and

---
[1] Psalm xxii. 1.

"*Therefore God thy God, hath anointed Thee with the oil of gladness above thy fellows*" (Ps. xlv. 7).

This correspondence of prophecy with passing circumstances is common, but it is not invariable. The prophecies are often presented in marked contrast and sharp antithesis. An element is often present in the prophecy which no circumstances, or at least no known circumstances whatever, could suggest, and herein we see the independence and absolute originality of Divine teaching. Isaiah, the courtly prophet, fitly tells of the Conqueror "*glorious in His apparel;*"[1] but what could have suggested to him the mournful portraiture of the Saviour's sorrow and death? Zechariah, as the prophet of the nation's restoration, gives scope to his patriotism as he sings "*Rejoice greatly, O daughter of Zion; shout, O daughter of Jerusalem: behold, thy King cometh unto thee*" (Zech. ix. 9). But whence could he have gathered the message "*Awake, O Sword, against my Shepherd, and against the man that is my fellow*"? (Zech. xiii. 7.) In these places it is the element of suffering that cannot be traced to natural suggestions; and hence it stands out as a proof of definite and absolute inspiration; a something so unique that it must come from above.

In other passages it is not the humiliation, but the transcendent glory, a glory too great for any creature, that gives the original colouring to the prediction and goes beyond the stretch of earthly or temporal suggestion. Thus the "Child born" is called the "*Mighty God*" (Isa. ix. 6). In Malachi, He who is called the "*Messenger of the Covenant*" (iii. 1) is also immediately before described as "*the Lord whom ye seek,*" and as coming "*to His temple.*" He who is David's Son is also "David's Lord."

Thus while we observe the prophecies of the Messiah wear the hues and bear the individual touch of the times and circumstances in which they were delivered; yet there is in them another Element that submits not to be so modified, but stands out in independent and unalterable shape. This Element is to the others surrounding it, what the Rhone is to the Lake of Geneva. Descending from the eternal snows into the lake, the river keeps on its individual course through the deep blue waters without losing in them its native distinctness. And so it is with the prophecies concerning the Christ of God. Many of them are like the waters of the lake that float around and over the margin of the national and even individual life; but others are like the strong and

---

[1] Isaiah lxiii. 1.

deep current of the River, and unmistakably descend from the Eternal Hills. They carry on their surface, as well as in their substance, the proofs of their Divine origin.

(II.) *The growth in distinctness of the prophecies concerning the personality of the Saviour.*

When I speak of prophecy pointing with ever-increasing distinctness to a personal Saviour, I do not forget those most ancient prophecies which represent His personality with a plainness, if not with a vividness, equal to that of the most recent. In the mother-prophecy of all, "*The seed of the woman shall bruise the head of the serpent*" (Gen. iii. 15), it is plain Salvation is to come by a person. In the promise given to Abraham, that "*in thy seed shall all the nations of the earth be blessed*" (Gen. xxii. 18), the personality is clear. To this class belong several other predictions, most notably distinct in their allusion to a personal Saviour. What I mean is, that if you will take up the writings of the prophets who are in the line of succession from Samuel to Malachi, whose messages were addressed to the people of Israel, whose ministry bore primarily upon the chequered history of that people—who consequently had to predict several acts of the deliverance, and tell of several successive deliverers—you will find that the lines of their predictions gradually converge, and meet in One Redeemer, who in His own person is to redeem Israel from all his troubles. As His presence becomes clearer and clearer in the vision, the vision widens and ceases to be local and national. He is seen to be the light of the nations, as well as the Glory of Israel: to be for Salvation unto the ends of the earth.

In the uprising of these prophecies it is most noticeable how the house of David becomes the point around which gather the fairest expectations. David, himself endowed with an unusual light of the Spirit, expresses the great hope with a minute clearness unsurpassed by any later seers. Indeed, it would seem that, after his days, dimness, for a time, instead of increased brightness, gathered around the theme. Taking the very oldest of the prophets, we find in Joel, a hope of "*a deliverance*" (Joel ii. 32), but not a deliverer; spiritual salvation, but no mention made of Him by whom the Spirit was to be gained. Amos, too (ix. 11, 12), merely sees the house of David brought to new honour; while Hosea (chapter iii. 4, 5) foretells the reunion of the separated tribes under a Davidic sceptre. But before the vision of Micah and Isaiah, a clearer light returns and increases, and what already in the

Assyrian period was unambiguously expressed, is soon in the Chaldean and Persian epochs inscribed with new traits. Especially do passages like Micah v. 1—4; Isaiah vii. 14—16; ix. 1—7; xi. 1—10;—the Messianic character of which is in our view incontestable—exhibit a preponderating importance. They put the Person or Kingdom of the Messiah before us in the light of the brightest glory, the suffering which is to precede that glory being by Isaiah, as well as by David, but gradually recognized. Only in the latter portions of Isaiah, in connection with the prospect of the redemption of the nation, is it declared that "the servant of the Lord," the genuine Israel, can but reach the appointed height through a dark abyss. As prophet, He is the Light of the Gentiles too; as Priest, He offers Himself voluntarily, and as an innocent Substitute for the sins of others; and thus He first attains the royal supremacy, and divides the spoil with the strong (Isa. liii. 12). Though all this may have found a commencement of its fulfilment in the heart of the people of Israel, the sketch is too concrete to be realized in any one less perfect than the suffering Christ. Only once do we find mention here of God's promise to David, though the highest Salvation is nowhere looked for, except from a King of the house of David. This continues the case, even in the time of the Babylonian exile; and striking is the certainty with which Jeremiah, in contrast with the apparent uncertainty of the Old Testament, predicts the glory of the new Dispensation. As it were out of the ruins of the destroyed Jerusalem, he sees the throne of David arising in glorious brightness, and sets forth at the same time all the spiritual splendour which the new Dispensation shall have above the Old. Ezekiel represents the Son of David under the beautiful images of a Cedar[1] and of a Shepherd,[2] and sees a stream of living water flowing out of the new temple.[3] Daniel stands as the world's prophet upon a height, whence in the stillness of the night he beholds how the image of earthly monarchy is broken before his eyes; and sees the Kingdom of heaven, symbolized under the form of a Son of Man, coming upon the clouds of heaven (Dan. vii. 13). He marks the time when the Messiah shall appear, and suffer and die. After the Exile the revived hopes of the returned captives are centred by Zechariah in the person of a Prince who should combine in Himself both the royal and priestly dignity (Zec. vi. 13). Is the second temple also less grand? Haggai predicts that its glory shall be greater than that of the first, by the coming of the "*Desire of*

---

[1] Ezek. xvii. 23.   [2] Ezek. xxxiv. 23.   [3] Ezek. xlvii. 1.

all nations" (ii. 7). Malachi sees Him as the Angel of God's Covenant, and at the same time proclaims the second Elias as His forerunner (Mal. iii. 1).

"Thus the course of the development of prophecy is fashioned, on the one hand, by the individuality of the prophets, and on the other, by the course of events, but at every turn the Person and work of the Messiah present themselves in a superhuman light before our eyes." ' Each prophet towers above his predecessor : all together point to the one who is the end (the final aim) of Law and Prophecy." "If the idea of the Messiah becomes ever more spiritual and universal, it becomes too, ever more Divine." "The mystery of the Incarnation rises resplendent in single points of prophecy, though the Old Testament consciousness of belief is not capable of retaining this ray" *(Delitzsch).*

(III.) *The Growth of particulars of the Saviour's life and death.*

Prophecy descends from sketching in broad outline the hopes of the Coming One, and minutely draws the most precise particulars. The multitude of these particulars is as remarkable as their variety. Among them we find marked the race from which He was to spring—from the seed of Abraham ; the tribe—from the lion-like tribe of Judah ; the family—the royal house of David ; the condition of His mother,— "*Behold a Virgin shall conceive and bear a Son, and shall call His name Immanuel*" (Isa. vii. 14). The place of His birth is set down with special care, the province and the town,—Bethlehem Ephratah, a little place among the thousands of Judah (Mic. v. 2). The troubles of His infant days are on the prophetic page, His flight to Egypt, and His return to His native land (Hos. xi. 1). Nazareth was the city where His youth was to be spent, and Galilee of the Gentiles where the dayspring of His ministry was first to gladden the people (Isa. ix. 1, 2). With what living colours is the character of that ministry itself drawn ! The Saviour's might in word and deed ; His grace and truth ; "His sharp arrows" piercing the heart of His enemies ; His gentleness to the suffering, coming down as rain upon the mown grass. Prison doors and captive chains give way before Him ; nevertheless, "*He shall not cry, nor lift up, nor cause His voice to be heard in the street. A bruised reed shall He not break, and the smoking flax shall He not quench : He shall bring forth judgment unto truth*" (Isa. xlii. 2, 3). The fortunes too, and the fruits of that ministry are written at large over all the prophetic page. The very character and conduct of his chosen followers and

THE UNFOLDING OF SALVATION IN PROPHECY. 159

friends are anticipated. At the last great crisis, when the Chief Shepherd is smitten, they all forsake Him and flee (cf. Zech. xiii. 7, Mark xiv. 27 and 50). The treachery of the traitor is singled out (cf. Ps. xli. 9, and John xiii. 18). He that eats bread with the Christ lifts up his heel against Him. The price that satisfies his avarice is noted down, and the ultimate use to which the accursed thirty pieces of silver are put (Zech. xi. 12, 13; cf. Matt. xxvii. 3—8). But it is when the Son of God enters within the inner and ever-darkening circle of His deeper sorrows that the Spirit of prophecy unveils His manifold light and brings before the wondering mind the never-failing love that bears the ever-varying scorn and suffering of that long agony.

Daniel tells the time when the Messiah shall be cut off (Dan. ix. 24—26). Isaiah foreshadows the mock trial which gave a semblance of justice to His condemnation (Isa. liii. 8), and draws the scenes of Calvary as if he had been one of those who sat down and watched Him there. The harp of the sweet singer of Israel mournfully resounds with the woes of the Cross, as if no longer touched by David's fingers, but thrilled by the sight, and vibrating to the deep heart throbs of the dying Son of God. Here we learn of His desertion by the Father (Ps. xxii. 1), of the piercing of His hands and feet (verse 16), of the division of His raiment, and the very method of that division (verse 18), the brutality and scorn of the multitudes of onlookers (verses 6, 7, 12, 13). We are told of His thirst, and the vinegar with which it was assuaged (Ps. lxix. 21), of His dying cry (Ps. xxii. 1), and of that which immediately broke the golden bowl of His life—"*Reproach hath broken my heart*" (Ps. lxix. 20). After the expiring cry, the hand of prophecy keeps guard, as it were, over the dead body. It prevents a bone of His from being broken; but points the soldier's spear to the broken heart (John xix. 36, 37; cf. Exod. xii. 46; Ps. xxxiv. 20; Ps. xxii. 16, 17; Zech. xii. 10). We see it describe with strange accuracy the manner of the burial, how He, who was with the poor in His death, yet rests in the virgin tomb of the rich man, Joseph of Arimathea.[1] It is the trump of prophecy that sounds the first note of the Resurrection, the first note of the world's Jubilee from death's long captivity: "*Thou wilt not leave my soul in hell; neither wilt Thou suffer Thine Holy One to see corruption. Thou wilt shew me the path of life; in Thy presence is fulness of joy; at Thy right hand there are pleasures for evermore*" (Ps. xvi. 10, 11).

---

[1] Isa. liii. 9. Cf. Matt. xxvii. 57—60.

I rely upon particulars of these, and all similar prophecies, as definitely pointing to Christ, and having their fulfilment in Him. I rely also upon the principle of interpretation which underlies the application of such predictions to the Saviour. Whatever may be urged against this principle, and by whomsoever objections may be brought, it has this in its favour, that it is a principle sanctioned by the practice of our Lord and His apostles. To all inducements to what may be a more excellent way, I reply, if there be an error here, I prefer to err with Christ, to go astray with Him who could unchallenged say, I *am the Truth, I am the Way* (John xiv. 6).

What is this principle? It were a poor account of it to say that it allowed a plurality of meanings in the prophetic words, and claimed one out of the many possible as applicable to Christ. It were still further from the mark to represent Christ's method as the mere accommodation of Scripture. Christ required not that man should dexterously apply the Scriptures, but humbly receive their testimony. He taught not His disciples to accommodate prophecy, but "*He opened their understanding, that they might understand the Scriptures*" (Luke xxiv. 45).

Testimony concerning any person can only relate to that person; it may in substance possibly be true of others, but as testimony it can only bear on that one. And it is in the nature of testimony that these prophecies of Christ, relate to Christ. They may, or may not, contain what is in substance true of others; but as testimony, as evidence, they relate solely to Him. "*Ye search the Scriptures . . . . . and they are they which bear witness of Me*" (John v. 39). "*To Him gave all the prophets witness*" (Acts x. 43).

The application of these prophecies to Christ I therefore regard as of the nature of the application of testimony to the person to whom it properly refers. It is not Christ among many; it is Christ against all.

As to the way in which this application of Scripture was made, the second passage quoted above leaves us in no doubt. It was by virtue of "understanding," of intelligently perceiving the sense and reference of the prophecies that rendered their application to the Christ not only possible, but also necessary. The Spirit of Christ which was in the prophets, was that very Spirit who enlightened the Apostle's understanding, and so Apostle and prophet, though ages intervened, saw eye to eye, concerning the things of Christ. There was thus in this their treatment of the Scriptures no diverting of their original meaning, but

THE UNFOLDING OF SALVATION IN PROPHECY. 161

a clear perception of it: no cunning accommodation, but an honest application — the rendering unto Christ of what already from of old bore his indelible mark and superscription.

In reply to this statement of the case, it may be said, it is only a removal of the difficulty concerning some of the Scriptures from the New Testament to the Old, from Christ and His Apostles to the ancient prophets themselves. I grant it; and in this there is a decided advantage. It traces the difficulty up to its primary source, and dealing with it there, we shall have the help of all its native attendant circumstances.

Whatever difficulties present themselves, they may be put into two classes. First, there are passages applied to Christ which seem taken clear away from their context. Secondly, there are passages regarded as prophetic, which do not appear truly so.

(1) With regard to those passages whose context does not bear on Christ, I have this to say, that this is the very peculiarity we ought to expect. The prophets had to speak of the Coming One in the midst of great national commotions and heart-stirring events. The word of hope would, therefore, often come with suddenness and abruptness, as the dying Jacob's, in the midst of blessing his children,[1] or Isaiah's, while speaking of the calamities of the days of Ahaz (Isa. vii., ix., xi.). When the events were themselves the subject of prophecy, the method of procedure was not altered, so far as the prophecy of the Christ was concerned. That only transferred to the future the relations that existed with regard to what was present. The prophets seemed to seize the events, and insert into them the graft of the Messianic hope : henceforth the events have the relation to the hope of Christ, that the wild stem has to the cultivated and good graft. The two parts are still distinct, the old stem and the new graft, and are very easily distinguishable. Weighing this relation well, instead of being amazed at prophecies of Christ occurring in out-of-the-way places, and in connection with events alien and foreign to them, being rightly prepared, we shall find no difficulty in separating the good graft borne on the wild stem. We shall also be prepared for an amount of enigmatical obscurity, arising from local and temporal surroundings, and darkening the prophecies themselves. Such surroundings we shall not allow ourselves to regard as unusual and unexpected, but on the contrary, as much to be expected, and as natural in the combination, as the quartz with the gold it contains.

---

[1] Gen. xlix. 10.

The rare discovery is the gold without the rock, in pure and unalloyed bulk. And the rare phenomenon in prophecy is when it separates itself, and stands out clear from the Jewish, the earthly and temporal circumstances in which it is wont to be enveloped.

(2) The second difficulty is in connection with those passages adduced as prophetic, which do not appear to have been originally so. Of these, the words, "Not a bone of Him shall be broken" (Exod. xii. 46), form a famous example. They originally occur in the description of the rites to be observed in preparing the paschal lamb. John regards them as relating to Christ, and as having been fulfilled when the Roman soldiers after having broken the legs of the dying malefactors on the cross, came to our Lord and finding Him already dead, refrained from doing so to Him (John xix. 33-36). To justify this application, and the application of all such Scriptures to our Lord, we have only to bear in mind that these words contain the law of a typical ritual, the ritual of the Paschal Lamb. That the Paschal Lamb, prefigured the Lamb of God who taketh away the sins of the world, needs no proof or argument. This being beyond all controversy, and as every type from its very nature contains a prophecy, the type being prophetic of the Antitype,—the justification of John's application of the words to our Lord is complete.

If to the recognition of the prophetic element in the types, we add the recognition of the typical element in the prophecies, every vestige of difficulty will vanish. Such types are taken from a larger field than the Ceremonial of the Tabernacle, or the worship of the Temple. Innumerable events, places, and persons are thus sanctified to a meaning and a purpose in connection with Christ and His Kingdom of Salvation, infinitely higher than any they could literally have reached. The Smitten Rock points to the smitten Christ,[1] Canaan to the rest that remaineth for the Sons of God,[2] Zion to the Zion which is above, and is the Mother of us all.[3] Taught by the Apostle in the last of these examples how to perceive the blending of the typical with the prophetic, we are prepared for the way in which Ezekiel describes the reign of Christ under the royal name of David (Ezek. xxxiv. 23; xxxvii. 24), and the Kingdom of Christ under the vast symbol of the Temple (chap. xli., etc.). Even John the Baptist, Christ's forerunner, was "*Elias, who was for to come*" (Matt. xi. 14).

Generally when the prophet's theme is the more spiritual, more

---

[1] 1 Cor. x. 4.   [2] Heb. iv. 9.   [3] Gal. iv. 26.

abiding and wider aspects of Christ's Salvation, he is shut up to the use of this typical form of description, if he would at all be understood by his contemporaries. And let it be remembered he had to minister Christ to them as well as to us. While yet in the Old Kingdom, he had to describe the New. While in the old world, he had in thought and in idea to construct, and create the New. The materials at his disposal had therefore to be taken from the Old, though fashioned to finer issues. If they are sometimes obscure, it was not intended they should always be clear. It they fail at times to equal with their words the Eternal Verities of which they speak, need we wonder? The wonder would be if they were always clear, if they always reached the height that we perceive to belong to their great argument. They themselves ofttimes felt they were speaking of what eye had not seen, of what ear had not heard, and of what had not entered into the heart of man (1 Cor. ii. 9; Isa. lxiv. 4).

Nevertheless our Lord and His inspired Apostles hesitate not to identify some of their most obscure predictions. And following the spirit of so perfect an example we shall enter upon the study of the Old Testament as David entered into the Tabernacle of old, with eye and ear expectant to behold the beauty of the Lord, and to hear where every one speaks of His glory. So shall Christ our Saviour be seen, and His voice heard at every turn of revelation.

LECTURE XIV.

THE SAVIOUR.

His Person.

In treating of the Person of Christ, no exact bounds have been adhered to by Theologians. Some, as Dr. Pye Smith in his famous treatise of *Scripture Testimony to the Messiah,* have used the phrase in a very wide sense, and included therein the whole of the Mediatorial capacities and dignities of the Son of God. Others have been content to discuss only the constituent elements of His person, adding as a supplement, the sinlessness of His character. A third class have considered it necessary to give in this connection a sketch of His life and work. A fourth, and with these I agree, have narrowed the enquiry to the different natures, and their combination in the Christ of God.

Whatever may be the range given to the subject, the subject itself is the vital centre of Christianity. The religion of Christ lives and moves and has its being in Christ. The personality of Christ is more closely interwoven with the Gospel, and more essential to its influence and propagation, than the founder of any system of philosophy or religion is to the system that bears his name. The philosophy of Plato is accepted or discarded on its own merits, independently of Plato. The scientific views of Newton bear sway, not because of what Newton was, but because they are, in the main, a truthful interpretation of nature. In the same way, the teachings of Mohammed hold their ground with Moslems, despite the shortcomings of Mohammed. The reason is obvious; none of them ever claimed to be, as Christ did, both text and interpreter. All these were expositors, and their two grand themes were,—nature for the philosopher, and God for the founder of religion. What, therefore, is essential to the validity of these systems is, not the founders themselves, but nature on the one hand, and God on the other.

Now this essential place of theme, as well as Expositor, is Christ's position in the Gospel. Our estimate of Christ, will therefore, in brief, be our standard by which to measure all that Christ did, or said, or suffered, or in other words, our measure of the Gospel, for these constitute the Gospel. We cannot assign to the Gospel a light, a life, an authority, not previously in Christ. Its measure of fitness and sympathy for humanity will be in proportion to the reality and elevation of His humanity. Its measure of binding force on the conscience will be in proportion to the Divine nature in Him. Its promise and power of drawing together into one, man, the transgressor, and God, the Holy Lawgiver, will find their measure and their type in the union of the Divine and the human in His own Person.

In discussing the Person of the Saviour, we are discussing Salvation. On this account it behoves us to keep as closely as possible to Scripture testimony, noting the order as well as the nature and proportion of that testimony. The whole doctrine may be summed up in the three brief propositions: (1) *That Christ is truly God:* (2) *That He is truly man:* (3) *That He unites these two natures in one personality.*

Before adducing the evidence of Scripture on each of these propositions, it may help us to view this great matter aright to observe how Scripture introduces the Christ to our knowledge. In the order and method of the Evangelists there is instruction, no less than in their definitions and facts. Their method and order give us their view-point of the natures and powers, and their relations to one another in the Christ. In fact, we may glean thence their ideas as to the *genesis* of His person. Before delineating any of His powers, Scripture directs a light from another sphere, a light of Divinity upon Him. Before we see Him, we see the Heavens opened. In Luke, the angel announces to the Virgin Mother the descent of Supreme Deity: "*The Holy Ghost shall come upon thee, and the power of the Highest shall overshadow thee: therefore also that Holy thing which shall be born of thee shall be called the Son of God*" (Luke i. 35).

In John, wider vistas, if that were possible, are opened to view. Before declaring "*the Word was made flesh, and dwelt among us,*"[1] the Evangelist traces the history of His eternal existence: "*In the beginning was the Word, and the Word was with God, and the Word was God*" (John. i. 1). Then he describes the outgoings of His creative energy: then he portrays the radiance of His life, which is the light of men.

---

[1] John. i. 14.

Aroused by these successive stages of advance, from the inmost recesses of the ineffable glory of the Godhead along the path of creative wonders, the mind is not only prepared, but would suffer unspeakable disappointment—deeming it but a lame and impotent conclusion—if, when He appeared as a man, we did not behold His Glory—"*the glory as of the Only-begotten of the Father, full of grace and truth*" (John i. 14). With this Divine halo surrounding Him, ever inseparable from His person, but distinguishing and separating Him from all other men, we must always contemplate His humanity itself. This was peculiar to Himself alone, though in all other respects, sin alone excepted, He shared in common with other men. He was both universal and unique.

In arranging the evidences from Scripture on His divinity and humanity, I shall endeavour to follow this order: first, to give the definitions and descriptions; and secondly, those passages which record the *facts*, which may be regarded as generalized in the definitions.

(I.) In proof of the first proposition, that *Christ is truly man*, we find Him called in express terms, "*the man Christ Jesus*" (1 Tim. ii. 5): "*He was made of a woman*" (Gal. iv. 4): "*He was made of the seed of David according to the flesh*" (Rom. i. 3): "*The Word was made flesh*" (John i. 14).

This last statement is very significant, as showing that it was not in appearance, as the Docetæ were then beginning to teach, but in reality that the Son of God became man. "Flesh" ($\sigma\grave{\alpha}\rho\xi$) is in some respects the most universal of all terms applied to our nature in Scripture. It stands, it is true, for our nature in its frailty and mortality, and thus it shows the condescension of the Logos. But it is more comprehensive than body ($\sigma\hat{\omega}\mu\alpha$), which is the antithesis of soul and spirit ($\psi\upsilon\chi\grave{\eta}$ $\kappa\alpha\grave{\iota}$ $\pi\nu\epsilon\hat{\upsilon}\mu\alpha$), and in its wider sense it includes both, and is the visible representation of the whole man. The Son of God, therefore, while dwelling among us, wore something more than a mask of humanity, something more than a partial humanity. "*He became flesh*," and therefore a real, a complete, and a sympathizing suffering man.

These definitions are supported by a vast array of facts. "*He increased in stature*" (Luke ii. 52). Toil brought fatigue to Him as to others, "*being wearied He sat thus on the well*" (John iv. 6). Want of food made Him hungry, and the heat and pain made Him thirsty. His constant companions had trial of Him by the senses of sight, touch and hearing : " *That which we have heard, which we have seen with our eyes, which we have looked upon, and our hands have handled of the Word of life,*" says the Apostle (1 John i. 1). Even after His resurrection He challenged the test of the senses, "*Behold My hands and My feet. . . . Handle Me, and see; for a spirit hath not flesh and bones, as ye see Me have*" (Luke xxiv. 39). In the closing scene, fact upon fact is given: the soldiers found a real body to scourge, a real head to crown, real hands and feet to nail to the cross, and a real side to pierce with the spear. His death and burial give the last proofs of His mortality.

Connected with these bodily sensations was a soul capable of being the seat of all human emotions: "*In that hour Jesus rejoiced*" (Luke x. 21). When He looked upon the young ruler He loved him. "*Jesus loved Martha, and her sister, and Lazarus*" (John xi. 5). At the grave of His friend, and over the city of His foes, He wept, and groaned, and lamented. In the prospect of His own decease, He confessed and hid not His feelings from His friends, " *Now is my soul troubled*" (John xii. 27).

His intellectual powers are as truly human as His emotional. "*He increased in wisdom*" (Luke ii. 52), and the word implies advancement in the face of difficulty. He marvelled at the faith of the Roman Centurion, and at the unbelief of His own townsmen.

We have seen He acknowledged the claims of friendship; and He felt Himself equally bound by the ties of kindred. He was subject unto His parents. He bore Himself obediently towards all the law of righteousness, and worshipfully in all the Divine ordinances of religion. He attended Divine service, both at the village synagogue and at the Temple of Jerusalem. He kept the annual feasts, and was baptized of John. We have already seen how He rejoiced in spirit, and the joy of that occasion was the reverent joy of one who worships the Father in spirit and in truth. With a sense of dependence, He offers His gratitude to the Father for His goodness, His power and sovereignty. He was a reader of the Scriptures, and relied on both their word and spirit. He cultivated social piety, and gave thanks before meat. He cultivated private prayerfulness. In the desert, on the mountain top, He spent whole nights alone with God. In His supplications there was a true exercise of faith, as is evident from His open request to be heard at the raising of Lazarus; from His agony in the Garden; from His cry on the Cross. His last words were the words of one who knew whom He had believed, "*Father, into Thy hands I commend My Spirit*" (Luke xxiii. 46).

Thus, however we survey the essential attributes of humanity, our Lord made good the ancient boast of the heathen, I am a man and nothing pertaining to man is foreign to me.

(II.) Our second proposition is *that Christ is truly God.* The Scriptures show that there is in Christ a nature superior to the human; that that superior nature is pre-existent to the human; that that pre-existent nature is Divine; that that Divine nature is the Deity of the Son of God, the Second Person in the Trinity; and finally, that as the Son, He is co-equal with the Father.

Those passages that establish the doctrine, that the Son is equal with the Father in Essential Deity, also go to establish the truth, that it was the Son that was made Flesh. It is this Second Person that descends, in order that He may ascend far above all heavens. Accordingly the title, "Son of God," given to Christ designates something more than character, which is its use when believers are called Sons of God. It pertains to something higher than office, on which account rulers in the Old Testament are termed Sons of God. When Moses, the very highest of them all is contrasted with Christ, the words are, "*Moses as a servant . . . But Christ as a Son over His own house*" (Heb. iii. 5, 6). The title reaches beyond His miraculous birth, as Adam, on account of his immediate creation by the hands of God, was called the Son of God. It carries us back to an existence prior to His incarnation, as it is said, "*When He bringeth in the First-begotten into the world*" (Heb. i. 6). As the Son, He is sent from the Father into the World (John iii. 17; x. 36). These same passages prove that it was not the Father who became incarnate under the name of the Son, but the Son who was in the beginning as the Word, and therefore Eternal; who was with God, and therefore distinct in personality; who was God, and therefore in essence equal with the Father. For this reason He is called, "*Emmanuel . . . . God with us*" (Matt. i. 23).

(1.) Looking now into the five heads under which we have arranged this proposition, we will begin with the first, *that there is in Christ a nature superior to the human.*

Most truly human as we have seen Christ was, His humanity cannot account for all that He suffered and did. The mark He has left on history is broader and deeper than any mere man could have left. What the Baptist, than whom no greater arose among men, says of Him, may be echoed of all Earth's great ones, "*One mightier than I cometh, the latchet of whose shoes I am not worthy to unloose*" (Luke iii. 16). As the Revealer of God, He is placed in a rank superior to all human messengers (Heb. i. 1, 2). In the parable of the Vineyard, He is at once the Messenger, the Son and the Heir of the Owner thereof (Mark xii. 1—9).

He claims legislative authority equal to that which enjoined the Mosaic code (Matt. v. 22, 28, 32, 34, 39, 44). He is styled "*the Holy One of God*" (Luke iv. 34), and simply "*the Holy One*" (Acts ii. 27; iii. 14; Rev. iii. 7). He is "*One with the Father*" (John x. 30, 33, 38), in a oneness of power which implies a oneness of nature. The Kingly dignity of Matthew xxv. 34 is peculiar to Himself alone: "*He is the Son, and the Lord*"; "*the Root and the Offspring of David*" (Matt. xxii. 42—45; Rev. xxii. 16). He is called "*the Truth, the Way, the Life*" (John xiv. 6). He is "*the Light of Life*," "*the Light of the World*" (John i. 4, 5; viii. 12; xii. 46). He bestows all spiritual life, true holiness and happiness (Gal. ii. 20; Col. iii. 4; Phil. i. 21). He is the Giver of all Divine and saving knowledge (Luke xxiv. 45). He is "*the Resurrection and the Life*" (John xi. 25); and the only sure hope of the resurrection of the body is in Him (1 Cor. xv. 12—23).

He is "*the Image of God*"—"*of the invisible God*"; "*the Brightness of His glory*"; "*the express Image of His Person*"; "*He is in the form of God*" (2 Cor. iv. 4; Col. i. 15; Heb. i. 3; Phil. ii. 5, 8). He is the First-born of the whole creation (Col. i. 17), "*the Prince* (ἀρχηγός) *and Captain of Salvation*" (Acts iii. 15; Heb. ii. 10). He wrought miracles by virtue of His own power; He exercised dominion over evil spirits; He claims rule over the holy angels (Matt. xiii. 41; xvi. 27; xxv. 31; 1 Peter iii. 22): and it is expressly said, "*Let all the angels of God worship Him*" (Heb. i. 6).

(2.) In the second place, *this superior nature is pre-existent to the human.* In John xvii., Christ speaks of the glory He had with the Father before the world was. In John v. 17—27, He speaks of being commissioned and sent into the world by the Father, and yet as possessing a self-existent, internal, and independent principle of *life*, the same as that of the Father. The passage, John vi. 33—42, refers to a personal coming; and to the same effect is Romans viii. 3: "*God sending His own Son in the likeness of sinful flesh.*" When He came unto the world, He came not to a strange place, but to His own property. "*He was in the world, and the world was made by Him. . . . . All things were made by Him; and without Him was not anything made that was made*" (John. i. 3, 10). He descended before He ascended (Eph. iv. 9). He was rich in a former state, before He became poor as a man (2 Cor. viii. 9).

(3.) Again, *this pre-existent nature is also Divine.* The above-mentioned dignities raise Christ not only above humanity, but also above every creature. He not only stands nearest the Throne of Deity, but He is the Lord of the Throne. He is described as "*the Lord from heaven*" (1 Cor. xv. 47); "*the Lord of all*" (Acts x. 36; Rom. x. 12); "*the Lord both of the dead and living*" (Rom. xiv. 9); "*the Lord of Glory*" (1 Cor. ii. 8). He is called "*the Alpha and the Omega,*" "*the First and the Last,*" "*the Beginning and the End*" (Rev. i. 17; xxi. 6). Even the doubting Thomas addresses Him as "*My Lord and my God*" (John xx. 28). John affirms, "*He is the true God and Eternal Life*" (1 John v. 20).

Both the Psalmist and the Apostle exclaim, "*Thy throne, O God, is for ever and ever*" (Ps. xlv. 6, 7; Heb. i. 8). Seeing, too, that Κύριος is the Greek equivalent of Jehovah, there is let in thereby a wide stream of evidence from the Old Testament in favour of His Divinity. Jehovah is the ineffable, the incommunicable name of God, and by this name Christ is continually described. As an example, Isaiah xl. 11 may be taken, where the prophet's name for Him who "*shall feed His flock like a shepherd, and gather the lambs with His arm and carry them in His bosom*" is the *Lord Jehovah*. This combination of title with work is similar to what we find in Titus ii. 13, where He is called "*the great God and our Saviour Jesus Christ.*"

In fact, there is no title, no dignity, no perfection, no attribute, no work, no homage, ascribed to Supreme Deity, but is also ascribed to Christ. The proof arising from these Scriptures is peculiarly cogent, for every attribute peculiar to Deity supposes the corresponding nature. He could not be omnipotent, and at the same time less than Divine as to the same nature. Nothing but the Infinite could be omnipotent. This, too, applies to all the other perfections. Were only one of them ascribed to Him, it would prove His Divinity; but seeing every one in detail is said to be His, the argument is cumulative and irresistible. God can be no more essential than Christ has been and is to the Church in all generations.

Apart from the substance of what the sacred writers say of the Deity of Christ, their manner might be taken as a separate argument. They appear so pervaded with a sense of His Deity, that they attribute to Him everything that is properly Divine with the most perfect ease. They never hesitate or falter, as if their phrases could go too far, and overleap the bounds of His rightful glories. This freedom of utterance about His Deity, is conspicuous on many occasions when His humanity, even in its weakness, is brought into prominence. Yet they never betray a sense of incongruity, of uttering what is self-contradictory or paradoxical. They speak as men who have lived in the very presence of the harmonious action of the different natures, and evermore bore the impression of the fact of their reality, their distinction and their union. Herein the language of the New Testatment exhibits the same characters as that of the Old. Writers in both speak of what they saw; the prophets saw His glory in vision, the apostles in fact. But in the vision and in the fact, there was the same manifestation of Supreme Deity incarnate in human nature, the infinite in the finite.

The perfect agreement, too, of all parts of Scripture in this kind of representation, leaves no foothold for doubt. It is an agreement, in the midst of endless variety. It is an agreement too, among men who have all been, without exception, nurtured in the fundamental truth that *God is One;* and yet in the Scriptures given through them, we read, "*The Lord said unto my Lord, sit Thou at My right hand, until I make Thine enemies Thy footstool*" (Ps. cx. 1). Jews were the authors of the doctrine of the Trinity, as well as of the Unity of God.

(4.) *This Divine nature is the Deity of the Son of God.* With this proposition I may join the fifth, *that as Son, Christ is co-equal with the Father.*

Since it has been shown that Christ is very God, the proof of His being the Son will necessarily carry with it the proof of His equality, as Son, with the Father. He could not be very God and the Son, without possessing also this perfect equality. The question of His personality, as the Son divinely subsisting with the Father, may be taken therefore as decisive as to His true rank, the virtue of His work, and the homage which is His due. To this single question of personality I now invite your attention.

Christ is called simply "*the Son,*" "*the Son of God,*" "*the Only Begotten,*" "*My Beloved Son,*" "*the Son of the living God,*" "*the Son of the Most High God,*" "*the Son of the Blessed*" (Mark xiv. 61). The Tempter was the first to throw a doubt on His Divine Sonship

("*If* Thou be the Son of God")[1] and to draw a false inference therefrom. The meaning of these titles was so clear that the Jews accounted the mere implication contained in them blasphemy. The priests condemned and slew our Lord on the confession of this truth. It is not contended, that in all places, and on all lips, the name has the same breadth or height of meaning. A glimmering only of its great import we may suppose dawned on the pagan mind of the Centurion (supposing him not to have been a Proselyte) as he exclaimed at the foot of the cross, "*Truly this man was the Son of God*" (Mark xv. 39). The glimmering of the truth may have been dim, for he was in the outer court; but John was in the inner court, when he said, "*We beheld His glory, the glory as of the only begotten of the Father*" (John i. 14). Beyond even where John stood and gazed there is an inmost, a thrice-holy place, veiled as yet, with excess of light, for "*great is the mystery of godliness*" (1 Tim. iii. 16). The outer leads to the inner, the holy to the Holy of Holies. The wider and the lower lead to, as they include or are included in, the most strict and elevated meaning of the title, "*Son of God*,"—a title that is given to Christ considerably over a hundred times in the New Testament. I proceed now to touch upon some particular instances.

The statements, already quoted, of His being sent by the Father into the world, show on the one hand, that it was not the Father who became incarnate under the name of the Son. In that case it could not be said, "the Father sent," if it were meant, "the Father came"; neither could it be said, "the Father sent the Son," if "the Father Himself came," was meant. On the other hand, Christ receives not the title "Son of God" from any of His mediatorial offices or relations, or from any elevation of His humanity; but carries that title from above into His offices, and even into His human existence. Men are called "Sons of God" from their character; Christ is called "The Son of God" from His nature. Men are called "Sons of God," from the offices they have held; but with Christ the title "Son," is personal and inherent. Adam was called the "Son of God," because of his immediate creation by the hand of God; but Christ owed not the dignity to His miraculous birth into this world. He had it before, yea, before all worlds.

Were we even to grant with Dr. Pye Smith, that in the passages, Luke i. 32—35; Matt. iii. 17, xvii. 5; John i. 34—49, the term "*Son of God*" has a special reference to His mediatorial rank, and includes His

---

[1] Matt. iv. 6.

humanity; yet it does not therefore follow, that in these instances the epithet is brought down to the level of the official designation of the most exalted men. In His Kingship, His Priesthood, His Prophetic Office, He stands above all, both in kind and degree. He is real, true, archetypal and supreme; all others are at best subordinate, shadowy, and typical. And though His humanity is included, His Divinity is by no means therefore excluded. In each of these passages cited, some circumstance is given as an index of this higher note in His being. In Matt. iii. 17 it is the description "*My beloved Son*,"—ὁ Ἀγαπητός is here equal to, my only beloved, or beloved in a unique sense. The occurrence therewith of the manifested presence of the Father and the Spirit, may surely be taken as shadowing forth the Trinity in that one baptismal act. In relation to the Father and the Spirit, the term "Son" designates, not what is official, but what is essential. It is with respect to this essence or Divine nature that the full meaning of the epithet, "*My Only Beloved*," is seen. In no other sense is He "The Only Beloved" of the Father. In Matt. xvii. 5, the command to "hear" the Son shows Him to have higher authority than Moses and Elias over the Church. How this dignity comes not from the office to His Person, but spreads from His Person to His office is clear from Heb. iii. 5, 6, wherein Moses is declared to be "*faithful in all his house, as a servant.* . . . . *But Christ as a Son over His own house.*" What is said in John i. 34, ought to be compared with the baptismal scene as described by Matthew, and the phrase "Son of God" taken in the light of John's own exalted view of Christ, as given in verse 30, which completes his testimony,—"*for He was before me.*" As this latter phrase clearly points to His antemundane, and so to His eternal existence, that eternal existence must enter into the Baptist's idea of the Son of God. When verse 51 is used as a commentary on verse 49, as was clearly our Lord's intention, His exaltation above angelic nature leads to the same conclusion—His being divinely the Son of God. Taking into account all that is said in Luke i. 34 and the context, there is a light of glory about Him, who is there called the Son of God, that comes not from His investiture in our nature, or with the offices for which it rendered Him fit, but is inseparable from His Divine nature. Even when He stoops to become the Son of Man, He cannot cease to be the Son of God.

Our argument, however, does not rest on these passages alone. I have brought them forward, because they are claimed as giving a meaning to the name "Son of God" something below the highest. My remarks will have accomplished their object, if they have shown that the highest meaning is not necessarily excluded from these passages. And if they do not exclude this highest meaning, they may be connected in proof with other Scriptures which are more definite and explicit. This is the very position which our Lord took in dealing with the Jews. They accused Him of blasphemy for saying, "*I and My Father are one*" (John x. 30), and thus claiming to be God. Our Lord does not deny their inference; but He rebuts the charge of blasphemy by showing that Scripture has a lower meaning for the word God, and in that lower meaning it may at least with safety be applied to Himself. He goes further. He asserts a better title to it than any other could have. His argument is, if to them, how much more to Me, the Son, can this title be given. Thus He lays down the basis of fact for drawing the clear and obvious conclusion, although He holds back, as is His wont, the direct assertion of His highest dignity as Son of God. Of what He does here assert, and of what the Scriptures to which I have alluded do assert, the doctrine of His Divine Sonship, in the very highest sense, is the only true complement.

While some passages reveal this doctrine in part only, others show it in its completeness. The Apostles, taught of the Spirit, drew the conclusions of which the facts of Christ's life had supplied the premises. In this way we are to understand Romans i. 4. The fact of Christ's resurrection the Apostle regards as the *incontrovertible manifestation of His being the Son of God*. The new, and doubtless the true reading of 1 Timothy iii. 16, inclines the testimony of that most important statement to support the distinct personality of the Divine nature of Christ. On the same side, also, is John i. 1: "*In the beginning was the Word*" —there is His eternity: "*The Word was with God*"—there is the personal distinction: "*The Word was God*"—there is His Divinity. That all this is applicable to the Son, and to none other, is plain from what follows in the chapter; but verse 18 enlarges our knowledge of the relations between the Father and the Son: "*No man hath seen God at any time; the only-begotten Son, which is in the bosom of the Father, He hath declared Him*" (cf. Matt. xi. 27). The same personal distinction, and the same oneness of essence, are asserted here, enhanced by the ineffable radiance of mutual love and knowledge between the Filial and Paternal Deity—"*the only-begotten Son, which is in the bosom of the Father.*"

It is by virtue of His Filial Deity, that Christ, and Christ alone, is the competent Revealer of the Father. He has certain and direct knowledge,—He sees the Father: He has true and perfect sympathy,—He is in the bosom of the Father. The same truth is expressed in our Lord's own words, rendered the more profound and impressive by the addition of their proper converse: "*No man knoweth the Son, but the Father*" (Matt. xi. 27).

But whither does this Divine reciprocity of feeling, this incomprehensible interchange of knowledge lead? To what conclusion are we drawn concerning Him, who is by turns the Subject and the Object in this highest mystery of alternate knowledge and contemplation? Can the Son be in such a case, at the same time, and under the same idea, both Subject and Object? Can there be reciprocity where there is only one? Or could there be an equal mutual knowledge without an equality of capacity and nature?

It only remains to be observed that His Divine intercourse must include the eternal existence of the Son as Son of God. Any lower sense would limit the Son's knowledge of the Father, and depreciate it in comparison with the Father's knowledge of the Son; but Christ has said, "*As the Father knoweth me, even so know I the Father*" (John x. 15). Eternal Sonship is the least idea that will satisfy these words; and eternal Sonship is implied by eternal Fatherhood. But here reason touches its limit, analogy breaks down, and thought is prostrated. It is the threshold of the Infinite: it is the point of humble, reverent and believing adoration. It is sufficient for faith, and enough to rebuke unbelief, that He who took up the seed of Abraham *is* the Eternal Son of God. As to *how* He can be eternally the Son, that is the mystery over which the veil rests, and perhaps for ever will rest. So firm is the truth, nevertheless, that it is wrought into the very badge of all who would fully obey Christ; for they are baptized into the name of the Father, into the name of the Son, and into the name of the Holy Ghost. It is set down in the ultimate aim of Christ's work, "*That all men should honour the Son, even as they honour the Father*" (John v. 23). From starting to goal, from beginning to end, from Peter's grand confession till to-day, this is the faith of the Church, that *Christ is the Son of the Living God.*

(III.) We come now to consider the proposition, *that Christ unites the human nature and the Divine in one personality*. The question as to the way the Divine and human are united in Christ, no less than the question as to the reality of these natures, goes to the very centre of Christ's fitness to be a Mediator, and of the value of His mediatorial work. I do not hope to explain everything involved in the above proposition. We cannot explain everything involved in the union of matter and spirit, their mutual action and reaction in our own personality. But is not every man conscious of the fact? And what sane man hesitates to accept the fact until he has received the explanation? Neither shall we hesitate to accept the fact of the personal union of the Divine and human in Christ, although we cannot lay bare the very link by which these natures are united. Scripture affords copious examples on this subject.

Everywhere the language is that of true personality. The "I" on the lips of Christ is the expression of the self-conscious union and harmony of the differing natures that meet in Him. Its usage, however, prevents the slightest suspicion of a rent between the two natures in any given act, although that given act may be proper only to one of His natures.

Christ says, " I *thirst,*" [1] and also, " *Whosoever drinketh of the water that* I *shall give him shall never thirst.*"[2] He says, "*Give* ME *to drink,*"[3] and also, "*If any man thirst, let him come unto* ME, *and drink.*"[4] He says, " I *and My Father are one,*"[5] and also, " *My Father is greater than* I."[6] To the servant of the High Priest, Christ says "*Why smitest thou* ME?"[7] and in His prayer to the Father, He says, " *Glorify Thou* ME *with the glory which I had with Thee before the world was.*"[8]

When we look at these affirmations, we find they belong to two classes, one referring to His humanity, the other to His Deity; and we cannot transpose them. The affirmations of the humanity do not hold good of the Deity, nor do those of the Deity hold good of the humanity. Yet both are true of Christ; they are both appropriate predicates of the " Ego," that is the Speaker throughout. Their personal union in the Speaker is the only adequate explanation of the appropriate and free use of such predicates. No notion of contiguity, however close, no contact of the two natures, no idea of the indwelling of the Divine in the human, will satisfy the force of such language.

Nor is there in these expressions anything foreign to the correct language of every-day life. Herein our Lord shows the same personal unity and harmony of powers that are seen in the common language

---

[1] John xix. 28.   [2] John iv. 14.   [3] John iv. 7.   [4] John vii. 37.
[5] John x. 30.   [6] John xiv. 28. [7] John xviii. 23. [8] John xvii. 5.

of mankind respecting the combination of the material and rational, the animal and the spiritual, in the union of every man's personality. From the self-conscious unity of our being we say, I see and I think ; I hear, I remember ; I eat, I understand ; I walk, I imagine. But, at the same time, we are conscious that the powers by which we see, hear, eat, and walk differ from the powers by which we think, remember, understand, or imagine. We are conscious that our sense of sight cannot think ; that our sense of hearing cannot imagine ; nor can the faculty of memory walk, or eat, or hear. Yet we are conscious of these powers. Thus also it is that powers and substances, in themselves diverse, have in the " Ego " their centre of unity and harmony. All belong to the " Ego," though none of them may singly express the " Ego." " I " have a body ; but " I " am not a body. " I " have a spirit ; but " I " am not a Spirit. Yet whatever is true of the body or spirit is true of the " Ego." Thus in ourselves, and in the frame of our daily thought and speech, we find some distant analogy of the manner in which Christ speaks of His complex nature. There is, therefore, no violence done to our reason, there is nothing at variance with our most familiar modes of thought, in representing either the Deity, or humanity, or both, by the personal " I."

It may be well at this point to observe, *that the union of the two natures in Christ forms a single personality.* I use the word "single" in what might seem a pleonastic sense as applied to personality, were it not remembered that some in their zeal for the integrity of the two natures have asserted a duality of persons. Did not the humanity of our Lord, they ask, as well as His Divinity, possess its own personality ? If that were so, then undoubtedly there would be in Him a duality of persons. Then the one would be capable of addressing the other, as Thou, Thine ; but neither would be able to speak of the other as Himself, or of its powers as His own. The humanity could not say of the act of Deity, " I " acted ; nor Deity of the suffering of humanity, " I " suffered. No trace or shadow of such a duality appears anywhere in Scripture. It is next to impossible to square the notion with what we find in Scripture. It leaves out of view the facts of the Incarnation. The personality of our Lord's Deity is as Eternal as His existence ; but His humanity never had a separate existence apart from His Deity. From the earliest dawn of its existence, from the first movements of its life, the Eternal was one with it ; and in consequence the seat of self-conscious subsistence would be in the Divine, that is, the higher nature, just as in man the seat of self-conscious individuality is in his higher rational nature, though he is possessed of the lower animal life.

Connected with the singleness of His personality, and in proof of it, is the continuousness of self-consciousness everywhere attributed to Christ. Its language comes to us from all the successive stages of our Lord's existence. We hear it in the prophecies before the Incarnation, "*Lo, I come . . . . I delight to do Thy will, O my God.*"[1] We hear it from His own lips, "*I came forth from the Father, and go to the Father.*"[2] It is found in the challenge to His enemies, "*I was daily with you in the temple;*" and in "*Before Abraham was,* I AM."[4] Amid the fury of the storm on Galilee, it brings peace and safety to the disciples: "*It is I; be not afraid.*"[5] It is the essence of the good confession made before Pilate: to his reply, "*Art Thou a King then?*" came the answer "*To this end was I born, and for this cause came I into the world.*"[6] It is the language of the Cross, "*Into thy hands I commend My Spirit.*"[7] It is the language of the Resurrection and Ascension, "*I ascend unto My Father.*"[8] It falls upon us from the skies, "*I am He that liveth, and was dead; and behold, I am alive for evermore*" (Rev. i. 18).

Where is duality of person to be detected in such language? The introduction of it would be at once gratuitous, and break up the unity both of the individual life and of the mediatorial work herein set forth. The fair, and I may say, the only interpretation of such Scriptures as these is that contained in the Apostle's words, "*He that descended is the same also that ascended up far above all heavens, that He might fill all things*" (Eph. iv. 10). There is one, and one only personality, speaking, acting, suffering, glorified throughout: one life-centre is the spring of all energy and light and grace: one self-conscious subsistence unfolds itself in the ineffable love of the Father's bosom, and throughout all creation in the omnipotent might and wisdom of the Logos. It unfolds itself in our fallen nature, as "*the Lamb of God which taketh away the sin of the world,*"[9] and thenceforward, and for ever, in the Zion above, as "*the Lamb, the Light thereof.*"[10] To allude to the figure of the Apostle in Romans xi. 16—24, where the wild branch of our nature is grafted upon the Divine, it does not become an individual centre of life and growth for itself; if such were the case, it might as well never have been grafted. But being grafted, while its distinctness as a graft remains unimpaired, it yet becomes a partaker of the goodness and richness of

---

[1] Ps. xl. 7, 8. [2] John xvi. 28. [3] Luke xxii. 53. [4] John viii. 58. [5] John vi. 20.
[6] John xviii. 37. [7] Luke xxiii. 46. [8] John xx. 17. [9] John i. 29. [10] Rev. xxi. 23.

the Divine nature. Nor is the individual life of the Divine Root interrupted. On the contrary, it finds new scope in the new graft, and, pouring forth through the new boughs and branches, grows those very leaves which are for the healing of the nations, and that very fruit which is the Fruit of Life to all mankind.

One consequence of this view of the subject is, that we are saved from all vain speculations as to the time when the consciousness of His having a Divine mission, or a Divine nature, dawned upon the Christ. It must first be shown that He ever lost such consciousness, and so was without it, before it is time to enquire as to when He found it. The supposition of Christ being destitute of this consciousness, and, according to the showing above, destitute because He lost it, is in some form or other the laying of the axe to the root doctrine of the Incarnation of the Son of God. From the orthodox point of view, it involves the impossible supposition of the suspension of the self-consciousness of Deity, or else that there was no true unity of life established in the Incarnation between the Divinity and the humanity. Either supposition is fatal to the true doctrine of the Incarnation. The speculation, however, is not born of orthodoxy. It owes its origin to Socinian views of the Christ. It cuts off the descent of the Son of God, and presents only the development of the Son of man. Only from such a one-sided, and therefore false view, could the speculation gather the mere semblance of pith or moment. The Scriptures which I have quoted represent the self-consciousness of the Son of God as remaining unbroken and undisturbed, both in His becoming a man, in His suffering death, and in His subsequent glorification at the Father's right hand; they shut and bar the door at the very threshold of such an enquiry.

While we thus contend that the human and Divine are united in a single personality in Christ, we must not lose sight of the ever-continuing distinction between these natures. Unity of personality does not imply a co-mingling of natures, nor the transmutation of one into the other, neither transubstantiation nor consubstantiation. In the grafted tree, root and graft both retain their individual distinctness, though the life is one. In our own persons, the material does not cease to be material, and subject to the laws of matter, either chemical or mechanical, though united in one personality with spirit. So with the two natures in the Person of our Lord. They lose in that union none of their distinctness, none of their essential and peculiar properties or attributes. The Deity is not humanized, the humanity is not deified. The Godhead is there; a Godhead not limited or weakened, but with all its essential attributes. Humanity is there; but it is a humanity in the full and free exercise of its capabilities, under the limitations of its own laws of growth and development, of action, thought and emotion, neither expanded beyond itself, nor transmuted into Deity. The Deity stoops, stoops to the lowest depths of human humiliation; but it is still Deity in all its effulgence. The humanity rises, rises to the right hand of the Eternal Throne; but ever amid the burning splendours of that Throne it is still true humanity.

Were this distinctness not retained, were the natures co-mingled and transfused in the Person of Christ, the result would be that He would be a something, neither properly Divine nor properly human. A clear loss would thence ensue in His capacity as Mediator, and so a clear loss to all the universe. He would be God-ward something less than Divine, and man-ward something other than human. He could therefore neither rise to the full height of Deity in the satisfaction required in His sacrifice, nor stoop to the lowliest depth of humanity in sympathy with our misery. What we find, however, in the Person of the Lord Jesus, and what constitutes His singular glory, is that the human in Him can suffer the lowest indignity of humanity—it can *die*. The Divine can wield the highest prerogative of Deity, it can give *Eternal Life*. These capacities belong, like opposite poles, to the one perfect sphere of His Being, dominated by the one Ego. By this undivided virtue, He could say, "*I am the Good Shepherd: the Good Shepherd giveth His life for the sheep;*" and at the same time, "*I give unto them (the Sheep) Eternal Life; and they shall never perish, neither shall any* MAN *pluck them out of My hand.*" (John x. 11 and 28).

It is true that here we touch the borders of the greatest of all mysteries submitted to the mind of man, the mystery of godliness. How can the Infinite dwell in the finite and retain its infinitude? How can the Almighty reside in feeble flesh and remain almighty still? How can the Omniscient have His home in a limited intelligence and lose nothing of His omniscience? Yet to the accomplishment of these, to our minds impossibilities, to the reconciliation of these contradictions, to the union of these opposites, the Scriptural evidence leads us on. It leads us as the Star led the wise men to the Christ, and over Him it rests and shines, Emmanuel—God with us—giving light to the truly wise, to believe, to worship and adore.

THE SAVIOUR.

But while we adore, let us draw as near as may be to contemplate. It is certainly a step nearer to recognize that the nature into which the Son of God descends is of no alien growth, for man as a creature is also God's offspring. It is also another step to remember that though man is formed of the dust, there is yet a Spirit in man. This created spirit may, in point of nature, claim lowly and distant kinship with the Creator Spirit, the finite with the Infinite. And reverently we say it, yet we humbly conceive that in this Spiritual element, originally formed for communion with God, there is a native fitness already prepared for the living and personal union that is consummated in the Incarnation of the Son of God. Further than this we cannot go, and the great mystery, as to how the Infinite can be one with the finite, remains hidden behind the veil.

We turn now to the results that follow from this doctrine.

(I.) *It throws light on certain passages of Scripture.*

We have seen how the affirmations made of His humanity, and also those of His Deity, find their harmony in the one personality of Christ. This prepares the way to view Scriptures of another complexion. I refer to what I may call the *mixed expressions* concerning Christ. The peculiarity of these expressions is, that while His Person is named from one of His natures, either the human or the Divine, yet what is said of Him in the one nature is true of Him in the other or in both. There are therefore four kinds of *mixed* expressions.

(*a*) *Those in which Christ is named from His Deity, what is said belonging properly to His humanity.*

Paul says, "*Had they known it, they would not have crucified the Lord of Glory*" (1 Cor. ii. 8). In Revelation we read, "*Our Lord was crucified*" (Rev. xi. 8). In Acts xx. 28, Paul says *of the Church of God*—and the preponderance of evidence is in favour of "*God*" rather than "*Lord*"—that He had purchased it with *His own blood*. Recognizing the unity of Christ's personality, there is no difficulty in such expressions. For though, as Peter says, "*Christ was put to death in the flesh*"[1]—as to the flesh—yet, seeing the mortal flesh was as truly a constituent part of His Person as the immortal Spirit, it was most divinely true, *the Lord, the Lord of Glory, was crucified.*

In the same way, it is, and has been held by the Church from the

---

[1] 1 Peter iii. 18.

earliest ages, that she is redeemed, not with "*corruptible things, but with the precious blood of Christ,*" the blood of God.[1] Ignatius writes to the Ephesians of being *kindled into energy by the blood of God.* Tertullian, in his address to women, speaks of being bought with a price, and what a price!—*the blood of God.* This kind of language, or rather the ideas underlying it, has been dear to the hearts of believers in every generation. It pervades all Christian literature, and forms the sweetest fragrance of many a prayer and many a hymn, and yields the motive and inspiration of many a noble life.

(*b*) Secondly, we have *those expressions in which the title belongs to the humanity, and the predicate pertains to the Divinity.*

In John vi. 62, we read, " *What and if ye see the Son of Man ascend up where He was before?*" Again, "*No man hath ascended up to heaven, but He that came down from heaven, even the Son of Man which is in heaven*" (John iii. 13). Did the Son of Man, as such, possess an existence previous to His birth at Bethlehem?—So we might ask concerning the first passage. Can the Son of Man, as Son of Man, be in heaven and on earth at the same time?—Such might be the question concerning the second passage. It will be seen that such Scriptures bring up a difficulty which is the very converse of what we have just been considering. They seem to attribute the perfections of Deity to Christ's humanity. But this difficulty finds its solution also in the same truth,—the unity of Christ's personality. Just as what the manhood does and suffers belongs, by virtue of personal unity, to the Deity, though the Deity of itself may not suffer; so by the same unity the acts of the Deity belong to the humanity, though the humanity has neither an everlasting nor an ubiquitous existence. That Person who is described as the Son of Man was with the Father before the birth at Bethlehem, and is now in heaven, because to that Person always belonged Eternity and Omnipresence. We may find an example of this in language we often see used. We read of the Duke of Wellington receiving his first lessons in the tactics of war on the Eton cricket-field; we read of the first exhibition of his powers as a general in the Indian campaigns. Yet the Duke of Wellington, so far as the record runs, never played a game of cricket at Eton, nor led any army in India. It was Arthur Wellesley that did both. But seeing that he rose to be the Duke, the actions of his life are truly said to be the actions of the Duke.

---

[1] 1 Pet. i. 18, 19.

In the same manner we see the Son of God descending to become the Son of Man, but that descent does not cut Him off from all His glorious past, from all He was and is as Son of God. The personality being the same, the actions of the Son of God belong to the Son of Man.

(*c*) There remains yet a third class of passages in which *Christ is named from His Divine nature, where the predicate is true of His whole personality as the God-Man.*

The Apostle writes: "*And when all things shall be subdued unto Him, then shall the Son also Himself be subject unto Him that put all things under Him, that God may be all in all*" (1 Cor. xv. 28). This passage cannot be fully understood if taken apart from what goes before; and as this is of great importance to the whole subject, it will be well to dwell on it a little. The Apostle is describing the reign of the Mediator. The work of subduing, spoken of in this verse, is Mediatorial subjugation, and therefore all questions as to the subordination of the Persons of the Trinity are here out of place. The work is the same as that mentioned in verses 23—25; but in the 23rd verse the Apostle gives to Him "*who puts down all rule*" the full mediatorial title of the Christ. In our verse, he contemplates that work as it reaches its grand consummation, when "*the last enemy*" is put down. And he anticipates the natural question of every man who has begun his life of grace and glory by looking to the God-Man. That question is: Shall the Son sever the tie with His humanity, and resume, apart from His humanity, the glories of His Deity in equality with the Father? Nay! says the Apostle, the Mediator shall be Mediator still. Having been the Servant of the Father even in His reign; having served Him in that reign till the last object of it is accomplished, and the full triumph won, He will be Servant in the triumph, as well as in the struggle. The kindred tie with His lowly Bride, the Church, so dearly bought, He will still own and cherish throughout all ages. When all are subject, He will be subject to the Father. The very name of "Son" given to Him in this subjection, confirms and seals the precious hope that the Christ of Bethany and the Christ of Calvary is the same, yesterday, to-day and for ever. It is only as the "Son" we could fear or expect Him to break the bond; but as "the Son" He abides by it, and so renders it to all eternity indissoluble.

(*d*) Finally, there are passages *in which the name given belongs to both natures, and the predicate belongs to the Divinity.*

We find here an example in Romans ix. 5 : "*Whose are the Father's, and of whom as concerning the flesh Christ came, who is over all, God blessed for ever. Amen.*" Here, Christ is the name applied to our Lord's Person; but the predicate, "*God over all, blessed for ever,*" is used of His Divinity.

Looking at these four classes of Scripture passages, I know not how they can be rendered consistent with one another, or with themselves, by any other means than by recognizing the cardinal truth of the *Oneness of our Lord's personality.* This truth applied silences all discrepancy. With this as a clue in our hand, we can find a sure way through all the diverse descriptions of our Lord's deeds, capacities and character.

(II.) The second use of this doctrine is, *to throw light on the acts and sufferings of Christ.*

According to it, there is one Divine Ego—one unbroken personality—exerting itself, and fulfilling itself in every phase of our Lord's career. It forbids us to say, here the God spake, there the man: here the God acted, there the Man suffered. For all sufferings and acts there is one life-centre—one life-centre whence the acts proceed, one life-centre where the vibrations of suffering strike home. One self-conscious individuality, moved by an undivided oneness of principle, pours itself forth in unbroken continuity of existence—

> " From the Throne of highest glory
> To the Cross of deepest woe."

In the conscious possession of various powers it broadens out, on the one hand into infinitely tender human sympathies, and on the other, into infinitely holy and perfect obedience to the Will of God. Christ's is an ocean-like life, whose tides are swayed by the power of an Everlasting love flowing between the shores of the Divine and human; and while His fulness, rising on the shore of our emptiness and sin, pours forth freely the riches of His grace, it breaks in the infinite beyond, at the foot of the Eternal Throne, in the loud thunders of delight and holy joy : "*I delight to do Thy will, O my God*" (Psalm xl. 8).

(III.) This doctrine helps us *to form some estimate of the rank of Christ.*

Retaining the integrity of both Deity and humanity, as Christ does, and presenting both in the Unity of a single person, we are forced to ask, Where is the place of that Person in the scale of being? His is true humanity, but to Him belongs what is above humanity. His is perfect Deity, but to Him belongs what is below Deity. A perfect, the One perfect man, He is at one with man, and yet He ranks higher than all men by the exact measure of His infinite nature. Divine, He is one with the Father and the Holy Spirit; and yet by taking humanity into union with Himself, He has not obscured, but manifested Deity. His descent is a revelation, His humiliation a proclamation unto the principalities and powers, of the manifold wisdom of God. By the assumption of our nature, the stream of life has flowed further from its Eternal Spring: the beams of light have penetrated further from the Central Sun. And just so far as our nature is below the Divine, and sinful man distant from God, by this exact distance is the kindness of God, our Saviour, revealed to the joy and contemplation of the universe.

In the Person of Christ we have therefore to contemplate, not a loss either on the side of humanity or Divinity, but an infinite gain on both. The humiliation was an advance, and leads to an advance—the suffering to the reward, the Cross to the Crown. This is the invariable strain of Scripture concerning the results of the manifestation in the flesh, as gathered up in the Person of the Redeemer.

We read, that He is "*highly exalted;*"[1] that He is set down "*on the right hand of the Majesty on high,*"[2] the place of supreme power and supreme honour; that there is given unto Him "*a name which is above every name.*"[3] What is of chief interest in the fact of His exaltation is that it is connected with His humiliation. The infinite glory of the Son could not be added to in the glorification, as it could not be diminished in the humiliation; and yet the taking to Himself of our nature, and the redemption of our race, form the occasion of a unique display of the personal glory of the Son, and of the Father and Holy Ghost in Him, more splendid than the universe had ever beheld. Hence the important "*wherefore*" in the inspired statement: "*Wherefore God also hath highly exalted Him*" (Phil. ii. 9). Higher than the glory He had before the world was, the glory that was to follow could not be, for that was supreme. For this reason Christ addresses the Father, "*Glorify Thou Me . . . . with the glory which I had with Thee before the world was*" (John xvii. 5). Although our Lord refers to that "one glory" which

---

[1] Phil. ii. 9.   [2] Heb. i. 3.   [3] Phil. ii. 9.

was peculiar to Him as the Son, and which He had before His Incarnation, let us not therefore imagine that the possession of it after the Incarnation was exactly the same as before. The Incarnation gave a new constituent element to the personality of the Son, which placed Him in new relations. This new element clothes the prayer with meaning, and shows its necessity. The fulfilment of the prayer meant the extension to Him, as the Possessor of humanity and the Redeemer of man, of that glory which the Son of God had as dwelling in the bosom of the Father, or as the Logos. The prayer seeks the revelation of the Divine glory in the God-man, and so an immeasurable increase compared with all former unfoldings of it.

To sum up, the Incarnation increased the lowliness of the Son of God, and so the depth of His being: it added a creaturely to an uncreated existence. It added a life that stooped to the lower parts of the earth to that which filled the highest heavens. It enabled Him to associate with Himself those whom He intended to save, and, by the very compass and variety of His personal capacities, to be the Vital, as well as the Kingly Head, over all things to His Church, which is His body. He has thus lifted up our degraded nature, and in Himself crowned it with many crowns. This was the joy that was set before Him, and which shone beyond, if not through, the darkness of Calvary. Hence it is, that for evermore Christ's glory must be measured by the depth as well as by the height; for the depth has increased the height.

(IV.) *This doctrine indicates the homage that is due to Christ.*

Christ being a Divine Person, though humanity is also comprised in His nature, it is evident that no inferior homage can comport with the rank of a Redeemer. Whatever grades of adoration Divines have noticed in the Scriptures, we claim the very highest for Christ. In Scripture, however, there are broadly speaking only two forms of worship—civil and religious—that due by an inferior to a superior, and that due by man to God. Throughout the Bible, that Book which forbids all idolatry, there is accorded to Christ, as His due, the supreme worship rendered to Supreme Deity. We have the loftiest examples of it. His disciples rendered it to Him, and Christ received it. If such had been above His right then it were treason in Him to the Eternal Throne to so receive it. Every doubt, however, on the point is set at rest, for the Father Himself commanded it—and that to higher creatures than man; for "*when He bringeth in the First-*

begotten into the world, He saith, And let all the Angels of God worship Him" (Heb. i. 6). The Apostle declares the object of Christ's reign in the words, "*At the name of Jesus every knee should bow* .... *and every tongue should confess that Jesus Christ is Lord, to the glory of God the Father*" (Phil. ii. 10, 11). Christ Himself, in His outlook into the far distant future, anticipates the result of His work and sufferings, and their purpose to be, "*That all men should honour the Son, even as they honour the Father*" (John v. 23).

If it is asked what these superlative qualities are which demand supreme adoration, it will be found they all meet in Christ. If the object of adoration must be supremely perfect, then all perfections dwell in Christ; all the fulness of the Godhead is His. *This shows that Christ is entitled to the homage of the mind.* If supreme adoration supposes supreme goodness, and the communication thereof to the worshippers; then behold how the Saviour loved the Church, and gave Himself for it. Thus the Baptist witnesses, "*And of His fulness have all we received, and grace for grace*" (John i. 16). *Here is His right to the worship of the heart.* If, finally, He who receives supreme worship must have supreme rule over all things, then all power in heaven and earth is Christ's: His is the power of Creation; He hath the Keys of government: His throne is for ever and ever. Here is reached our unlimited dependence upon the empire of Christ, and in that dependence the reason for our unlimited submission to His will.

Thus to the person of the Christ, because of the excellences that dwell in Him in their perfection, is due the supreme homage of mind, heart and will—all that is wisest, purest and strongest within us, expressed not merely in fervent prayer and hymn, but embodied in the service or sufferings of consecrated lives. It is not so much a question as to whether this Divine tribute shall be paid to Him. It is paid to Him. From every land, wherever the true Israel are scattered, or have been scattered, all down the ages to our own, "incense and a pure offering" of adoration continually ascend to the Redeemer. Though now His worship is spreading its fragrance in every clime, and its melody in every tongue, yet all this is but the gathering of the Choir, the training of the Choristers, the sounding of the first notes of that undying adoration that shall wrap heaven and earth in unbroken harmony. For could we remove the intervening ages, and listen to the song of God's heroes as they return from the great conflict crowned with victory, it would be—Praise unto the Lamb. Could we push onward the march of events to the final issue, and see the new heavens and the new earth, the new Jerusalem with no light of sun or moon, and no temple therein,—for the Lamb is the light thereof. Were we permitted, like John, to be witnesses of that perfect worship, we should hear the new song sung unto the Lamb, "*Thou art worthy.*" We should hear the voice of many angels round about the Throne, the living creatures and the elders, the ten thousands of the pure and the strong, saying, "*Worthy is the Lamb that was slain to receive power, and riches, and wisdom, and strength, and honour, and glory, and blessing*" (Rev. v. 12). We should hear "*every creature which is in heaven, and on the earth, and under the earth, and such as are in the sea, and all that are in them, saying, Blessing and honour, and glory and power be unto Him that sitteth upon the throne, and unto the Lamb for ever and ever*" (Rev. v. 13). Yes, we should hear the loud Amen to those acts of homage from the living creatures and elders,—

>. . . . . . " Sound
> From the centre to the skies
> Wake above, beneath, around
> All creation's harmonies." [1]

We should there find it revealed and acknowledged, as we now with Conder sing :—

> " Throughout the universe of bliss,
> The Centre Thou and Sun,
> The eternal theme of praise is this,
> To Heaven's Beloved One :—
> Worthy O Lamb of God art Thou,
> That every knee to Thee should bow.'

With such a Saviour, highly exalted, and so universally adored, we can understand the Gospel that reveals Him to be indeed "*the glorious gospel of the blessed God*" (1 Tim. i. 11). We can anticipate that this Gospel will satisfy the yearnings of every human mind and heart, and prove itself to be "*worthy of all acceptation.*"

---

[1] Montgomery.

LECTURE XV.

ANCIENT AND MODERN VIEWS AS TO THE PERSON OF THE SAVIOUR.

I CANNOT pass away from the Person of the Saviour without dealing in some way, though necessarily short and meagre, with the history of the views held on this subject. This may be divided into three sections: *the first* extending from Apostolic times through the dark ages: *the second* beginning with the reformation and extending to the rise of modern Rationalism: *the third*, including modern speculations.

FIRST SECTION OF THE HISTORY FROM APOSTOLIC TIMES TO THE DAWN OF THE REFORMATION.

The first section may be sub-divided into two almost equal periods: the one terminating with the Council of Constantinople, A.D. 681, the other with the dawn of the Reformation. In the first the orthodox doctrine may be said to be militant, in the second triumphant.

Going back to the times immediately following the Apostolic age, we shall be disappointed if we ask for definition; these were not the days of definitions on this, or any other doctrine. We have evidence of the truth in practice. The reception given to the first erroneous teachings as to the Person of Christ, proves how thoroughly Christians were imbued with this truth, and how dearly they prized it. They had not minutely traced out all that belonged to the union of the Deity and humanity in the Redeemer, but they insisted on certain great essentials with the sureness of instinct. The union of the Divine and human in the Person of Christ was a truth absolutely new to the world, and opposed to the tendencies of both Jewish and Gentile thought. The Jewish teachers placed a chasm between God and man; the Heathen taught a deification of nature and man in which humanity lost its character. When these opposing views joined issue with "*the truth as it is in Jesus,*" we find them developing themselves, on the one hand into a denial of the Divinity of Christ, and on the other into a denial of His humanity.

So early as the days of John and Paul, these views had gained some standing in the Churches. Paul writes against them in the first verses of his first epistle; and John aims against the same heresies. Under the names of Ebionites and Nazarenes, the rejectors of the Divinity of Christ are known in Church history. Whether the name came from Ebion, a leader, or was a name descriptive of the sect, is not known; but of its Hebrew origin from אֶבְיוֹנִים, *i.e.*, poor people, there is little doubt. The Nazarenes took their designation from the epithet Nazarene applied to Christ. Both parties appear to have had their founders in those men who in Apostolic times held by the Mosaic law. To them Jesus was a man of singular holiness and gifts, a loftier Abraham, a mightier Moses. Most of the Ebionites looked upon Him as the Son of Mary and Joseph, whereas the Nazarenes admitted His supernatural birth, and unusual measure of the Spirit of God. Hence they owned in Him a dignity above that of all other men.

Cerinthus, the great antagonist of John the Apostle, seems to have mixed the views of the Ebionites as to the humanity of Christ with the Gnostic ideas, teaching that at His baptism the Redeeming Spirit came suddenly upon Him, and used the Man Jesus as an accidental vehicle of the work of redemption.[1] The human was thus only a temporary mark for the Divine. "When Jesus was apprehended *Christ* flew away, so that only the Man Jesus was put to death."[2]

Amongst the Gnostics themselves, there was great variety of opinion. Some denied the reality of Christ's human life, holding that the Divine alone was real, and the human but a mere appearance: hence their name Docetæ. Of this party Marcion was a notable leader. Speculations of this sort prepared the way for the appearance, at a later period, of the wild theories that passed under the name of Manicheism. Here the great moral revelation of God was degraded into a mere question of physics, the Incarnation was the coming of the Spirit of the Sun, and the Crucifixion a symbol of a soul suffering in combination with matter.

On the other hand, the Valentinians held that Christ's human life was real, but that His body, being of an ethereal texture, was not

---

[1] Cf. Neander, *Church History*, Vol. I, p. 393.
[2] Mosheim, *Church History*, Vol. I, p. 117.

subject to sensuous human affections. He ate without feeling hunger, He drank without thirst, He slept without the weariness of fatigue. All in Him was imperishable, and therefore needed no repair. In this, however, as in all the other theories, the Church only saw another way of taking away her Lord, and she still insisted on the retention of the true humanity of Christ. Teachers in both the Eastern and Western Church insisted on the veritable humiliation to the form of a Servant of the Son of God. It is a curious proof of the extreme to which they carried their views, that they represented, from Isaiah liii. and John viii. 57, the bodily form of Christ as ill-favoured, and that He looked much older than He really was: thus setting in the Person of Christ the holy in contrast with the idea of the beautiful. The contrast serves as a landmark in the opinions of the Church.

As we read the statements in defence of orthodox views, we can trace how simplicity of argument grows into profound theology. The Ignatian Epistles, and Apologies of Justin Martyr are followed by Irenæus; and Irenæus by Tertullian and Origen. The truth was attacked by increasing subtlety of logic, and by equal subtlety of reasoning was it defended. Christian teachers like Origen and Gregorius, well versed in the philosophies of the day, called the principles of these philosophies to their aid. They smote the philosophic Pagan with a deeper and purer philosophy, and the rationalistic heretic with a loftier and a sounder reason.

As, however, we observe the field of controversy clear, and the various bands of heretics retire broken and dispirited, a new gage of battle is thrown down, and a fierce fight follows. Arius, a Presbyter of Alexandria, rises in his place in the presbytery to challenge the statements of his Bishop respecting the Trinity. The dispute, thus begun, spreads throughout the Church, and convulses the whole Roman, which under Constantine had now become the Christian World. Arius' own statement of his position, as taken from his letter to Eusebius, Bishop of Nicomedia, is this :—

"We have taught, and still teach, that the Son is not unbegotten, nor a portion of the unbegotten, in any manner: nor was He formed out of any subjacent matter, but that in will and purpose He existed before all time, and before all worlds, perfect God, the only begotten, unchangeable; and that before He was begotten, or created, or purposed, or established, He was not, for He was never unbegotten. We are persecuted because we say, the Son had a beginning, but God was without beginning. We are also persecuted because we say that He is from nothing, and this we say inasmuch as He is not a portion of God, nor formed from any subjacent matter."

This was the doctrine condemned at the first General Council of the Church, held at Nice, A.D. 325. Great as was the influence of the decision of this venerable assembly, it soon became apparent that all the points involved had not yet passed through the fire of discussion. Thus the philosophic spirit introduced into the Church led to a new series of errors. While, by the unavoidable springing up of systems in her own camp, the truth seemed endangered by the conflict, the Church was really winning her way thereby to a nearer and closer view of it, and to a more tenacious grasp.

The fluctuations of the Arian controversy occasioned a constant agitation, and furnished an opportunity for putting forward new theories. Among these, Marcellus and his pupil, Photinus, held a conspicuous place. Marcellus taught that the Son was but an *Emanation* from the Father; that this Emanation dwelt not in a perfect human nature, but in a body, and would return into the Divine Unity. This latter is the point at which Photinus differed from Marcellus, he maintaining that the personality would not cease, but continue throughout all eternity. He taught that Jesus Christ was a *mere* man, who had no previous existence, but began to be when He was born of Mary by the Holy Spirit: that a special influence came upon Him called the Word, or Understanding of God: that on account of His excellent gifts and virtues, God took this Man into the place of a Son: and that therefore He is called the "Son of God," and God. Both the Arians and the Orthodox joined in condemning these doctrines. He was deprived of his bishopric, and driven into exile.

While Photinus was languishing in exile a new error appeared. One of the most acute and scholarly on the side of the Orthodox was Apollinarius the younger, who, with his father, had rendered good service to the Church in providing Christian Classics when Julian interdicted the reading of the heathen Classics by Christians. Feeling the pressure of the Arian controversy, he endeavoured to make the personal union of the two natures more clear than Origen had done, and in this effort, fell into a new error. He asserted that the effect of Origen's teaching was, not to make the union of the natures real, but to make two Sons of God—the Logos and the God-Man. Holding the Platonic view that there is in man $\lambda o \gamma \iota \kappa \grave{\eta}$ $\psi \upsilon \chi \grave{\eta}$, $\mathring{\alpha} \lambda o \gamma o s$ and $\sigma \tilde{\omega} \mu \alpha$, he taught that in

VIEWS AS TO THE PERSON OF THE SAVIOUR. 193

the Person of Christ the Divine Logos took the place of the natural λογικὴ ψυχή; and thus in the manhood of the Christ a prime essential was extinguished.

In reply Athanasius maintained, "Christ could not exhort us to imitate Him if His human nature had not been like ours. If He had not perfectly assumed this, He could not have redeemed it."[1] Gregory Nazianzen held a similar contention: "The Logos," said he, "connected Himself with human nature in order not only to reveal Himself to man in a visible manner, but to redeem and to save it in its totality, and therefore none of its essential parts could be wanting to Him."[2]

The error continued to spread throughout the East, and for about twenty years added another element to the strife of tongues in the Church and in the State. To obtain uniformity of speech, the Council of Constantinople was summoned by Theodosius in 381 A.D. It was a Council of very variable reputation. Some, with Dr. Cave, term it "Venerandum Concilium Œcumenicum:"[3] others incline to Dr. Jortin's judgment that it was as little entitled to veneration as a "Council of Gladiators held in an Amphitheatre."[4] Gregory Nazianzen himself who was present, being Bishop of Constantinople at the time, and an opponent of Apollinarian doctrine, passes upon it the severest censure. In spite, however, of all these drawbacks from a theological point of view, the Council was formidable as an imperial assembly. Its decision dealt another blow at Arianism and Semiarianism generally, and against Apollinarians in particular. These latter subsequently dwindled into obscure sects, and faded out of all recognition.

The decisions of the Council did not, however, mean agreement of opinion. The causes of variance were only veiled by such means, but not eradicated. Those who opposed heresies were themselves divided against one another concerning the grounds of opposition. They who concurred in the putting down of the Apollinarian heresies were all orthodox; but as soon as they began to hold up and establish their own views, the latent estrangement became visible, and the orthodox began to anathematize the orthodox. This difference of sentiment had its origin mainly in the character of the errors that had to be met. To dispose of the Apollinarian doctrine it was necessary to set forth the completeness of the two natures in Christ. This led to the habit of keeping these natures asunder, and hence it was that theologians of this

---

[1] Neander, *History of Christian Dogmas*, Vol. I, p. 323. [2] Ibid, pp 323-4.
[3] Jortin, *Eccles. Hist.*, Vol. 2, p. 38. [4] Ibid, Vol. I, p. 354.

school saw in Christ, not so much the symbol of the unity as of the co-operation of the Divine and human. Theodorus Mopsuestinus, the ablest leader in this style of teaching, claimed for Christ not only the the possession of two intelligences and two wills, but virtually two persons as well. His words are: "In reference to the Union of Divinty and Humanity we acknowledge one person, just as we say of a man and his wife that they are one." This is union, but not unity, as becomes apparent when he continues, "but in reference to the distinction, we acknowledge two natures and two persons (ὑποστάσεις), God and man; for we cannot conceive of a perfect nature without a perfect person." Accordingly he can say, "the proper Son of God made use of the Man Jesus as His organ, and dwelt in Him as a Temple."

It was in conflict with Photinian and Arian errors that the opposite mode of treating the doctrine of Christ's person was developed. Here the centre of importance was the unity of the two natures. Arianism required to be met by a declaration of the Divinity of Christ; and they who were so engaged were inclined to look upon Christ exclusively from this standpoint. The brightness of the Deity hid the humanity. In the abstract they admitted the distinction of the natures, but they refused to analyze them while they recognized them as present in the actual Christ. Their favourite formula was, "Christ is of, but not in two natures." To them He had not only one person, but also one nature. Hence by a strange anticlimax they called the Virgin Mary Θεοτόκος.

This was the word which brought the two parties into open hostilities. It was a common epithet for the Virgin Mary in Constantinople when Nestorius came from Antioch to be Patriarch of that see. Anastasius, his presbyter, took offence at it; and as the quarrel grew, Nestorius himself was gradually drawn into it. In order fully to understand the position of Nestorius, it must be borne in mind that this word, Θεοτόκος, was the symbol of a growing superstition, as well as of a school of thought. It was a sign of that excessive veneration (?) for saints and relics which began, in east and west, to lay its dead hand on the vital religion of the churches. To this incipient worship of the Virgin and the saints Nestorius was a determined foe. It ought also to be kept in mind that Nestorius himself cannot be fairly charged with all the opinions which go to make up what is called Nestorianism in Church History. Nestorianism is the name for the doctrine of a dual personality in Christ, and although, as we have seen, the tenets of the Antiochian School, to which Nestorius belonged, might lead to such conclusions, Nestorius himself did not teach the doctrine. With regard to the word Θεοτόκος, he was perfectly willing to admit it in the right sense of the union of Deity and humanity; but he denied that a "*Creature* could bring forth the Creator." He proposed a middle term, Χριστοτόκος, as free from the objections to which Θεοτόκος is exposed

Had truth been the aim, and peace desired by all the parties to the controversy, this moderation of Nestorius would have healed the dispute. But he had to deal with a man who was fighting for victory. Cyril, Bishop of Alexandria, carried into the conflict at the very first, "the heat of an unholy passion." By covert attack in his writings, by court intrigue and bribery, by trickery and violence, he brought about the Synod of Ephesus in 431 A.D., whereat he secured the condemnation of Nestorius. This decision was snatched at a party meeting before the arrival of the Eastern bishops, who, when they heard of it, refused to be consenting parties, and treated the proceedings as irregular and nugatory. This lame and impotent conclusion of the Council, left the quarrel to rankle undecided for some time, till the party of Cyril, gaining the upper hand at Court, "through fanatical monks and female intrigue," Nestorius was deposed and driven into exile, where he died in 440 A.D. His followers spread towards Central Asia, many as brave-hearted missionaries to India and China. While till this day the Nestorian Christians survive as a sect on the borders of Persia.

The putting out of this controversy scattered some sparks that in a little time kindled another. The success that the Alexandrian School had gained against Nestorianism gave an impetus to the ripening of the error latent in their own teaching. Cyril had maintained that the nature of Christ was one. His successor, Dioscuros (444 A.D.), insisted with greater imperiousness on making paramount the doctrine of one nature in Christ. The monks, among whom fanaticism took the place of discrimination, detected blasphemy in any distinction of the two natures. Led by Eutyches, of Constantinople, they said, "The *Logos* became flesh: it was an ineffable miracle. It was more than the assumption of human nature, the Logos had not changed Himself: He was still the same; but everything human might be attributed to the Logos; God was born; God suffered; All was Divine in Christ, even His body; but no human reason can explain *how*." As Nestorianism was the error of carrying the distinction of the two natures too far, so this new error of Eutyches arose from not carrying the distinction far enough,—from allowing it to disappear and leave the two to merge into one, the human to vanish into the Divine, to be lost in it as a drop of vinegar in the ocean. Theodoret, Bishop of Cyrus, assailed the new heresy in his treatise called Ερανιστής, or the Mendicant, because it seemed to be made up of contributions from several ancient ones.

Eutyches was brought before a Council summoned by Flavian, Patriarch of Constantinople, and condemned. This being a virtual condemnation of himself, Dioscuros laboured to bring about a new Council, and obtain a different decision. The Council of Ephesus, 449 A.D.—"the Robber Council"—was called; the condemnation pronounced at Constantinople revoked, and Eutyches reinstated in his office. The character of these proceedings marked them as but temporary. A rapid turn in the political scale afforded an opportunity of reaching a more satisfactory settlement. The Emperor, Theodosius II. died, and his daughter Pulcheria and her husband Marcian were his successors. With them that party came into power which sought the truth between the two extremes ot the rival theories. To this party Flavian, Patriarch of Constantinople, belonged. He entered into correspondence with Leo of Rome, and the hope was cherished that with his co-operation peace might be secured. A new Council was arranged to meet at Chalcedon in 451 A.D. The whole controversy turned on the point, whether Christ was to be regarded as consisting *of* two natures, according to the Egyptian mode of doctrine, or *in* two natures. Conference after conference proved futile, till at length Leo's letter to Flavian was taken as a basis of a doctrinal statement, to which all parties gave a superficial consent. The doctrine of Eutyches was rejected as well as that of Nestorius, and the epithet Θεοτόκος was retained.

By Nestorianism, was meant the separation of the two natures or Sons of God; by Eutychianism, the mixture of the two natures. The dogmatic decision arrived at was, "that Christ the only Son of God is of equal essence with the Father according to His Divinity; but like man in all things according to His humanity. The one and the same Christ is in two Natures, without mixture, without change, without division, without separation." This creed met the wishes of the Western Church; but both the Antiochian and Egyptian parties saw in it a compromise in which something had been lost. The Egyptians, in particular, quitted the assembly in dissatisfaction, and renewed their strife for the ascendancy of their favourite doctrine.

For more than two centuries a struggling controversy was kept up, which now and then seriously threatened the peace of the empire. It ultimately took the form of the question whether there are in Christ two wills or only one. Heraclius, and his successor Constans, tried mediation and the force of imperial edicts, and thereby embittered the dispute. The controversy had spread too far, and presented this peculiar phase,—that while in the Western Church the doctrine of the two wills had been established by the first Lateran Council, the same doctrine was being put down by an iron despotism in the East. The difference was by degrees assuming the dimensions of a schism, and to put an end to it the Emperor Constantine Pogonatus, with the consent of the Bishop of Rome, called, in 680 A.D., the sixth General Council to assemble at Constantinople.

The doctrine of a single will was rejected, and its adherents, the Monothelites exposed to persecution. Their views of the Person of Christ were stated in this form: "We proclaim Christ to be One and the Same, Son, Lord, Only-begotten, in two natures without mixture, without change, without division; the difference between the two natures is by no means removed by their union; but the peculiarities of each nature are preserved, and meet in the one Person; and we declare two essential ($\phi \upsilon \sigma \iota \kappa \acute{o} s$) volitions or wills in Him, and two essential ($\phi \upsilon \sigma \iota \kappa \acute{o} s$) modes of operation, without division, mixture or transmutation, so that no contradiction can exist between them; but the human will is always subordinated to the Divine." Thus by the thorny road of controversy, and the somewhat suspicious machinery of a General Council, a definition of doctrine was obtained that cleared the theological atmosphere, and afforded to all sections of the church a solid resting-place for faith till the days of the Reformation.

As for the Adoptionist Controversy in the end of the eighth century, it hardly left a trace behind. The speculations of Anselm and Abelard as to whether Christ had a *non posse peccare* or a *posse non peccare*, did not disturb the Church doctrine as settled at Constantinople. Anselm held that "Christ could have sinned if He had so willed; but this possibility is only hypothetical; He did not and could not so will." Abelard held that if Christ be considered as a man, simple and by

Himself, we may speak of His having a *posse non peccare*, which was first determined by the action of the will: but if we speak of Him in the concrete, as being at once God and man, a *non posse peccare* alone is to be admitted.[1]

SECOND SECTION OF THE HISTORY, COMPRISING THE PERIOD OF THE REFORMATION.

When the Reformation was in its first stages, the chief aim of its leaders was to present the saving and practical truths of the Gospel in a fresh and vigorous manner. They perceived that these truths had been so overlaid with subtleties by the School-men, that the people generally could not feel or perceive their force. They laboured therefore to unbind them from their metaphysics and set them free, like Samson liberated from his bonds to work deliverance for Israel. For this reason, they were content to leave the more abstruse doctrines, such as those of the Trinity and the Person of Christ, out of the arena of public debate. Melancthon, with this view, in the first edition of his *Loci Theologici* (A.D. 1521) omitted the chapters on the Trinity.

But the mighty fermentation concerning traditional beliefs that was making itself felt in every part of Europe very soon compelled a re-statement and defence of the Church doctrine of the Person of Christ. The person of Christ soon became the centre of interest, as it ever must when men's minds are deeply stirred about the Gospel and its claims. Our Lord's own question, "*What think ye of Christ?*" seemed propounded anew to Europe, and in some respects the replies brought back the old heresies one by one to life again, disguised by a new dress and in new combinations.

Accordingly we find in the various Confessions of the Reformed Church—notably in that made at Augsberg, and in the second Helvetic, etc.—an express repudiation of the Ebionite, Gnostic, Arian, Nestorian, Eutychian, Monothelite and other forms of error, as if they constituted a present danger. Those churches which ultimately acquired the names of the Reformed, Swiss, Dutch, French, English and Scotch, kept to the lines of the ancient definitions, and maintain in their standards the same form of doctrine till this day.

But this result did not obtain without prolonged and repeated discussions. These were brought about, on the one hand by Luther's views of the presence of Christ in the Eucharist, and on the other, by

---

[1] Neander, *History Christian Dogmas* Vol. 2, pp. 512—4.

VIEWS AS TO THE PERSON OF THE SAVIOUR.

the teachings of Servetus and Socinus. In the sermon published by Luther in 1526, entitled, "*A Discourse of the Sacrament of the Body and Blood of Christ against Visionaries,*" he based the presence of Christ in the Sacrament on the words of promise. In the following year, he took up the same position in another discourse on the theme, —"*That the words, 'This is my body,' still stand fast.*" It was not till Zwingle had pointed out that behind Luther's doctrine of the presence of Christ in the Eucharist lay another, the ubiquity of Christ's humanity, that Luther affirmed that Christ's body is ubiquitous. This he did in the year 1528, in his "*Confessions concerning the Eucharist.*"

The Conference of Marburg followed in 1529; and the divergence of views thus begun in these occasional discourses received a fixed shape at the Eucharistic Controversy between the German and Swiss Reformers.

Luther and his followers now clearly committed themselves to the doctrine of the "ubiquity." After the middle of the sixteenth century, Brenz, the bosom friend of Luther, revived the controversy, by writing a set treatise on the subject. The way in which Luther conducted the discussion could give satisfaction to none but partisans. In the doctrine of the ubiquity he left the German Church an evil heritage. From this false conception of our Lord's humanity, there have continually arisen successive sceptic exhalations that have overspread and poisoned, as with a miasma, much of German theology.

Melancthon, the profoundest theologian of the German reformers, early felt that in such a treatment of the subject, food was being furnished for future controversies. Four years after the Marburg Conference, and two years after the publication of the treatise of Servetus, *De Trinitatis Erroribus*, he says, in a letter to Camerarius (about 1533): "You know that, in reference to the Trinity, I have always feared that these things would again break out. Good God! what disturbances will be raised in the next age, whether the Logos or the Holy Spirit are Hypostases. I abide by these words of Holy Writ, which direct us to pray to Christ, and attribute to Him Divine honours; but I do not feel compelled to examine more essentially the assertions respecting Hypostases."[1] In a letter addressed to Brenz, in the same year, he says, "περὶ τοῦ λόγου, εἰ ἔστιν ὑποστάσις—non dubito quin paulo post magnæ de hac re controversiæ exorituræ sint."[2]

The doctrine of Servetus was a strange medley. He denied the

---
[1] Neander, *Hist. Christian Dogma.*, pp. 650, 1.   [2] *Dorner*, Vol. 2, p. 407.

eternal generation of the Son; and so agreed with the Arians. He taught that the Logos and Spirit were only Divine modes of manifestation; and so agreed with Sabellius. In this way Christ occupies in his system a very lofty position, but it is at the expense of the doctrine of the Trinity. He holds that out of Christ, God cannot be known; and so He cannot be worshipped except through Him. In the adoration of God in Christ consists the worship of God in spirit and in truth. In handling the Old Testament he revived the principles of the Antiochian School: in working out his views he interspersed ingredients of Gnosticism. The system, on the whole, is a form of Sabellianism tempered with Pantheism.[1] He adopted a tone of arrogance and temper towards received opinions that provoked the aversion both of the Roman Catholics and of Reformers of every school. We recoil from the impiety of his doctrines; but we abhor the method of replying to them. His death fixed a foul blot on both Papist and Protestant. Neither truth nor error can be burnt out at the stake. It has been gravely doubted whether Servetus left behind him one genuine disciple.

Sixteen years later there appeared at Racovia in Poland a man destined to be the leader of a new sect, endowed with far greater tact and powers of organization, although of inferior genius and learning. This was Faustus Socinus, nephew of Lælius Socinus. The doctrines the uncle had for the most part thought out and left in manuscript the nephew developed and published, and gradually drew the Unitarian brethren of Cracow to accept. The Arians or Unitarians thus became Socinians. Socinus acknowledged in Christ no pre-existent Divine nature; but taught that Jesus Christ was a man born of the Virgin Mary through the Divine power, and endowed in an extraordinary degree with the Divine energy called the Holy Spirit; that He was caught up to heaven, as Moses was called to the Mountain-top, and instructed and equipped for His public mission; that after His Resurrection He was exalted to power and dominion next to God; and that by God's command worship was due to Him. Thus the doctrine of Socinus is the doctrine of Photinus revived.

THIRD SECTION OF THE HISTORY, COMPRISING MODERN SPECULATIONS.

As one of the links connecting the mass of the opinions of the present with those of the past, the doctrine of Swedenborg (1688-1772),

---

[1] Cf. *Dorner*, Vol. 2, p. 105.

deserves notice. He applied his theory of human nature to the Divine. He held that man has two bodies, a material and a spiritual, an external and an internal. The spiritual body is the immediate clothing of the Spirit, and grows with its growth till the time of death; the material is then thrown aside, and the ethereal henceforth becomes the Spirit's enduring home. Beyond this he admitted no resurrection. So far, this is a revival of the Stoic doctrine of "the Subtle Chariot of the Soul." He reasoned, that as the Spirit of man forms for itself a spiritual body as a vehicle of action on external nature, so is it also with the Divine essence. God has surrounded His essence with a spiritual body, and that body being in form human, "God is the eternal God-Man." Admitting only one person as one essence in Deity, he taught that the Incarnation consisted in God taking upon Himself in the womb of the Virgin Mary, a sentient material body, in addition to the spiritual body He had from eternity. This material body in its growth and death resembled that of mankind; but after death it differed from all others in that the material was gradually etherealized; and absorbed in the glory of the spiritual. He thus recognized two bodies, one spiritual and eternal, the other material and transitory. In this respect he is not alone, but is joined by others, such as Barclay the Quaker, and Poiret, of Amsterdam, who do not share his views concerning the one personality of the Divine essence. This Sabellian doctrine of the Trinity leads him to deny that the death of Christ was a satisfaction to justice.

It is not a little singular to find the name of Dr. Isaac Watts tainted with the suspicion of heresy respecting the person of Christ. Though he stands unrivalled as a master in putting sound doctrine into melodious verse, though he has written a powerful treatise on "*The Christian Doctrine of the Trinity*," though he was the author of that admirable piece of persuasive reasoning, "*The Arian invited to the Orthodox Faith*," yet he was accused by some of being little better than an Arian himself. The occasion for this charge was found in the sentiments expressed in "*The Glory of Christ as God-Man.*" Dr. Watts was not satisfied with asserting the eternal existence and supreme dignity of Christ's Divine nature, he went much further. He wished to show that Christ's human nature had a share in these dignities, both before, as well as in consequence of the Incarnation. He pleaded that "the human soul of our Lord Jesus Christ had an existence, and was personally united to the Divine nature, long before it came to dwell in flesh and blood."[1] Beside the union of the Soul with the Second Person of the Trinity prior to the Incarnation, he taught the pre-eminence of this soul over all other created spirits. His words are: "The human soul of Christ is the brightest image or copy of the Divine nature that is found among mere creatures."[2] "Such thoughts as these," the Doctor contended, "spread a new lustre over all our former ideas of the glory of Christ." Yet we are not dependent upon "such thoughts as these" to enhance our ideas of the proper glories of the Mediator. "Such thoughts as these" transpose, rather than elucidate or exalt the glories of Christ.

What "such thoughts as these" add to one part of our Lord's glory they take from another. The soul which they add to His prior existence, being thus taken up before His Incarnation, makes that Incarnation the assumption of a body, and not of humanity. At this point there is an approach to the Swedenborgian view. "Such thoughts as these," while adding to the dignity of the Soul of Christ, at the same time necessarily increase its separation from mankind, and detract from its perfect sympathy with those for whom Christ is Mediator. They require, as they have received at the hands of their author, a forced interpretation of Scripture to support them. The Divines Dr. Watts calls to his aid are indeed distinct enough in their testimony to the ordinary doctrine; but with respect to Dr. Watts' peculiar thoughts they are resolutely silent. Bishop Bull, Dr. Goodwin, Dr. Owen, and Dr. Waterland are all mute when the Doctor comes to the point. And though Goodwin's venerable name is invoked with special entreaty, and one of his works, "*The Royalties and Glories that belong to Jesus Christ considered as God-Man*," abridged and put into an appendix, yet all the grave Doctor will admit about the previous existence of the soul of Christ is a prolepsis—a treating of the Son of God in the Divine Councils as if He were what He was to become, the Son of Mary— a pre-existence which could not be denied to any creature throughout the wide universe. The point of greatest interest which Dr. Watts' theory presents to my mind is the use he makes of the pre-existence of the Soul of Christ to account for that humiliation, that emptying of Himself, which Christ endured in the Incarnation. Christ's human soul having been "vested with a Godlike form and glory in all former ages" was divested "of this Godlike form, this Divine Shekinah," when Christ took upon Himself "the likeness of man and

---

[1] *Works*, Vol. 5, p. 382.   [2] Ibid, Vol. 5, p. 365.

the form of a servant." But "such thoughts as these" create greater difficulties than they remove. Besides, the theoretical pre-existence of Christ's Soul offers a very meagre and dubious account of that grand act of self-humiliation compared with what is obtained when we use the uninterrupted personality of the Christ as the key to unlock the wonders of grace in His being made the Son of Man.

I do not for a moment wish to establish any connection between the views of Dr. Watts and the Christianity of modern Germany. Yet it is certainly worthy of notice that from his own starting point Dr. Watts has anticipated those problems that most agitate German Theology, notably the doctrine of the *Kenosis*.

The centre of development for the modern German Christianity was the Lutheran doctrine of ubiquity. Gradually the ubiquity ripened into the transference of the Divine attributes to the human nature of Christ. Then the distinction between the natures vanished. A Pantheistic philosophy stepped in and, denying that there were two natures, proclaimed that the fundamental idea of the Universe and of Religion is that God and man are one. Some of the Pantheists claim that man is the highest existent form of God; that the incarnation is from eternity; and that it is still going on in every individual. The difference between Christ and others is only one of degree; God was more fully manifested in Him than in any other of the race.

Strauss will not even concede this solitary pre-eminence to Christ; but asserts that Christ is only one among many exemplars. "Mankind, the human race, is the God-Man. The key to a true Christianity is, that the predicates which the Church applies to Christ, as an individual, belong to an idea, or to a generic whole." Others, of a dye less deep, are content to claim that human nature is capable of the Divine: "*Natura humana capax est naturæ divinæ.*" Man may become God.

It is in this sentiment that Pantheism and modern Theism begin to mingle together. Dorner asserts that the principles underlying modern Theistic Christianity are two: *first*, that there is but one nature in Christ; and *secondly*, that human nature is capable of being made Divine. There must, however, be added a third, as Dr. Hodge has pointed out, that the Divine is capable of becoming human. This last is indeed of prime importance to their theories. For their idea of the Incarnation is that the Son of God has no life or activity, no knowledge, no power, outside of or apart from His humanity. The life and consciousness within His humanity they reduce to the lowest elements. They teach that He grew through infancy, childhood, and youth in the ordinary way; that He was sinless; that the knowledge that He was a Divine Person gradually dawned upon Him; that it was not until His resurrection and ascension that He became truly and for ever Divine; and that since His exaltation He is still a man, and only a man. Nevertheless He is an Infinite man; a man in whom all the powers of humanity, and all the perfections of Deity meet.

The account given of the way in which the Divine becomes identified with the human in the person of Christ is twofold. According to Dorner, there is a human soul to begin with, to which the Eternal Logos without change gradually communicated His Divine perfections according as it was able to receive them. Thomasius asserts that the Eternal Logos divested Himself of all His Divine attributes, and for the time ceased to be omnipresent, omniscient and omnipotent. He reduced Himself to the dimensions of humanity in its infantile stage. Ebrard varies the doctrine. He holds that the Logos reduced Himself to the dimensions of a man; but at the same time retained and exercised His Divine perfections as the Second Person in the Trinity. Gess, in order to avoid such a contradiction as Ebrard's theory presents, teaches that the Eternal Son laid aside His Godhead in becoming a man. He says the substance of the Logos remained, but remained in the form of an infant,—with an infant's knowledge and power. During His earthly career, the communication of Divine life from the Father was suspended, although power was given as required. His Divine self-consciousness fell asleep at the Incarnation, and when it awoke through ripening growth, awoke in the form of a human self-consciousness. With His Divine self-consciousness were also laid aside His omnipotence, omniscience and omnipresence.

It serves as an instructive commentary on this whole system of doctrine to remember that Thomasius and Gess, its two chief expositors, came professedly to substantially the same conclusions by different ways: the one by way of philosophic speculation, the other by way of Scriptural interpretation. How then can the two following questions be answered? Is He likely to be the Christ of God who is built up out of the inner-consciousness of a philosopher? Or is that a sure interpretation of Scripture which can produce no higher result than philosophic speculation?

On a careful examination of these two theories, it will be found that they contain elements which, besides being self contradictory, are at variance with some of the most cherished and fundamental truths in natural and revealed religion. They destroy the immutability of the Divine Essence. The Omnipotent can cease to be omnipotent. It needs only one more step to reach the supposition that God could cease to be. If He could denude Himself of Omnipotence, He could also of existence. These theories destroy also the verity of Christ's humanity. In His humiliation, Christ's soul is not a human soul, but the Logos lowered to the form of a human soul. Christ is thus without a true human soul, and so without humanity. In His exaltation, His body becomes ubiquitous, and His soul infinite. Thus neither in His humiliation, nor in His exaltation is Christ truly " *Like unto his brethren.*" His Divinity is disrobed of its glory; His humanity of its kinship and sympathy. The unity of His Person is expressly attained by these theories at the expense of the distinction of the natures. The Alexandrian teaching, that Christ is *of* two natures, is advanced upon: there are not natures, there is one only nature in the Christ. In plain terms there is here no true Incarnation.

Theories that thus set out from false premises, that advance by the rejection or forced interpretation of Scripture, that reduce to chaos fixed principles concerning the Divine nature, that create difficulties in the name of simplicity, and spread darkness in the name of light, only require to be candidly stated in order to be rejected. Grasping the skilfully woven drapery of learning and laboured logic, and pulling it aside, the form we see is not the form of "the Mighty God" incarnate, as seen by the prophet; nor does His voice sound like the voice of the Man Christ Jesus, as heard by the Apostles.

The teachings of Schleiermacher deserve a brief separate notice. They had for the Germans and many others all the attraction of that romantic enthusiasm, poetic temperament, transparent honesty, and elevation of aim that dwelt in their author. Despite the many changes of his opinions, and his readiness in casting down what he had formerly set up, he held his followers by a certain fascination. It was said of him that "he first betrayed philosophy to theology, and then theology to philosophy"; yet it was confessed on the occasion of his death, "He gave up everything that he might save Christ." The latter we must interpret from the standpoint of Schleiermacher's followers, which widely differs from our own. The doctrine he held was a form of Sabellianism tempered with Pantheism. "God was to him an undivided absolute unity, inconsistent with any

Trinitarian distinction." Christ was the perfect revelation of God, bearing relation to the entire creation-circle of humanity, whose Head He is. With him, God in the world is the Father; God in Christ is the Son; God in the Church is the Spirit.

In his denial of the existence of an immanent Trinity in the Godhead, his doctrine was confessedly Sabellianism. Comparing his teaching with the views of Bushnell and Maurice, we find them tinctured with the same leaven, although in different ways. Bushnell strives to get rid of an immanent Trinity, and to preserve at the same time the advantage of a Trinitarian exhibition of the work of God in man's salvation, not for the purpose of giving a more natural interpretation of Scripture, but to make Divine things agree better with an enlightened reason, and the feelings and affections of a spiritual mind. Maurice holds a doctrine of the Trinity, not because of its Scriptural basis, but because of the light it throws on man's relation to God. By the doctrine of the Father we can see the common paternity of the Godhead; from that of the Son, the filial relation; and from that of the Spirit we are led to feel and act suitably to this relation. This is a Trinity of operations, rather than a Trinity of natures.

How largely such views in their endless modifications have leavened, and are leavening, the opinions of the day, it requires little keenness of observation to detect. Our periodical literature is saturated through and through with them; and not infrequently do we hear them in public discourses in places which were once the homes of a pure and better theology. They are given forth under the name of a more advanced and scientific theology—a theology that has trampled down the mistakes and dense ignorance of former generations, and is gradually smoothing the way for enlightened progress. Their real classification in this country is with the Socinian propaganda, which, under ever-changing forms since the publication of Biddle's Tract in 1652, has been sending forth what professed to be enlightening, but have ever proved to be blighting and deadening influences, upon the religious life of England. Such teachings came in historic sequence to that first Socinian piece of literature, to Locke's *Reasonableness of Christianity*, to the Deism of Woollaston, Chubb, and Tindal, to the Unitarianism of Whiston, Whitby, and Dr. Samuel Clarke, and to the still more degenerate Unitarianism of Priestley and Belsham. Error beaten off the field, and shamed and silenced for the time under the blaze of truth witnessed by Owen, Bull, Waterland, and Horsley, comes back again in its new Sabellian dress, cunningly hiding its old wounds and past disgraces. But it always has the same end in view, to rob in some way the Person of Christ of some of its essential properties and so devastate the whole Evangelical System. It has always the same deception on its lips. It wishes to remove the corruptions of Christian doctrine, and to return to a primitive truth, about which, if questioned, it is not very sure. Its plan is to keep beliefs in a constant state of flux, to reduce fixed doctrines to as slight a basis as possible, to be proving all things while holding none, to be ever learning and never coming to the truth.

But, brethren, "*Ye have not so learned Christ; If so be that ye have heard Him, and have been taught by Him, as the truth is in Jesus.*"[1] "*And we know that the Son of God is come, and hath given us an understanding, that we may know Him that is true, and we are in Him that is true, even in His Son Jesus Christ This is the true God, and Eternal Life. Little children, keep yourselves from idols. Amen.*"[2]

---

[1] Eph. iv. 20, 21. [2] 1 John v. 20, 21.

LECTURE XVI.

THE WORK OF THE REDEEMER.

IN the previous section, I have endeavoured to trace some of the attributes of the Person of the Saviour. In these attributes lie the capacity and fitness of Christ for "*the work set before Him*"; and it is by a due consideration of these that our expectations are raised as to the magnitude and nature of that work.

When the Son of God appears we may be sure He comes not to do what a creature could accomplish. There is a task worthy of His Divinity. When, too, we hear the declaration, "*Behold the Lord God will come with strong hand, and His arm shall rule for Him*" (Isa. xl. 10), when we call to witness the preparations of the Lord—how He put on righteousness as a breastplate, and salvation as an helmet upon His head, and how "He travels in the greatness of His strength"—we may conclude that the effects shall correspond with these great preparations and exertions. As the work is worthy, so shall the results also be worthy of God: all things are set to the scale of a Divine grandeur.

What is that work? In the broadest generalization it wears two aspects: It is a *manifestation* and a *representation*. It is a manifestation of God to man: it is a representation of man to God. From the Divine side it is a manifestation: from the human a representation. "*God was manifest in the flesh*,"[1] declared the invisible Father. If the manifestation was confined to teaching, we might say that this manifestation lay within the scope of Christ's prophetic office. But it is not so. He showed us heavenly things : Christ's life as well as His doctrine in the light of God. The revelation shines from the character, the purity,

---

[1] 1 Tim. iii. 16.

and elevation, the deeds, the suffering and even the death, resurrection and ascension of the Christ. The primary aspect of God revealed in all this is Love. Those imperishable words, "*God so loved the world that He gave His only begotten Son,*"[1] explain the initial motive : God's love is the spring of the Son's work.

But while it is thus a declaration and a manifestation of God to man, the work of Christ also assumes another form. There is a point at which the Christ turns as it were His face from earth and directs it to heaven ; He withdraws His regard from men, and fastens all His attention upon God. In this phase of His work Christ recognizes only one Presence, and that is His Father's. He ministers as the Father's Servant ; from the Father He receives "the command" ; to the Father's Will he renders a joyous obedience. It seems as if here the tide of love and light and holiness which had been rising higher and higher upon the shores of our misery turns in another direction, and rolls its onward course direct to the Eternal Throne.

Christ offers Himself without spot to God. In this aspect of His work, He appears as a Representation—a representation of man to God. And it is while thus acting or suffering as man's Representation to God, that God's righteousness is so conspicuously displayed and honoured. But while we keep the ideas distinct, we must not so sever the Representation from the Manifestation, as if they stood apart. They are intertwined and interlaced with one another. Representation is one of the chief ingredients of manifestation. It is wrapped up in its very heart. Christ, the *Representation* of man, is the grand and central Object in the *Manifestation*. All those Scriptures which declare He was the Manifestation of God, express or imply that this Manifestation was in and through the Representation; and where the Representation was the most exact, close, and perfect, there was the Manifestation brightest and most glorious. On the Cross both culminated; Christ most perfectly identified Himself with man, and became his representation to God. Thus Christ's manifestation of God, which had its origin in Love, goes on by way of His Representation of man to blossom out into the grandest display of righteousness. On the Cross Infinite Love and Eternal Justice meet, and the harmony of these attributes is revealed not effected.

What is the nature of this Representation, is then the question which brings up that of the Mediatorial Work.

---

[1] John iii. 16.

REPRESENTATION.

I have, I confess, chosen this term because of its width, and if there be something of vagueness as well, it can be no objection to its use. The very vagueness may represent the mystery that never can be expressed. I employ it to cover all those complex relations in which Christ stands and acts God-ward on man's behalf. The term is sufficiently ample to embrace His most universal position in the "New Man," the Second Adam, and sufficiently definite to be applicable to Christ in His most peculiar (?) relation as the Head of the Church. Christ is equally our Representative when He wears our nature, and when He bears our sins. The value of one such general term I deem to be considerable, chiefly because it enables us to look at Christ's work as one grand whole, and forbids us to look at its several parts as being disjointed, simply because they are diverse and distinct. The vital connection, the harmony and unity of the several offices more readily impress the mind; and it is more clearly seen that His work is not composed of pieces wrought out from different centres, and then fixed together. It has only one centre of life and grace: one inner pith extending to its outmost bough: it is one even as the seamless robe woven from the top throughout. The offices and dignities of redemption are many, but there is One Head, and One only that wears the many crowns.

In favour of this particular term *Representation*, I hope it may be said that it will exclude from the mind all thoughts of Christ's work ever being merely personal to Himself—ever being merely declarative of God to man, ever being disconnected from those on whose behalf it was accomplished, ever being simply a transaction between the Two Persons of the Trinity; and that on the contrary it will suggest to the mind that from its first inception the work of Redemption was wrought out within the lines of an indissoluble connection with the redeemed. Into the nature of that connection I shall not just now make any enquiry. It is enough to note the fact of the connection. The importance of recognizing the fact is very great; as the recognition or non-recognition of it will be sure to affect our sentiments concerning some part of Christ's work itself. If we ignore or deny the existence of this relation while Christ was working out Redemption, and insist that the connection began only when Redemption was completed, and its benefits applied by Christ to us, we are bound either to fall into the governmental theory of the Atonement on the one hand, or into

Socianianism on the other. If, however, we recognize a connection existing between Christ and the redeemed before their redemption was completed, and while it was being wrought out, it is unavoidable to suppose that the work and sufferings of Christ must have borne the marks of that relation. His relation to a fallen sinful race would necessitate work and suffering of a special character. Christ's representative work on man's behalf must bear the marks of the conditions and obligations of those whom He represented to God. If this connection existed before Redemption was completed, then the guilt and demerit, the misery and exposure to wrath of those to be redeemed must necessarily appear as the dark threads in the texture of the work and sufferings of the Redeemer, just as afterwards when Redemption is completed the merits and grace of the Redeemer are transfused like beams of light throughout the lives and experiences of the redeemed. The connection on the one hand brought about His shame and death, and on the other our justification and life.

THE RELATION OF CHRIST AS OUR REPRESENTATION IN WORKING OUT REDEMPTION.

If Christ wrought out redemption as a Representative of men, He must in some way have been connected with man during the work. The great question then is, Do the Scriptures recognize or establish a relation or connection of this kind? A careful and unprejudiced examination will shew that they not only recognize it, but also almost uniformly describe the work as the outcome of the relation. The relation is established by Scripture at various points, just as the redemptive work is to be effective in different phases and directions. The relation between Christ and our race is established in the outer circle of our common nature; it is also formed in the inmost centre of individual choice and love, and runs its lines of connection all the way between the vital centre and the uttermost circumference. Not one point of contact ought to be omitted in our survey, as each is possessed of its own proper significance.

First then we note,—

(I.) *Christ is connected with the world as a world.*

He came to the world: He was in the world: He dwelt among us, and pitched His tent here. He became a citizen of earth. He thus became related to this world in distinction and contrast with the other worlds of the boundless creation; in contrast with that bright world from which He descended. And when by virtue of this earthly connection He offered His obedience and sacrifice to the Eternal Throne, He stood out most truly, and meekly suffered as *"the Lamb of God which taketh away the Sin of the world"* (John i. 29). The acceptance of His sacrifice brought with it the return of the world, as a world, from her long alienation from God, from her long severance from the harmonious family of worlds, and secured her restoration to peace with the Holy Creator and Governor of all worlds. The virtue of His work ensured the breaking of Creation's bondage to vanity, the coming of the sweets of liberty with the hour of glory, the transformation of earth's woes, her pains, her long servitude, into the birth pangs of unspeakable bliss. What John the Baptist saw on the banks of the Jordan—*" the Lamb of God which taketh away the Sin of the world"*—has its glorious outcome in what John the Divine saw in the vision of the New Jerusalem—the Lamb enthroned. That enthronement marks the complete and perfect efficacy of His sin-bearing; and as a consequence we immediately read, *" There shall be no more curse"* (Rev. xxii. 3). The curse that fell upon the ground for the sinner's sake is removed. Instead of the sway of death there flows from the Throne the river of the Water of Life; and instead of the thorn and the thistle there grows the Tree of Life bearing twelve manner of fruits, yielding its fruits every month, while its leaves are for the healing of the nations (Rev. xxii. 2).

(II.) *Christ is connected with men as a race.*

The terms used by Scripture to express this condition are of the most universal description *"He was made flesh"* (John i. 14). In the most ancient promise He is *"the seed of the woman"* (Gen. iii. 15), the Offspring of her who was the mother of all living, and thus the true Brother of all mankind. *"He was made of a woman"* (Gal. iv. 4), is a statement that carries with it the same broad import: in one of the latest doctrinal statements also, He is brought into the same relation: *"Forasmuch then as the children are partakers of flesh and blood, He also Himself likewise took part of the same"* (Heb. ii. 14). His own chosen title—a title reserved in the days of His flesh for His own lips alone, and only once afterwards used by another—is *"Son of Man."* It is in this connection that the Apostle displays the sovereign and gracious preference of God for man over angels. The human race as a race is through its participation in the sufferings of the Son of God lifted up from its ruin and bondage to the place of glory, honour and dominion from which angels are excluded.

Among the Angels, as well as throughout the race of mankind, sin had entered and brought ruin in its train. If man had fallen by his iniquity, there were angels, also, who had not kept their first estate. If mankind were "subject to bondage," there were angels who were held in " chains of darkness." Yet in stooping to effect a restoration from sin's devastations, the Son of God formed no relation with the Angelic race, but passing that race by, "*He was made a little lower than the angels.*"[1] It was not to angels that He extended the helping hand; nor is it in consequence through the angelic nature that the healing balm, the renovating virtue of Redemption, is poured throughout God's moral universe.

But as it is to the human race that the Son of God has humbled Himself, and among us has made Himself of no reputation, being found in fashion like a man, so it is that to this race, and not unto the Angels, is to be given the dominion of "the world to come," of which the Apostle spake. This world reconstituted by Christ is, as Alford expresses it, " the whole new order of things brought in by Christ—taking its rise in His life on earth, and having its completion in His reign in glory." From this " glorious hope," no nation, no tribe, no family, no class, no rank, no condition, no character of man is excluded. As a Man and Brother to the race, Christ says, "*I, if I be lifted up from the earth, will draw all men unto me*" (John xii. 32). When the Apostle bids us behold Jesus as "*made a little lower than the angels,*"[2] he shows us the comprehensiveness of that condescension to our race in all its divisions and subdivisions, and the effectual grace that shall, through Christ's death, ultimately spread to every part : "*He tasted death for every man.*"[3] In Christ, the race rises again, and mankind comes back to God. As the world is prevented from withering for ever under the curse of God, and is promised a day when " *There shall be no more curse,*"[4] so the race, through Christ's work, is prevented from perishing as a race, and mankind recover their way to the chief end for which they were created—to glorify God and enjoy Him for ever. Instead of being a race lost to the other orders of holy and happy beings that form the hosts and choirs of God's true servants and sons ; instead of being a race lost to the Father of Spirits, with its place for ever void in

---

[1] Heb. ii. 9. [2] Heb. ii. 9. [3] Heb. ii. 9. [4] Rev. xxii. 3.

this great family, its name erased from the Book of Life, and its voice unheard in joy and praise—mankind in Christ rejoins the hosts of God, and appears before God as sons; and the music of their praise is the sweetest and loudest of all others before the Eternal Throne.

(III.) *Christ is connected with the Jews as a people.*

Here we come within a narrower circle of relations; but we shall soon perceive that the pressure of the relations thus becomes more intense upon the Redeemer. Christ was *"made of the seed of David according to the flesh"* (Rom. i. 3). The woman of Samaria recognized Him as a Jew, and in return He claimed for the Jews a special prerogative. In estimating the significance of His relation to the Jews, it is not enough to let the mind dwell on the distinction, the separation and isolation of that people from the rest of mankind. They were the hermit nation but it was not for the purpose of being the Hermit of the hermits that Christ became a Jew. Nor would it be possible to find a full account of Christ's connection with the Jews in His blood, lineage, and national history. In their carnal confidence the Jews made it their boast that they were the children of Abraham. But Christ made light of such ancestry on the carnal side, as Moses had done ages before, when he told the tribes that their father was a Syrian ready to perish (Deut. xxvi. 5).

Now it would be impossible to imagine that Christ, while thus making light of kinship on its carnal side in the case of the Jews themselves, could, in His own case, have found therein the chief reason of His being born a Jew, when He had all the tribes and tongues of earth from whom to make His choice. The chief attraction the carnal kindred of the Jew had for the Son of God was that He would, by being born a Jew, come into contact and connection with an element that was not after the flesh. That element, as it existed amongst the Jewish people, was to be found in no other section of the human race. The Barbarian, Grecian, and Roman tribes possessed it not. Had the Lord been born of any of the barbarous tribes, He would have been connected with an effete civilization bordering upon or plunged into the darkness and cruelty of savage life. Had He been born a Grecian, He would have been linked to that empty philosophy which, while spiritually powerless with men, is foolishness with God. Had He been born a Roman, He would have been united with the Roman lust of power, and with that iron rule that trampled on the freedom of the world. In all these, the great divisions of the human race, the paramount and reigning elements were more or less ignoble, earth-born and transitory. For the highest and noblest elements that can enter into the rule and inspiration of human existence, and point to humanity's true dignity and glorious destiny, we must turn to the Jew. In the guardianship of the Jew, we discover this supreme element, *Divine law*. This was the loadstone that attracted the Son of God to enter into ties of blood with the Jew. If it be asked, What of the prophecies that Christ should spring from this race? I reply that the fact of the Jew being the only custodian of Divine law, when the fulness of the time arrived, is only one other proof of the way God provides for the full and punctual fulfilment of His own word.

But while we thus hold that it was the Divine law, and not the mere lineage of the Jew, that occasioned Christ's birth as a Jew, we must not fail to recognize that this connection is to reflect on the Jews as a people an exceeding brightness of glory. Christ, who turns every point of connection with us into a means of blessing, has given us unmistakable indications that the Jew, as a Jew, shall not be the exception to the rule. The giver of a cup of cold water to a disciple is not to be without his reward. Our Lord would not use Peter's boat as a pulpit from which to deliver His discourses without giving him as a recompense the great draught of fishes. Shall then that human stock from which our Lord derived His own humanity receive no corresponding advantage? He is to be "*the Glory of His own people Israel.*"[1] This implies, in its truer and deeper significance, that His own people shall glory in Him, that they shall regard Him as their one true and only Glory. That glad event we do not yet see. We only see that they looked upon Him as their shame, and that He has put them to shame. They cried, "*Away with Him*," and He has scattered them to the four winds of heaven. But their present fall is not eternal. "*The Deliverer shall turn away ungodliness from Jacob*";[1] and when that shall take place, the heart of the Jew shall turn to Christ; and then shall their dawn of glory be. For in the words of the Apostle, "*Now if the fall of them be the riches of the world, and the diminishing of them the riches of the Gentiles; how much more their fulness?*" (Rom. xi. 12, and cf. v. 15).

---

[1] Luke ii. 32. [2] Rom. xi. 26.

(IV.) *Christ is connected with Divine law as a covenant of life.*

I have already anticipated this in tracing His connection with the Jew; but I wish now to shew more fully that Christ's ultimate purpose in becoming a Jew was to come within the claims of Divine law. We have seen that in order to find out the divinely bestowed privilege of the Jew we must turn away from his seclusion and exclusiveness. "*What advantage then hath the Jew?*" is the Apostle's question, and his reply is, "*Much every way*" (Rom. iii. 1, 2). These advantages he proceeds to enumerate in Rom. ix. 4: "*To whom pertained the adoption, and the glory, and the covenants, and the giving of the law, and the service of God, and the promises; Whose are the fathers, and of whom as concerning the flesh Christ came, who is over all, God blessed for ever. Amen.*" Now if after examining these several particular advantages we ask ourselves which was supreme to the people as a people, apart from their connection with Christ, should we not agree with the Apostle when he adds to the "*much every way,*" "*chiefly, because that unto them were committed the Oracles of God?*" (Rom. iii. 2.) Herein lay both the summary and the sum of God's favours to the Jews, and herein, too, their tremendous responsibility. But what are "*the Oracles of God*" referred to? Clearly all the direct revelations God had up till then made of Himself; and chief among them that revelation of Himself which had been made in the Law. That this was the primary idea of "*the Oracles of God*" before the Apostle's mind is clear from the application which he makes of his argument in Rom. iii. 19. His whole reasoning in verses 1—18 has been drawn from the Jews' possession of "*the Oracles of God*"; but in verse 19 he applies this argument: "*Now we know that what things soever the law saith, it saith to them who are under the law . . . . .*" To the Apostle's mind therefore the sayings of "*the Oracles*" were the sayings of *the law;* so that his first conception of these oracles was in their legal aspect, as declarative of the righteousness of God. The prime distinction then of the Jew was that to him the Law was given. It was of this he boasted before the rest of mankind. "We have Moses' law," they boasted to Christ. Again we read "*Behold thou art called a Jew and resteth in the law*" (Rom. ii. 17), and in verse 23 "*Thou that makest thy boast of the law.*" It was in this indeed that the Jew believed the chief glory of his nation to consist. The ministration of the law which the Apostle calls "*the ministration of death, written and engraven in stones, was glorious, so that the children of Israel could not steadfastly behold the face of Moses for the glory of his countenance*" (2 Cor. iii. 7). He that uttered anything contrary to the law was treated at once as both a blasphemer and traitor. The law was the basis of the nation's life, as well as the standard of the national religion. To be a Jew was therefore to be above all other things a recipient and subject of the law.

Now when our Lord became a Jew, He became therefore subject to the law. "*When the fulness of the time was come, God sent forth His Son, born of a woman, born under the law*" (Gal. iv. 4, Rev. Vers.). In the first statement we have Christ's relation to humanity; in the second, Christ's relation to the Jew. The way in which this relation is described shows us that Christ's principal object in becoming a Jew was that He might be born under the law. To be a Jew, and to be born under the law were synonymous terms. Christ was born a Jewish Child and grew up a Jewish Man because of that which was most peculiarly Jewish, and the chief glory of the nation—the possession of the law of God. The lineage and the blood of the Jew, and "Israel after the flesh" in any form, were all of secondary importance in this high concern, and indeed bore no significance, and presented no attractions whatever to the Son of God, excepting so far as "Israel after the flesh" had been made the vehicle of God's revelation of His righteous and holy law. As God had chosen "Israel after the flesh" to be the recipients of that law, so the Son of God chose "Israel after the flesh" to be the bond of connection and subjection to that law.

What was the meaning of Christ's connection with that law? Here we touch upon a question of vital import, not only to the Jews, but to all mankind, and the whole remedial plan. It will help us considerably to a clear understanding of this point if we remember that the law has two sides, command and sanction, precept and penalty. Let us then consider first Christ's relation to law on its preceptive side, and then in its penal view.

(1.) *Christ's relation to the Precept.*

The law was the wisest, the most complete and perfect expression of God's righteousness that the world had ever received. In His visible works, in His rule and Providential dealings with mankind, in the constitution of Society, and in the instincts of Conscience, God as Creator and Moral Governor of the Universe had written in detached portions His Code of Righteousness. Since this writing could not always be clearly deciphered, and part fitted to corresponding part, God gave on Sinai His own complete version, with the sound of trumpet and the flash of lightning, that thenceforth none should ever be in doubt as to the eternal principles of right. In becoming subject to this law, our Lord came under obligations to be righteous, and to fulfil righteousness in the most strict and perfect form promulgated to the Universe. If our Lord had fulfilled the law of Righteousness only in so far as it was known to the Barbarian, Greek or Roman, such a fulfilment would have fallen far short of the requirements of that law as revealed to the Jew. But our Lord fulfilled the highest and most complete form of law, and this fulfilment covers therefore the lower forms, and includes every principle of righteousness, wherever found among men. Christ, as a Jew, was bound to fulfill "*all righteousness*," and He was enabled to magnify the law, and make it honourable. His righteousuess was of the nature of an universal righteousness: neither Eternal Justice on the one hand, nor conscience on the other, can demand anything further. Both God and man find therein a sweet savour of rest.

(2.) *Christ's relation to the penalty.*

Hitherto we have regarded law, and our Redeemer's connection therewith, only in one aspect; but the law has two: it is *preceptive* and *punitive*: it is a two-edged sword. It is the light that shines on the path of duty; but it has, also, the flame that consumes the transgressor. Its promise is, "*That the man which doeth these things shall live by them*" (Rom. x. 5); but its dread sanction proclaims, "*Cursed is every one that continueth not . . . to do them*" (Gal. iii. 10).

In this latter aspect, we see the law as it is violated, as the majesty of Divine righteousness therein had been assailed, and as it stood clad in complete armour to vindicate the rule of God against all transgressors. Anything short of such a vindication would be a tacit confession of previous unrighteousness in the precept. This line of reasoning would have the effect of raising transgression to an equality with obedience. And if both be equal, why should obedience be demanded at all? Carried out universally, this would mean the dethronement of all law, and the blotting out of the distinction between right and wrong. At least, it would imply that wrong might enforce itself against right, so as to limit and stay its course; while, at the same time time, righteousness would have no right to enforce itself against wrong. The penalty, therefore, is as truly of the nature of righteousness as is the precept, and the way in which the sentence takes effect is by making life painful, and death penal.

Now it is very clear from the nature of the case, that though our

Lord was made under the law, as it enjoins what we ought to do, yet this connection did not of itself necessarily require that He should come under the penalties of law. His obligation to suffer did not and could not arise from His obligation to obey. Instead of this being the case, the more perfect the obedience the further was He removed from suffering. Had there been failure, of course even the Mediator—we say it reverently—would have been exposed to wrath for Himself. But since in Him was no sin, His obligation as a Jew to obey did not carry with it the obligation to suffer. For our Lord therefore to place Himself under the penal sanctions of the violated law was an act of the purest freest grace, even in comparison with His other acts of grace. It was grace within grace. His holiness gave Him absolute power over His own life. As the Holy Man, He had power to lay down His life; as Son of God He had power to take it up again. Every reason that evinces the perfect righteousness of the Redeemer, and the perfect voluntariness of the sufferings of Christ goes also to show that they were entirely vicarious. Had they in aught been endured by way of satisfying a just claim upon Himself personally, so far would they have lost their vicarious character, and so far have convicted Him of indebtedness to the law. But as they were wholly voluntary, they were wholly endured on behalf of others. If these conclusions be not accepted, then the only alternative left is that Christ's sufferings had nothing to do with righteousness.

We may take it therefore as clear that our Saviour was bound by no personal legal obligation to suffer and die; and as it is equally clear from Scripture that He did suffer and die in discharge of the penalty of the broken law—He was made a curse for us—it remains to enquire in what way He came under that penalty. I do not now so much ask why He became obnoxious to the curse, or for what purpose He endured it. I ask rather, in what capacity He encountered the sufferings and death denounced by the violated law. On this point, as in the others, a reference to the Jewish legal system will help us. That system was the stalk and husk in which the precious grains of the truths of redemption grew.

How was it made known to the Jew that the penalty of the law was suffering and death? In many ways this was intimated throughout their civil code; but never by way of extinguishing the offence by the infliction of the penalty. But where the civil Code failed, the religious enactments came into the foreground with profuse abundance. Here it was ordained that the penalty should be met by means of sacrifice. That death was the wages of sin was enforced in the most solemn manner day by day and year by year, in every dying victim, bleeding at the altar, and burning thereon in continual sacrifices. In the death of every victim was revealed how the penalty for transgression was exacted, how wrath against the offence and the offender was exhausted, and how, in consequence thereof, the offender might return to the favour of a God at once holy and merciful.

It did not lessen the force of this style of teaching to know that the custom of sacrifices did not originate with Moses; but rather enhanced it, giving it a greater antiquity and demonstrating God's plan as being one and invariable from the beginning. The custom appears to have been instituted by God, either when He gave to our first parents the promise of a Redeemer, or shortly afterwards. Amongst the heathen it became corrupted, and the true purpose of sacrifice was obscured; but in the worship of the Patriarchs, and afterwards in the Mosaic Economy, the rite itself was preserved with scrupulous care, and the purpose and meaning rendered apparent to the faithful worshipper. The immediate aim of sacrifices was to sanctify to the purifying of the flesh, and so far they were valid and effectual. The sprinkled blood of the victim purified the Jew bodily, and enabled him to appear in the temple of God. But their ultimate aim was to point to another sacrifice, whose effectual virtue should reach the heart and conscience, and purify the whole inner man before the gaze of God.

It is at this point that we see our Redeemer establish His connection with the law on its punitive side. He came in succession of the great system of sacrifices established from the beginning. He came in the line of priestly intercession and expiation for sin ordained by God for the vindication and reparation of the Divine Commands. And as He so came, His own sacrificial character and priestly office are brought to light. He appears as one invested with a priesthood, called of God as was Aaron. He appears to consummate and perfect all priestly work, both by expiation and intercession.

Coming thus, He had something in common, and much in contrast, with all the priests and sacrifices gone before. That He was to be a priest appointed of God; that He was to offer a sacrifice; that He was to intercede: these He had in common. But almost in these few points the resemblance ends. Like Aaron, called of God; but, unlike Aaron, He was appointed by the Oath of God. Unlike Aaron, too,

He sprang not from the Levi, but from the tribe of Judah, of which, no priest ministered at the altar. Being unlike Aaron, He could not sacrifice at the altar, He could not burn incense in the Holy Place, He could not sprinkle the atoning blood within the Holy of Holies. It is deeply significant of all His priestly work that, being thus under no legal bond to serve under the example and shadow of heavenly things, He was free to exercise a priesthood of a wider range and more exalted influence. Unlike Aaron's, our Lord's priesthood was not after the law of a carnal covenant, and in this the Apostle traces its true resemblance and type to Melchisedec, the King Priest, who appears in Sacred History, "without beginning of days or end of life." Unlike both Melchisedec and Aaron, and all other Divinely-appointed priests, Christ was both the Sacrifice and the Priest, the Victim and the Intercessor: His was the sprinkled blood, and His also the pleading voice. Thus it is that Christ, in the exercise of His priestly office, transcends all other priests and all other sacrifices; and as the High Priest, the great High Priest, appears suffering, dying without the gate ("*made a curse for us*"); offering Himself without spot to God; and once for all in the end of the world, putting away sin by the sacrifice of Himself. It is in this way Christ is connected with the penal sanctions of the Divine law. As He fulfilled the precept, so also He exhausted the penalty.

(V.) *Our Lord is connected with the redeemed as they are given Him of the Father.*

There is indeed a large number of Scriptures representing the connection between Christ and His people as the result of His work and sufferings. We are made Christ's by faith in His name, and by the renewing of the Holy Spirit. This connection is vital and practical, and through it we become partakers of the merit and moral power of the life, death and resurrection of Christ. This connection no one will deny. But there is also a large number of Scriptures declaring that the work and sufferings of Christ were undertaken because of His connection with His people. Because they were His, He became their Redeemer. This is the connection which we now wish to trace. It is a connection established by the eternal decree of the Father, by His choice, by His deed of gift to the Son, and by the Son's own free and eternal choice and love. This is the inmost circle of all our Lord's relationships, and it is in response, and in full discharge of these relationships, that our Lord pours out the infinite wealth of His doings and sufferings. This is the unmistakable meaning of many passages that contain, not mere incidental allusions, but formal expositions of the subject. When, in Heb. ii. 6—9, the Apostle had exhibited the outer circle of our Lord's connection with the *race*, he immediately carries us within the inmost circle of His union with the *Children*. Our Lord is connected with *the sons that are to be brought to glory* (verse 10); He is not ashamed to call them *"brethren"* (verse 11). Of them He says *"I will declare thy name unto My brethren, in the midst of the church will I sing praise unto thee"* (verse 12). In verse 13, they are the *"children"* which God gave to Him. In verse 16, they are *" the seed of Abraham."* And as the Apostle exhibits these tender ties existing between Christ and His people, he describes the work of Christ in a great variety of phases. But it will be observed with what unvarying fidelity it is shewn that to every part of that work Christ was moved by His union with His brethren. He turns with an unwearied sympathy, that vibrates at their need, to suffer, to teach, to praise, to extend the helping hand, to die. Because of bringing many sons unto glory, He was made perfect through sufferings. Because He was one with them, He was not ashamed to call them brethren, to declare the Father's name unto them, and in their midst sing praises unto God. Because the *Children* were partakers of flesh and blood, He also Himself took part of the same. The Apostle sums up thus, " *Wherefore in all things it behoved Him to be made like unto His brethren"* (Heb. ii. 17).

Who then are these *"children,"* these *"brethren,"* this *"seed of Abraham"* ? The explanation of this last designation throws light upon all the others. They are not all Israel which are of Israel; neither because they are the seed of Abraham are they all children; but *"In Isaac shall Thy seed be called,"* we read in Gen. xxi. 12. *"That is, they which are the children of the flesh, these are not the children of God : but the children of the promise are counted for the seed "* (Rom. ix. 6—8). Again the Apostle says in Gal. iii. 29, *" And if ye be Christ's, then are ye Abraham's seed."* The more we examine these passages, and the general course of thought and expression running through them, the more evident it will become that *" the children of God"* are His chosen ones ; the sons are *" the elect "* ; the brethren of Christ are those who are *" chosen to Him from before the foundation of the world."*

The tenor of our Saviour's own language is the same when He teaches on this theme, and it is very noticeable that it was when He was on the very point of entering within the darkest circle of His sufferings

His words grew in definiteness and emphasis. He most manifestly unveiled and explained His union with His people, and the effect that union had on all He had done, and was about to do. When His soul was about to be poured out as an oblation, He tells who they are upon whom its affections are set. When His love is about to be proved, even unto death, He makes known who they are on whose behalf that love passed through the ordeal. The vehemence of our Lord's love, in His intercessory prayer became so strong, that it put a double edge on many of His expressions, which, while it defends and secures "*His own*," even goes the length of cutting off "*the world*" from the special benefits of His work. "*I pray for them: I pray not for the world, but for them which Thou hast given Me; for they are Thine*" (John xvii. 9) . . . . . "*And for their sakes I sanctify Myself, that they also may be sanctified through the truth*" (verse 19). . . . "*Neither pray I for these alone, but for them also which shall believe on Me through their word*" (verse 20). In these expressions we get a glimpse of the breastplate of our great High Priest, and read the names of those for whose sake He approaches the Altar of Sacrifice " deep graven on His heart." The opinion of some of the Fathers, that whilst on the Cross, all the redeemed ones were in vision personally brought before the gaze of the dying Saviour, while of course it carries us into an unknown region, at the same time affords a striking commentary on this point, and also a remarkable testimony to the realistic manner in which the early Church understood the personal love of Christ to every believer.

But, indeed, we are not allowed to wait to the closing scenes; the very strongest evidence of the existence of a bond between Christ and His people is given us ere He suffers for them. The discriminative and elective feeling induced by such a bond wells up on several other occasions. It gives shape to our Lord's controversy with the Jews recorded by John. It inspires His gratitude to the Father, and moulds His mighty joy as a Redeemer, in Matthew xi. Before it defines His priestly Mediation, it is seen giving outlines, ample and full, but fixed and immutable, to His love and work as the Great and the Good Shepherd. The sheep are His before He calls them; and they hear His voice, because they are His. The sheep are His, before He dies for them; and He dies for them because they are His. They are His as the gift of the Father (John x. 29), and the objects of His own love. All the way through the variations of the discourse, Christ's loved ownership of the flock stands out as anterior to what He does on their behalf. At no point does He appear as a Shepherd in search of a flock to make it His; but because this flock is His, and in peril, He lays down His life to save them. It is in this very particular that our Lord places the successive contrasts between Himself and the stranger, the hireling, and the thief and robber. The sheep will not follow but will flee from a stranger (verse 5), *"for they know not the voice of strangers";* but the Shepherd of the sheep *" calleth His own sheep by name, and leadeth them out"* (verse 3). The thief and robber having no right of open entrance to the fold *"climb up some other way";* but the Shepherd enters by the door to His own sheep. The *"hireling"* flees when he sees the wolf coming, because the sheep are not *" his own," " because he is a hireling "* (verse 13); but the Good Shepherd encounters all hazards on their behalf, and gives His life for the sheep, because they are His own. If, therefore, you disallow this previous ownership of the flock, you remove the pivot on which the whole shepherdly care and sufferings of Christ turn, and you leave that care and those sufferings, so far as Christ's teaching in these passages is concerned, without reason and explanation. Either the reason given by the Good Shepherd Himself is true, or there is none. Does any one then say he has found another and a better reason than that rendered by Christ?

In that famous passage in Ephesians v., the same relation of cause and effect obtains. The previous bond between Christ and His Church develops into an all-controlling motive for everything that Christ does and suffers on her behalf. Here it is not ownership, as in the case of the flock, but something of a more tenacious and imperious nature: it is personal love, the bond of perfectness. In the entire passage, from verse 22, the Apostle is instructing Christian wives and husbands in the way they are respectively to fulfil the duties, and preserve the high sanctities of married life. The Church in her subjection to Christ is the model of the Christian wife's submissiveness to her husband: Christ in His love to the Church is the Model of the Christian husband's affection for his wife. The force of this lesson is enhanced, and additional insight is gained into the great truth the Apostle is applying, by observing that his argument is not based upon the assumption that human marriage is the figure of the Divine relation of Christ to the Church; but upon the ground that the relation of Christ to the Church is the grand archetype, the Divine and perfect pattern of human marriage.

Of the many and deep matters presented herein to our contemplation, I refer only to that which pertains to our present subject. The Apostle exhibits Christ as the Divine Archetypal Husband in the two aspects of *acquisition* and *fruition*. In verses 29—32, there is revealed the love of Christ in its fruition in those who are the members of His body, flesh and bones. In verses 25—27, the love of Christ in winning the Church, and making her His own, is portrayed. In this latter case, it is abundantly clear that Christ's love to the Church is no afterthought. He did not acquire, and then love; neither did He love the Church only because He had suffered. The application to her of the benefits of redemption was not incidental, or even as a mere consequence. Neither is it for one moment suggested that one great purpose dominated the sufferings of Christ, and quite another the application of the merits of those sufferings. On the contrary, one purpose pervades the sacrifice of Christ and the sanctification of the Church. One mighty motive inspires both—the great love wherewith He loved us. In the original design of that love, the presentation of the Bride *without spot, or wrinkle, or any such thing*, her purification and sanctification, and all her future glory, are as certainly inherent and essential parts as was the giving of Himself. The nuptial day, the Marriage of the Lamb, is the last of an unbroken series of redemptive acts, the first of which is the sacrifice of Himself, and the whole initiated, as it is ruled and consummated by His own Eternal love to the Church. The expression of this great truth for the Old Testament Church was, " *I have loved thee with an everlasting love . . . with lovingkindness have I drawn thee* " (Jer. xxxi. 3).

From these three typical Scriptures it was clear that there was a connection of choice, right, and love between Christ and His people before He entered upon the work of redemption.

(VI.) *Christ's relation to the Father.*

These, then, are the ties into which Christ has entered, and by which Christ is bound on the side of the creature—ties with the world, with the race, with the Jew as the recipient and transgressor of the law, and with the chosen race. But before considering their relation to one another it may be useful to bring into view for a moment what I have already alluded to, the bond between Christ and the Father. In His work Christ is a Mediator, but it is an axiom that a mediator is not of one, so there must be another side than the human on which we must look for claims and obligations. Christ is in league and covenant with

His Father in His mediation. He is the Father's Representative. He came in the Father's "name," He came "*to reveal*" the Father. He came as the Father's "*Servant*" to do the Father's "*will.*" From the Father He received a "*command*" to fulfil. By the Father a "*work*" was assigned Him to do. And though His condition in the Father's service was still that of a Son—a Son over His own house, and as such possessed of and invested with a dignity incommunicable to even the highest of God's ministers—yet His official rank was in "*the form of a servant.*" Of Him, Jehovah says, "*Behold My Servant*" (Isa. xlii. 1). Thus Christ is bound to the Father.

But while it is evident that Christ is thus bound to the Father, it is equally evident from Scripture that the bonds which bind Him are in respect of the gracious work that He accomplished for men, and in respect of no other. The very same Scriptures that show that Christ was charged to do the Father's Will, show also that that Will was the redemption of men. Scripture has revealed no work accomplished by Christ for the Father that is not connected with that redemption. There may have been profound purposes served in His Mediation, above and beyond the human, but of these we know nothing, and perhaps are incompetent to know anything in our present state. The mere supposition of such purposes, quite separate from human redemption, and God's glory therein, seems contrary to the constant tenor of Scripture. The Divine intent is, "*that now unto the principalities and powers in heavenly places might be known by the Church the manifold wisdom of God*" (Eph. iii. 10). As this redemption advances throughout the ages to accomplish its mission in all ways, only in connection with and through the Church, so also it had its beginning in the same human connection. As Christ served the Father, He served and honoured Him, clothed with the claims and obligations—whatever they were, and however numerous and various—represented in His wearing our humanity. The very essential virtue of His mediation lies in its being wrought out in discharge of these claims and obligations. Without the supposition of His human relations, how is it possible to vindicate for Him any right of place, any *locus standi*, either to do or suffer, even as God's Representative? So little separate are the two series of obligations, the Divine and the human, that the one could not be met and righteously discharged without the other. In fulfilling His task as God's Servant, Christ was fulfilling His work as the Redeemer of Man. In the same acts and sufferings by which the love and righteousness of the Father were manifested, mankind was ransomed. It is as impossible on the one hand to form a just estimate of Christ's work in glorifying the Father, by considering it apart from His union with man; as it is to judge His redemption of men aright, by considering it as disconnected from the Father's purpose and commission. The covenant of the Father with the Son has its final issue outward from Deity in the release of the redeemed from all evil, and their elevation to Eternal bliss. Christ's relation to man has its final result, inwards and upwards towards the Eternal Throne, in enhancing the glory of God and raising to a higher pitch His praise. Thus it comes about that the joyous shout of a world's redemption is also the loftiest anthem of God's praise. This marvellous harmony of man's supreme good with God's greatest glory is brought about by the double relationship of Christ, and His complete fulfilment of every claim, Divine and human.

LECTURE XVII.

THE RELATION BETWEEN CHRIST'S ENGAGEMENTS;
OR,
THE RELATION TO ONE ANOTHER OF THE VARIOUS TIES BY WHICH CHRIST IS BOUND.

THE subject is intricate; but it has this attraction, that if we can succeed in only partially opening it up, we shall thereby gain very considerable insight into many important questions, and especially into the question of the extent of the Atonement.

In order to perceive the correlation of the ties that bind Christ as a Representative, it is needful to bring also into view the claims and responsibilities arising from these ties. This I now attempt very briefly. As Christ is connected with the world, and as Creation's Heir, He is its Emancipator from the bondage of corruption. As He is connected with the race, He is the New Man, the Second Adam. As He is connected with the Jews, He is their glory, the Star of Jacob, David's Son and David's Lord. As He is connected with the law on its preceptive side, He is the Righteous One, the End of the law for righteousness: and on its punitive side, He is the one real Sacrifice, the Great High Priest. As He is connected with the Church, He is the Elder Brother, the Redeemer, the Good Shepherd, etc.

Now, if we have the authority of Scripture for believing in the existence of these relationships, and their corresponding duties and responsibilities, we ought to allow the full weight of every one of them to be felt in any theory of redemption we may form. If our system is not large enough for all of them, let us enlarge it. If it is not varied and comprehensive enough, let us add to it, rather than narrow the grace of our Lord Jesus Christ. But everything must be in its own order, and in its own proportion.

The recognition of these different points of connection will also compel us to classify the statements of Scripture, while supplying the principle on which the classification may be made. The texts pertaining to the relations of Christ to the world will not be applied to His relations to the Jews as a nation, nor to the Church as the chosen people of God. Confusion will hereby be avoided; and we shall be able to see that, while there are many purposes secured, each is distinct, and all are harmonious one with another.

So far we have the plain teaching of Scripture on our side; but Scripture does not leave us here. It does not merely state the fact of Christ's various connecting ties. It goes much further. It exhibits the order in which Christ stands to all these relationships. It shows a gradation in the parts and objects of His work, and reveals some of them as lying more distant, and others as nearest to His heart. It is in discovering and adjusting the relative positions of the various parts to one another, and to the whole of Christ's representative work, that the chief difficulty is encountered. A careful and delicate hand is needed to trace the intricate lines of these relationships as revealed in the Word of God. Not that there is any lack of certainty, but because the subject is so profound, and so liable to be handled under the influences of strong passions and prejudices.

I think it will be found that there is in Scripture a principle of co-ordination, and also of subordination or gradation in Christ's various relationships.

(I.) *The relations of Christ are co-ordinate.*

They all meet together in the one Person, the one life, the one death; they all meet together on such terms of equality, that not one of them is excluded while the others are admitted and satisfied. While Christ is fulfilling His purpose towards the Jews, He is not severed from His design towards the race. While He redeems the world, His heart is not diverted from the Church. It seems a simple truth that there is one only Christ for all; and yet in connection with these questions, it is too little heard, and needs to be repeated again and again. In His one righteousness, His one passion, His one resurrection, Christ contemplates and secures all the manifold aims of redemption, however wide or minute, however cosmic or personal they may be. Christ did not redeem the race by one act, and the Church by another; the same redemptive act is a fountain of virtue for all. This unity in

Christ implies a harmony in all the objects of His compassion. The interests of the Church, therefore, and of the world, of the elect and of the universal race, do not clash, but are combined in the one redemption. If we prove that Christ's redemption is general, we do not therefore disprove that it is particular. If we prove that Christ loved the Church and gave Himself for it, we do not therefore disprove that He is the Lamb of God that taketh away the sin of the world. Both are true, each in its proper order; both are essential and integral parts of one great whole. The system of exposition that presents them at irreconcilable variance and perpetual feud with one another is as false in logic as it is unfaithful to Scripture.

(II.) *The relations of Christ are subordinate.*

I do not mean by this that any one of the relations of Christ is subordinate in the sense that it could be omitted, or only partially met or imperfectly fulfilled. The idea is not that there was any part or purpose of His work of so little account that it could be treated with indifference, or left to hap-hazard; on the contrary, I hold that for Christ's work to be efficacious at all, and accomplish even its humblest purpose, it must be perfect and entire, wanting nothing in any part of it.

What I mean is that there is in Christ's one Mediatorial work such a subordination, or gradation if you will, of part to part, and of purpose to purpose, as we see between the foundation of the Temple and its superstructure and topstone; as we observe between the root, trunk and branches of a tree and its bloom and fruit: as we perceive in the Sabbath which was made for man, and not man for the Sabbath; as we can discern in Creation,—the world, prepared through long ages and by great processes, fitted and adorned for man, and arriving at its chief end in being man's kingdom and home. When this principle is applied to redemption it assigns to each part thereof its true place and significance, and enables us more clearly to see what that place and significance may be. The Apostle adduces it, and incidentally illustrates it, when rectifying the notions of the Corinthian converts concerning different ministries : "*for all things are your's,*" he declares, "*whether Paul, or Apollos, or Cephas, or the world, or life, or death, or things present, or things to come; all are your's; and ye are Christ's; and Christ is God's*" (1 Cor. iii. 21—23). The great principle underlying the Apostle's words is what has been called the *doctrine of final causes.* Here are the tributaries, the main stream and the eternal ocean, into which all finally flow, as from it they all had their first existence and activity.

The subject, however, is not exhausted by observing the convergence of all parts of the Saviour's work to the one great end. There is room for deepest meditation over the nature of the connection one part holds to another in the remedial plan. We find one part forms the basis of another : one part contributes to another, or is as a means to an end, that end in turn becoming the means to an end still higher ; and so the scale ascends till the very highest is reached. This ascending scale is most instructive and suggestive. Had not the Son of God come to our world, He could not have formed a connection with the human race. Had He not partaken of our nature, He could not have been a Jew. Had He not been of the seed of Abraham, He could not have been under the Mosaic law. Had He not been made under the law, He could neither have fulfilled the precepts nor borne the penalty. Had He not rendered perfect obedience and complete satisfaction, He could never have been the Redeemer of the chosen race. Had He not been the Redeemer of the chosen people, He could never have been the Author of the New Creation, the Prince of the Eternal Kingdom which is for ever to express to the Universe the very brightness of the moral splendour of Deity. Though I mention this last step, it is, however, a degree beyond Christ's proper capacity as the Representative of man to God. As the Representative, the chief and supreme of all His relationships is His relation to the brethren, the flock, the Bride, the Lamb's Wife. This is at the one end of the series where Grace begins to ripen into glory, just as at the other end is the great descent, when He bowed the heavens, and came down and tabernacled among us.

As we note each member of the series of relationships, we see that as Christ realizes it, He develops a capacity to fulfil the next. His incarnation develops the capacity to fulfil all righteousness: His fulfilling all righteousness develops the capacity to bring in an everlasting redemption. And so, since these capacities, growing and multiplying, increase in importance all along the series, it is when Christ arrives at the very chief, that of Representative of the Redeemed, that we should expect to see His power in its most multiform exhibition, and most mature and perfect degree.

This great principle runs through a large number of Scriptural statements. In one of the most general descriptions of Christ's work, it is divided into two parts—a great humiliation, and a great exaltation ;

and it is in the great humiliation into the lower parts of the earth that Christ develops the capacity for the great exaltation. The same order and sequence are observed in such passages as Phil. ii. 5—11; Heb. ii. 9, 10, 17, 18; v. 7—10; and Eph. iv. 9, 10. When we come to descriptions of the way in which His mission and work took effect, we find the effects traced from their broader phases up to their most direct and individual forms. Thus we find its broadest phase in "*He was in the world*" (John i. 10); and its narrower aspect in "*He came unto His own*" (John i. 11); and though his own kindred after the flesh received Him not, yet His own kindred after the Spirit—those born of God—receive and believe in His name. Here, then, we see its most direct aspect. In receiving "*All power .... in heaven and in earth*" (Matt. xxviii. 18), He received universal authority over the world and all that it contains, to shape, to guide, and to control all forces and events in the physical frame of things and in the life of nations, as the necessary condition of rendering effectual His own mission, and the mission of His Church throughout the ages (John xvii. 2).

He obtains power over all flesh by being made flesh, as the indispensable prerequisite for giving "*Eternal Life to as many as Thou hast given Him*" (John xvii. 2). Besides the purpose stated in Gal. iv. 4, 5—"*to redeem them that were under the law*"—the graduated conditions of fulfilling this purpose are also revealed in that He was "*made of a woman, made under the law*" (verse 4). He is made a little lower than the angels, He is made perfect through sufferings, He is made partaker of flesh and blood. He suffers through temptation, He offers up strong cryings and tears, He learns obedience by the things He suffered. He is in all things made like unto His brethren, so as to develop and mature His power to be a Merciful and Faithful High Priest in things pertaining to God, so that He may be touched with a feeling of our infirmities, have compassion on the ignorant and those out of the way, "succour them that are tempted," and lead "many sons unto glory" (Heb. ii. 7—18).

But while we thus trace the development of Christ's capacity as a Mediator in an ascending scale, we must never forget that there is a descending order of influence of no less importance. The final outcome of the Redemption Work has influenced the first step, no less than the first step has pointed to the summit. Let us only consider that that outcome is the result of intelligence, that God saw the end from the beginning, and that the end which He saw was within His own free Sovereign Choice, not forced upon Him by external violence. Being within His free choice, it was also wisely chosen; so that being intelligently, freely, and wisely chosen, He had the power, without being Himself coerced in any particular, to accomplish it exactly as it was determined. The evidence, then, is abundantly clear that it was to that final issue God subordinated and directed all previous arrangements and acts. The finished plan of the Temple thus regulated the laying of the first stone: the final issue of Redemption, contemplated in a past Eternity, modifies its initial stage in time. Because Christ was to be the Head of the Church, therefore He came to overthrow the usurped authority of the Devil in this world. Because He was to be the New Man, the quickening Spirit, therefore He came in the likeness of sinful flesh (Rom. viii. 3, 4). Because He was to purify unto Himself a peculiar people, "*He came . . . . to give His life a ransom for many*" (Mark x. 45; Matt. xx. 28), and "*He gave Himself for our sins*" (Gal. i. 4).

In proof of this a large body of Scriptures can be quoted:—

"*And ye know that He was manifested to take away our sins*" (1 John iii. 5).

"*For this purpose the Son of God was manifested, that He might destroy the works of the Devil*" (1 John iii. 8).

"*In this was manifested the love of God towards us, because that God sent His only begotten Son into the world, that we might live through Him*" (1 John iv. 9; cf. verse 14, also John iii. 16).

"*Herein is love, not that we loved God, but that He loved us, and sent His Son to be the propitiation for our sins*" (1 John iv. 10; cf. ii. 2, iii. 16, John xv. 13, and 2 Tim. i. 9, 10).

"*Who gave Himself for our sins, that He might deliver us from this present evil world, according to the will of God and our Father*" (Gal. i. 4).

"*Forasmuch as ye know . . . . . who verily was foreordained before the foundation of the world, but was manifest in these last times for you, who by Him do believe in God*" (1 Peter i. 18—21).

These Scriptures, and many others of the same mould, while not hiding from view the broader bearings of Christ's work, direct the eye over all and through all upward to where all converge in the believing, sanctified and glorified Church. To the Church Christ Himself directs His ultimate aim. If He attacks the outer walls and fortifications of the world, it is to capture the Church, which is as the Citadel. If He purchases the field of the world, it is to reach, and righteously make His own, the Church which is the hidden treasure there.

From a comparison of these two methods of describing our Lord's mediatorial work, it will, I think, strike every mind most forcibly (1) That Christ *could not* have been the Church's Redeemer unless He had been the world's; and (2), That Christ *would not* have been the World's Redeemer unless He had been the Redeemer of the Church. This view of the case will prevent Christ's work in relation to the world at large from appearing as an unimportant appendage. It will impress us with the idea that its universal scope was an essential part of the entire scheme, so essential that without it there could be no fulfilment of the particular design. On the other hand, it will be evident that Christ's ultimate relations to the Church are no afterthought, coming into view when the broader work had been planned or finished, nor are the numbers of the saved determined finally by the unconquerable obstinacy or yielding pliancy of the human will. Christ's relations to the Church inspire the generous freeness of His work, and enlarge it to its utmost expanse over the world and race. He is Head over all things for the Church. The benefits of His redemption do not dwindle down from being universal in aim to be limited in their effect: it was because the purpose was originally fixed and particular that the work was set to so grand a scale. Thus it results that Christ's work has universal scope, because it has a particular design.

Therefore, though it sounds somewhat paradoxical, if you would see the work of mediation where it is broadest and most comprehensive in its bearings, you must consider Christ as the Representative of the Church. The reason is, that this being the "supreme office" Christ bears, it includes all the other parts of His work; it is to this all the other parts contribute and converge, and in this they culminate. It is this principle that underlies the Apostle's words (1 Cor. iii. 21—23), "*All things are your's; whether Paul, or Apollos, or Cephas, or the world, or life, or death, or things present, or things to come; all are your's; and ye are Christ's; and Christ is God's.*" Christ in being the Head of the Church is the Head of all things. When, therefore, we behold Him stand forth as the Representative of the Church to be her Redeemer, we see Him in that high undertaking necessarily burdened with the weight of a world's reparation, charged with the task of restoring a race, and face to face with the duty of bringing in all righteousness, and making an end of sin. It is in her cause that His mightiest works are to be done, and for her sake His great sorrow and sufferings are to be endured. And as where anything exists in highest perfection, there its nature and properties can be best discerned; so, since it is in relation to the Church that the perfection of Christ's mediatorial work is reached, it is in that relation we may hope to gain the clearest and deepest insight into its nature and effects.

We shall, therefore, henceforth consider Christ *in His mediatorial work as the Representative of the Redeemed.* I have already sketched in general outline what is meant by the connection, it is now needful to be more particular. As Christ is the Representative of the world there is nothing of a personal character in the relation. This also applies to His relation to mankind; for He is the Representative of the race as a race, and not of the individuals of that race. It is true also of His relation to the Jews; it is the nation as a nation, the people as a people, that find in Him a Representative. But when we come to the Church we find a discrimination with regard to the individuals of which she is composed, to which the world, the race, and the Jewish nation are alike strangers. These are no longer spoken of or treated in the mass, but personally, singly, individually. If wider terms are used, they are so qualified as to leave no doubt as to Christ's union with every one of them individually, so that there is no exception whatever allowable in their number. If spoken of as a "*generation,*" they are a "*chosen*" generation; if as a "*people,*" they are a "*peculiar*" people, a people most intimately God's own. They are said to be "*chosen,*" "*elected,*" "*called,*" "*foreknown,*" "*predestinated,*" "*sanctified,*"—language which can be only fairly interpreted to mean an individual choice and personal predestination of the redeemed. Seeing that it is the constant teaching of Scripture that this choice is in Christ, it follows that Christ in His mediatorial work is the Representative of the Church in all her membership personally considered. To this there is no exception; in this, no omission; of this, no diminution. As the whole human family are without exception comprised in Adam as the natural head of the race, so in the case of the Redeemed, Christ is individually and collectively their Representative before God. But this comparison with Adam suggests the intimate nature of Christ's Representation of His people, and warrants the application to it of a stronger term. Adam is the natural head of the race: Christ is the federal, spiritual, and vital Head of the ransomed race, and is thus its Representative.

In reference to this intimate nature of Christ's relation with His people, a vast array of metaphors, types, and illustrations of every kind is found in Scripture; and with some of them we are very familiar.

Union of support.
   He is the Foundation . . . . They the building.
                                1 Cor. iii. 10, 11.
                                Eph. ii. 20, 21.
                                1 Pet. ii. 4—6.

Union of sustenance.
   He is the Vine. . . . . . . They the branches.
                                John xv. 1—5.

Union of guardianship.
   He is the Shepherd . . . . . They the flock.
                                John x. 3, 4, 9, 11, 14, 15.

Union of kindred.
   He is the Elder Brother . . . They the family.
                                Heb. ii. 10—14.

Union of love.
   He is the Husband . . . . . They the bride.
                                Eph. v. 25—32.

Union of life.
   He is the Head . . . . They the members.
                                1 Cor. xii. 12, 27.
                                Eph. v. 30; i. 22, 23; iv. 15, 16.
                                Col. i. 18—24.

Christ does not sustain these relationships with His own people in common with others. The believing and the elect are alone thus intimately united with Him. Believers exclusively are the "*living stones,*" built on Christ, the elect and precious foundation, the branches in the Vine, and the members of the body of which Christ is the Head. In reference to this last particular Headship, Christ is said (Eph. i. 22) "*to have all things under His feet*"; this would seem to bring in others as sharers with the redeemed; but this is not on a par with His Headship of the Church, being indeed subordinate to it. He is "*Head over all things* to the Church"; the redemption of the Church is the chief of all God's purposes and achievements. If we trace up the saving virtue that was diffused throughout all these relations, we shall find its first elements to be lodged in Christ's priestly work. The river of living water flows from beneath the Throne of God and of the Lamb (Rev. xxii. 1).

The reasons why I now draw attention to this phase of our Lord's work are two: the first is derived from Scripture; the second, from the nature of the case.

(I.) Scripture never severs any portion of our Lord's work from connection with those who ultimately receive the benefit of it. It insists with an additional emphasis on this relation at all points of our Lord's career, when His suffering comes into view, and when shame and death are endured. His work of mediation which belonged to His whole life on earth implies, indeed, this connection. It is impossible also to fully explain our Lord's sufferings and death apart from His connection with those to whom such suffering and death were justly due. It is not to be explained by saying He became a man; it is not human to suffer and die. That is the doom of sinful humanity; but Christ was free from sin. His connection with the race will not explain it, for in this particular He had nothing in common with the rest of mankind. On the one hand, His miraculous birth secured His freedom from the hereditary taint of other men, and on the other hand, His righteous life defined Him to be the Holy One of God. The fact, admitted by most, that His sufferings and death are the greatest exhibition of God's righteousness, will not explain the death and sufferings themselves; for they, in some form, constitute the penalty of sin. There must be a most righteous bond connecting Christ in a most righteous manner with these same sufferings and death, that is, with the penalty of sin; otherwise what is represented as a supreme manifestation of righteousness cannot be cleared from being the perpetration of supreme unrighteousness. It is not enough to show that He voluntarily undertook to bear the penalty; His right so to will must be demonstrated. What *locus standi* had He in the matter? What righteous, what legal footing did He occupy?

Observe the difficulty is not on the Divine side: all admit His perfect union in purpose with the Father in enduring the penalty. The point to be cleared up is His connection with the penalty. For if He was not legally connected with the penalty, He could not righteously endure it, and His sufferings and death could never count in the scale of righteousness. To represent that the penalty of sin considered in the abstract,—sin as the great injury and dishonour done to God, the Moral Governor of the Universe,—apart altogether from those creatures who committed the sin, was righteously inflicted because it was voluntarily endured, is to render an explanation which leaves unexplained what most requires it—the legal right Christ had as the Sin-bearer. On this ground Christ might as well have taken upon Himself the nature of angels as of men. This hypothesis ignores the invariable teaching of Scripture which connects Christ with "sinners" as well as with "sin." To this conclusion then we are driven, that the only thing that can give a rational and righteous account of Christ's endurance of penal sufferings is to be found in His federal union with His people. They were sinful; yet He came to their help. He voluntarily espoused their cause; He identified Himself with them before the eye of the law; and submitted to all the conditions by which they could be lifted up to God. *He loved them and gave Himself for them*.[1] This same federal bond which made it a righteous thing for Christ to suffer, also prevents the final condemnation of any for whom those sufferings were endured.

(II.) Having thus shown that our Lord occupied a legal position by virtue of His Headship, we now proceed to examine what He did in fulfilment of that position.

(1.) The first demand on Christ as the Head, comes from the *vast and pressing need of man for reconciliation with God*. Over and above all the moral institutions, the unrest and misery, the weakness and darkness of sinners, there is the deep need for peace with God. Alienation from Him is the root of the world's woes. Sin has shown itself to be exceeding sinful, by making the alienation entire, and dissolving the created harmony between man and God. Sin has rent man from the Eden of God's presence, driven him as a prodigal from the Father's home into a far country, separated him from the Tree of Life and the Fountain of Living Waters, and turned him who was formed for fellowship into a fugitive. The friend has become an enemy, the child an alien, the law-abiding subject a rebel against his King. It is this self-inflicted exile, this voluntary going astray from God, this enmity—wilful, yet fruitless and impotent, that fills the sinner's lot with fears, and surrounds it with terrors. Until this alienation is removed in its root and cause, until the stranger is "*brought nigh*," "*reconciled*," "*made one*" with God, and the enmity destroyed, nothing of a thorough or permanent nature is effected for man's safety and regeneration. Could the conscience of mankind be quickened to feel and express its first and deepest

---

[1] Cf. Gal. ii. 20, i. 4; Eph. v. 2; Tit. ii. 14.

need, it would put it into the publican's cry, God be merciful, God be propitious, be reconciled to me, a sinner.

(2.) *What is the reconciliation needed?* To ascertain this, we must look at the elements of the alienation, both from the Divine and human standpoint. On God's part, indeed, no cause of offence was given, the injury to His character was gratuitous; His law was just and good, and the basis of the well-being of the universe. His separation from man is the separation of the offended from the offender; His ground of displeasure, His own outraged majesty, the dishonour of His law, and the injury done to the cause of good order throughout the universe. On the side of man, the alienation is the alienation of the offender, the holding aloof from guilty shame and dread, the separation of distrust, hatred and rebellion.

It is very apparent that if a reconciliation would be effective in both directions, it must contain elements of a most diverse kind. On the one hand, it must be adapted to the offended Moral Ruler, who has, in upholding His own dignity and the authority of His law, to guard the wide interests of the universe. On the other, it must be fitted to eradicate from man the distrust and disobedience springing from his sin and departure from God. In a word, *it must combine reparation and persuasion, satisfaction and regeneration.* On the side of God, it must meet the demands of violated law; on the side of man, it must vanquish his depravity. If the reparation offered to God can also be the most potent persuasive addressed to man, we shall see herein the consummation and masterpiece of Divine wisdom. For the Mediator to confine Himself to only one side would be to leave the work half done, and the chasm of separation as wide as before. The utter insufficiency of a one-sided scheme of reconciliation becomes glaringly manifest, especially when it is claimed that only man needs to be reconciled. Is the glory of the Moral Ruler to meet with no consideration? Is the authority of His law worthy of no regard? Is the welfare of the universe menaced by sin to count for nothing in the scale? The mere mention of these high considerations justifies their title not only to a place, but to one also in the first rank of those things which must be dealt with in bringing about a true reconciliation. Until God is satisfied, where can man find safety?

(3.) *What then are the means by which Christ effected reconciliation?* Had reconciliation been requisite only on the side of man, then it might have been effected by means of the sinner's repentance. In that case atonement and conversion would have been synonymous; faith would be the propitiation; and repentance the offering up of oneself without spot unto God. If any process of action or teaching that could have brought about such a moral change in man would have been a valid reconciliation, one fails to see the need of the Incarnation, and must come to the Apostle's conclusion—"*Christ is dead in vain*," *i.e.*, gratuitously (Gal. ii. 21). But all this proceeds on the latent assumption that justice is not injured, which is another form of saying that sin is not a transgression of law. If, however, sin be allowed to have any moral character, if our definition—a transgression of law—be allowed, then a mere change in conduct or character—even were that possible—would leave the ancient offences and injuries just where they were before. Inasmuch as the claims of the injured righteousness were still outstanding and had to be met, inasmuch as the majesty of the law had to be asserted and vindicated with reference to the past,—it is very evident that something more than an alteration in man's disposition must be accomplished, since he is the violator of the majesty and justice.

Both Scripture and the human conscience insist on reparation. The instinctive sense of right in the human breast refuses to admit that the repentance of the wrong-doer is a valid atonement for his wrong. That instinct is so embodied in the laws of mankind that the thief is not allowed to go free on an expression of sorrow for his theft. The creditor is not satisfied by the debtor's contrition; nor is it allowed that the crime of murder is sufficiently expiated by the remorse of the murderer. Were the bonds of right manufactured or elastic, it would not require much calculation to forecast the time when law would be denied even a faint resemblance of respect and acknowledgment, while the thief, the debtor and capital offender would give full play to their evil propensities without the slightest twinge of compunction. Such a justice for transgressors would be brought about in that day when right had lost its might. When justice has lost her sword, she may also cast down her scales. But since Eternal Justice has not cast away either the unerring scales or the two-edged sword, since she cannot relent or abate anything of her demands—for that would be a departure from the right and a sanction of the wrong, and anything less than justice would be injustice—since God has declared that "*the wages of sin is death*" (Rom. vi. 23), that "*He will by no means clear the guilty*" (Ex. xxxiv. 7), and that "*the soul that sinneth it shall die*" (Ezek. xviii. 4), we cannot, we ought not to hope for reconciliation at less cost than a perfect obedience of the precept, on the one hand, and on the other, by less rigorous means than are shadowed forth in the great axiom, the constitutional law of the Mediatorial system—" *Without shedding of blood is no remission*" (Heb. ix. 22). That reparation must be made is therefore clear, and it is equally clear from the passages just adduced, what the nature of that reparation to Justice must be, by which God is reconciled to man. It is a reparation made by means of death and the shedding of blood; for only through these can man receive the fruit of reconciliation which is the remission of sins.

From the beginning to the end, from Genesis to Revelation, under the Law and under the Gospel, Scripture is constant on this point. If history can make a doctrine certain, no doctrine can be more certain than this. From the days of Abel, the first believer who died, till the moment when the festal assembly of the redeemed shall meet in immeasurable multitude before the Eternal Throne, there is no variation, there is no weakness, there is no exception discernible in any instance in her testimony to this being the divinely revealed way of reconciliation. Abel's more acceptable sacrifice, offered outside the Gates of Eden, finds in the New Jerusalem its antitype and realization in the Lamb enthroned, and the curse for ever removed. " WITHOUT SHEDDING OF BLOOD IS NO REMISSION" might fitly be inscribed on the whole course of reconciliation in all its phases from *Paradise Lost* to *Paradise Regained*. If anywhere the letters are unusually large and plain, it is in connection with the work of the one Mediator between God and man.

(4.) We may therefore advance with a growing conviction of certainty to our fourth point, *Christ effected reconciliation by means of His death*. We find this stated almost in so many words: "*And you, that were sometime alienated and enemies in your mind by wicked works, yet now hath He reconciled in the body of His flesh through death*" (Coloss. i. 21, 22). In relying on this, or on kindred passages, to show that by Christ's death God is reconciled, I cannot be charged with taking for granted the thing to be proved; because the Apostle speaks in the passage of two reconciliations, the one as accomplished, the other to be accomplished; the one the basis of the other; the one supplying the motive power to bring the other about. The one which is accomplished is the reconciliation of God; the other to be accomplished is the reconciliation of man. Should this not be conceded—and how can it be denied?—then we are forced to think both reconciliations refer to man, so that a man can be reconciled and not reconciled: he can be the subject of a complete reconciliation which is to form the motive and basis for another and further reconciliation. The same absurdity is involved by applying this sense of reconciliation to the similar passages (Eph. ii. 13—17, and 2 Cor. v. 18—21). In the former, Christ is represented as preaching and imparting peace because He had made peace. But what weak and meaningless theology it would be if the peace that is the basis of the preaching is the same as the peace that is the result and fruit of the preaching! If already they had it, why preach it, why impart it by preaching? In the latter (2 Cor. v.) there is a "*reconciliation*" and a "*ministry of reconciliation*" (verse 18). There is a reconciliation offered to God, and there is a "*word of reconciliation*" addressed to man. The work of reconciliation with God consisted in Christ having been made sin for us: the work of reconciliation of men is "*that we might be made the righteousness of God in Him*" (verse 21). Hence the word of pardon is grounded on the work of mediation. Upon this same ground the ambassadors take their stand, and from it draw their prevailing entreaties and moving supplications. Hence reconciliation is finished and yet unfinished: "*God hath reconciled us to Himself by Jesus Christ*" (verse 18), and yet we are besought on behalf of Christ, "*be ye reconciled to God*" (verse 20). But if reconciliation is only to be taken in one sense throughout this fervent and vigorous appeal, and that too in the sense of man being the subject of reconciliation, we cut the nerve of all its strength, and turn what is possessed of Divine energy into chaotic jargon. I take it therefore as our indefeasible right to use these, and all such Scriptures, in support of the doctrine that Christ reconciled us to God by His death. His work was first objective and then subjective. He has made reconciliation for us; He now works it within us.

(5.) The fact being plain that Christ did effect reconciliation with God by His death, we next propose to enquire, *Under what view could His death have accomplished reconciliation?* If we regard His death as natural, as coming about in the ordinary course from purely natural causes, it could in this sense effect no reconciliation, unless we are prepared to believe that all natural death makes reconciliation with God. Where then would be the need for the dread warning, "*After death the Judgment"*? Where the room for future penalties, if death discharges the debt of justice, as well as pays the "debt of nature"? Either Christ's death considered as in the course of nature could make no reconciliation for us, or else all death reconciles; and if this be so, Where was the need for Christ to die at all? Why die to do for others what everyone in death could and must do for himself?

Nor can we see how reconciliation could be brought about if the death of Christ be regarded as necessary, wherever that necessity be p'aced, either in the powers of evil which He encountered, or in what is called the Law of Being. If we place the necessity of Christ's death in His conflict with the powers of evil, we run counter to the reiterated declarations of our Lord Himself. Again and again He repudiates the compulsion to the subordination implied in such necessity, and asserts His freedom and sovereignty of action over the powers of darkness, even while He yielded to them. "*No man taketh it* (My life) *from Me . . . . . I* HAVE POWER *to lay it down*" (John x. 18). He maintained in every single act of suffering up to the very last His perfectly free volition, and never lapsed into the condition of helpless submission to the inevitable. Such a surrender would, on the one hand, rob His final sufferings of their moral value, where that moral value culminates, that is, as those sufferings mature into death. On the other hand, to have given up the helm when the storm of enmity was at its height would have been, in plain and naked verity—whatever fine words and phrases may be employed to disguise it—the shipwreck, and not the victory of virtue. For Christ to be driven and to drift on that storm's billows would have been the crowning triumph of evil, and instead of inspiring the hope and strength of a new life, would have taken all hope away, leaving the gloom of an eternal despair. To say that Christ was borne down to death by the irresistible violence of the evil He assailed, is simply to say that He was conquered, and that His life and death were an impotent protest against that evil. To say such a death was a martyrdom, the sealing of His testimony with His blood, is to use a very thin disguise of that impotency. Besides which it misrepresents the whole nature of martyrdom as known among Christians. Whence did Martyrs arise? What formed their inspiration and their strength in the days when their blood was the seed of the Church? It may have been the great example of Christ as the faithful and true Witness, or Martyr, but this in a subordinate degree. If this were so, it would be a hard problem to solve, why the death of Socrates was so barren and that of

Christ so prolific. What first and principally kindled the zeal of the martyr host, came from Christ in His death being to the martyrs something more than a Martyr. It came from that very element to which they who say Christ's death was a mere martyrdom deny existence, viz., that He bore (sacrificially) our sins in His own body on the tree (1 Pet. ii. 24). As the Sin-bearer, our Lord was the Victor, though necessarily the Sufferer. As the Sin-bearer, He was the Redeemer, and it is the Redeemer that makes the martyr. To represent Christ's death as a martyrdom is to rob it of that virtue which made the martyr element therein operative and contagious. The very essence of that virtue lay in Christ's entire voluntariness in submitting to death. For this reason, we must resist and reject all necessity, coming from the antagonism of evil, as offering a true or complete account of the way in which Christ died. Here, however, it is only fair to say that they who represent Christ's death as fully accounted for by the action of natural causes, or the violence of evil, do not feel the pressure of this difficulty. They deny Christ made reconciliation with God for us; they deny that there was any opposition by Justice to the sinner's acceptance; and consequently they can lightly pass over the question whether Christ was or was not held in the iron grip of necessity when He died. For us who hold that reconciliation was needed, that Christ by His death effected that reconciliation, it is of the first importance to demonstrate His complete moral freedom, and mastery over Himself, even in His death; for therein lies one chief requisite—*the moral efficacy of His death as a means of reconciliation.*

The remaining necessity that is alleged is of a more subtle kind. Its pressure is traced up to the Eternal Law, to the Eternal Being. "It was the will of God, the dictate of the Eternal Nature. He could not but have acted thus." It is claimed that "vicarious sacrifice is the law of Being." "It is a mysterious and fearful thing to observe how all God's universe is built upon this law, how it penetrates and pervades all Nature, so that, if it were to cease, Nature would cease to exist."[1] It is admitted, indeed, that Christ freely came under the force of this law *consciously*, and voluntarily obeyed it as the law of man's existence."[2] But even with the addition of the elements of "consciousness and freedom" to His submission to this law, His death, if due to the behests of this inexorable law, is thereby incapable, no less than by other kinds of necessity, of effecting reconciliation. The incapacity came from

---

[1] Robertson's *Sermons*, Vol. 1, p. 138.   [2] Ibid, Vol. 1, p. 139.

a different cause, but is as certain if due heed be paid to this statement. In this account, Christ's death is said to be due to a law that is never broken, consciously or unconsciously. Now, if Christ's death be only traceable to a universal law, acting with the universal precision, and of the same nature as the laws of the material universe, then the suffering of death is no longer a penalty on account of disobedience, but becomes the most illustrious example of obedience. It thus excludes the idea of reconciliation to God, for there could be no wrath were there no offence against law: and this law is such that none can transgress, for it enforces itself. This is the very thing the framers of this theory wish to do. They wish to teach that Christ did not reconcile God and satisfy for transgression; but that He exhibited the self-denial of Deity in His death. The only purpose answered thereby, is to demonstrate the righteousness of this inexorable law by submitting to it, thus reconciling others who are forcibly under it to the misery of their lot, and to acquiesce in it as the best thing for them. Men would thus be led to do voluntarily what they now submit to through necessity. The things themselves would remain the same : the necessity to suffer would remain unaltered,—to suffer just as Christ did, to die just in the same sense as Christ did. And the law would gain in additional strength through the honour done to it by Christ. This being so, everyone who, either with or without the force of His example, voluntarily acquiesced in this law would, in his death, be as true a sacrifice as Christ was; his sufferings and death would be as real an atonement as Christ made. This, indeed, is the result which is represented as the one, and the only one, contemplated in the humiliation of our Lord.

Without denying that there are some grains of truth scattered here and there throughout this theory, I charge it with being utterly erroneous and false as a complete account of Christ's death. It turns the meaning of such Scriptures as "*By whom we have now received the reconciliation*" (Rom. v. 11), into "by ourselves we have received the reconciliation." It leaves no room for the plain meaning—which is also the vital sense of many other passages—but contradicts it. We must no longer read, "*But now once in the end of the world hath He appeared to put away sin by the sacrifice of Himself*" (Heb. ix. 26); Sin is put away by our self-sacrifice. It is not true that "*Christ was once offered to bear the sins of many*" (Heb. ix. 28); every one bears his own iniquity and meritoriously puts it away.

It also gives a false view of death. Suffering and death are represented as having their origin in the force of a preceptive law; a law that is never broken, for it enforces itself. But Scripture traces this dominion over mankind not to law, but to the violation of law; not to a self-enforcing precept, but to a divinely inflicted penalty. Death is not the embodiment of Eternal righteousness, but "the curse" denounced upon the transgressors of that righteousness. Our Lord therefore did not suffer and die by keeping to the footsteps of Eternal law, but by standing in the room of law-breakers; not by developing an Eternal righteousness, but by suffering the just for the unjust; not because of His own infinite love, but because in that love He was made a curse for us, as it is written, "*Cursed is every one that hangeth on a tree*" (Gal. iii. 13). We see His holiness in all these sufferings, and His love sustaining them all, as we see the sun in an eclipse; the darkness of the eclipse comes not from the sun, for he shines with undimmed ray behind it all. The darkness comes from another source, another orb intervenes with its bulk of gloom and shuts the brightness out. And so in the eclipse of the Sun of Righteousness, the horror of darkness overspreading Him arose not from His own burning beams, but because our iniquities were made to meet upon Him. His love bore the suffering, but the suffering had not its origin in the love. His righteousness endured the death, but death had not its source in His righteousness, but in human sin. By sin came death, the death of Adam, and all his children, and the death also of the Second Adam—the Son of God.

And so on all the occasions when Scripture touches upon this momentous theme, it employs a like careful discrimination. And this most necessarily and justly: for while it was essential to show Christ's character was free from every stain, it was equally necessary to show that so absolutely holy and good a being—the Holy One of God—was not smitten, and did not suffer, by virtue of His own holiness, but because of His union with the unjust and the sinful.

But all this reasoning proceeds on the assumption that the alleged law of self-sacrifice is the true reading of the constitution of nature. Is it so? Is it indeed true that this law "penetrates and pervades all nature, so that if it were to cease, Nature would cease to exist"?[1] Let it be remembered that the question is not whether one order of creatures is nourished and sustained by another—the higher by the lower, the animal by the vegetable, and the vegetable by the mineral. This is a

---

[1] Robertson's *Sermons*, Vol. I, p. 138.

fact open as the face of day. The question is whether this is done by way of self-sacrifice. Do the lower forms of life sacrifice themselves to the higher? Does the vegetable sacrifice itself to the animal, and the mineral to the vegetable? What is self-sacrifice? If it means anything that is at all pertinent to this matter, it must, on the most cursory view, signify a surrender of happiness, of life, or even of existence for the good of other and higher orders of creation; and the essence of the matter is that this should be done consciously and voluntarily. These are the very least of the elements that can give us an adequate idea of self-sacrifice. But when they are stated who does not see that we are ascribing to Nature something to which she has no just claim, something that is not found within her whole domain, something of which Nature is not even capable. Who can speak in sober language of the consciousness of the mineral as it yields its nourishment to the vegetation of the Earth? Has the Sun, the most potent and universal benefactor of our material world, the gift of consciousness, the sense of free benevolence, when he floods the heavens with light and the Earth with warmth? Has the Sea consciousness when it sends its vapours to the sky to be the fertilizing treasures of thirsty lands and parching crops? Is the corn conscious and free as it falls beneath the sickle, or the grass as it is cropped by browsing flocks and herds? Do these same flocks and herds immolate themselves at the feet of man, or in a martyr spirit seek the knife and the shambles freely and voluntarily, in utter self-negation and self-sacrifice, crowding to suffer and die for his higher good?

The hard facts of nature hold another and a far different language and meaning. The truth rather is that no creature obtains its supply without exacting it, and capturing its food as its prey. The vegetable makes the mineral contribute to its support; the animal captures and slays the vegetable; and man conquers and subdues all to his own purposes; and there is nothing which he or any other creature uses or consumes, that he must not win by superior skill or strength. This was the original law imposed on man at his creation, the very character of his being and well-being; and all life, in all its grades, is in its measure, and after its kind, under the very same law. All nature teems with evidence of the existence of this law; but when nature is put on the rack to disclose this other law—that of self-sacrifice—upon which her very being is said to depend, she remains obstinately silent and shows no sign that it exists in any of her realms, whether mineral, vegetable, or animal.

Only by one of two errors, or by a combination of both, can there be attributed even the semblance of true self-sacrifice. We may poetize the interdependence the Creator has established between the different orders of being for the purpose of mutual sustenance. This is imagination, not interpretation of nature; fiction, not science or law. Or else we may borrow the ideas and language proper to the Redeemer and redemption, and by the aid of fancy clothe Nature in garments not her own, hiding what she really is, and making her appear what she is not, a practical exponent of the grace of our Lord Jesus Christ. Only when we have misread Nature on the one hand, and on the other read into her pages a language taken from a higher source, can we obtain from her even a broken and faltering utterance of the faintest semblance of self-sacrifice as it appears in the sacrifice of the Son of God for the redemption of men. But the law of self-sacrifice is itself utterly absent from Nature in all her operations. Thus the very basis of this kind of necessity, when examined, crumbles and disappears, and with it all the theories and speculations built upon it concerning the Saviour's death.

(6.) Our way is now open to enquire how we must regard Christ's sufferings and death *as they merit and procure reconciliation with God.* What was the character or quality that gave them this efficiency? This has already suggested itself in the foregoing observations:—

(*a*) *Christ's sufferings and death were penal.* They were endured as the doom appointed and inflicted by God on account of the violation of law. They came upon Him, it is true, through the ignorance and malignant envy of wicked men; but this is only part of the truth. They came as an infliction from a higher and holier Hand. As we read, "*He hath put Him to grief*"; and again, "*It pleased the Lord to bruise Him*" (Isa. liii. 10). They came as the consequences of contact with evil, permitted by the Father for disciplinary purposes. But this also is only part of the truth; it must be added that they came as the allotted punishment denounced against sin. Christ died *because* (διά) of our sins, *for* (περί) our sins, and *on account of* (ὑπέρ) our sins. In what He suffered there was so complete a revelation of the righteous displeasure against sin, such a judicial exaction of the penalty due to the infringement of law, that it is said, "*He hath made Him to be sin for us, who knew no sin*" (2 Cor. v. 21), and also that He was "*made a curse for us*" (Gal. iii. 13). And, indeed, without the visitation of judicial displeasure be admitted, we must leave the most peculiar and striking facts in the sufferings and death of Christ without an adequate explanation. Without the cloud of righteous wrath, without the penal curse, without the "awakened sword" smiting the man that is Jehovah's fellow, the mystery of the Cross is wrapped in deeper mystery still. So far as the humanly inflicted sufferings of Christ are concerned, if these comprised all He endured, we might see, as we all do and must see in them, the perfection of a serene trust in God and benevolence to man. In these, indeed, Christ has given such a display of a divinely pure, elevated and harmonious godliness and philanthropy, that they must impress and inspire all who contemplate the decease He accomplished at Jerusalem. But His encounter with the mere human and earthly sufferings is the very least of all He endured. The stress of His struggle, the agony of His passion began where these ended. His bodily calamities and the wrongs inflicted by wicked men were only the dark shadow cast around Him by a substance of grief that pressed His soul in sorrow even to death. It is there that we are conducted to the margin of the vast ocean-like woe, against which He had to contend ; its mighty waves break and resound in our hearing, but its profound depths are to us unfathomable and invisible. That exceeding great and heart-rendering cry " *My God, My God, why hast Thou forsaken Me ?* "[1] comes as an echo from His invisible conflicts, and were there no other evidence, this would of itself infallibly testify to the penal character of His sufferings and death. This cry brings before us an element belonging to this penalty which deserves consideration, as it is instructive on the whole subject of punishment, and especially so in relation to the passion of our Lord. I refer to the element of *separation* or *exclusion* of the criminal from the good. This appears in the first stage of Adam's penalty—he was driven forth from Eden from the presence of the Lord. It appears in Cain, who went forth from the presence of the Lord, a fugitive. It appears in the penalties denounced by human authority on criminals against society. The prison embodies it ; the distant penal settlement points to it ; exile and banishment are its exponents. It culminates in this world in the death penalty—separation that bodes no reunion, an exile that anticipates no return, a banishment that forbids recall. It reappears in the world to come, when Angel reapers shall separate the tares from the wheat, and the Great Shepherd divide the sheep from the goats. It culminates there in the sentence of the Judge of all—" *Depart from Me, ye cursed, into everlasting fire, prepared for the devil and his angels*

---

[1] Matt. xxvii. 46.

. . . . . *and these shall go away into everlasting punishment"* (Matt. xxv. 41, 46).

This very element is found in the sufferings of the Saviour. It forms the dread basis and background of His cry from the Cross, " *Why hast Thou forsaken Me ?* " Nothing could so certainly seal the conviction that Christ experienced at that moment a hiding of the Father's face, which was of a penal nature, and inflicted because He " *bare our sins in His own body on the tree.*" [1] It marks the uttermost aversion and detestation of sin on God's part; it shows that He is of purer eyes than to behold iniquity. When the gaze of the Eternal Judge is turned away even from the Spotless Son as He bears sin, it is the last proof given to the universe that sin is that abominable thing which God hates.

(*b*) *Christ's sufferings and death were sacrificial.* While the infliction of the penalty may testify displeasure at transgression, and make right terrible in the eyes of sinners, the object of sacrifice is of a much wider scope. In the sacrifice, it is true, the idea of penalty appears in the sufferings and death of the victim. But sufferings and death are only subsidiary to the main purpose. The main purpose of sacrifice is not to show the heinousness of sin, but to remove it; it is not to display the Divine displeasure against sin, but to avert it,—to avert while revealing the wrath of God against sin. The transgressor bears the penalty; the sacrifice bears it away. The endurance of the penalty comes through the vindication of God's righteousness; the sufferings of the sacrifice aim at the restoration of His favour. Hence it is that, while all sacrificial sufferings must be also penal, all penal sufferings are not necessarily sacrificial. The suffering victim requires a character of which the penal sufferer is, as a rule, destitute. What is that character? What is it that can turn the penal sufferer into the sacrificial? Absolute freedom from guilt, complete absence of a reason why it should suffer at all. Christ as the holy, harmless, and undefiled; Christ as the Lamb without blemish and without spot, is the Sacrifice. Christ is " *the Lamb of God which taketh away the sin of the World* " (John i. 29).

That Christ's sufferings were *sacrificial* as well as *penal* is very evident from the plain sense of Scripture. Thus in Isaiah liii. 10, we read, " *When thou shalt make His soul an offering for sin.*" He was to make " *reconciliation for iniquity* " (Dan. ix. 24). " *Christ our Passover is sacrificed for us* " (1 Cor. v. 7). " *Whom God hath set forth to*

---

[1] 1 Pet. ii. 24.

be a propitiation through faith in His blood" (Rom. iii. 25). "*He is the propitiation for our sins*" (1 John ii. 2). "*As Christ also hath loved us, and hath given Himself for us, an offering and a sacrifice to God*" (Eph. v. 2). "*Who needeth not daily, as those high priests, to offer up sacrifice, first for his own sins, then for the people's: for this He did once, when He offered up Himself*" (Heb. vii. 27). "*Now once in the end of the world hath He appeared to put away sin by the sacrifice of Himself*" (Heb. ix. 26). "*This man, after He had offered one sacrifice for sins for ever, sat down on the right hand of God*" (Heb. x. 12). "*Worthy is the Lamb that was slain to receive power, and riches, and wisdom, and strength, and honour, and glory, and blessing*" (Rev. v. 12).

So constantly and so strongly is the sacrificial character of Christ's sufferings enforced through every part of the New Testament, that an impartial writer (Soame Jenyns), himself emerging from infidelity, has said that "whoever will seriously peruse those writings, and deny that it is there, may, with as much reason and truth, after reading the works of Thucydides and Livy, assert that in them no mention is made of any facts relative to the histories of Greece and Rome."[1]

But it is alleged that though Christ's death is spoken of as sacrificial, such language is an accommodation to Jewish ideas, and the death is not sacrificial in a real, but in a figurative sense. Against these allegations the express teaching of the New Testament (Heb. viii.) is, that so far from the language ever used of Christ's passion being toned down to Jewish notions, the whole framework of the Jewish ceremonies of sacrifice was set up as the type of Christ's sacrifice. Instead of the Jewish sacrifices being real and Christ's figurative, Scripture declares the Mosaic offerings were only a " shadow," whereas Christ's is the "substance," and His death the one only real sacrifice. Yet the patriarchal or Levitical sacrifice illustrates in a most vivid and impressive manner the essential truths clustering around the death of Christ. A victim is selected, the best of the flock or the herd, without blemish or defect. It is brought before the altar of the Lord; its owner lays his hand upon its head; its life-blood flows upon the ground. It is divided and burned with fire, while the conscious sinner sees his own desert and prays, "Now, O Lord, I have sinned, I have committed iniquity, I have rebelled: thus and thus have I done. But I return in repentance to Thy presence, and be this my expiation."[2] In this solemn ceremony

---

[1] Dr. Pye Smith's *Four Discourses.*   [2] Ibid, pp. 13, 14.

with what boldness is it set forth that sin is an offence against God; that it must be punished; and that its proper punishment is death: that the sinner is of himself unable to escape the penalty; yet that God is merciful and will pardon: that the way of pardon is through substitutionary sufferings and death: that the victim must be the suppliant's own, in order to derive benefit therefrom: and that the suppliant should have such a moral disposition as to cordially acquiesce in the punitive acts of Divine Justice. A closer observance of the peculiarities of these sacrifices will make the essential virtues of the Great Sacrifice more plainly visible. The Divinely appointed sacrifices were to be creatures having life, that they might bear the death penalty. They were to be creatures having freedom from guilt—a reason why the animals appointed could not be guilty of man's sin. They were to be clean animals—because the food of man, and hence his life. They were to be without blemish, to show that, after their kind, they were perfect. This innocence, cleanness, and freedom from blemish were the emblems of conformity with law; the suffering death, a confession of sin; conformity with the law of God, the reason of their acceptance with God. Here then comes into view another difference between the sacrificial and general sufferer. The penalty represents the violation, the sacrifice represents, in addition to the violation, conformity with law. The penalty represents wrath due to disobedience; the sacrifice represents, in addition, favour and good pleasure due to obedience. The transgressor may pass through the penal fires, and still retain his character as a transgressor; and hence it is that such sufferings never take away sin. While the character endures, the penalty falls. The sacrificial victim, however, is pure, innocent, and spotless in the eye of the law to begin with: his contact with guilt is not through complicity with crime, but by his peculiar position through entire freedom from crime. In the case of Christ, indeed, this lay in the very perfection of His holiness, His love to God and man; and in the case of all sacrifices, as of Christ's, in their vicarious position. The sin on account of which the sacrifice suffered, was the sin imputed, so that when the penalty falls on account of this, the victim remains the same. The sacrifice does not lose its purity, etc., while the fire burns and consumes it. It was pure when death overtook it, and remained pure in the agonies of death, which were the penalty of sin. It continued pure till that penalty was exhausted: the sins laid on the victim expired when the victim expired; its last quivering agony was the last of sin's penalty and consequently of sin. It was thus the flowing blood that cleansed away sin; or even when the victim did not die, that departure of the scapegoat, which represented death, bore away sin into a land not inhabited. It was here that the ceremonial validity lay in the case of sacrifices offered under the law. This was the reason why the *blood of bulls* did avail to the *purifying of the flesh*. The sufferings and death of clean animals thus possessed the requisite fitness, and were divinely appointed to remove the guilt and pollution of sin, so far as it pertains to the body, and inflicted bodily, that is, external and ceremonial disabilities. The impure, who through his impurity had been debarred from the society of the pure, and from the camp or courts of the Temple, could, through the bleeding victim, be brought again within the sacred precincts of God's house, and to the enjoyment of all his rights as an Israelite. Thus through sacrifice the whole nation could be rendered ceremonially clean, and thus come nigh to God. So far such sacrifice availed : that is, sin was removed to the extent of the innocence and purity of the sacrifices. Further than this cleansing could not be obtained.

How far then was this? Was it a complete removal? The Apostle tells us that "*every priest standeth daily ministering and offering oftentimes the same sacrifices, which can never take away sins*" (Heb. x. 11). Wherein then lay this impossibility to remove sin? How far did they fall short of taking away sin from conscience and heart? They were incapable of bearing human sin away to the whole extent by which they fall below man in the scale of creation. They fell short to the whole extent by which they are incapable of rendering a moral conformity to the holy law of God. Destitute of moral nature, they could not even apprehend the moral requirements of God, much less acquiesce in, delight and satisfy them. Theirs was only an animal, not a moral innocence; a carnal and not a spiritual purity. Corresponding with the inadequacy of animals to yield conformity to the morality and spirituality of the law, was also the inadequacy of their sufferings. The sufferings of the animal could not fully represent the penalty due to the intelligent, the moral and spiritual transgressor. They were carnally clean, and hence could avail to the purifying of the flesh. But the victim that would purify the conscience and heart, must himself have a conscience and heart, a conscience without spot, a heart delighting in the law. Such a sacrifice must be as truly without blemish in the moral and spiritual sphere, as the lambs were without blemish in the lower sphere of the carnal, external and ceremonial. Such a sacrifice must also undergo the sufferings due to the higher nature that had sinned and was to be purified. As the soul has sinned, the soul must suffer; as the spirit has rebelled, the spirit of man must sustain the stroke of righteous wrath. The nature that has transgressed can alone be the sacrifice to make an end of transgression.

This being the case, two things become the more plain and impressive. On the one hand, the insufficiency of animal victims is written legibly as with a sunbeam; and we see how it was that God could not with them be well pleased. We see how it was that numbers could never give value to such sacrifices, that though Lebanon were made to burn and the beasts thereof offered as a burnt offering; though thousands of rams and ten thousand rivers of oil were offered to Jehovah, yet thereby the sin of a single human soul could not be removed. The sufferings of the soul can alone atone for the sin of the soul.

But, on the other hand, we see the reason why human victims were not appointed by God to supplement the deficiency of animal sacrifices. All down the ages, in every branch of the human family, amidst all the teeming millions of Adam's descendants, the cry was, "*All we like sheep have gone astray*" (Isaiah liii. 6), "*The whole head is sick, and the whole heart faint*" (Isaiah i. 5), "*There is none righteous, no, not one*" (Rom. iii. 10). From the midst of the unclean no pure victim could be found; hence the resort to the pure though inadequate animal sacrifices. But when the Holy One appeared, what had been an impossibility in all ages became possible. The nature that had sinned might suffer, a human soul might suffer for human souls, mind for mind, heart for heart, and spirit for spirit. The just might be offered for the unjust. An all-perfect human victim, without blemish or spot, might be offered as a sacrifice for our sins. In the end of the ages He appeared whose whole soul burned with a perfect love to God and man, whose life shone with a spotless holiness, and delight in the law of God; and as "*He was led as a Lamb to the slaughter,*" His feelings were "*Sacrifice and offering Thou didst not desire . . . . . I delight to do Thy will, O My God: yea, Thy law is within My heart*" (Ps. xl. 6—8).

But while dwelling on these important contrasts between our Lord as a sacrifice and all other sacrifices, there is one important point of resemblance. Since all sacrifices must be innocent of that for which they suffered, they could have no sense of blameworthiness or guilt. The lamb that was led to the slaughter could have no feeling of ill-desert while suffering and dying for a nation's sins. What has just been said of Christ's rank as the " Holy One " gives this the greater prominence. Since the Lamb of God, while bearing the sins of the world, was without blemish; and since, too, He occupied that position voluntarily, He could feel nothing of the contact of remorse from the sin he bore. His was the contact of undefiled benevolence. As from His life rebounded the charge of wrong—Who could convict Him of sin ?—so from the Eternal rock of His conscious purity must have recoiled, broken and dispersed, each and every suggestion of remorse, could they ever have been made. The poignant self-reproach that storms the inmost soul of the criminal in his sufferings, could never mar or disturb the serene peace of our Lord's purity. With wretched criminals one leading ingredient in their sufferings is that "*they eat of the fruit of their own way, and be filled with their own devices*" (Prov. i. 31). " A most material part of their misery," says Dr. Pye Smith, " consists in the unrestrained power of sinful passions, for ever raging but for ever ungratified. Their minds are constantly torn with the racking consciousness of personal guilt; with mutual aggravations and insults ; with the remorse of despair ; with malice, fury, and blasphemy against the Holy and Blessed God Himself; and with an indubitable sense of Jehovah's abhorrence and rejection of them. No such passions as these, nor the slightest tincture of them, could have place in the breast of the Holy Jesus. That meek and purest Lamb offered Himself without spot. His heart, though broken and bleeding with agonies to us unknown, ever felt a perfect resignation to the hand that smote Him, and a full acquiescence in all the bitterness of the cup which was appointed Him to drink : the resignation and acquiescence of love and conviction. He suffered in such a manner as a being perfectly holy could suffer." [1]

Thus to the whole extent of the perfections required in the sacrifice of Christ, that is, as far as infinite holiness is from unholiness, infinite love from hatred and malice, infinite obedience from rebellion, so far did Christ in His sufferings differ from the personal transgressor. When He suffered to the utmost for the wrong, He never ceased to love the right. When the reproaches of sin and sinners were crushing Him to death, He never wavered in the purpose of His pity, but cried,

---

[1] *Four Discourses*, p. 41.

"*Father forgive them, for they know not what they do.*"[1] And when the sword of Justice was at length unsheathed, and the Father with averted face smote the Son in whom He was well pleased, He wavered not in His love to Him who smote, but clung to Him with unflinching trust, "*My God, My God, why hast Thou forsaken Me?*"[2]

But here let us not suppose that Christ's freedom from the reproach of personal guiltiness, and the scorpion-sting of remorse, diminished His sensibility to suffering while bearing our sins. It shut one avenue, but it opened another and a wider one to pain. His perfect purity enabled Him to behold the majestic terrors of God's detestation of sin in a way criminals never can. His infinite love of God, on the one hand, and His infinite pity of man, on the other, developed an exquisite sensibility of the horror of His position. Forsaken of God, whose moral glory He most exhibited, and that in the moment of brightest manifestation; despised and reproached of man, whom He redeemed, and that in the crucial moment of that redemption; other sources also, above and beneath, poured forth their sorrows. As none could see to the uttermost depths of man's guilt, nor fathom the consequences of the misery resulting therefrom, so no heart could be thrilled with a horror and pierced like His with a grief commensurate with the sin and its consequences. His love of righteousness being infinite, infinite also must have been His loathing of the iniquities that were laid upon Him; yet His love for the sinner helped Him to endure this loathing for his sin. As no being ever loved the Father with a love like His, infinite in tenderness and truth, or took such unspeakable delight in God; so no nature but His could ever thrill with so infinite an agony in every line, when it pleased the Lord to bruise Him and hide from Him the light of His countenance. Thus, while by the perfection of His holiness, He is for ever raised to an infinite degree above the criminal sufferer, He is yet thereby raised also to an infinitely higher grade of suffering. The Altar is raised higher, but its fires instead of being thus abated are intensified. Suffering finds a leverage, never to be estimated, in the very purity of His love to God and man, and in his boundless grace and goodness. Every virtue that led him to the Cross, all the transcendent excellences that fitted him to be the Sin-bearer became the occasions and channels of the most inconceivable parts of our Lord's passion. But here we can only pause and wonder and adore. Neither sympathy nor thought can carry us within the veil, the veil

---

[1] Luke xxiii. 34.   [2] Matt. xxvii. 46.

not of darkness but of light, with which the moral perfection of the Sufferer conceals the perfectness of His personal agony. For, as the brighter the daylight that clothes the sky, the more completely does it veil and hide from view the massive worlds that move in the depths of space, so the visible perfection of Christ as a sacrifice—as the Lamb without blemish and without spot—renders invisible and inscrutable to us those passages of His sufferings wherein the principal stress and horror lay. But what is concealed from us was clear to the Almighty and All-holy Ruler, and these things made up in the Eternal esteem that greater and more perfect sacrifice, that *one* sacrifice by which Christ put away sin.

(*c*) The third reason why the sufferings and death of Christ effected reconciliation is because they rendered *satisfaction*. We have seen that Christ's sufferings came on account of His connection with violated law making them penal. We have seen that He bore them innocently as a sacrifice, and so, in bearing our sins, bore them away. This brought into view the good pleasure, the savour of rest, God found in that sacrifice. It is this virtue in the sacrifice that yielded to God this sweet savour of rest that has been called by Theologians *satisfaction*. The term is derived from the legal usages of the Romans, and signified *the security given to a creditor on behalf of a debtor, the payment of a debt*, or *reparation rendered for an injury*. As used by Theologians it still retains something of the colour of its ancient meaning. Tertullian, whose early training and practice as a lawyer made him familiar with the word as a law term, is the first to use it of Christ's work. He says, " *Christus peccata hominum omni satisfactionis habitu expiavit* "—"Christ atoned for the sins of man by a satisfaction perfect in every respect." He illustrates the meaning he attaches to the term, when he says that our Lord, by healing the wound of Malchus, repaired the injury; "*sanitatis restitutione ei, quem non ipse vexaverat satisfecit*" (*De Patientiâ*, cap. iii). Pretty much in this way Thomas Aquinas, and after him the Divines of the sixteenth and seventeenth centuries, employed the word. As used by the Reformed Divines, *Satisfaction* meant, " such act or acts as shall accomplish all the moral purposes which, to the infinite wisdom of God, appear fit and necessary under a system of rectoral holiness, and which must otherwise have been accomplished by the exercise of retributive justice upon transgressors in their own persons." Dr. Pye Smith, in briefer form, calls it " a compensative resource . . . . by which the salvation of the sinner shall be obtained in consistency with the honours of the Divine Government."[1]

Dr. Jenkyn, taking atonement as synonymous with Satisfaction, says, "ATONEMENT is an expedient substituted in the place of the literal infliction of the penalty, so as to supply to the government just and good grounds for dispensing favours to an offender."[2] Andrew Fuller, giving preponderance to the result, says, "That a way was opened, by the mediation of Christ, for the free and consistent exercise of mercy in all the methods which Sovereign Wisdom saw fit to adopt."[3] Wardlaw put it in the form of a question—"IN WHAT MANNER may forgiveness be extended to the guilty, so as to satisfy the claims of infinite justice, and thus to maintain, in their full dignity, free from every charge of imperfection or mutability, the character of the Governor, the rectitude of His administration, and the sanction of His law?" To this, on reflection, he added the clause, "*And to provide, in the pardoned sinner, for the interests of holiness.*"[4]

I only notice, at present, that in these definitions it will be seen that the satisfaction rendered by Christ is said not only to be retrospective, but prospective. In rendering satisfaction, Christ appears not only to remove sin, but as the Author of a new righteousness. He obtains justification as well as absolution. He delivers from hell, and also wins meritoriously "*the inheritance, incorruptible, and undefiled, and that fadeth not away*" (1 Peter i. 4).

(*a*) The first point to which I wish to call attention is, the *nature of the Satisfaction that is demanded.* So obvious is it that it must be of a moral kind, that it may appear superfluous to mention the subject. I do so, however, because the moral character of what Christ has done and suffered for us has not always been consistently kept in view, and especially in respect of the inferences which may naturally be drawn therefrom. Being moral, it is evident that the satisfaction rendered by our Lord is to be estimated by a moral standard, and not by any material method of computation. Were the satisfaction capable of being paid in corruptible things, such as silver and gold, it would be possible to estimate their commercial value as being more or less. But, seeing we have been redeemed with precious blood, and satisfaction has been rendered, as it alone could be, in moral worth, purity, and obedience,—to which things weight, and measure, and number are

---

[1] *Four Discourses*, p. 193.   [2] *On the extent of the Atonement*, p. 2.
[3] Gospel its own Witness (*Works*, notes, p. 39).   [4] *Atonement*, pp. 12, 13.

inapplicable, being mere physical tests,—all mention of a possible greater or less satisfaction is worse than misleading. To introduce, in this connection, the question as to whether they were many or few on whose behalf Christ made satisfaction, as if that could affect the satisfaction itself, betrays a lamentable confusion of ideas. Numbers can neither affect the kind nor the degree of satisfaction. Being moral, it is incapable of limitation, whether given for tens or for myriads. Being moral, it must be perfect. Were the satisfaction not morally perfect in the eye of Infinite Righteousness, it would be utterly valueless. But to be morally perfect, it must be the loving service of all the heart, and all the strength, and all the soul, and all the mind of the person who undertakes to satisfy God. Anything less than that which is the highest falls to the lowest; for anything short of this is less than what is due. The principle is not altered in the case of Christ. Stooping to be "*made under the law*," He pledges Himself to fulfil all righteousness. Because He did so, because the righteousness of His life and death was complete and perfect, the Apostle, refusing to recognise parts or partitions, calls it the "*one righteousness*" on account of which justification is secured for "*many offences*" (Rom. v. 16—18). Moreover, when we consider the Person of Him who rendered satisfaction, how harsh and unworthy of Him and of His work are those reasonings that suppose or suggest that the incarnate Son of God throughout His humiliation and death dealt with the Father, or that the Father dealt with Him, as one has said, "ledger in hand." The moral nature of the satisfaction excludes all such commercial views.

(β) The next particular on which we must keep our minds steadily fixed is the *Capacity in which Christ rendered satisfaction*. The difficulty that has here been raised, of God satisfying God, is perfectly gratuitous. One marvels how clear-sighted men could for a moment admit it. Only by sheer perversity of rhetoric can the slightest incoherence be shewn. The doctrine is not that God as such satisfies God, that the Second Person of the Trinity satisfies the First, that the Son satisfies the Father; but that He, though the Second Person of the Trinity, though the Son and equal with the Father, rendered satisfaction to all the demands of righteousness as Son of Man, being found in fashion as a man. It is in response to the new relations and claims devolving upon Him, through His incarnation, that the Son offers Himself to the Father. All the distinctions between Godhead and humanity exist in the person of Christ, and operate to make His work distinct from what would be the sole work of Divinity; while all the perfections of Deity are therein to render it congruous and worthy of the Infinite Mind.

(γ) The third point on which I wish to insist, is *to give due weight to the language and even to the imagery used by Scripture to set forth the satisfaction of Christ*. We must not allow ourselves to undervalue the language in which this work is described, because much is figurative, and the words separately are inadequate. Because Christ's work is more than "a *ransom*," more than "a *substitution*," more than "a *propitiation*," it were a fatal conclusion that therefore He did not truly give Himself a ransom for many, did not die for us, and is not a valid "propitiation for our sins."[1] Nor must we imagine because these images are different, that therefore they are incompatible, and may not find an appropriate place in one harmonious theory. Red differs from blue, and blue from orange, but there is one white beam wherein all hues and colours are blended, and all differences vanish. The crank acts on one principle, the wheel on another, and the lever on a third; but one piece of mechanism may be constructed which shall not mar, but utilize and harmonize the action of each and all. In variance with this very obvious proposition, Dr. Dale would have us suppose that "these representations of the Death of Christ as a Ransom, as a Vicarious Death, as a Propitiation, though they illustrate the cause of His sufferings and their effect, and contain all that is necessary for faith, do not constitute a theory. As they stand they are not consistent with each other."[2] In reference to this last remark, I suggest in passing, that we must be careful to form no theory that will stand without these representations, much less one that will stand against them. The theory of the death of Christ that excludes the element of the Ransom, Substitution, or Propitiation, is for that very reason defective, vicious, false, and misleading.

But what reason does Dr. Dale give for the incongruity of these representations? "For a good citizen to bear the punishment of a convicted criminal is one thing; for a generous philanthropist to pay the ransom of a slave, is a different thing; for a friend or a relative of a man who has done wrong to propitiate the anger of a powerful superior, is a different thing again."[3] I admit the three differences; I admit them to the whole extent of their possible divergence; I admit them

---

[1] Trench on *Various Approaches*. [2] Dr. Dale: *The Atonement*, pp. 355, 356.
[3] Ibid, p. 356.

as I admit the difference between the colours red and blue and orange, as I admit the difference between lever, crank and wheel. But I deny that these differences mean inconsistency and incompatibility. Red, blue and orange may be blended; lever, crank and wheel may be combined; and so, though not by the "rough process," which Dr. Dale thinks only applicable to such a case, it is possible to draw together the Ransom, Substitution and Propitiation without jarring or conflicting one with another. It is possible to find a common measure for these fractional descriptions, and it can be done with perfect ease and success by following out Dr. Dale's own illustrations. It is only necessary to suppose man is in the position of Onesimus, and that in man as in Onesimus, bondage, personal offence and crime meet; that God is He against whose supreme authority man is a criminal, whose Person he has offended; and that he is under bondage to the curse of God's broken law · then corresponding with these three elements of misery in man's sinful condition, corresponding with the threefold claim of God there may, yea there must necessarily be, in the death of Christ, the three elements of ransom, substitution and propitiation, if that death would do for man all that man requires for his salvation. If these three elements are consistent in the sinner,—and who that knows himself, but knows also their terrible consistency?—if these threefold claims of God do not conflict with each other, by what process of correct reasoning can it be made to appear that because the virtue that is in the death of Christ goes out in these three forms, therefore they are heterogeneous and inconsistent? Instead of following Dr. Dale in setting these representations of Christ's death in dialectic strife,—every man's sword against his fellow's, for their mutual destruction; instead of making one integral part jar with another, let us seek their harmony, for that is of God. Let us seek the luminous arch spanning the heavens where every colour is combined, the bow of mercy where all are mutually illuminated.

(δ) Having seen that these various Scriptural representations of Christ's satisfaction are not incoherent and inconsistent, I proceed to enquire *what it was on God's part to which Christ rendered satisfaction.* Satisfaction must be made in relation and proportion to the claims upon it. What were those claims which Christ satisfied? In a general way, it may be answered, they were the claims of righteousness. But what are we to understand by righteousness in this connection? Righteousness has various forms: Are we to look upon righteousness as simply punitive or vindicatory, while exacting a penalty because of transgression? Or are we to regard it as exemplified in the acts of the Divine Government? or, still further, Are we to hold that it is embodied in law? And, if so, what is that law?

As to whether it is simply punitive or vindicatory righteousness whose claims our Lord satisfied, you will find that while Scripture recognizes this element, as has been shown, its sense of the requirements of righteousness is much broader. If you refer to what is the *textus classicus* on this doctrine, its language will be found unmistakable. In Rom. iii. 25, 26, Paul says of Christ Jesus, "*Whom God hath set forth to be a propitiation through faith in His blood, to declare His righteousness for the passing over of sins that are past, through the forbearance of God; to declare, I say, at this time His righteousness: that He might be just, and the Justifier of him which believeth in Jesus.*" In this most vital statement there are three aspects of righteousness.

(I.) In the fact of the propitiation there is exhibited righteousness in its punitive character.

(II.) One of the purposes served by that propitiation was to reveal the righteous character of the Divine rule, in passing by sins during the time of forbearance.

(III.) There is also the declaration of God's righteousness not only in pardoning, but in justifying "*him which believeth in Jesus.*"

These three phases of righteousness are perfectly distinct. But as perfectly clear is it, that in all three phases, righteousness was satisfied in Christ. But since Christ satisfied the requirements of righteousness in respect of the dealings of God in times of forbearance, and also with regard to the justification of the ungodly; to the whole extent to which both of these great objects exceed the purpose of merely punitive justice did Christ satisfy the demands of righteousness.

Now if these two phases of righteousness are examined—beyond the vindicatory—it will be found that though they refer to different acts of God, and thus are distinct, yet from one point of view they may be classed together. They both pertain to the rule of God over His moral creatures, and may therefore come under what has been denominated rectoral or public righteousness. In its very broadest sense, "public righteousness" may comprise every form of righteousness revealed in the Divine government of the universe. Whether justice be distinguished into commutative or distributive, punitive or vindicatory, relative or absolute, all have their fitting place in the manifold rule of God. But in none of these phases can we admit that righteousness is a mere arbitrary scheme or device of government, which might be laid aside in favour of some other plan or policy. As God cannot lie, so by the same moral necessity, His righteousness shows itself the same in all its acts, and that necessarily, for God cannot be otherwise than He is. Unless we concede this absolute and essential character to the righteousness of God's rule, we must deprive the sufferings of Christ of the character of a real satisfaction. If righteousness is a scheme or a policy of government of the universe on God's part, then it follows, on the one hand, that the chief reason for the Cross, and indeed for the Incarnation, is taken away; and on the other hand, since the Cross is a fact, it can only rank as a part of a policy of moral rule, other policies having been possible.

Closely allied to the essential nature of "rectoral righteousness" is the question of the necessary harmony of all its forms of manifestation. Because in the hands of the magistrate punitive justice is sometimes far from equitable, and because among men vindicatory righteousness is too often steeped in the prison of revengeful passions, a deep-rooted prejudice is cherished by some against the very name of vindicatory righteousness. This, however, is to reason from the abuse, rather than the use of retributive justice. It is not only using human legal procedure as a mirror to reflect what is divine, but also allowing the imperfections of the mirror to distort and misrepresent the spotless perfections of Divine righteousness. Shall not the Judge of all the Earth do right? Shall He not give to every one his due? Taking this to be the necessary character of the rule of God, it is just here that there comes into view the need of vindicating and satisfying His rectoral righteousness.

On the one hand, God had passed by transgressions, He had let sins slip, as it were, without punishment; and so far as this had happened, so far His righteousness appeared impaired. On the other hand, He had raised the ungodly to the position and privileges of the just and the good and holy; and here again His righteousness seemed compromised. He appeared not to give every one his due. These are the two cases supposed by the Apostle; and they tell all the more strongly when it is remembered that the claims of righteousness terminate in the person. Did man stand in the position of a debtor alone, the claims of his Divine Creditor would extend to what is his.

Man, however, is in the condition of a criminal, and the claims of the Divine Legislator and Sovereign extend both to himself and to his. In the case of debt it matters not who pays, provided payment be made. But in the case of the criminal, the one thing essential is that he in his own person should satisfy the law in respect of his crime. Now as all this was in full force in the case of those sinners whom God had not visited as He visited the angels who sinned, as He visited the world in the days of Noah, as He visited the guilty cities of the plain with the terrors of retribution; as all this was in full force in the case of the sinners whom God not only spared, but justified; it became needful that the rule of God should be cleared from every shadow of suspicion, and that He should be shewn to act both in the one case and the other on the grounds of perfect righteousness. The Apostle declares the propitiation of Christ was the righteous foundation on which were based these acts of forbearance, and these acts of justifying grace. It results, therefore, that Christ satisfied righteousness in bearing the penalty due to sin; He satisfied righteousness in respect of Divine forbearance of the unrighteous; and, above all, Christ satisfied righteousness in respect of the sinners who were made the righteousness of God in Him.

It is now sufficiently apparent what is meant by public righteousness and the satisfaction rendered to it. But at this point we must be careful not to allow ourselves to regard this righteousness in any restricted sense. We must not confine it exclusively to the administrative acts, or even principles, of the Divine Government. It must also include that law which is to men the supreme expression of Divine righteousness in words. It is this law which enables us to know with certainty what is morally right. It is this law which furnishes the perfect standard whereby we can estimate the rectitude of the Divine procedure. It underlies the whole Government of God. In the sublime language of the Psalmist its position is this, "*Justice and judgment are the habitation of Thy throne*" (Psalm lxxxix. 14). In the equally sublime imagery of the Holy of Holies, the tables of the law were enclosed in the Ark of the Covenant, and lay beneath the golden Mercy Seat, where the Shekinah shone between the Cherubim. It is this law that is presented to us by Revelation, and enjoined by the authority of God. Higher than this, when fully interpreted, as it has been by Christ, no righteousness can rise, no holiness can reach. It is the expression of the Divine nature and of the Divine will. Therefore it is in its principles eternal and of universal obligation. For all the changing phases of the Divine Administration, there has been no change in the principles of the law. The expression may have altered, but not the precepts. These have been one and the same both in Eden and outside its guarded gates; the same to the world before the Flood and in Patriarchal times; the same from Sinai to Calvary; the same from Calvary right onward till the Great White Throne appears, and then the same for ever. This law, that comes from above, is the true objective counterpart to that which is within the human breast, and is subjective in the conscience. To the meaning of the handwriting of God, the Divine hieroglyphics in the human soul, this is the only and the infallible key. When touched by this, the heart of man discloses its inmost secrets, and admits the authority of the Divine Legislator, bowing before the presence of the Judge of all. This is the law by which we discern the righteousness of the Government of God, the law which forms the constitution of God's Sovereignty, and this we understand to be that law of righteousness whose claims the Saviour satisfied.

It is in this and no other sense that Scripture speaks of Christ's work in relation to law. It was prophesied of this law, "*He will magnify the law, and make it honourable*" (Isa. xlii. 21). Christ Himself said, "*Think not that I am come to destroy the law, or the prophets: I am not come to destroy, but to fulfil*" (Matt. v. 17). The Apostle said, "*Christ is the end of the law for righteousness to every one that believeth*" (Rom. x. 4).[1]

What, then, were the claims of this law which our Lord satisfied? They descend from the two elements contained in the law as from two sources, its precepts and its sanctions. We may view them both as to their nature and their extent.

(I.) *We view first the claims of law in regard to their nature.*

Here we have not been left to grope our way by the light of ethical or metaphysical reasoning. Our Lord Himself has shewn us the inmost nature of that law which He was to satisfy. In answer to the question, "*Which is the great commandment in the law?*" He said, "*Thou shalt love the Lord thy God with all thy heart, and with all thy soul, and with all thy mind:* . . . *And the second is like unto it, Thou shalt love thy neighbour as thyself. On these two commandments hang*

---

[1] Cf. Gal. iii. 24.

all the law and the prophets" (Matt. xxii. 36—40). The whole sum of moral truth and the whole of moral obedience are supported by love to God and love to man.

In this great induction, the greatest ever made in practical religion, it is before all things apparent that love and righteousness are not contrary principles, but mutually complementary. Our Lord's exposition would seem to convey that love is more than a condition of obedience, more than a motive to obedience. It is itself obedience : to love is to obey. According to the Apostle's inspired commentary, "*Love is the fulfilling of the law* " (Rom. xiii. 10).

Are we, therefore, to suppose that love can dispense with the precepts? By no means. The propelling power of the engine does not enable it to dispense with the firm metal rails, nor does the swiftness of the vessel render it independent of the helm. On the contrary, the greater the swiftness, the firmer must be the guidance of the helm ; the mightier the engine's force, the more need there is for its course to be shaped by the undeviating line. So the sacred passion of Divine love within the heart cannot afford to part company with the precept of the law. To come to such a conclusion would be altogether contrary to our Lord's meaning. Dealing with those who saw only the outside of the law, our Lord opened up the precepts, and showed them what was within. They wanted to know how to fulfil the law of righteousness. The answer was, to love God and man. But when showing those who did love Him how they were to love Him, He said, "*If ye love Me, keep My commandments*" (John xiv. 15). Thus "*the commandment is a lamp ; and the law is light*" (Prov. vi. 23) : it is a "*lamp unto my feet, and a light unto my path*" (Psalm cxix. 105).

The conclusion, then, to which we come is, that law contains the principle of love, that love is to be guided by the light of law. Advancing another step, if such be the nature of law, does it not reflect a light in turn upon the inner principle of the Divine Government, upon the very character of God, and also upon the satisfaction which Christ rendered to God? If there is love in the precept, what is there in the heart of the Lawgiver? If love fulfils, what is it that commands? If God expects love in us, will He disappoint us when we seek it in Him? If love be the principle on which the whole of our life is to move, is it not also the pivot on which the whole of the Divine administration turns? Is it not thus that John reasons, carrying the inference right up to the nature of God, " *Beloved let us love one another, for love is of God*

. . . . *God is love*" (1 John. iv. 7, 8). The principle of law conducts us up through the Divine rule onward to the central Eternal Love that originates and controls all things. What, therefore, God demands in the law, that He is Himself. What He enjoins, that He will be to those upon whom the injunction is laid. To those who in love serve and obey, He will be found to be Eternal Love.

Thus far the principle of the law leads us. It corresponds with the principle of Divine Government, and is one with the nature of God. But on their side the precepts of the law, by shewing the way and means of our love to God, shew also the objects of the Divine love. God's love is righteous. His goodness takes shape in the form of holiness. His love pours its living and healing waters along the channels of righteousness. He loveth righteousness. Upon Himself, as the only supreme and perfect Being, the Divine love is fixed as its only infinitely worthy object; but thence outwards to all His creatures who bear the likeness of His moral perfections does it extend. All who walk in the commandments and ordinances of the Lord find Him in their path, and meeting their advancing footsteps they see Everlasting Love.

In God's eternal and immutable love of righteousness we recognize the firm foundation of moral order and bliss throughout the universe. But we must remember the terror that is implied in this love of righteousness, this Scripture expresses when it says, "*Thou hast loved righteousness, and hated iniquity*" (Heb. i. 9). Though this is said of the Son, yet in this, as in all else, He has shewn us the Father. The infinite love of righteousness necessarily implies the infinite hatred of unrighteousness. To the obedient He appears through the medium of the righteous precepts as the Giver of the joyous reward of Eternal life. To the transgressor through the broken commandments, "*Our God is a consuming fire*" (Heb. xii. 29). The claims of law are therefore *obedience* or *death*.

As the case stood, our Lord had not only to meet the one, but He had to satisfy both. He sought the reward of obedience, as well as to remove, by bearing it, the wrath due to disobedience. But as we have seen that the one principle of the Eternal love of righteousness lies behind both the reward and penalty of law, so we shall find that it was by virtue of an undivided love of righteousness that Christ won the reward and endured the Cross.

The claims of law conduct us to a perception of the *manner in which Christ rendered satisfaction.* With the Lawgiver He was at one as to the Eternal love of righteousness. He alone, of all the race, was in everything, and at all times, controlled by an immutable and perfect love of God. Of all the race, He alone had a perfect perception of the requirements of righteousness, both in relation to God and man. He was the first who could say of the whole law in its two unbroken tables, "*Thy law is within My heart.*" In His life and death He loved the Lord His God with His whole heart . . . . . and His neighbour as Himself. Thus serving in love under the precept, and in love also suffering under the penalty, Christ, when that suffering is over, finds in God that love which, like the Shekinah in the Holy Place, shines within all the outward ordinances of righteousness.

For His obedience unto death He receives the great reward, which is life for evermore. But as Christ herein is the Federal Head of the new race, a new and living way is opened up to the Father, and every sinner who approaches the Majesty on High, in Jesus has the assurance that God is Love.

(II.) *The extent of the claims of law.*

The law demands the love of all the heart, soul and mind, and demands that love always. "*God requires that we should walk in all His ways*" (Deut. x. 12); which means at least to continue in them, and, as it is expressed in Deut. iv. 9, not to depart from them all the days of our life. The claims of righteousness know no end. There never can come a moment when it shall be right to cease to do right, to cease to love God. If such a time could come, then it would at that moment be wrong to love God: if wrong at that time, what could make it right now or at any time? Hence to suppose the claims of the law terminable would be the virtual abrogation of all law. But seeing this is manifestly absurd, seeing that the claim to love God can never cease, another and a further consequence will follow. Should any refuse that love, should any render hatred and disobedience instead, then the man who does so cuts off from God what is unceasingly His due. He withholds the revenue of love and dutiful service that should perpetually flow into the Divine treasury. He is thereby doing God an unending wrong. This is the case of the sinner; and in this respect, his sin is an infinite injustice.

How do these unending claims of righteousness and this unending wrong of sin bear upon the question of satisfaction? In the first place, they cannot be separated in the case of him who stands in the stead of sinners, as Christ did. And in the second place, when put together, they render it imperative that suffering and obedience must be joined in a perfect satisfaction.

We hear it sometimes stated that the law must be satisfied either by obedience or suffering. No such alternative is open, if the claims of law have just now been truly described. It is a matter of course, indeed, that if a man obeys he is free from penalty. But it does not follow that because the disobedient undergoes the penalty, that he is therefore free from the command. Were this the case it would put a premium on transgression, and place the sinner in a position of unrestrained action, denied to the obedient and law-abiding. The transgressor violates, but does not relax the right of law. His endurance of the penalty will not enable him to avoid the precept, any more than the convict can, because he is a convict, obtain for himself a perpetual and indefeasible right to do wrong. It is true, indeed, that a man must either obey or suffer under the law. But when a man has refused to obey, and thereby made himself obnoxious to suffering, he may certainly suffer; but as certainly his suffering can never satisfy. And for this reason: suffering that is not animated and qualified by obedience partakes of the character of disobedience; and such suffering continues to add new offence to the old indebtedness and guilt. Such suffering to be acceptable would suppose the suspension of the precepts while it was endured. But, as we have seen, the precepts can never be suspended. Here we see the deep necessity for the holy life of Christ, in that He should fulfil all righteousness.

On the other hand, to obey alone could not satisfy, so long as there was an outstanding penalty against sinners. There must therefore be a suffering that shall obey, and an obedience that shall suffer; and both these must meet in the Substitute of sinners. Take away the obedience from the suffering, and the suffering is insufficient, as is the suffering of lost souls. Such can never say of their payment of the debt of justice, "*It is finished.*" Take away the suffering from the obedience, and the sanctions of the law remain unfulfilled. In our Redeemer both meet. The crimson hues of suffering coloured all His life and service; and throughout all His manifold sufferings the deep pulse of an infinite love to God and man kept beating; and never with so strong and true a beat as when those sufferings matured into death. In the profoundly significant words of Scripture, which sum up both sides of

His satisfaction, "*He became obedient unto death, even the death of the Cross*" (Phil. ii. 8).

If it be urged that our Lord's sufferings were not lasting like those of the lost, the reply is at hand, that it was not needful they should be so prolonged, because they had a character far transcending the sufferings of the lost. Christ's sufferings were pure, obedient and loving, and therefore rendered a satisfaction to a pure and loving God, though endured for but a limited duration; but this the sufferings of the lost can never do, seeing they are still mingled with unholiness and rebellion. Besides, the law of righteousness can at once fulfil itself through obedience, but never through disobedience. On this account the sufferings of our Lord needed not to last like the sufferings of sinners. His sufferings, also, were those of a Person who is infinite as well as finite. Upon Him, therefore, could be poured forth, *in intenso*, that wrath which must be poured out on the lost *in extenso*. Thus the sufferings of the Infinite, if but for a moment, infinitely surpass the woes of lost souls, since these can never be other than finite. The infinite and intrinsic worth of His Person communicated itself to all He did and endured, and enabled Him to concentrate into years, and days, hours and moments, and fragments and drops of time, what impenitent finite sufferers could not compress into ages, however prolonged. It is in this unique quality of our Lord's work and sufferings that, in company with nearly ll Evangelical Christians in all ages, I humbly deem there lies the essential virtue which satisfied righteousness, and so procured reconciliation.

LECTURE XVIII.

THE EFFECTS OF CHRIST'S RECONCILIATION UPON MEN.

HAVING tried to describe the satisfaction Christ has accomplished, I now wish to shew, that upon this satisfaction depend all God's gracious methods of liberating sinners from their sins.

We might indeed mention that Christ's work, it is true, gives a form and colour to the whole of the administration of righteousness throughout the universe. No creature can ever impugn the righteousness of the law, seeing that the Son of God has stooped to come under both its precept and its penalty. And since it is ordained that the Sufferer of Calvary shall be the Judge of All, it is the highest demonstration of His equity, that He has first satisfied in His own Person what He shall bind upon others. In the presence of the sufferings of the Son of God, no intelligent being can ever dare to do other than regard righteousness as most vital to the government of the world. In a word, Christ has magnified the law and made it honourable. But let us understand that these are rather the effects of the satisfaction of Christ than the satisfaction itself. The satisfaction lies not in conciliating the minds of men to the goodness and majesty of law as an instrument of rule and government, but in meeting the requirements of the law as the expression of the Divine mind; and from that source springs all the honour done to Divine law and Divine government throughout the universe. All the ends of righteousness being thus secured by Christ's work, it becomes the ground of pardon and justification to all who come unto God through Him.

In freedom from sin, the reconciliation fulfils itself in the individual. And here let me say that I take for granted that, without a spiritual connection with Christ, of which faith is the conscious sign and proof, no man can claim to be a recipient of the saving benefits of the Cross. That the believer is "the heir," I take to be the teaching of Scripture from first to last.

Assuming, then, this vital link of faith in the individual, I observe that, in the widest and most general descriptions of the Word of God, Christ's mediation is made the meritorious ground for the removal of sin. He is the one Mediator—the one Priest of whose Person and work, the kingly Priest Melchisedec and the whole order of the Aaronic priests were types. His sacrifice is alone efficacious to remove sin; and when all besides had failed, "*Once in the end of the world hath He appeared to put away sin by the sacrifice of Himself.*"[1] Viewed in the Divine purpose His sacrifice underlies all human history, and especially all God's forbearance of the race; for He is the "*Lamb slain from the foundation of the world.*"[2] From the depths of all the ages before His manifestation, penitent and believing men looked to Him as the woman's Seed, as God's Salvation. They saw His day, and were glad. From the ranks of all generations succeeding the Cross, believers have turned to Him as the "*Lamb of God that taketh away the sin of the world.*" In the Apostle's esteem, Christ crucified was the Foundation, other than which no man could lay, the Foundation of the sinner's hope, the Foundation of the Church's safety (1 Cor. iii. 11). Therefore it was, that though this truth was to the Greeks foolishness, and to the Jews a stumbling-block, the Apostle kept on preaching the Crucified, and "*determined not to know anything among (men) save Jesus Christ, and Him crucified*" (1 Cor. ii. 2).

Passing from the more general to the more definite teaching of Scripture, the same virtue is assigned to Christ's work. In every way in which it is possible for sin to be removed, it is removed through, and on account of the work and sufferings of Christ. Christ's obedience unto death supplies the righteous basis of both pardon and justification, and likewise all the moral force by virtue of which men are to be "renewed in the spirit of their mind" (Eph. iv. 23). It may not even be an over-refinement to trace a connection and correspondence between the various effects of Christ's work in His people and the several parts of that work itself. Though we must ever regard His mediation as one and inseparable, yet a distinction may be observed between its several parts. So, also, though the salvation conferred is one and undivided, yet it is imparted in divers parts and sundry blessings. Is it

---

[1] Heb. ix. 26.   [2] Rev. xiii. 8.

not, therefore, reasonable to suppose that there is a connection and correspondence between the several parts of Christ's work for us, and His work in us? Between the ways in which He made satisfaction for us, and the ways in which He frees us from our sins? Between the forms of His mediation and the manner in which we are restored? Scripture itself affirms the connection in more than one notable passage. In saying, He "*was delivered for our offences, and was raised again for our justification*" (Rom. iv. 24, 25), the principle is established: and other passages afford illustrations of it.[1] Generally it may be stated, that to the comprehensive priestly work corresponding comprehensive effects are attributed. Over against His sufferings, more particularly the shedding of His blood, pardon of sins is placed. His righteousness has its equivalent in our justification. So, probably, the personal character of Christ, as to holiness and love, reappears and reasserts itself in the moral influence of His Cross and passion.

To take the most comprehensive first :—

(I.) *Sin is removed sacrificially.*

In those grand comprehensive phrases born of the priestly office, this is especially made clear :—

(1.) Those expressions sometimes affirm the objective removal of sin—*sin as guilt before God.* "*Christ was once offered to bear the sins of many*" (Heb. ix. 28). "*He bare our sins in His own body on the tree*" (1 Peter ii. 24). "*He is the propitiation for our sins*" (1 John ii. 2). "*Christ our Passover is sacrificed for us*" (1 Cor. v. 7). "*By His own blood He entered in once into the holy place, having obtained eternal redemption for us*" (Heb. ix. 12).

(2.) Sometimes there is set forth the subjective removal of sin—*sin as pollution in man.* "*Unto Him that loved us and washed us from our sins in His own blood*" (Rev. i. 5). "*Wherefore Jesus also, that He might sanctify the people with His own blood, suffered without the gate*" (Heb. xiii. 12). "*How much more shall the blood of Christ, who through the Eternal Spirit offered Himself without spot to God, purge your conscience from dead works to serve the living God?*" (Heb. ix. 14.)

(3.) Sometimes both are combined. "*Who* . . . . *when He had by Himself purged our sins, sat down on the right hand of the Majesty on High*" (Heb. i. 3). "*Ye are come* . . . . *to the blood of sprinkling, that speaketh better things than that of Abel*" (Heb. xii. 22 and 24).

---

[1] Rom. v. 10; viii. 32—34.

(II.) *Sin is removed by pardon.*

God removes the guilt of sin by the act of pardon, and the consciousness of sin by the assurance of pardon. Without the assurance we could not be aware of the act; and this assurance is conveyed by faith, and by the testimony of the Word of God and of the Holy Spirit with our spirits. In conferring both blessings He acts in a perfectly free and sovereign manner, having "*mercy on whom He will have mercy*" (Rom. ix. 15). But as this mercy vindicates its sovereign freeness in respect of the objects on whom it lights, so also is it in regard to the way by which it descends. That way has been one and the same from the beginning. The Old Testament knows nothing of pardon but by way of sacrifice; neither does the New Testament, except through the redemption that is in Christ. In both Old and New Testaments it is an axiom, that "*without shedding of blood is no remission.*" Accordingly Christ speaks of His blood as "*My blood of the New Testament which is shed for many for the remission of sins*" (Matt. xxvi. 28). The language of the inspired Apostle is, "*In whom we have redemption through His blood, the forgiveness of sins*" (Eph. i. 7). It is part of the honour with which He was crowned, because of tasting death, that He should be exalted to the Father's right hand to grant repentance to Israel and remission of sins (Acts v. 31).[1] "*In His name*," His last injunction before the Ascension ran, "*repentance and remission of sins should be preached among all nations*" (Luke xxiv. 47). The same truth is conveyed also when we are told that "*He is faithful and just to forgive us our sins, and to cleanse us from all unrighteousness*" (1 John i. 9); for this cleansing is connected with the blood of Christ (verse 7), and the forgiveness is connected with the Advocacy of Christ the Righteous, and with His propitiation (1 John ii. 1, 2). Hence John says (1 John ii. 12), "*I write unto you, little children, because your sins are forgiven for His name's sake*"; and Paul exhorts the Ephesians, "*Be ye kind one to another . . . even as God for Christ's sake hath forgiven you*" (Eph. iv. 32). One of the most precious clauses of the New Covenant, which marks its superiority over the Old is, "*I will be merciful to their unrighteousness, and their sins and their iniquities will I remember no more*" (Heb. viii. 12). But this clause, as the Apostle argues, like every other clause in the testament, is of no strength at all while the Testator liveth (Heb. ix. 17), but obtains its validity

---

[1] Cf. Acts x. 43; xiii. 39; xxvi. 18.

through the death, through the sprinkling of the blood of Christ (Heb. ix. 18, 23 and 24; x. 14—19). The blood of Christ is the seal of the New Covenant, and the seal of forgiveness.

That the pardoning mercy of God should thus lean upon the Atonement, does not detract from its free and sovereign character. Who gave His only begotten Son? Who spared not His own Son but delivered Him up to death? Whose wisdom was it that framed the whole merciful design? Whose grace is it that connects the sinner with the benefits of Christ's work? Where is the sinner's right to demand a share in the redemption that is in Christ? And whence arises that right? Did not our sins pierce the Saviour? And is He not a Saviour, a Redeemer, possessed with power to remove sins, contrary to the expectation of a sinful world, and in spite of all that wickedness could do to prevent it? It were surely an unaccountable hardship and perversity of things, if the Grace that planned forgiveness in a certain way—a way most righteous and loving—and provided for its bestowal in that way, should because of so doing lose its character of grace, and be turned into a narrow exacting commercial selfishness. Let us rather reason from the Sovereign Love displayed in the plan of redemption and the gift of Christ to the boundlessness of God's lovingkindness and generosity. Christ is God's—God's Anointed : and that we or any should share in the least of His fulness of redemption is of God's infinitely free compassion.

(III.) *Sin is removed by justification.*

The evil effects of sin are not only felt in exposing us to wrath, but also in despoiling us of a title to life, and the privileges and inheritance of the Children of God. While Mercy avails to release us from punishment, the grace of God is revealed in conferring upon us through the "one righteousness" of the One Man, justification of life. This act peculiarly attributed to the grace of God, though never separate in any individual from regeneration, is yet radically distinct from regeneration. This latter is a moral change, a change of nature; whereas justification is a legal or forensic change, a rectification of our relations to the law.

By justification a believer is put in the place of a righteous man in the eye of the law, and is entitled, on Christ's account, to all the advantages of righteousness. As these advantages comprise peace with God, His favour, and access to Him, His guardian care for this life, and for the life to come the unfading inheritance and Eternal

Kingdom,—it is evident how unspeakably rich is the grace given to us in justification.

And as the blessings are manifold, so also are they conditioned on the manifold work of Christ. In Rom. iii. 24—26, our justification rests on Christ as a propitiation. In Rom. iv. 24, 25, our justification rests on His resurrection; He was delivered for our offences, but raised again for our justification. His sufferings won pardon for us, His resurrection—life. But that resurrection was His justification, the seal of God's acceptance of what He had done and suffered, and therefore the justification of all who believe in Him. "*And if Christ be not raised . . . . ye are yet in your sins.*" [1] In Rom. v. 9, our justification rests on His blood; in verse 18, on His righteousness; in verse 19, on His obedience; and again, in verse 21, Grace prevails over the effects of sin, and reigns through righteousness unto Eternal Life by Jesus Christ our Lord.

That the justification of believers should thus be attributed severally to the chief factors in our Lord's mediation—His righteousness, His blood, His death, His resurrection, His obedience—is accounted for first of all by the essential unity of that work, and then by the necessity of adding suffering to obedience, and a sacrificial death to a holy life in the satisfaction He rendered unto righteousness.

And just as certainly as justification rests on the work and sufferings of Christ as its righteous basis, so also is it certain that it is a free and pure act of Divine Grace. They who are justified are in no way of themselves entitled to the place of righteous ones. They are the "ungodly," the "condemned," those whom God has "concluded under sin," those who are morally impotent, the chief of sinners. How, then, is righteousness maintained in the act that makes the unrighteous righteous? By what method, or on what principle? The answer of Scripture is, that it is by the *principle of imputation*. As to this principle, whatever may be said for or against it, we must not forget that it is not invented *ad hoc*, as applicable to this case alone. Neither is it a mere theory or hypothesis. It is a universal law. It enforces itself throughout the whole fabric of society, and uses as its channels of communication the kindred ties that bind the race together in nations, and in families. There is no section of mankind, whether naturally, artificially, or legally constituted, there is no individual on the face of the earth that does not receive either good or evil, praise or blame, happiness or misery, by means of imputation. Life teems with

---

[1] 1 Cor. xv. 17.

examples. When, therefore, we adduce this principle, we are not invoking a legal fiction, nor an exploded theological figment. We are not introducing something repugnant to reason, because it is a paradox to our experience of life. The whole frame of human society, the operative beliefs of the world in all departments of life, stand out as living witnesses to the potency and universal rule of this principle.

Since the principle itself is not new or strange, neither is it a new or strange thing to apply it to the higher sphere of the spiritual condition of man. Already, according to Scriptural teaching, had this been done in reference to Adam and the whole race, as a necessary result of the federal relationship. Already also in the case of the Lord Jesus it had been applied as a necessary accompaniment of His spiritual Headship. What principle, other than this, can render even an approximation to a satisfactory account of Christ's sufferings and death? Scripture seeks for no other, and mentions no other. "*The Lord hath laid on Him the iniquity of us all*" (Isa. liii. 6); "*He hath made Him to be sin for us, who knew no sin*" (2 Cor. v. 21); "*He was made a curse*" (Gal. iii. 13). Of this imputation of sin to the Holy Christ, the imputation of righteousness to the ungodly is the true counterpart. How is it possible to justify the sufferings of Christ, the just for the unjust, unless by raising the unjust to the place of the just? Reason and equity demand that Christ's death for sinners should be justified by justifying sinners. The justification of the ungodly is needed as a counterpoise of the death of the "Holy One and the Just." That righteousness should be reckoned "without the works of the law" is the true equivalent of making "*Him to be sin for us, who knew no sin.*" Otherwise, where is Christ's "portion", His "spoil", His "reward", "the joy that was set before Him"?

This great blessing of justification, coming thus by means of imputation, is all comprehensive in relation to law. It never needs to be repeated, but for ever places a believer at one with the demands of righteousness, even as Christ is. While it includes the past and the present, it has a special reference to the future, to the result of life, the reward and inheritance. Pardon rescues from guilt and hell, justification raises to heaven.

(IV.) *Sin is removed by Sanctification.*

By sanctification I understand the infusion and development of the holiness in the heart, character and life. When we speak of the removal of sin by sanctification, in addition to pardon and justification, it ought to be ascertained in what sense the words are used. Pardon removes sins committed, and so is a negative good by removing positive evils. Sanctification first regenerates the sinner, and is a positive good, and thus is the negative of evil—that which is born of God sinneth not. Justification sets us right in the eye of the law, and is objective. But sanctification is subjective, and confers personal holiness.

If we trace sanctification up to its root in regeneration, or onwards to its ultimate fruits in bringing every thought into captivity to Christ, we find it comes altogether, root, fruit and branch, from His mediation. The Spirit Himself, by whom holiness is infused, is the gift and the Witness of Christ; and His work lies in quickening us together with Him. Shining like a lamp, whose self-denying office is not to render itself but other objects visible, the Holy Spirit directs His beams in such a way as to render the Lord Jesus visible to the eyes of the heart as the Christ of God. And it is Christ, Christ in the personal glory of His infinitely holy love which transfused all He did or suffered, who stands out under the Spirit's light as the sole Object of contemplation, by whose power we are transformed, and to whose image we are to be conformed.

Not only is the Holy Spirit bestowed, but also the blessings of the Christian life—and chiefly those of which we have been speaking, pardon and justification—are given in such a way that they cannot but promote holiness and loyalty to God in Christ. Bestowed on one side through a godly sorrow, a repentance that needeth not to be repented of, a faith that purifies the heart; they are on the side of God connected inseparably and in every part with what Christ is, or has done, or suffered for us. These gifts are so closely and intimately connected with the humiliation and the tremendous griefs of the Son of God, that it is no less an awe than a joy to be forgiven and restored. To be pardoned by an arbitrary decision of the Divine Will would bespeak the clemency of God, and evoke our gratitude. To obtain release from sin and its consequences, by any means or in any manner, would be prized as an unspeakable boon by the sinner. But when pardon comes to him by way of the Cross a higher sentiment than gratitude is raised. The sorrows of the Son of God invest pardon with a sacred preciousness; and every pang, and every tear, and every wound plead with the heart not to misuse what has been so dearly won, nor sin at the expense of such wondrous love, and such amazing grief. A pardon, perfumed with such memories, written with a pierced hand, and sealed with such precious blood, is not only life, but also holiness, and the inspiration of a new devotedness. "*Because we thus judge that if One died for all . . . . . that they which live should not henceforth live unto themselves, but unto Him which died for them and rose again*" (2 Cor. v. 14, 15).

And as the release and emancipation are conferred with a pierced hand, so it is with the privileges of the New Kingdom. They all spring up around the Cross under the bedewing influences of its sufferings. The graces cultivated by the Holy Spirit in every believer have their seeds in the work and Person of the Redeemer. In the disciple they are transplanted growths; in Christ they are native: the Spirit takes of the things of Jesus and shews them to Christ's people. The persuasions, as well as the aids to prayer, are derived from Him; for by Him we have peace, and by Him access. He is the new and living way; He is the ever-living Priest. From Him hope springs; from Him comes assurance in the contemplation of Providence and Eternity. The most cogent arguments to brotherly kindness, love, duty and faith are derived from Him. The strongest arguments that can move to patience, humility, endurance and faithfulness are marked by His hand, and coloured with the hues of Calvary.

The whole tendency of the Gospel is to teach us to seek in Christ the centre and life of that truth which sanctifies—that unfolding of the character of God which both attracts and subdues, ennobles and humbles, awakes to a sense of sin and ruin, and yet inspires with a hope of attaining Eternal life. Nor are the influences of Christ restricted to this present state of sorrows, conflict, unfulfilled desires, weakness and sin.

In the Revelation the imagery used of the future life shews that the moral influence of the Cross has not spent itself in time or on earth, but will extend to heaven and reign through all the ages. For inasmuch as Christ is represented as doing this in the character of the Lamb, to the exclusion of everything else, it is fair to conclude that the virtue which came to maturity on the Cross will distinguish Christ's heavenly leadership of His people and be eternally paramount in their affections. This at least I take to be within the meaning of those passages which tell us that the Redeemed shall follow the Lamb whithersoever He goeth;[1] and that He shall lead them to living fountains.[2]

---

[1] Rev. xiv. 4.   [2] Rev. vii. 17.

The moral glories of the Lamb give shape and direction to the activities of the sanctified. Beneath the influence of Christ, heaven itself discloses its fountains of unalloyed joy, and pours forth its streams of blessedness. In the last vision of the ransomed and triumphant Church, when the terrors of judgment have passed, and the New Jerusalem descends out of heaven, there is no temple therein, for the Lord God Almighty and the Lamb are the Temple thereof; the City shall have no need of the sun, neither of the moon, for the glory of God shall lighten it, and the Lamb be the Light thereof. (Rev. xxi. 22, 23). If light be taken for wisdom, then it is the wisdom centred in the Crucified, that shall shine its beams over the pursuits of the Redeemed. If light be taken for holiness, then it is the unblemished holiness of Christ, as the Sacrifice, that shall inspire their worship. If light be taken for love, then it is the Love of God, commended to us on earth in the Great Passover slain for us, that shall encompass their lives. Whatever that light may stand for, life or power, glory or beauty, all shall be diffused from Christ as the Lamb of God, as from a sun that never sets, and the nations of those which are saved shall walk in its light.

LECTURE XIX.

THE ASPECTS OF THE ATONEMENT.

I WILL now endeavour to draw together the results we have reached. To do this I must briefly recall and shew the connection of the main joints of the whole argument concerning the Atonement.

From the broadest point of view, we have seen this Atonement contains a *manifestation* and a *representation:* A manifestation of God to man, and a representation of man to God. These are not separate, but interpenetrate one another. In Christ's representation of man to God, we have seen that this presupposed and included bonds of connection with all on whose behalf Christ was to perform the representative office. He was to be the Representative of the world as a world, the race as a race, the Jews as under the law in its precept and penalty; the Church as Her Head and Redeemer. We have seen that while these ties are all co-ordinate, meeting in the One Mediator, the One life and death; they are also subordinate or graduated. The outer circle of connection with the world is subordinate to the union with the race; that with the race is subordinate to His relation to law; His relation to law merges and issues in His redemption of the Church. It is here Representation ripens into *Federation*, and the Son of Man becomes the Head of the new and redeemed race. This is the order of final causes—of design and Eternal purpose. Selecting, therefore, this union with the Church as that which was the very core of all Christ's relations, we judged it as the best fitted to disclose information concerning the Atonement He has made. This union with the Redeemed in the Eternal purpose or covenant secured for the Incarnate Son of God a legal standing before the law of righteousness. By virtue of this position He could righteously undertake to make provision for the great need of sinners, which is reconciliation with God: reconciliation in its double aspect—as it relates to God as the Righteous

Ruler, and to man as the transgressor and rebel; and as it required the suffering of death. We have seen how our Lord met all requirements, by enduring the penalty, by suffering as a Sacrifice, by rendering complete satisfaction in righteousness and in death. Finally, we have seen that this reconciliation is completed by the release of sinners from their sins, by the elevation of believers to be heirs with Christ, and by making them meet to be "*partakers of the inheritance of the saints in light*" (Col. i. 12).

The advantages accruing from the method of presenting the Atonement which I have adopted are these :—

(I.) *It affords an adequate account of the sufferings and death of the Son of God.*

No one can obliterate the fact of that death; it remains, and must remain the central fact of human history, whatever theory of it men may form. By a false theory, however, its significance may be much obscured. Sunder the ties between Christ and His people, which have been formed in federal relationship from eternity, and you reduce Christ to the position of a private person. Any connection with others which His work may subsequently acquire becomes purely arbitrary. Suppose that He appears on God's behalf only to vindicate His righteousness, Wherefore should He suffer or die? In this case, sufferings and death would be purely arbitrary, and destitute of the moral character desiderated in enduring them. Were Christ not connected with sinners, How could He be connected with their sins, or the consequences of them? Sever Christ from legal union with a "people laden with iniquity," and how can you vindicate the righteousness of that rule that allows the innocent to suffer, and the holy die an ignominious death? Finally, place Christ apart from federal relation with His people, and you stand at variance with the unanimous testimony of Scripture concerning the causes of Christ's death. But admit that this relation exists between Christ and His people, and every incident and circumstance fall into their proper order, and are possessed of their due import. Christ is no longer only a vision of righteousness disclosed from the heavens—much less is He a drop in the wave, or a wave in the great tide of humanity: His death is no longer the blind result of contact and conflict with evil, it is the righteous infliction of the penalty due to sinners and their sin. He rises on the shores of the desolations of sin as the Rock of Ages to stem the further advance, and bear the fury of the storms of wrath on their account. But from the very cleft the storms leave there issues for every thirsty pilgrim the stream of Eternal Life. Satan coming in like a flood recoils before the dying Saviour. Our Lord appears in death as a Substitute, and becomes the Leader of a new race, the Head and Captain of Salvation.

(II.) *It reveals the true and perfect philanthropy of Christ's work.*

If union with sinful men brought upon Christ sufferings and death, it is abundantly clear that in all these, as well as in His incarnation, and all that followed therefrom, He aimed at man's salvation. Love for them could never for a moment have been absent from His heart in aught He did or suffered. In this the love of Christ ran parallel with the Father's to the same object. The gift of His Son was out of love to the world—" *God commended His love toward us, in that, while we were yet sinners, Christ died for us*" (Rom. v. 8). There is a way of placing in a kind of competition with this as the great object of Christ's advent in this world, first God Himself, and secondly, the glory of His righteous government. But here we do not separate the design of the salvation of man, from the glory either of God's nature or of His government. We do not deny that God's love can have for its only adequate and perfect object His own adorable Being; but that men should be the objects of Divine love does not divide this necessary ineffable internal and supreme love. The salvation of man is in connection with the manifestation of God's love outward from Himself in Creation. It is the supreme manifestation of love; the height and depth of which passeth knowledge. What, too, if the Church, in all her purity and completeness in the body of Christ, the Head, is, after all, through the fulness, the "all fulness" that dwells in Him, able to give a meet—I say it in all humility—even a meet response to the infinite love of God! If this be so, how unspeakably godlike are the purposes served by the Incarnation and Redemption! How profound the meaning given to the ancient prophecy concerning the joy of God in completed redemption : "*He will rest in His love, He will joy over thee with singing*" (Zeph. iii. 17).

Neither do we deny that the righteousness of the Divine rule attains its brightest manifestation through the salvation of men. But we hold that the peculiar glory shed around the throne of God was not the glory of righteousness in itself considered, but the righteousness of God as concerned in the salvation of sinners. From eternity, all things—

and notably the overthrow of the angels, and the destruction of the ancient world—had proclaimed God to be just. But this was the justice of destroying the transgressor. Now in the Gospel a new phase of righteousness is revealed. God is shewn to be just, and the Justifier of the ungodly, a just God and a Saviour. This is the peculiar glory that Redemption shed on the Divine rule, and towards this goal all the purposes of the Incarnation travel. Never, indeed, did the sword of Justice appear so terrible as when it awoke and smote the Shepherd, the Man that was God's fellow; but it was not then unsheathed to display its lightning terrors or reflect them around the Eternal Throne. It was to open up a way for the passage of Mercy, and to render it possible righteously to extend to sinful men the golden sceptre of Divine forgiveness and favour.

(III.) *It brings out clearly the truth of the parallel existing between Christ and Adam.*

The name of "Second Adam" given to Christ is mere fancy, unless Christ occupied from the very beginning of His life a position exactly parallel to Adam's. The Apostle, in Rom. v. and 1 Cor. xv., does not establish a barren comparison between the two as individuals, but between the moral and physical causes they set in motion, and the effects that follow therefrom to the race. But as evil effects could not follow justly on the side of Adam, unless his rank had been that of federal head, and unless he had been charged with all the obligations of that office from the very first; so neither on the side of Christ could the effects of goodness righteously descend to any, unless a federal relation had been established between Christ and them, and Christ charged with their responsibilities from the first. But by recognizing these obligations, we recognize His public character in its full significance. We recognise that between Christ's and Adam's leadership the whole history of the race is divided, the one in the natural, the other in the spiritual sphere. We regard Christ as charged to restore, as Adam had been charged to keep. The various interests received under the one are taken up to be reconstructed in the other. In the one the world had been cursed, in the other the curse is removed. In the one the race fell, in the other the race is to be redeemed. In the one righteousness is violated, in the other all righteousness fulfilled. In the one we see death, in the other Eternal Life. In the one Eden forfeited, in the other

Paradise regained. The persistency, too, of the effects from the one are seen in the other. Nothing has ever diverted the headship of Adam from operating on the race naturally; nothing therefore we may gather shall impede the efficacy of Christ spiritually. If the ruin sin induced in nature has been effectual, how much more the righteousness of Christ! Each spreads his influence in his own sphere. The first man was of the earth, earthy; the Second is the Lord from heaven. The children of the first man have his likeness, so also it is promised to Christ that "*He shall see His seed; He shall prolong His days, and the pleasure of the Lord shall prosper in His hand*" (Isa. liii. 10); and also that He shall be the Father of Eternity or the Eternal Age. It is promised that His people shall be as numerous as the dew-drops in the morning, and that they shall be conformed to His likeness. But Christ does not pass over to the natural sphere of Adam, any more than Adam can pass over to the sphere of the Redeemer. Therefore it is that the lines along which the efficiency of Each Head runs, differ as much as the nature of their spheres. Christ communicates not His grace through natural channels, any more than Adam transmits his corruption through spiritual. "*That which is born of the flesh, is flesh; and that which is born of the Spirit is spirit;*"[1] and they who receive Christ and are His, are "*born not of blood, nor of the will of the flesh, nor of the will of man, but of God.*"[2] Christ is a quickening Spirit and "*hath quickened us together*" with Him and "*raised us up together*" with Him.[3] "*If any man be in Christ, he is a new creature*" (2 Cor. v. 17).

Here I cannot forbear referring to the frequency and emphasis with which the Apostle gives expression to this grand truth (Eph. ii.). It is with him the vital bond of the constitution of the Kingdom of Mercy.

(IV.) *It reveals the true basis of the justification of sinners.*

Justification is wrought, as we have seen, by means of imputation. But whenever there is imputation of good or evil, there is supposed to exist a union or community between the parties. The imputation of good or evil, going on all the world over, from father to son, from one member of a family to another, from friend to friend, from partner to partner, proceeds on the basis of the ties of kindred, friendship, partnership, or nationality. The imputation of Adam's guilt rests upon his natural and legal relation to the race. If the common sense of mankind

---

[1] John iii. 6.   [2] John i. 13.   [3] Eph. ii. 5, 6.

recognizes it, and acts upon it in the one case, why not in the other? In the same way, the imputation of Christ's righteousness has its righteous basis in His federal Headship of His people. In the days of His humiliation on earth, this union operated so as to cover Him with dire demerits and sufferings. Now that He is raised to victory, it operates in making Christ to be their wisdom, righteousness, sanctification, and redemption. He was bound by this union when He went out to the conflict; He generously acknowledged it on His return, in the distribution of the spoils and rewards of victory.

By thus making the union with Christ to underlie the imputation of His righteousness, all the glory of our justification is given to God in Christ, and all boasting on the part of man is excluded for ever. This is so. For in the first place the union itself depends upon the good pleasure of God; it is first formed in design by His Eternal choice, and afterwards effected by His Spirit. In the second place, the justifying act of God is shewn not to rest upon the improvements men may make in what is called common grace, nor upon the natural towardliness of any individual, but solely upon what Christ is and has done, upon His righteousness without the deeds of the law. In the third place, provision is made for the personal holiness of all who are justified. Their personal reception of justification is through faith; and faith works by love, and purifies the heart. Lastly, faith itself is made to appear in its true and proper character. It is wrought in us as the result of our decretive union with Christ, and is thus, as the gift of God, an evidence and proof of that union. In this, as in all other things, it is the substance of things hoped for, and the evidence of things not seen. But it is not the things hoped for, nor is it the things not seen. The things hoped for and the things not seen are in this case the grace of justification and the righteousness of Christ. And since faith is the substance and evidence of these, it cannot be itself the righteousness on the grounds of which we are justified. That is no kind of Evangelical righteousness which is but a good work or a development of self-righteousness. "*Where is boasting then?*" we may ask with the Apostle, and with him reply, "*It is excluded.*" "*By what law? Of works? Nay: but by the law of faith*" (Rom. iii. 27). And if any should boast of their faith, let not the thing formed boast against Him who formed it. We are chosen in Christ to the obedience of faith. Thus Christ Crucified appears as He is—the Lord our Righteousness and the only ground of our justification.

(V.) *It enables us to perceive the true scope and grandeur of the work of Christ.*

When we think of the grand scale indicated in some parts of the Mediatorial work, we may surely judge that all other parts will correspond with them. To begin with, there is the infinite worth of Christ's own Person. He is to emancipate a world, to restore a fallen race, to magnify righteousness, and reveal the love of God in such a way that all the universe shall admire. What do these parts promise of the proportions of other parts of His work? Has Christ had the world placed under Him (Heb. ii. 8) in order to sway but a fragment of it? Shall He be content with merely touching the margin of human history? Shall Satan and sin run riot for thousands of years, and Christ's saving operations be compressed into the mere fag end of time? Shall Satan have his millions, and Christ only His scores out of the human family? I believe all such narrow representations are unreasonable, unworthy of Christ, and directly opposed to the spirit and letter of Scripture.

How does the Spirit of inspiration forecast the day of Christ? Christ appears as Heir of all things, the Head of the new race, the Author of a new life, the Founder of a new kingdom. The heathen are to be His heritage and the uttermost parts of the earth His possession.[1] Righteousness is to cover the earth as the waters cover the channels of the sea.[2] His ransomed subjects, gathered out of all nations and tribes, and tongues, and families, are to be so numerous that no man can number them; and His Church composed of these is to reign with Him through a long millenium of triumph,[3] and to exhibit unto the principalities and powers in the heavenly places the manifold wisdom of God.[4] Finally death is to be destroyed, and the renovating power of Christ extended to the grave and the whole outward frame of creation.[5]

Charged with all these vast purposes when He appeared, need we wonder that Scripture employs the loftiest and most sublime language of our Saviour's advent? Yet even the ardour of the loftiest strains grows weak, and their boldest and highest flights shrink and fail in comparison with "the work" itself which was "set before Him." No wonder that catching a glimpse of the Divine designs, multitudes of angels heralded His approach, and from the silence of the midnight sky allowed their wonder to burst into unusual song. No wonder that the Lord Himself contemplating this work from afar, is smitten with a rapturous joy, and

---

[1] Ps. ii. 8. [2] Isa. xi. 9. [3] Rev. vii. 9, etc. [4] Eph. iii. 10. [5] Rev. xxi. 4, etc.

exclaims, "*Lo! I come.*"[1] It dimned not the brightness of that joy, though He foresaw that the weight of a double world would rest upon Him—the old world of transgression, the new world of righteousness, and peace, and joy in the Holy Ghost. Upon that brief life He was to live, upon that death He was to die, and upon every incident of both, what momentous and eternal issues hung! So vast is the work that only the Incarnate Son of God may scarce rise to its infinite dimensions; so vast and elevated as not to be unworthy even of Him. Pursuing through the revolving ages His mighty and merciful purposes, He will make His moral victory complete, and will make full proof of the "all power given unto Him in heaven and in earth"[2] by bringing the very last and the very least of God's sons from afar, and the last of His daughters from the ends of the earth. And when even He, with all the unutterable yearnings of His eternal love, shall look upon the mighty family of the redeemed and sanctified, "*He shall see of the travail of His soul, and shall be satisfied*" (Isa. liii. 11).

(VI.) *It frees us from difficulty in presenting the Gospel to sinners.*

The difficulty felt, is that of a contradiction between the free invitation of the Gospel and every limitation of the work of Christ. The difficulty presses upon every theory of the Atonement which acknowledges a limitation of any kind which the hearer of the Gospel does not make, or which, though he does make, is known before the offer of Salvation is made to him.

The Hyper-Calvinist disposes of the difficulty by not giving the invitation, and thus hides his Lord's money in the earth. One section of Moderate Calvinists, admitting the design of the Atonement to be limited, solves the difficulty by basing the universal call upon the infinite worth of Christ's Atonement; another, by alleging that provision has been made for all. Both only shift, but do not dispose of the seeming contradiction. Whether the limitation be placed in the Atonement or in the destination, the limitation has been fixed before the Gospel call is issued to all. He who thus views the matter must be conscious all the time he indiscriminately invites sinners, that he is issuing an invitation that runs beyond the decree of election.

The Arminian does not escape the pressure of the difficulty; for though rejecting predestination, yet, by holding foreknowledge, he admits that God knows who shall receive and who shall reject the

---

[1] Ps. xl. 7.   [2] Matt. xxviii. 18.

Gospel, before it is offered, while still sending the offer to all. The unscriptural supposition that the Gospel must be preached to secure man's condemnation settles nothing, but introduces a new element of confusion.

The difficulty is best met, first of all, by admitting that the mercy of God is turned towards the world, the race, and the Church. According to the views of Christ's relations, which I have sketched, it is most vitally true that, "*God so loved the world, that He gave His only begotten Son, that whosoever believeth in Him should not perish, but have eternal life*":[1] Christ is the Propitiation for our sins: the Saviour of all men, and tasted death for every man. It is most essential that every line of the Divine purpose in the manifestation of mercy should travel onwards to its definite fulfilment. The world becomes Christ's world, and the race through Christ is rescued as a race from destruction. And upon this we ought to insist. But the way in which the purpose of mercy fulfils itself in these respects is in the salvation of the believer. All these passages either express or imply this. "*He is the Saviour of all men, especially of those that believe*" (1 Tim. iv. 10); so, also, in John iii. 16. The world and the race are saved in the believer. Who, then, is the believer? A man who is in Christ, chosen in Him; and consequently one of His brethren, and one of the Church for whom Christ laid down His life. Thus there is no antagonism between the Scripture which says "*God so loved the world . . . .*" and "*Christ loved the Church*" (Eph. v. 25). Instead of antagonism, the one contributes to the other. We can therefore consistently affirm the wider bearing of the work of Christ, and also the more definite.

As strengthening this position, we ought also to take into account the prophetic element in the Scriptures relating to Christ's work. When we read of the "*Lamb of God which taketh away the sin of the world*,"[2] and look upon the iniquity abounding throughout the ages, we are fain to seek some more natural sense for the expression. Is it necessary or right to do so? Is there not promised a time when the balance between right and wrong shall be redressed? Surely the Sun of Righteousness shall not always fall on barren sands, or the dew of mercy distil upon the wastes? From the testimony of Scripture already adduced, May we not anticipate a time when the Lamb of God shall have taken *away* the sin of the world? When He shall be in fact the Propitiation and the Saviour of all? What else is meant by the

---

[1] John iii. 16.   [2] John i. 29.

declaration that "*every knee should bow* . . . . and *that every tongue should confess that Jesus Christ is Lord?*" (Phil. ii. 10, 11.) To that day when all shall know the Lord, the language of the Gospel is adapted, and in view of it, we can give the broadest presentation of the bearings and influences of His work.

The next consideration that clears our path in freely inviting the Sinner is the great aim of preaching the Gospel. That aim is to lead to faith in the Lord Jesus Christ. Preachers of all schools of doctrine, high and low, narrow and broad, agree in this, though they may differ in their manner of presenting the truth. They also agree that the Gospel has some influence in producing faith. But it is of the very genius of the Gospel message, which in one aspect is God's great entreaty, His great persuasion addressed to the heart and mind, that it must be carried by man to his fellow men, by the saved to the unsaved. Now when God for weighty reasons made choice of man, in preference to angels, as His messenger, He chose a being of a limited intelligence, who was unacquainted with the elect as such, no discerner of spirits, and ignorant of the secret purposes of God. The message fitted to such a messenger must be general—addressed to all whom he may meet. This also enters into the nature of faith, which is in no sense physical, but is a willing acceptance of Christ. But this general bearing of the message is in harmony with the general bearing of Christ's work upon the world and mankind at large. Upon all this there comes the command and promise of God; and this command is addressed to all —"*God . . . . commandeth all men everywhere to repent*" (Acts xvii. 30). This word of God is the true warrant of faith, and it is the measure of our duty; for no man has to enquire what is the secret decree, but what is the express command. It comes to the sinner clothed with every form of reasonableness that might secure its acceptance. Corresponding with this universal call to faith addressed to the sinner, there is the universal command addressed to the Church to preach the Gospel to every creature; and he who is wise above that command is wise at his own risk and peril.

While no thought of the secret purpose of God may come in to change the terms of the invitation, it yet may assure us that the invitation shall not be in vain. The thought that God's purpose is being fulfilled in the faithful proclamation of the Gospel is immense strength to every preacher. Despite all appearance to the contrary, despite opposition, despite indifference, there is assurance that the counsel of God shall stand, and that He will do all His pleasure. The Omnipotent Spirit is in secret at work, and sooner or later the signs must follow. The presence and powers of that Spirit are the guarantee against failure.

Let us therefore have no hesitation. Let us not fear to overstep the limits of our commission by making the invitation large and wide. Let us sound the great trumpet and blow an alarm. Let us go into the highways, and let us cry, "*Ho, every one that thirsteth, come ye to the waters;*" and assure them that him that cometh to Christ He will in no wise cast out.

(VII.) *It enables every believer to perceive the direct personal love of Christ to him.*

We perceive Christ entering upon His work as the Elder Brother drawn by kindred ties to redeem His brethren : as the Good Shepherd with the glance of compassion discovering every lost sheep in the wilds, and seeking their individual salvation. His people come not before Him as a secondary care, or to share a reflected benefit. In the midst of all the multiplicity of His obligations, through all the claims of other interests, steadily and singly His love shines forth towards each and every one. The whole company can sing, "*Unto Him that loved* us, *and washed* us *from our sins in His own blood* . . . . . *be glory and dominion for ever*" (Rev. i. 5, 6), and each one can adoringly say, "*He loved* ME *and gave Himself for* ME."

www.ingramcontent.com/pod-product-compliance
Lightning Source LLC
Chambersburg PA
CBHW022052160426
43198CB00008B/203